Unvarnishing Reality

UNVARNISHING REALITY

Subversive Russian and American Cold War Satire

DEREK C. MAUS

The University of South Carolina Press

© 2011 University of South Carolina

Published by the University of South Carolina Press
Columbia, South Carolina 29208

www.sc.edu/uscpress

Manufactured in the United States of America

20 19 18 17 16 15 14 13 12 11   10 9 8 7 6 5 4 3 2 1

Library of Congress Cataloging-in-Publication Data
Maus, Derek C.
  Unvarnishing reality : subversive Russian and American cold war
satire / Derek C. Maus.
    p. cm.
  Includes bibliographical references and index.
  ISBN 978-1-57003-985-0 (cloth : alk. paper)
  1. American fiction–20th century—History and criticism. 2. Russian
fiction—20th century—History and criticism. 3. Satire, American—
History and criticism. 4. Satire, Russian—History and criticism.
5. Cold War in literature. 6. Politics and literature—History—20th
century. 7. Cold War—Influence. I. Title.
  PS374.S2M38 2011
  817'.5409358282—dc22

                                    2011001616

This book was printed on Glatfelter Natures, a recycled paper with 30 percent
postconsumer waste content.

CONTENTS

INTRODUCTION

> I only ever cared about the man. . . . I never gave a fig for the ideologies.
> . . . I never saw institutions as being worthy of their parts, or policies as much
> other than excuses for not feeling. Man, not the mass, is what our calling is
> about. It was man who ended the Cold War in case you didn't notice. . . . And
> the ideologies trailed after these impossible events like condemned prisoners,
> as ideologies do when they've had their day. Because they have no heart of
> their own. They're the whores and angels of our striving selves.
>
> John le Carré, *The Secret Pilgrim* (1990)

Since the dissolution of the Soviet Union in 1991, relations between the
United States and Russia have progressed through several stages. From the
initial flurry of optimism about (and monetary investment in) Russia's future
as a new democracy and global trading partner, through fears of a return to
Communism (or worse, the hypernationalism exemplified by Vladimir Zhiri-
novsky during the mid- to late 1990s) and an initially warm but increasingly
strained friendship between Vladimir Putin and George W. Bush, American attitudes toward its former enemy have vacillated considerably since
George H. W. Bush's proclamation of a "New World Order" in January 1991.
To be sure, things have changed, and all-out nuclear apocalypse has been
largely forestalled—if only to be replaced by a host of alternate, less totalized,
but no less immediate (at least in the popular imagination) threats, ranging
from so-called rogue nations to stateless terrorist organizations such as al-
Qaida. I believe this tendency is a dual effect of governments peopled largely
with individuals who cut their teeth during the cold war and an incomplete,
perhaps intentionally hobbled, effort to understand the ways in which the
cold war was conducted.

As a result the philosophical and political landscape of the post–cold war
world is dominated by volatility, from the economic catastrophes threatened
by the 1997 Asian economic crisis and again by the international banking
meltdown of 2008–9, to regional conflicts with global significance (such as
NATO's 1999 military intervention in the Balkans, the resurgence of the Pales-
tinian intifada, and the long-standing Kashmir border dispute between India

and Pakistan), and finally to the growing influence of various forms of religious fundamentalism reacting against the generally secularist and rationalist tendencies of the past century. Despite one of its greatest periods of sustained economic growth through the 1990s, the United States also witnessed bitter political infighting at the national level and localized outbreaks of violence such as the Oklahoma City bombing or the Columbine shootings that seemingly alluded to disturbances in the ostensibly healthy national psyche. As the boom years subsided, these disturbances were exacerbated, first in the bitterly contested presidential election of 2000 and later in the national and cultural response to the terrorist attacks of September 11, 2001, especially the decision to go to war against Iraq in March 2003. Russia has likewise proceeded erratically in its efforts to move away from the unpleasant past of the cold war, including its continuing problems with rebellion in Chechnya, its lingering tendency toward authoritarianism in suppressing internal dissent, and its mixed results in retaining a preeminent role in global politics and economics.

Although only a small and relatively reactionary minority in either the United States or Russia advocates a return to the superpower rivalry of the cold war, the tumultuous situation of the early twenty-first century hints at a lingering social unease about the two nations' recent past. Given the nuclear tension of varying intensity that existed from 1949, when the Soviets successfully exploded their first atomic bomb, until 1991, when the cold war effectively ended along with the Soviet Union, one obvious source of this cultural trauma is not difficult to identify.[1] Any diagnosis of contemporary cultural maladies must consider the shortcomings of the exalted (and exaggerated) rhetorical edifice of the "New World Order" the cold war's victors erected atop the rubble of the Berlin Wall and innumerable toppled statues of Lenin. If the initial American cultural response to the end of the cold war was understandably celebratory (if perhaps overly self-congratulatory), it also lacked substantive inquiry into the potentially deleterious after-effects of nearly fifty years of extreme anxiety. Likewise the furious dash to "de-Sovietize" Russia under the iconic prodemocracy figure of Boris Yeltsin in the early and mid-1990s tempered widespread efforts to delve deeply into the past.[2] As statesman George Kennan, whose 1946 "Long Telegram" to Harry Truman from Moscow indirectly helped define the cold war in its earliest days, argued in a *New York Times* op-ed piece on October 28, 1992, the end of the cold war "is a fit occasion for satisfaction but also for sober re-examination of the part we took in its origin and long continuation. It is not a fit occasion for pretending that the end of it was a great triumph for anyone" (A21).

My response to Kennan's call for such "sober re-examination" specifically involves reexamining a group of socially conscious writers of satirical fiction who began, well before 1992, to question the various forces that contributed to the "origin and long continuation" of the cold war. Although the literature of the cold war period has been studied extensively, in terms of not only its literary lineage but also its historical context, precious few critics have compared works by both Russian and American writers of satirical fiction that endeavor to condemn and in due course subvert the established power structure. Such a comparison yields a complex of thematic and structural similarities that transcends specific national/cultural origins. The cold war was a conflict that inextricably linked the governments and citizens of both countries, even as they ostensibly separated themselves from one another with ideological barriers. Similarly the literature that resisted and/or rejected the premises that guided this conflict is not confined by national borders, even though many of its creators and its physical manifestations—that is, printed texts—were. Together these works represent a thoroughgoing humanistic refutation of the cold war and its operative doctrines, an alternative to the exclusionary binary logic of the time. My goal in this book is first to reveal the existence and the scope of such nonaligned critiques and then to evaluate their philosophical merits. In my view such a process is an important step in addressing the cultural damage of living for so long "under the nuclear Sword of Damocles," as John F. Kennedy called it in his September 25, 1961, address to the United Nations.

Although triumphalist discourses, especially those associated with neoconservatism, are perhaps the most robust forces affecting the retrospective cultural attitudes toward the cold war in the United States, they are not the only ones whose insistent nationalism threatens to oversimplify and thereby distort the legacy of the cold war by marginalizing anyone who refused to take sides in the conflict, to say nothing of those who cast their lot with the "losing" side. A substantial number of condemnations have originated from within the intellectual Left as well. Of especial interest to me are the denunciations of literary authors who question(ed) fundamental notions of American self-image. Such allegations generally imply that raising such doubts during perilous times such as the cold war is at worst treasonous, at best woefully misguided.

In his *Achieving Our Country* (1998), for example, Richard Rorty singles out Richard Condon's *Manchurian Candidate* (1959), Thomas Pynchon's *Vineland* (1990), Leslie Marmon Silko's *Almanac of the Dead* (1991), and Neal Stephenson's *Snow Crash* (1992) as "novels not of social protest but rather of rueful acquiescence in the end of American hopes" (3). Rorty's interpretation is predicated on the belief that pride in American national identity is a necessary precondition for ethical national policies: "Those who hope to persuade a nation to exert itself need to remind their country of what it can take pride in as well as what it should be ashamed of. They must tell inspiring stories about episodes and figures in the nation's past—episodes and figures to which the country should remain true" (3–4). I believe that his claim that writers such as Condon, Pynchon, Stephenson, and Silko fail in this task because

they "view the United States of America . . . as something we must hope will
be replaced, as soon as possible, by something utterly different" (7) is wildly
off the mark in equating strident criticism of a system's flaws with rejection
of that system in toto. The writers that Rorty censures—as is the case with
all of the writers included in this study—revisit the assumptions that under-
lie the moral imperative to "remain true" to particular "episodes and figures"
in the nation's past and present. They no more rule out the possibility of
national pride than Sinclair Lewis did in satirizing the Babbitts of the 1920s;
however, they also suggest, from a variety of perspectives, that there are ethical and moral standards that trump parochially nationalistic ones, *especially*
those that have, for whatever reason, become resistant to scrutiny.

Silko articulated such a perspective in her novel *Ceremony* (1977), in
which she describes the atomic bomb—developed, constructed, and tested
on land taken from Native Americans—as "witchery's final ceremonial sand
painting." This grave situation has created a new, if also perhaps unrecognized, universal alliance that transcends race or nationality: "From that time
on, human beings were one clan again, united by the fate the destroyers
planned for all of them, for all living things; united by a circle of death that
devoured people in cities twelve thousand miles away, victims who had never
known these mesas, who had never seen the delicate colors of the rocks
which boiled up their slaughter" (228). Although Silko suggests earlier in the
novel that European colonization was also an effect of the "witchery" that
resulted in the bomb, she also makes it clear that the "destroyers" mentioned
in the above passage are not *just* white people. In fact Betonie, an old medicine man and the moral center of *Ceremony*, corrects Tayo, the novel's protagonist, when he tries to make precisely such an association: "The old man
shook his head. 'That is the trickery of the witchcraft,' he said. 'They want us
to believe all evil resides with white people. Then we will look no further to
see what is really happening. They want us to separate ourselves from white
people, to be ignorant and helpless as we watch our own destruction. But
white people are only the tools that the witchery manipulates; and I tell you,
we can deal with white people, with their machines and their beliefs. We can
because we invented white people; it was Indian witchery that made white
people in the first place'" (122). Betonie's words certainly suggest a state of
existence that would be "utterly different" from the status quo of the novel's
post–World War II American setting; however, there is also a clear imperative to find and to redeem a shared identity that is more inclusive and less
destructive than that of the segregated, nationalistic society that produced
reservations and atomic bombs. Silko ardently derides the United States of
the early cold war as an outgrowth of an older "witchery" but equally ardently
rejects *any* tribalistic moral exceptionalism in formulating a cure to this condition. Betonie's insistence on the need for change in traditional ceremonies
articulates Silko's position succinctly: "Things which don't shift and grow are

dead things. They are the things the witchery people want. Witchery works to scare people, to make them fear growth. But it has always been necessary, and more than ever now, it is. Otherwise we won't make it. We won't survive" (116). Silko's tone in *Ceremony* is neither one of "rueful acquiescence" nor righteous vengeance, but of insistence that one must break the spells that promote violence and division before peace and goodness can return to the world. In this regard she stands in rhetorical solidarity with many, if not all, of the writers I will examine in this study.

Rorty defends his support for the cold war by invoking his pedigree as part of "the anticommunist reformist Left in mid-century," a comment that illustrates what I find to be an overly reductive attitude toward antiauthoritarianism common in the aftermath of the cold war. While attributing a kind of reform-minded patriotism to himself and to others like him, he claims that the new generation of leftists abandoned all hope of changing their own country into something better: "They wanted to hear that America was a very different sort of place, a much worse place, than their parents and teachers had told them it was. . . . For if you turn out to be living in an evil empire (rather than, as you had been told, a democracy fighting an evil empire) then you have no responsibility to your country; you are accountable only to humanity" (66). The rigid binary within Rorty's rhetoric—are one's choices truly limited to an "evil empire" or "a democracy fighting an evil empire"?—is not so different from the more overtly nationalistic "my country, right or wrong" thinking that he presumably encountered in his activist days and that vigorously resurfaced in American political discourse in the aftermath of the September 11, 2001, terrorist attacks. If all flaws within national behavior *must* be signs of either something irreparably (because "deeply") wrong or "mistakes correctable by reform," then branding someone as a "revolutionary" (and subsequently dismissing them, as Rorty does) becomes a simple task. Rorty matter-of-factly denies the possibility that the atmosphere of the cold war might have created or exposed problems within the country that actually did make it "a much worse place" than it had been or that it claimed to be.

I concur with Rorty's assertion that "nothing a nation has done should make it impossible for a constitutional democracy to regain self-respect. To say that certain acts *do* make this impossible is to abandon the secular, antiauthoritarian vocabulary of shared social hope in favor of . . . a vocabulary built on the notion of sin" (32). However, Rorty overlooks the extent to which the cold war was perpetuated *by both sides* using precisely this latter kind of rhetoric, usually attributing "sin" of some kind to the enemy while claiming "purity" for oneself, whether through dialectical materialism or puritanical nationalism. Many of the American writers examined in this study explicitly satirize exactly this sort of self-sanctifying rhetoric in its cold war setting. Furthermore the deflation of Marxist-Leninist propaganda about the inevitably glorious future of Communism is practically inescapable in dissident Soviet satire. The point, thus, is not that such writers themselves "abandon . . . [the] vocabulary of shared social hope" but that they very clearly *do* adhere to and even defend it by demonstrating the ways in which various powers-that-be have callously misused the "vocabulary built on the notion of sin" to further their own ends. The writers I examine herein may feel themselves account-able to their country (if not necessarily to particular institutions and leaders) to some extent, but any "social hope" they invoke is shared among humanity as a whole, not merely a subset thereof.

Refusing to fight the cold war, regardless of which side one was being asked to fight on, meant rejecting an ideological conscription that required the acceptance of a particular rhetoric of national, political, economic, and often cultural superiority. Rorty complains that writers like Pynchon, Silko, and Stephenson were either unable or unwilling "to formulate a legislative program, to join a political movement, or to share in a national hope" (8–9), as though these three were both equivalently reform-minded gestures and the only forms of meaningful sociopolitical action. His insistence on separat-ing participation in political *processes* from participation in political *dialogue* is problematic precisely because it denies any reformative power to a writer who does not propose a course of action that can be applied directly to im-proving existing political institutions. This book argues that the act of satiri-cally recontextualizing the language of the public sphere during the cold war is *inherently* political because of the extent to which that language was inten-tionally controlled and, by extension, corrupted by the political elite of both superpowers. In my view it was satirists, both Russian and American, who acted as genuinely conscientious objectors to the cold war by pointing out the fallacies, self-serving fabrications, and otherwise disingenuous rhetoric and policy that kept it alive for nearly fifty years. I find dismissal of passion-ate criticism of a half-century's dangerous and occasionally deceitful policy as "rueful acquiescence in the end of American hopes" disturbingly close to jingoism, no matter the location on the political spectrum from which such an interpretation arises.

A Working Definition of Russian Literature

Any discussion of Russian literature during the Soviet era must take into account the complex issues surrounding "Russian" identity during this period. The frequent synonymous use of "Russian" and "Soviet" suffers from three major flaws: it ignores the vast diversity of nationalities and ethnicities con-tained within the Soviet Union; it discounts the political, rather than national, origins of the term "Soviet" (in order to be a Soviet citizen, one must comply with the policies of the Soviet state, not simply be born within its borders); and it downplays the internationalism that is central, in theory at least, to Marxism-Leninism, especially in its earliest stages. While it is true that ethnic Russians dominated the political and literary landscape of the Soviet Union, other ethnic/national groups exerted a substantial influence on Soviet life, even if it not always openly acknowledged (as in the case of Stalin's Georgian origins). As Andrei Sinyavsky notes in *Soviet Civilization: A Cultural History* (1990), constant tension existed in the Soviet Union between the theoretical internationalism of Marxism-Leninism and the inherent "great-power chauvinism" (239) of Russian ethnic dominance in the Soviet Union. This tension remained essentially unresolved throughout the history of the Soviet Union and contributed greatly to its eventual downfall. Its repercussions can also be seen clearly in the regional conflicts (Nagorno-Karabakh, Abkhazia, and Chechnya) that have plagued Russia since 1991, although many of these disputes predate the birth of the Soviet Union, much less its demise.

Throughout the Soviet era, writers of at least partly non-Russian ethnicity or nationality[3] continued to figure prominently in both the official and the unofficial strains of Russian literature. It is noteworthy, though, that the vast majority of official Soviet literature was written in the Russian language, regardless of the authors' ethnic origins. This was almost exclusively the case from the 1930s through the 1950s, when the Stalinist program of "Russification" was at its peak. With the establishment of the state-controlled Soiuz pisatelei SSSR, or Writers' Union of the USSR,[4] in 1932, literature explicitly became "official business" and was therefore written in Russian with increasingly fewer exceptions. Only after 1956 did officially sanctioned publication in non-Russian languages resume, but even during this time most literature was still written in Russian, the acknowledged *lingua sovietica,* With few exceptions, any work of literature that sought nationwide publication through official channels would need to be written in Russian, even if the author of the work was treating non-Russian subject matter. Several generations of non-Russian Soviet citizens grew up with little or no formal training in their native languages, so Russian became dominant. Despite the relative linguistic uniformity, the mixture of non-Russian cultural influences found in Russian-language literature in the Soviet Union nevertheless expanded Russian literature's thematic range between 1917 and 1991. Stories that were previously marginalized in terms of both geography and ethnicity—such as Fazil Iskander's semifolkloric "Sandro" tales about Abkhazia or Chingiz Aitmatov's fictionalized accounts of life in Soviet Kirghizia—could now, at least in terms of the language in which they were written, be called Russian.

There was no universal moral or ethical imperative for non-Russian writers (especially those seeking a broad audience) to write in their native languages, even though many of their sentiments undoubtedly corresponded to those of Vassily Aksyonov's fictional Armenian émigré Aram Ter-Aivazian from *Novyi sladostnyi stil'* (1997; *The New Sweet Style*): "[He] preferred to speak English. Or, if possible, Armenian. I'm only thirty-five, he would say, there's still time to forget all that Komsomol jargon—that is, Russian" (85). For Ter-Aivazian the Russian language is directly, and negatively, associated with

Soviet state organs. Upon leaving the Soviet Union, he simultaneously emigrates across both its linguistic and its geographic boundaries. Russian cultural supremacy within the Soviet Union ensured that a writer's choice of language would not only shape his or her *cultural* identity but also his or her *political* identity—a much more important consideration in terms of prospects for publication.

Thus a linguistic definition (that is, "Russian literature is literature written in the Russian language") provides a more inclusive scheme than a strictly geopolitical one (that is, "Russian literature is literature produced within the borders of Russia / the Soviet Union"). Such a definition does not, however, address the important variations in this body of literature produced both by stringent state control over literary form and content and by the large number of writers who were forced into foreign exile. Many influential writers of the Soviet era were published largely or, in some cases, solely in *samizdat* (self-publication, usually in the form of secretly circulated mimeographed or hand-copied texts) or *tamizdat* (illegal foreign publications of manuscripts smuggled out of the Soviet Union). Boris Pasternak, Andrei Sinyavsky, and Yuli Daniel were among the most famous of the authors who were vigorously persecuted by the state during the 1950s and 1960s for allowing their works to be published in foreign countries. In a system that considered publishing a literary work without official approval a seditious act *regardless of that work's content*, it comes as no surprise that the unofficial Russian-language literature of the cold war was filled with works that express outspokenly dissident and subversive points of view.

The penalties for ideological divergence were certainly less harsh during the 1960s, 1970s, and 1980s than in Stalin's time. In the 1930s an offhand comment about the skill of the officially scorned émigré writer Ivan Bunin earned Varlaam Shalamov more than twenty years of hard labor in Siberia, and numerous other writers were shot for ostensibly "counterrevolutionary" sentiments in their works. Although the post–World War II era was still repressive—even during the comparatively more tolerant "Thaw" that immediately followed Stalin's death in 1953—physical punishment was gradually replaced with severe professional and psychological sanctions. From Pasternak's refusal to denounce the foreign publication of *Doctor Zhivago* in 1957 until the relative freedom of glasnost in the late 1980s, authors who were judged to have committed ideological indiscretions in their writing were subject to a fairly standard course of events. The threat of censure by or outright expulsion from the Writers' Union was used to coerce writers who had strayed back into accord with official policies. The former made official publication more difficult, and the latter made it impossible. At times, though, these professional punishments were not considered harsh enough, as in the case of the trial and imprisonment of Sinyavsky and Daniel in February 1966. The treatment of Sinyavsky and Daniel triggered an international outcry, after which Soviet authorities began to favor exile over the potential creation of additional martyrs for the dissident cause. This change in strategy precipitated what would come to be known as the "third wave" (*tret'ia volna*) of emigration.

Communities of literate Russian émigrés already existed in parts of Western Europe and the United States after World War II. Their presence was mostly a result of the wave of writers and intellectuals who had left Russia during the "first emigration" around the time of the Russian Revolution and Civil War (1917–21). As a result many foreign outlets were available for Russian-language publication, especially in the United States, Great Britain, France, and West Germany. Several writers precipitated their own ruin within official Soviet literary circles by publishing extensively in *tamizdat*, and many of them were eventually exiled, voluntarily or involuntarily. Aksyonov's involvement with the foreign publication of the *Metropol'* almanac (fictionally depicted in his 1985 novel *Say Cheese!*) led directly to his exile from the Soviet Union and his subsequent immigration to the United States in 1980. The majority of the Russian-language works that I examine in this study were first published *outside* the Soviet Union. Presses such as Ardis (originally located in Ann Arbor, Michigan) and such émigré journals as *Kontinent* (Paris and Berlin), *Ekho* (Paris), *Grani* (Frankfurt), and *Novy zhurnal* (New York) were invaluable in disseminating the work of authors who had fallen out of favor with the Soviet authorities, whether or not these authors were still physically within the borders of the Soviet Union.

There is as yet no definitive answer to the question of how the work of these displaced writers fits into the tradition of Russian literature. During a 1990 panel discussion, Sergei Dovlatov comically, yet tellingly, outlined the difficulty in defining his status as an émigré: "I am from the Soviet Union; I was born in Bashkiria. My father was half-Jewish, and my mother Armenian. I now live in the German quarter of New York City. I speak, and more important, write, only in Russian. My books are translated into English by a Polish Jew. In brief, I am more or less a typical Russian émigré writer" (Glad, *Literature in Exile*, 96). To help resolve such identity issues, I am defining Russian literature very broadly herein, both because such a definition reflects my personal feelings about the fluid relationship between national identity and literature and, more important, because the central purpose of my study is to establish commonalties between Russian and American literature from the cold war era that transcend national, linguistic, and ideological boundaries. A broader categorization naturally allows for a wider selection of texts in which to look for such concurrence. Simply put, I believe that all the non-American authors from the cold war period who are covered in this study exhibit characteristics in their works that make them distinctively and *primarily* conversant with the Russian tradition in literature and therefore a part of Russian literature. This distinction and primacy does not exclude dialogue with and influence from and on other national traditions—such supranational dialogue and influence is, after all, an inherent part of my argument—but it does provide a useful historical framework for *initial* contextualization of their works.

Note on Translations, Quoted Materials, and Titles

Wherever possible, I have quoted published English translations from Russian primary texts. If necessary, I have also commented in footnotes about any semantic or substantive changes that occurred in the process of translation in order to retain as much of the original Russian context as possible while making the material accessible to an audience including both those who read Russian and those who do not. Rather than retaining the original Cyrillic for Russian words and phrases that appear in the text (since that hinders almost any recognition of cognates or common roots for readers unfamiliar with Russian), I have used the standard Library of Congress transliterations, meaning that the Cyrillic character й is transliterated as "y," the character э as "e," the character ё as "è," the character ц as "ts," and x as "kh." The "soft sign" (ь) and "hard sign" (ъ) are respectively rendered with single (') and double (") diacritical apostrophes. The only exception to this general rule is proper names, for which I have generally used the most familiar form of transliteration into English in order to keep what is already somewhat unfamiliar material for non-Slavists from seeming even more exotic. This means, for example, that diacritics have been removed and "-ii" endings have been condensed into "-y" (so "Gorky" rather than "Gor'kii" and "Aleshkovsky" rather than "Aleshkovskii"). Likewise the "ks" cluster has been rendered as "x" (so "Maxim" rather than "Maksim"). I have retained the original transliterations for both proper names and other Russian words if they occur in direct quotations from other sources, thus variants such as "Aksenov," "Aksënov," and "Aksyonov" are all present here.

When first referencing Russian works, I have mentioned them first in their original Russian, with the first date of publication (in whichever language this first publication occurred) given immediately thereafter, followed by the title (or titles) under which the work was published in English translation, if indeed it has been. All subsequent references refer to the English title for the benefit of readers not familiar with Russian.

1

The Role of Literature during the Cold War

In [Gertrude Stein's] probing of nothingness and in her undoing of dichotomous paradigms, she establishes one fundamental role for the imaginative
writer . . . in the nuclear age: to confront annihilation's otherness without
capitulating to its seductive power.

John Gery, *Nuclear Annihilation and
Contemporary American Poetry* (1996)

The Historical and Cultural Context
of the Cold War

The widespread adoption of satire as a medium for fictional expression stems
from a number of factors that arose in both the United States and the Soviet
Union during the years of the cold war. Scholars from a variety of disciplines
have attempted to unravel the dynamics that altered the American and Soviet
cultural landscapes so drastically between 1945 and 1991. Although they often
differ greatly in their ideas about the means by which cultural phenomena
influence artistic representations, scholars of the cold war generally agree
that these two factors are part of a cause-and-effect cycle. Satirical literature
reflects aspects of the culture(s) in which it is produced and subsequently
aspires to bring about changes in that/those culture(s), an endeavor that in
turn instigates new literary developments, and so on. Such notions concerning the relationship between literature and culture have attained especial (but
not exclusive) credence among the New Historicist school of literary criticism. In *Figural Realism: Studies in the Mimesis Effect* (1999), Hayden White
states his understanding of New Historicism: "[It] has advanced the notion
of a cultural poetics and, by extension, a historical poetics as a means of
identifying those aspects of historical sequences that conduce to the breaking, revision, or weakening of the dominant codes—social, political, cultural,
psychological, and so on—prevailing at specific times and places in history.
Whence their interest in what appears to be the emergent, episodic, anec-
dotal, contingent, exotic, abjected, or simply uncanny aspects of the historical

record" (63). All of the cold war satires discussed in this study diverge from and often seek to undercut the aesthetic and political norms (that is, the "dominant codes") of their time, which is why I have adopted White's notion of a "historical poetics" to analyze them.

In my view a comparative historicist approach is essential to greater understanding of the nature of satirical fiction in an era during which control of language became a powerful (arguably, the primary) weapon for conducting the cold war, both domestically and internationally. Self-contradictory expressions such as "It became necessary to destroy the town to save it" were commonplace in the governmental and military rhetoric of the United States and the Soviet Union, and the extreme propagandization of language during the cold war drastically destabilized the semantic and semiotic values of words. The formal and thematic qualities found in the satires that arise from this cultural context are directly linked to their creators' distrust of language (sometimes including, in true postmodernist fashion, that of their own satires) in the post–World War II world.

Whether considered as the dawn of the "atomic age" or as the "first cold war," the historical period following the Hiroshima- and Nagasaki–induced conclusion of World War II created a radically new cultural context in both the United States and the Soviet Union. E. B. White's comments from the August 18, 1945, issue of the *New Yorker* clearly convey the unsettling sense that a new era has suddenly begun: "For the first time in our lives, we can feel the disturbing vibrations of complete human readjustment. Usually the vibrations are so faint as to go unnoticed. This time they are so strong that even the ending of a war is overshadowed" (108). White understood that the significant shift in the military balance of power was minimal compared with the necessary recalibration of cultural norms in the wake of the atomic bomb's creation and use. During the late 1940s he advocated tirelessly for a unified "world government" as a pragmatic response to the state of global affairs in the nuclear era.

The intensifying political and military rivalry between the Soviet Union and the United States was not the only source of "disturbing vibrations" resonating through the cultural landscape after 1945, though. Postwar literature about the Holocaust implicitly responds to Theodor Adorno's oft-quoted assertion that it would be "barbaric" to continue to write poetry as though Auschwitz had never happened; a similar principle holds true for nuclear-themed literature after Hiroshima and Nagasaki. As in the literature of the Holocaust, a transformation takes place over time in the language of fiction that attempts to come to terms with the significance of the atomic bomb. In both cases the emphasis shifts appreciably from largely mimetic (usually realistic or biographical) narratives toward more abstract representations. Whereas Holocaust literature serves primarily as a simultaneously reproachful and memorializing chronicle of a hitherto unimaginable atrocity from the past, the bulk of nuclear fiction speculates about a future global atrocity that could result from prevalent attitudes.

Lawrence L. Langer and Sidra DeKoven Ezrahi clarify the connection between works about the Holocaust and works about Hiroshima/Nagasaki. Langer writes in *The Age of Atrocity: Death in Modern Literature* (1978) that the "Hiroshima bomb, perhaps even more than Auschwitz, changed the quality of war and hence the quality of life and of survival itself" (61). He expands this analysis in the introduction to *Art from the Ashes: A Holocaust Anthology* (1995): "Language, of course, has its limitations; this is one of the first truths we hear about Holocaust writing. . . . The question we need to address, dispensing with excessive solemnity, is how words help us to imagine what reason rejects—a reality that makes the frail spirit cringe" (3–4). Applying this assessment of the potential of language to Holocaust texts, Langer writes that the "most compelling Holocaust writers reject the temptation to squeeze their themes into familiar premises: content and form, language and style, character and moral growth, suffering and spiritual identity, the tragic nature of existence—in short, all those literary ideas that normally sustain and nourish the creative effort" (6). In *The Age of Atrocity*, Langer posits the dilemma facing the post-Auschwitz / post-Hiroshima world in terms of a "disruption": "With the disruption of a familiar moral universe, the individual must find 'new' reasons for living and 'new' ways of confronting the prospect of death introduced into reality by atrocity. Such disruption mars not only an ordered universe, but the identity of one's self, one's conception of where he fits and how (and why) he is to act as a human being in a dehumanized world" (62). Thus the "familiar premises" of literature are rendered "barbaric" in the sense that the "familiar moral universe" that they described has been revealed to be literally and figuratively atrocious.

Ezrahi uses a similar idiom of dehumanization in *By Words Alone: The Holocaust in Literature* (1980) as part of a discussion of Saul Bellow's work, stating that he "deplor[es] the threat to the self, the loss of identity, which both the Nazi and the nuclear forms of mass extermination represented" (177). Albert Einstein's 1946 admonitions about the widespread failure to recognize the altered state of the postbomb world serve as yet another point of comparison: "The unleashed power of the atom has changed everything, save our modes of thinking, and thus we drift toward unparalleled disaster" (quoted in Dewey 7). These comments all indicate the value of language — including fiction—as a medium in which to track how and why "modes of thinking" changed in response to events that established forms of reasoning cannot comprehend.

In essence the Holocaust generated literature aimed at making it impossible for its readers to forget what happened or to allow something similar to recur, whereas most early nuclear literature served as a warning to prevent the apocalyptic events it depicts from ever occurring. As Stanley Kubrick explained in describing his motivations for making *Dr. Strangelove, or How I Learned to Stop Worrying and Love the Bomb* (1963), "It was very important to deal with this problem dramatically because it's the only social problem where there's absolutely no chance for people to learn anything from experience" (quoted in Whitfield 219). The subversive satirists who wittingly or unwittingly followed Kubrick's lead extended this task toward a general critique of the dehumanizing processes at work within the cold war.

The cold war period is unusual in the way that both Russian and American literary cultures responded to the inherent novelty of the times. Whereas American literary expressions of the post–World War I zeitgeist generally adopted the "high" artistic forms associated with modernism (as with the fiction of the Lost Generation or the highly intellectual poetry of Eliot, Pound, and others), a substantial part of the initial literary response to the cold war occurred in "low" or "popular" forms such as science fiction and espionage thrillers. The vastly decreased cost of mass-producing books coupled with the burgeoning film and television industries assured greater opportunities for publishing and consuming literature in the decade after World War II than in the decade after World War I. The traditional university-educated and/or university-employed American literary elite began to engage extensively with cold war themes extensively in fiction only in the early 1960s, in the process drawing significantly on the "low" forms that came before. Whereas the initial responses generally engaged with the historical and political events of the early years of the cold war (or extrapolated the effects of such events into futures, usually utopian or dystopian ones),[1] the subversive satires that begin springing up in the early 1960s engage with the period in more oblique terms, critically examining the underlying philosophy and language that shaped the more visible historical and political domains.

Even though the later elite works have generally still become the canonical texts, the influence of popular culture is much more pronounced and direct because of this process of incorporation. Philip E. Simmons discusses the direct connection between mass culture and literature in his *Deep Surfaces* (1997):

> With the vertiginous self-consciousness and skepticism that belong
> to the postmodern historical imagination, writers as different in style
> and approach as Thomas Pynchon, E. L. Doctorow, Ishmael Reed, Don
> DeLillo, Nicholson Baker, and Bobbie Ann Mason not only write about
> the present while writing about the past, but construct histories of their
> own novelistic methods, of the conditions of their texts' production, and
> of their own approach to representing the past. In these constructions,
> mass culture—particularly film, television, and the consumer culture
> built on advertising—shows up as a significant historical development

in itself. Enabled by new technologies and multinational organizations of capital, mass culture has become the "cultural dominant"—the force field in which all forms of representation, including the novel, must operate. (1–2)

Simmons later includes literary forms such as science fiction and pulp magazines as part of "mass culture." While Simmons does not directly associate the cold war with the transition of the "cultural dominant" from the elite to the masses, many factors his study claims as distinctly "postmodern" are ones I attribute primarily to that sociohistorical correlation. The combination of greater and faster media saturation, increased literacy among the general population, and the tremendous rhetorical and physical power unleashed by the development of the atomic bomb all contributed to the rapid development and entrenchment of a belief that the world was in a radically new era.

In the Soviet Union, the sense of living in a fundamentally changed world was initially delayed by Stalin's continued rule. The rigorous state control over literature and the widespread annihilation of the intelligentsia during the "great terror" (*yezhovshchina*) of the late 1930s ensured that the post–World War II literary scene in the Soviet Union did not resemble that of the highly innovative 1920s in either its artistic or intellectual merit. Until Stalin's death in 1953, the party's control over literary form and content was relatively unquestioned and nearly complete. This situation improved somewhat during the Thaw (*Ottepel'*), a period of relaxed governmental control from roughly 1954 to 1963, but the relative candor of this time also contributed to discontent by continually providing reminders of how tenuous and restricted the new freedoms were.

Although token dissenting works such as Vladimir Dudintsev's *Ne khlebom edinym* (1956; *Not by Bread Alone*) and Yuri Bondarev's *Tishina* (1962; *Silence*) were published and a number of previously outlawed writers were rehabilitated (either in reputation, if dead, or in person, if alive), the Thaw's limitations were still exceedingly clear to authors who wished to criticize something other than the excesses of Stalin's rule. The relaxation of censorship never expanded beyond a few politically expedient internal targets,[2] thereby allowing the party and its organs to retain full control over legal means of publication, especially from the end of the Thaw through glasnost. Thus the literary response, satirical or otherwise, to the cold war inevitably remained divided into official and unofficial branches. This phenomenon implicitly imparted political undertones to nearly all works of Russian literature, undertones that were defined by the extent to which a work sought and/or received official sanction. The generation of young writers who got their first glimpse of what was possible beyond Socialist Realism during the Thaw included Aksyonov, Dovlatov, Iskander, Yuz Aleshkovsky, Sasha Sokolov,

Vladimir Voinovich, and Alexander Zinoviev, each of whom went on to produce subversive satirical works that were published outside the official literary organs of the Soviet Union.

"When night seems thickest and the earth itself an intricate absurdity": *Literature as a Reaffirmation of Life in an Increasingly Dangerous World*

According to many U.S. and Russian historians, the cold war reached its
zenith during the Cuban Missile Crisis in October 1962. The Soviet Union
and the United States came into unprecedented direct conflict over the place-
ment of Soviet missiles in Cuba as well as the United States' deployment
of missiles in Turkey.[3] In his exhaustive political memoir/history *Danger and
Survival* (1988), McGeorge Bundy, special assistant for national security
affairs in President John F. Kennedy's cabinet, maintains that this was the
"most dangerous crisis of the nuclear age," although he downplays the actual
danger by stating that "the largest single factor that might have led to nuclear
war—the readiness of one leader or another to regard that outcome as remotely acceptable—simply did not exist" (453). Whether or not this assertion
is accurate, the resonating aftereffects on the collective psyche of Russian
and American society demonstrate the power contained within the *perceived*
threat of imminent total destruction.

The extreme anxiety engendered by the standoff in Cuba served as a
stimulus for a literary response that followed closely behind. As Paul Boyer
outlines in his two excellent cultural histories, *By the Bomb's Early Light* (1985)
and *Fallout* (1998), fictional works with nuclear themes were fairly commonplace before 1962. Most of these works, though, had been classified in the
traditionally "low" literary category of science fiction and thus had flown
under the critical establishment's radar. Of the "familiar titles" of nuclear-
themed fiction from the precrisis period listed by Albert E. Stone in his *Literary Aftershocks,* only the works of two British authors, William Golding's
Lord of the Flies (1954) and Nevil Shute's *On the Beach* (1957), generated any
stir within critical circles.

Although the possibility of nuclear war had been the overt source of anxiety during the Cuban Missile Crisis, the satires that arose in its wake did not
necessarily limit themselves just to criticizing the dangerous practices of
nuclear brinksmanship; they also decried the underlying cultural forces that
made such risky practices possible in the first place. The number of works of
satirical fiction increased dramatically in the wake of the precrisis publication of Joseph Heller's *Catch-22* (1961) and the release of *Dr. Strangelove* in
1963. The eleven years immediately following the Cuban Missile Crisis witnessed the production and publication of the following works: Thomas Pynchon's *V.* (1963), Kurt Vonnegut Jr.'s *Cat's Cradle* (1963), John Barth's *Giles
Goat-Boy* (1966), Robert Coover's *The Origin of the Brunists* (1966), Pynchon's

The Crying of Lot 49 (1966), Donald Barthelme's *Snow White* (1967) and *Unspeakable Practices, Unnatural Acts* (1968), Vonnegut's *Slaughterhouse-Five* (1969), Walker Percy's *Love in the Ruins* (1971), Don DeLillo's *End Zone* (1971), Ishmael Reed's *Mumbo Jumbo* (1972), and Pynchon's *Gravity's Rainbow* (1973). All of these works of fiction, and many others like them, contain satirical elements that are part of a broad criticism of American cold war culture in toto in a period when a number of other factors (the Vietnam War, civil rights, and so on)[4] led to a "sudden fading of the nuclear-weapons issue . . . whether as an activist cause, a cultural motif, or a topic of public discourse" (Boyer, *Fallout* 110). Whereas Boyer sees the years between 1963 and 1980 as the "Era of the Big Sleep"[5] because of a "sharp decline in culturally expressed engagement with the issue [of nuclear war]" (*Bomb's Early Light* 355), I contend that this decline, if it can be said to have happened, was far from a comfortable slumber.

To his credit Boyer admits as much when he qualifies his remarks: "This is not to suggest that nuclear fear ceased to be a significant cultural force in these years. Robert Jay Lifton may well be right in his speculation that the denial of nuclear awareness . . . affects a culture as profoundly as acknowledging it does" (*Bomb's Early Light* 355). In my view this is precisely the phenomenon that the writers mentioned above exposed in the late 1960s and early 1970s. Pynchon rather disconsolately hints at such a viewpoint in the introduction to *Slow Learner* (1984) in the process of explaining the themes of his 1959 story "Under the Rose": "Our common nightmare The Bomb is in there too. It was bad enough in '59 and is much worse now, as the level of danger has continued to grow. There was never anything subliminal about it, then or now. Except for that succession of the criminally insane who have enjoyed power since 1945, including the power to do something about it, most of the rest of us poor sheep have always been stuck with simple, standard fear. I think we have all tried to deal with this slow escalation of our helplessness in the few ways open to us, from not thinking about it to going crazy from it. Somewhere on this spectrum of impotence is writing fiction about it—occasionally, as here, offset to a more colorful time and place" (18–19). Pynchon and other writers like him pointed out, among other things, the kinds of elaborate political and social manipulations that were involved in diminishing that "simple, standard" nuclear fear to levels that didn't threaten pervasive dissatisfaction with either the system or its masters, all while still allowing anti-Communist popular sentiment to produce strong support, at least initially, for otherwise dubious policies like the Vietnam War. Boyer's "Big Sleep" essentially represents a period of greater sublimation and abstraction in terms of the iconic vocabulary of cold war rhetoric, and this process is due, at least in part, to a concerted effort on the part of the Johnson and Nixon administrations in redirecting fear of Communism away from nuclear weapons (Johnson's [in]famous "Daisy" campaign ad notwithstanding)

and toward related issues fraught with less totalizing peril, such as preventing the spread of Communism into the Third World. By the mid- to late 1960s,
the shoe-banging, missile-brandishing Soviet bogeyman that Khrushchev represented in the early 1960s took a back seat to the Vietcong soldier as the predominant symbol of the Red Menace.

Nuclear motifs disappeared in the United States only in their *explicit*
forms during this period; however, implicit and/or metanarrative expressions
of nuclear and related cold war themes remained consistent and perhaps even
increased in number. Joseph Dewey addresses this issue in the introduction
to his *In a Dark Time* (1990): "The apocalyptic temper emerged strongest in
the very period Boyer dismisses. . . . However, the response did not under-
take the direct treatment of doomsday scenarios, but instead dealt directly
with how people adjust to life in perilous times" (48n18). Dewey's qualified
and insightful definition of "apocalyptic temper" in a post-Hiroshima context
rejects many of the pejorative labels that have been applied by hostile critics
to some of the most important cold war works: "The apocalyptic temper,
then, brings more than . . . the joy of plotting. It is more than a collective
paranoia, a defensive strategy affected by the scared against a terror that
seems to spin wildly out of control. It is more than a sugar pill for those who
in the dark moments seem to see the very beast itself slouching toward Beth-
lehem. It is more than simply supplying form to time, a shape when it seems
most defiantly shapeless. It is supremely an act of the moral imagination, a
gesture of confidence and even *defiance that challenges its own assumptions*
that history is itself tracked toward endings" (15; emphasis added). His formulation of the apocalyptic perspective on the cold war allows for a proac-
tive and politicized mode of fictional expression that overcomes both bleak
defeatism and the temptation to replace one flawed utopian scheme with
another: "When history, then, goes critical; when God seems withdrawn, or
silent, or, even worse, casketed; when, as in this century, the finest instru-
ments of our own technologies seem bent on destroying us; when night seems
thickest and the earth itself an intricate absurdity, the apocalyptic temper
refutes the bated breath of the cataclysmic imagination and the nonchalant
breathlessness of the millennialist spirit. It refuses either simple annihilation
or the simplistic spiral of inevitable progress to offer the oxymoron of humanity as a creature brave and timid" (15). Such refusal of "simple" or "simplistic"
solutions echoes the notion of satirical subversion that Steven Weisenburger
establishes in his *Fables of Subversion: Satire and the American Novel, 1930–
1980* (1995). Both Weisenburger and Dewey deny the existence of a single
"proper" alternative in place of the systems they refute. More important,
though, both schemes allow for wholesale dissent against norms without resulting in nihilism, meaninglessness, or hopelessness. For Dewey, the apocalyptic mode provides "reassurance that a dangerous present is fraught with as
much hope as it is with danger" (15). Weisenburger, using a semiotic context,

more abstractly claims that the works he analyzes in his book demonstrate that "no one, not even the least privileged among us, is ever really stripped of power over those messages that continually relocate one as sender, referent, and addressee" (6). Both modes of interpretation offer something more than cold comfort to readers, even as they acknowledge the grim potency of the debased and warped spirit of the nuclear age.

There are a number of significant problems with the literary histories of the cold war that have been published since the early 1980s. Not the least among these is an almost exclusive focus on American and, to a lesser extent, British works. This limited scope remains blind to a corresponding upsurge in "apocalyptic temper" in Russian literature in the late 1960s and 1970s. Aksyonov, Iskander, Voinovich, and Zinoviev, for example, all establish their dissident credentials during this period, primarily as a result of their satirical writings. Especially in the cases of Aksyonov and Voinovich, adoption of the subversive satirical mode represented a significant departure from their earlier, more ideologically acceptable forms of writing.[6] Each of these writers criticized Soviet (and occasionally American) governmental policies that led to, resulted from, and perpetuated the dangerous strategic shell game of the cold war.

Explicit instances of nuclear themes are scarce in both official and unofficial Russian literature—certainly far less common than in American fiction. In his *Red Stars: Political Aspects of Soviet Science Fiction* (1985), Patrick L. McGuire points out that while "after-the-bomb stories had been appearing in western science fiction since a time when the atomic bomb was itself fiction . . . no post-1920s Soviet story deals with the theme directly" (59). In fact McGuire lists only two novels that feature post-nuclear-war settings at all, *Obitaemyi ostrov* (1969; *Prisoners of Power*) by Boris and Arkady Strugatsky and *Posledniaia voina* (1970; *The Last War*) by Kirill Bulychev. In 1989 Vladimir Gakov and Paul Brians published a more extensive bibliography in the journal *Science-Fiction Studies* that lists fifty cold war–era Russian works "depicting nuclear war or its aftermath" (67) and another fifteen works that deal with the threat of nuclear war. Even with Gakov and Brians's expanded list—prefaced with the compilers' acknowledgment that "the theme has hardly been a popular one in the Soviet Union" and that the works they list are "for the most part . . . not major contributions to fiction" (67)—the number of Soviet texts explicitly engaging with nuclear issues is minuscule in comparison to the frequency with which this topos occurs in American science fiction.[7] Overt references to nuclear weapons occasionally cropped up in novels by dissident and/or émigré writers,[8] but such novels were generally written with little or no hope (or intention) of being published in the Soviet Union.

Rosalind J. Marsh also mentions the "tenuous" presence of nuclear themes in postwar Soviet literature in her *Soviet Fiction since Stalin: Soviet Politics and Literature* (1986).[9] Yet the scattered works she includes are never more than tangentially concerned with nuclear issues. Marsh attributes the general lack of nuclear themes in Soviet literature both to "a special military censorship [that] vetted all literary references to nuclear research" and to "the ambiguous Soviet position [on nuclear weapons], which can be defined as the combination of an avowedly defensive policy with an offensive posture" (195). Because ambiguous policies are inherently difficult to depict in an ideologically "correct" manner, most writers avoided altogether the possible pitfalls associated with the nuclear issue.

The immensely different relationship between the "average" citizen and the atomic bomb in the Soviet Union as opposed to the United States also helps explain the disparity in fictional representations of the bomb. First, the Soviet Union had no history of using its nuclear weapons in combat, thus sparing its citizenry the kind of moral dilemma that the Hiroshima and Nagasaki bombings represented.[10] In fact the Soviet Union and allied Communist organizations worldwide sponsored a campaign to outlaw atomic bombs entirely in the years immediately following the end of World War II. Although the Soviet Union was covertly working to produce its own bomb at the time, the pursuit of this policy was both good propaganda and a win-win political position: "If by chance the United States agreed to a paper ban without inspectors, Russia might feel a little more secure; meanwhile, provoking disgust toward atomic bombs would teach the world to despise the Americans who owned them" (Weart, *Nuclear Fear* 117–18).

Second, the quick onset of the cold war allowed Soviet authorities to claim moral superiority in the conflict by claiming that their own nuclear policies were simply a reaction to the demonstrated aggressive stance of the United States. Published opinion polls that showed the American public favoring the use of nuclear weapons in the Korean War served only to bolster this feeling and led to a rapid acceleration of weapons development and stockpiling on both sides (Boyer, *Fallout* 36–38).[11] In its early years, Soviet propagandists found it easy to justify the nuclear arms race as both a source of pride for the achievement of Soviet science and as defense of the Soviet motherland against American nuclear belligerence (a position that was predictably mirrored in American pronuclear, anti-Soviet propaganda). After the Cuban Missile Crisis, this tone moderated to the point that Soviet government official Mikhail Suslov openly stated in 1963 that in the case of nuclear war "the question of the victory of socialism would no longer arise for entire peoples, as they would have disappeared from the earth" (quoted in Weart, *Nuclear Fear* 238). Suslov and other Soviet officials who voiced similar opinions were careful to note that this was *not* the case for the Soviet Union; in keeping with Marxist-Leninist historical determinism, the governmental stance consistently, and irrationally, remained that nuclear combat would be regrettable but that the Soviet Union would survive and prevail.

Third, Soviet nuclear policy was part of general governmental policy and therefore virtually sacrosanct from criticism. This was somewhat less the case during the comparatively liberal years of the Thaw, but even then, the freedom to disapprove was generally limited to particular elements of nuclear policy rather than complete opposition. After Khrushchev's faction seized power from Molotov's comparatively more reactionary one in the wake of Stalin's death, the Soviet leadership advocated a purely defensive nuclear policy in public, even if that defensive posture did occasionally lead to serious "misunderstandings" like the Cuban Missile Crisis. Official Soviet policy from 1962 onward generally acknowledged the unprecedented destructiveness of nuclear war but maintained that the results would ultimately resemble "a radioactive Second World War, with large areas of their nation scorched yet once again struggling to victory" (Weart, *Nuclear Fear* 239). The repeated hard lessons of how to prevail despite the destruction of entire cities (as with Moscow in the Napoleonic Wars or Stalingrad in World War II) helped provide the Soviets with a propagandistic model for perseverance even in the face of the nuclear threat.

Finally the Soviet public had almost no visible antinuclear movement from which to take its example. There were few public figures who could parallel J. Robert Oppenheimer, Albert Einstein, Linus Pauling, or Leo Szilard, knowledgeable scientists who openly decried the risks of nuclear proliferation in the United States after 1945.[12] The physicist Andrei Sakharov, who was both the "father" of the Soviet atomic bomb and perhaps the most celebrated Soviet dissident, played this role as much as anyone could. His efforts were largely behind the scenes, frequently in the form of letters urging Khrushchev to stop atomic testing because of the dangers of radioactive fallout.[13] He also produced an article in 1957 for the popular magazine *Sovetskii soiuz* (*Soviet Union*) in which he outlined the biological effects of fallout from bomb tests. This article was contextualized in such a way as to criticize continued nuclear testing by the United States, which had already suffered international embarrassment in 1954, when radioactive fallout from the Castle Bravo hydrogen bomb test killed a Japanese fisherman, but Sakharov's unseen efforts to lobby Khrushchev make it clear that this propagandistic intention was not his. What small measure of public effect Sakharov's nuclear dissent had enjoyed, though, effectively ended in 1964 when Khrushchev was deposed in favor of the hard-line government of Leonid Brezhnev. From that point on, Sakharov's increasingly broad-ranging calls for peace, political reform, and nuclear disarmament were published and disseminated purely through unofficial channels and earned him the government's extreme ire.

Sakharov remained a relatively isolated figure, however, in his campaign to recontain the nuclear genie that he had previously helped set free. Outright antinuclear activism like that conducted in the United States by SANE

(National Committee for a Sane Nuclear Policy) and the Council for a Livable World would have been considered treasonous in the Soviet Union from the mid-1960s up to the glasnost era. Marsh notes that even though a "horrified reaction to nuclear weapons" was commonplace in the Soviet Union throughout the cold war, "at no time . . . has protest in the USSR approached the proportions of the CND [Campaign for Nuclear Disarmament] marches in Britain" (195). In short, state control of all discourse concerning nuclear weapons seems to have been designed to minimize their effect on everyday Soviet life.

This assessment does not imply that the Soviet people were ignorant or dismissive of the imminent threat of nuclear war. Weart summarizes the attitude of the Soviet populace toward the bomb:

> The belief that Soviet society would survive, as it had survived the Second World War, was still ritually invoked in military circles, but it was now [in the early 1980s] largely discredited among the public. A group of American psychiatrists who managed to poll some Soviet adolescents found them heavily concerned with the threat of global doom. Only 3 percent said that they and their families would survive a war, compared with 16 percent of a comparable sample of American students. . . . The Soviet civil defense program tried harder than ever, but its posters and textbooks, seen everywhere, offered precisely the same uncanny picture: a desert of rubble, through which somber figures moved, the few survivors shrouded in rubberized protective clothing and wearing gas masks, like a spectral procession commemorating the triumph of death.
> (*Nuclear Fear* 379–80)

Simply put, the atomic bomb was a palpable source of psychological stress for the average Russian, but one for which there were few, if any, outlets for relief. Since literary and other artistic expressions of the often dour fatalism engendered by the ever-present nuclear threat were not permitted during most of the cold war, the bomb provided fewer metaphors for life (and death) in Russian culture and literature than it did in the United States.

The paucity of atomic bomb–related metaphors in the Soviet cultural idiom points toward another common problem in the extant literary criticism about the cold war: a perhaps understandable but nevertheless problematic tendency to overemphasize the role of nuclear war in defining the cold war. Admittedly the cold war was the first period in human history in which the threat of nuclear war existed, but that threat has not disappeared along with the cold war, even if it has been lessened or altered appreciably. At least for the first few decades of their existence, nuclear weapons were intrinsically related to the cold war. As more states joined the nuclear fraternity and as the oversimplified black-and-white political divisions of the 1950s disintegrated, nuclear weapons ceased to be solely a subset of issues related to the cold war.

The primacy of nuclear weapons in the politics of the cold war also fails to define an absolute relationship between the two. The fact that the two superpowers repeatedly came into nonnuclear military conflict with one another—usually by proxy—over the course of more than forty years indicates that the cold war did not *inevitably* have a nuclear resolution, only the potential for one. The acknowledged military policy of both countries from the mid-1960s onward was shaped largely by the "escalation ladder thesis: war could and must be kept below the level of all-out destruction" (Weart, *Nuclear Fear* 379). Although the specter of the two countries' respective nuclear arsenals certainly hovered over the process (especially after the formulation and adoption of such policies as Mutual Assured Destruction), not all foreign policy decisions during the period were made with nuclear concerns exclusively or even foremost in mind.[14] Furthermore many issues unrelated or at most indirectly related to nuclear weapons (like the surveillance/detention of private citizens, trends toward technocracy, creation of sizable covert entities, growth and expansion of the military-industrial complex, economic globalization, and so on) stem from governmental and societal responses to stimuli intrinsic to the cold war.

Thus it is possible to speak of literary works dealing with cold war issues only tangentially related to nuclear issues. The neo-Stalinist domestic policies of the Brezhnev regime in large measure responded to the perceived weakening of Soviet power under Khrushchev. Since the balance of power during the cold war was chiefly predicated on the credibility of both the military arsenals and the political influence of its participants, any perceived damage to Soviet prestige, and the steps taken to repair such damage, implicitly became a cold war issue. The fact that Brezhnev's nuclear policy during the détente of the early and mid-1970s continued and even expanded Khrushchev's somewhat ambiguously conciliatory post-Cuba rhetorical stance serves to further demonstrate the potential autonomy of cold war issues from nuclear ones. As Marsh notes, "The USSR always regarded *détente* as a relationship of both cooperation and conflict: while agreeing that co-operation in such areas as arms control and trade was mutually beneficial, the Soviet leaders never contemplated changing their political system or modifying their foreign policy" (199). Thus détente was intended to reduce the nuclear danger of the cold war but had no bearing on the ideological struggle between the capitalist West and the Communist East, as shown by both sides' continued military support for warring satellite states.

Many of the Russian works included in this study, especially those written during the *zastoi* (stagnation) period of the mid-1970s, concern themselves with social and cultural deformations that result from this kind of duplicity. For most of these writers, the retreat from the Thaw concurrently signaled the end of any remaining belief that Communism could be modified to produce the positive ends that it promised. Their disillusioned works subverted not only Stalinism (as the most influential works of the Thaw had) but also Soviet Communism in general, frequently as part of a universal rejection of rigidly ideological value systems. Because the cold war was expressly "fought" in defense of such systems, this brand of subversion takes on a character particular to this historical period, much as the subversive critiques of the kind of knee-jerk nationalism that had previously led to World War I—such as Wilfrid Owen's "Dulce et Decorum Est" (1920), Jaroslav Hašek's *Good Soldier Schweik* (1921–23), and Erich Maria Remarque's *All Quiet on the Western Front* (1929)—were distinct products of that earlier time, despite numerous formal and tonal similarities with the works I will be analyzing herein.

I do not wish to overcompensate by downplaying the role of nuclear weapons in the cold war, either as a geopolitical conflict or as a literary milieu. My aim, rather, is to point out that there are ways of discussing the cold war that do not focus *exclusively* on the bomb, a position that has at times dominated the critical discourse. This study uses "cold war" broadly as an adjective to include consideration of cultural and especially linguistic issues relating to totalitarianism, control of information, technological innovation (nuclear weapons and other developments), sociological and/or psychological changes in cultures and/or individuals, and so on that arise especially during this period.[15]

A Brief History (and Working Definition) of Subversive Satire

In the introduction to *Fables of Subversion,* Weisenburger posits that satire in twentieth-century American literature works "in crucial opposition to the generative satires of a Pope or Twain . . . it functions to subvert hierarchies of value and to reflect suspiciously on all ways of making meaning, including its own" (3). He furthermore states that "narrative satire is a major form through which the postmodern writer interrogates and subverts authority" (6). And finally he affirms that "the concept of a degenerative satire can begin to map the landscape of contemporary American fiction in meaningful new ways, tracing lines of descent and differentiation that were previously fuzzy and indistinct" (3). I agree with him in this regard, but I also believe that one can glean a further level of meaning—the most important one, in my view—from these American "subversive satires" by comparing them with their Russian contemporaries. In my view the strictly American focus of Weisenburger's study creates an inherent limit to understanding the development of what he repeatedly and explicitly defines as a "postmodern" form of satire. While the aesthetic and philosophical concepts associated with postmodernism, which can also be rather "fuzzy and indistinct" at times, are doubtlessly germane to discussion of writers such as Pynchon, Coover, and Barth, I also believe that using the broader international context of the cold war as an interpretive lens provides even greater insight into a sustained collaborative (if not necessarily organized) effort at satirical subversion of the dominant political and cultural forces of the age on a global scale. Literary postmodernism's thoroughgoing drive to perceive, to expose, and frequently to undermine "master narratives" by scrutinizing how, why, and by whom they were constructed is a direct result of living in an era whose geopolitics, as George Orwell pointed out in the late 1940s, demanded belief in patent untruths, absurdities, and contradictions.

There are a host of formal and thematic similarities—including but not limited to depictions of processes that intentionally and clandestinely deform language, especially political language; depictions of science and technology being misused to serve political ends; "serial" and "systemic" dystopias, in which all seeming alternatives for social organization have catastrophic results; and depiction of the fabrication, literal and figurative, of history— among the works of satirical fiction written by Russian and American authors during the four decades after World War II. The ideological insularity of the two postwar superpowers restricts the likelihood that these correspondences stem from direct literary influence. Writers in Russia have had relatively free access to the works of their American contemporaries for only a few brief periods of the last two centuries. The few copies of illicit books smuggled into the Soviet Union during the cold war were irregularly circulated at great risk among an underground intelligentsia in a reverse form of *tamizdat*. Although Russian works were only occasionally subject to formal U.S. censorship, the availability and translation of Russian writers in the West from 1945 to 1990 was nevertheless heavily slanted toward those writers whose ideas fit, or could be made to fit, with the dominant anti-Soviet sentiment in the United States. As a result many of the writers this study examines have not gained a wide American audience, in part because they cast their satirical glance not only at the Soviet Union but often also at the West or at the world as a whole. With only a few exceptions, if their works have been published at all it is in relatively small English-language editions dwarfed by the massive printings of works by unambiguously anti-Soviet writers like Alexander Solzhenitsyn or seemingly apolitical writers like Boris Pasternak.

Yet the striking parallels between Russian and American satirical fiction during the latter half of the twentieth century stem first and foremost from the historically unique geopolitical situation of the cold war and its everpresent threat of complete nuclear annihilation. Satire in an age as filled with potential peril as the cold war provides a clear means by which to fulfill the simultaneously confrontational, analytical, and dissenting role that John Gery attributes to Gertrude Stein in the epigraph to this chapter. Weisenburger suggests a similar intention in the following passage: "If these fables of subversion can be said to target anything, it is fiction making, the very strategies of dissimulation by which the nuclear age seeks to mask its violent being" (19). Weisenburger stops short of articulating the explicit philosophical connection between this satirical mode and the deformed mentality produced when leaders ask people, among other things, to "stop worrying and love the

Bomb," but the historical role of Russian satire offers a model for extending his work in this manner.

In the opening section of her *Contemporary Russian Satire* (1995), Karen L. Ryan-Hayes affirms a number of Weisenburger's positions concerning the nature of satire (even as she engages in some of the "formalist" critique of satire against which he rails) in explicating Russian satire's idiosyncrasies: "While Western literary traditions have often deemphasized the didactic function of satire and viewed it as a forum for oppositionist commentary and mockery, Russian and Soviet criticism has emphasized the reformative nature of the mode" (3). She also claims (correctly, I believe) that the altered nature of satire produced under the threat of stringent censorship or even more severe official reprisal importantly distinguishes the development of Russian and especially Soviet satirical writing from that of the West. The government-approved satire produced under the watchful eye of the state (via the Writers' Union) functioned almost exclusively to "reform" in a strictly normative manner, usually in such a way as to denigrate "counterrevolutionary" elements in society. Such satire served to reinforce, and if necessary refurbish, the moral and political example of the original Bolshevik revolutionaries, especially Lenin. This basic intent remained the same whether the target of satire was the ineffectual NEP (New Economic Policy) of the 1920s, the "rootless cosmopolitans" of the 1930s, or the "Stalinist excesses" (as Khrushchev's famous phrase put it) that were briefly fair game for writers to criticize, albeit within defined limits, during the Thaw.

Satire of a somewhat less prescribed nature had appeared with some frequency in the earliest years of the Soviet Union. The decade between the end of the Russian Civil War in 1921 and the establishment of the Writers' Union witnessed the publication of a wealth of openly satirical works such as Mikhail Bulgakov's collection of short stories *Diavoliada* (1925; *Diaboliad*), several collections of stories by Mikhail Zoshchenko, Yuri Olesha's novella *Zavist'* (1927; *Envy*), Il'f and Petrov's novel *Dvenadsat' stul'ev* (1928; *The Twelve Chairs*), and Vladimir Mayakovsky's plays *Klop* (1928; *The Bedbug*) and *Bania* (1929; *The Bathhouse*). All of these works brought some measure of official censure to their authors for ideological waywardness. Even though the bulk of these works treated their subject matter wholly in keeping with the mainstream ideology of the time, their normative function was not fully achieved in the eyes of the official critics. Either they were too broad in satirical scope (that is, their targets included both ideologically correct and incorrect subject matter) or they were not explicit enough in their support for the Marxist-Leninist view of progress (that is, they failed to assert positively that Soviet Communism was the desirable—as well as the dialectically inevitable—way of the future).[16]

Mayakovsky's plays were critical of—among other things—the growing Soviet bureaucracy and the NEP, and his fervent support for the Bolshevik

Revolution did not shield him from a backlash by the Communist Party leadership. Both Zoshchenko and Bulgakov also brought the wrath of the government down upon themselves for criticizing the NEP.[17] Olesha's *Envy* satirizes overly positivistic Marxism-Leninism and the runaway bureaucracy even as it critiques the Russian intelligentsia for wavering in its commitment to the revolution. As Janet Tucker writes, "In *Envy*, we see that, having once gained control, revolutionaries have turned into their former nemesis, the autocracy; they are the new power structure. . . . *Envy* should therefore be considered anti-Soviet instead of anti-revolutionary" (20). Bulgakov's story "The Fatal Eggs" (in *Diaboliad*) contains a mild satirical critique of state interference in science. He revisited this theme more outspokenly in his satirical novel *Sobach'e serdtse* (*The Heart of a Dog*), which remained unpublished in the Soviet Union from its completion in 1925 until 1987.

Even though all of the works listed above (with the exception of *The Heart of a Dog*) were approved by the official literary organs of the state, they were all subject to suppression and/or substantial revision during the more stringent era of Socialist Realism that followed Stalin's rise to power. As the 1920s progressed, the relatively collegial attitude toward non-Communist writers who accepted the revolution or were at least sympathetic to it (known as *poputchiki* or "fellow travelers") changed dramatically. The more lenient view espoused by Trotsky and the critic Aleksandr Voronsky was replaced by the venomous denunciations of such "bourgeois" holdovers by the hard-line journal *Oktiabr'* (*October*), RAPP (Rossiiskaia assotsiatsiia proletarskikh pisatelei [the Russian Association of Proletarian Writers]) and other staunchly Communist groups.

Satirists were especially susceptible to censure during this time of backlash because their works were easily, yet often incorrectly, categorized as direct attacks on the principles of the revolution and the Soviet Union. As a result of this heightened ideological vigilance, virtually all satire legally published in the Soviet Union from 1932 until the mid-1980s corresponded to the "reformative" and "normative" mode designed to bring readers back in line with Soviet ideology.[18] Satire that threatened to subvert that ideology was inherently limited to *samizdat* or *tamizdat* publication.

In American literature the official source of judgment concerning the place of satire is not rooted so much in governmental machinations[19] as in the iconic status of certain literary critics or schools of thought. Many formalist critics dismissed satire as either a "dead" form describing only the works of such past practitioners as Jonathan Swift and Alexander Pope or as a "low" or "vulgar" form. If considered at all, it was generally only as an archaic discursive mode derived from Greek and Roman literature. Even Gilbert Highet views it as something of an artifact of bygone ages in his landmark 1962 book *The Anatomy of Satire*. Despite mentioning a few relatively minor contemporary satirists (such as Mary McCarthy), Highet's work leaves the reader with the clear impression that satire is almost entirely the domain of Juvenal, Aristophanes, Pope, Swift, and Voltaire. Highet's book opens, in fact, by stating that "satire is not the greatest type of literature" and that "it cannot, in spite of the ambitious claims of one of its masters [that is, Juvenal], rival tragic drama and epic poetry" (3). According to Highet, satire may make brief appearances in contemporary literature, but its heyday has definitely passed, a view that not only reflected but also bolstered the dominant critical attitude of the time.

Starting in the early 1970s, such critics as Leon Guilhamet, Jerome Klinkowitz, Linda Hutcheon, and others began to discuss satire, especially contemporary satire, in a new way, focusing on not only its narrative-destabilizing metafictional qualities but also its potential for political and cultural activism. Weisenburger adapts the works of these predecessors in identifying the subversive tendency in twentieth-century American satire. Weisenburger does not define subversion simply as making a target or set of targets seem absurd via satirical derision but as a wholesale exposure of destructive and insidious cultural forces. In this way he claims a greater power for subversion than its simple definition—that is, sabotage or rebellion—implies. His form of subversion is implicitly critical of *all* modern ideologies, even those that rebel against or undermine the status quo, as being consciously constructed fictions that aspire impossibly (or pretend) to be more or less absolute truths.

Weisenburger's study owes a notable debt to Hutcheon's *Poetics of Postmodernism* (1988). In that book Hutcheon articulated a definition of postmodernist literature that remains compelling two decades later. More immediately germane to this study is her definition of "historiographic metafiction," a subset of postmodernist literature to which almost all cold war subversive satire—Russian and American—inherently belongs. In terms of its opposition to what Jean-François Lyotard and others categorized as "master narratives," Hutcheon claims that postmodernism "is characterized by energy derived from the rethinking of the value of multiplicity and provisionality; in actual practice, it does not seem to be defined by any potentially paralyzing opposition between making and unmaking. . . . Postmodernist discourses—both theoretical and practical—need the very myths and conventions they contest and reduce; they do not necessarily come to terms with either order or disorder, but question both in terms of each other. The myths and conventions exist for a reason, and postmodernism investigates that reason. The postmodern impulse is not to seek any total vision. It merely questions. If it *finds* such a vision, it questions how, in fact, it *made* it" (48). More specifically Hutcheon argues that historiographic metafiction is "willing to draw upon any signifying practices it can find operative in a society. It wants to challenge those discourses and yet to use them, even to milk them for all they are worth" (133). This dual intent allows historiographic metafictions to first reveal the means of their own construction and then to disrupt them, thereby destabilizing *any* ideological potentialities found therein: "[The postmodern novel] begins by creating and centering a world . . . and then contesting it. Historiographic metafictions are not 'ideological novels' in Susan Suleiman's sense of the word: they do not 'seek, through the vehicle of fiction to convince their readers of the "correctness" of a particular way of interpreting the world.' Instead they make their readers *question* their own (and by implication others') interpretations. They are more 'romans à hypothèse' than 'romans à thèse'" (180). This unwillingness to provide a fixed substitute truth to replace the contested one(s) is precisely what has opened postmodernism up to being labeled a "nihilistic" or "empty" worldview by its detractors, a charge that echoes in Rorty's laments about the lack of "hope" in Pynchon, Silko, et al. Such a pejorative characterization is in my view a vestige of the moralistically binary worldviews that have predominated in the West since the Enlightenment, and the validity of such worldviews are intrinsically called into question by postmodernist philosophies.

Even though Hutcheon's approach does not directly engage with critical theories of satire,[20] her work still succinctly and compellingly delineates the subversively humanist and inherently nonbinary (or perhaps transbinary) intentions underlying most cold war satirical fiction, as her brief commentary on Ishmael Reed illustrates:

> Those in power control history. The marginal and ex-centric, however, can contest that power, even as they remain within its purvey. Ishmael Reed's "Neo-HooDoo Manifesto" [in *Mumbo Jumbo*] reveals these power relations in both history and language. But in several ways, he reveals the inside-ness of his insider-outsider marginalized position. On the one hand, he offers another totalizing system to counter that of white western culture: that of voodoo. And, on the other hand, he appears to believe strongly in certain humanist concepts, such as the ultimately free individual artist in opposition to the political forces of oppression. This is the kind of self-implicated yet challenging critique of humanism, however, that is typical of postmodernism. The position of black Americans has worked to make them especially aware of those political and social consequences of art, but they are still part of American society. (197–98)

This passage articulates precisely why I believe that subversive satire is not a dejected response but a strident affirmation of a need for a new worldview in the face of extreme circumstances resulting from pervasive ideological entrenchment. Given their utterly marginalized position vis-à-vis institutional power, both Russian and American subversive satirists find potency instead through their skill at creating and interpreting texts. They call, much as Kennan did in 1992, for a thorough and honest reexamination not only of how and why we arrived at the historical juncture of the cold war but also, and

more important, how and why we *think* we arrived there and who is ultimately responsible for conveying that conception to us: "Historiographic
metafiction . . . demands of the reader not only the recognition of textualized
traces of the literary and historical past but also the awareness of what has
been done—through irony—to those traces. The reader is forced to acknowledge not only the inevitable textuality of our knowledge of the past, but also
both the value and the limitation of the inescapably discursive form of that
knowledge" (Hutcheon 127).

Cold War Satire: *Genre, Subgenre, Mode,* *All of the Above, or None?*

A great deal of the critical work produced on satire in the past fifty years centers on the debate about whether satire is a mode or a genre. The modal
school of thought sees satire as a method that can be used in any particular
genre to create an atmosphere of ridicule that would normally not exist
within the conventions of that genre. Using this line of reasoning, Twain's
Connecticut Yankee in King Arthur's Court (1889) achieves a satirical effect
because of the modal application of satirical elements onto the existing semantic framework of the well-defined genre of the Arthurian romance, with
its recognizable characters, setting, plots, themes, and language. The satiric
mode transforms (or deforms) the meanings usually carried by a particular
genre conveying an alternate satirical meaning in its place. For the modal
critics, satire is generally the formal equivalent of an adjective in traditional
grammar: abstract at best or meaningless at worst without a genre/noun—
the picaresque novel, the epic poem, the legal drama, and so on—to modify.

On the other hand, those critics who contend that satire exists sui generis
argue that the didactic role of satire forms an expectation of meaning and
content regarding the satirical text itself. Such expectations hold true among
satires in general, even when their outward form seems to be that of another
genre. The genre itself may be perceived as being variable because the cultural norms from which individual satires arise are not consistent,[21] but the
underlying techniques and tropes remain essentially the same even as the
superficial form mutates. Brian A. Connery and Kirk Combe refer to this
process in their introduction to *Theorizing Satire: Essays in Literary Criticism*
(1995) as "satire's insistence on its historical specificity, its torrential references to the peculiarities of the particular individuals in the society that it
represents" (4). John R. Clark puts this "historical specificity" into an explicitly linguistic context, claiming that satirists are "vigilantes of crapulous usage
and abusage" who are "perennially sensitized to auditioning and preserving
the languages of Babel. They will never forgive the vocabulary of fools, the
punctuation of profligates, the syntax of disorder or disgrace" (21). Although
satire may thus be forced to "inhabit the forms of other genres" (Connery
and Combe 5), it is defined as a genre of its own by virtue of the consistency

of its basic and necessary technique of making meaning—in the form of critical commentary—through the tension between thesis and antithesis, or "straight" reading and satirical subtext (6, 11).

Leon Guilhamet's *Satire and the Transformation of Genre* (1987) attempts to mediate between these two camps of satire theorists. For Guilhamet, modal satire occurs largely as a distinction from the comic mode: "The basic difference between the satiric and the comic is that the satiric reinterprets the ridiculous in an ethical light. The satiric employs comic techniques of ridicule, but discovers harm and even evil in the ridiculous. The ridiculous that is proper to satire cannot be reconciled to the good at the conclusion of a comic plot" (8). He goes on to write that this form of satire is readily apparent but insufficient for the more expansive generic understanding of satire: "The essential integrants of generic satire are a combination of modal satire and variable rhetorical and generic structures which are borrowed and deformed. The dynamic of satire transforms these components into a new generic identity" (11). His emphasis on the "borrow[ing] and deform[ing]" of "rhetorical and generic structures" is what makes this definition especially valuable for my discussion of cold war satire, since many of these works explicitly appropriate and deform the nonfictional "genres" of cold war rhetoric, including political speeches, mass-media journalism, legislative and judicial deliberations, and a host of others.

Weisenburger crystallizes the utility of this approach when he notes that it "treats narrative fictions as manifestations of intertextuality or 'dialogism' in the Bakhtinian sense, thus as counterpositionings not only of different voices in the narrative itself but also of anterior texts and the codified elements of language and culture in general" (11). He additionally claims that this "approach coincides with the provisional definition . . . [of] degenerative satire as a form for interrogating and subverting codified knowledge and revealing it as a dissimulation of violence" (11–12). Weisenburger expands the parodic aspect of satire to include not only formal distortions of literary models but also thematic ridicule of social, political, psychological, linguistic, or philosophical knowledge and/or behavior—anything that can be reduced to "elements of language and culture" of some sort. In doing so, he again echoes Hutcheon, who argues that historiographic metafiction's "self-awareness of history and fiction as human constructs . . . is made the grounds for its rethinking and reworking of the forms and contents of the past" (5). She later describes the process by which postmodernist literature intertextually destabilizes the certainty of the past in order to stimulate a less constrained deliberation on received textual knowledge: "Postmodern intertextuality is a formal manifestation of both a desire to close a gap between present and past of the reader and a desire to rewrite the past in a new context. It is not a modernist desire to order the present through the past or to make the present look spare in contrast to the richness of the past. It is not attempt to void or avoid history. Instead, it directly confronts the past of literature—and of historiography, for it too derives from other texts (documents). It uses and abuses those intertextual echoes, inscribing their powerful allusions and then subverting that power through irony. In all, there is little of the modernist sense of a unique, symbolic, visionary 'work of art'; there are only texts, already written ones" (118). The dual process of interrogation and revelation that Weisenburger and Hutcheon (among others) identify is in my view the *fundamental* intention that links most cold war satire, whether Russian or American. As the later chapters of this book will show, what follows on that initial process not surprisingly varies from author to author, including calls for a return to a form of seemingly abandoned traditional values; exhortations to greater compassion or better judgment; rational arguments against the continuation of particular behaviors, policies, and so on; vociferous appeals for immediate political and/or social reform; incitements to rise up and overthrow the status quo by force; and sometimes just a cri de coeur that asks us collectively to step away from the brink of self-destruction for a moment.

2

The Intersection of Literature and Politics during the Cold War

The Landscape of the Cold War's "City of Words"

Tony Tanner's 1971 *City of Words* is one of the first exhaustive studies of how post–World War II American authors responded to cultural stimuli of their time. Although Tanner examines these developments primarily in terms of their departure from aesthetic and stylistic conventions in American literature, the underlying sociopolitical dimension also merits greater attention. As a growing number of relatively low-cost media radically increased the quantity of messages to which the average American was exposed during the early years of the cold war, the potential influence that language could exert also increased. This point was understood equally by Joseph McCarthy and George Orwell, although it led them to very different conclusions; where McCarthy saw Communist propaganda lurking masked in "genres" ranging from Hollywood scripts, insufficiently vigilant government legislation, and college lectures, Orwell saw a society increasingly willing not only to be told what it thought but also the words in which it was proper to have those thoughts.

As the cold war progressed, the discursive environment of the United States increasingly resembled Times Square with its whirlwind of messages bombarding the individual from every direction. Also like Times Square, though, the superficial diversity of these messages was subtly undercut by their homogeneous role as carefully constructed advertisements for some aspect of American consumer culture and its products. In such an environment, voices of dissent, criticism, and/or reform found it increasingly difficult to be heard as long as they participated in the extant forms of expression, given that such forms are designed, as Marshall McLuhan and others began pointing out volubly in the 1960s, to control or even to become "the message." Altering, subverting, or even altogether abandoning the conventional modes of expression thus becomes not only an aesthetic choice but also an inherently political one. Pynchon fictionally conveyed his understanding of this concept in *The Crying of Lot 49* via the mysterious Tristero organization (and its clandestine W.A.S.T.E. mail system), whose rhetoric contains echoes of nonfictional countercultures ranging from the civil rights movement and second-wave feminism to the Black Panthers and the Weather Underground.

In his introduction Tanner argues that all writers face a complex choice regarding their use of accepted forms of language: "If he wants to write in any communicable form he must traffic in a language which may at every turn be limiting, directing and perhaps controlling his responses and formulations. If he feels that the given structuring of reality of the available language is imprisoning or iniquitous, he may abandon language altogether; or he may seek to use the existing language in such a way that he demonstrates to himself and other people that he does not wholly conform to the structures built into the common tongue, that he has the power to resist and perhaps disturb the particular 'rubricizing' tendency of the language he has inherited" (16). While admitting that such authorial behavior "is not in itself a new position for the writer to find himself in," Tanner also asserts "that many recent American writers are unusually aware of this quite fundamental and inescapable paradox: that to exist, a book, a vision, a system, like a person, has to have an outline—there can be no identity without contour. But contours signify arrest, they involve restraint and the acceptance of limits" (16–17). Although Tanner repeatedly uses physical metaphors in these passages (resist, disturb, arrest, restraint) to describe defiance of linguistic conventions in literary works, he refrains from concretizing this symbolic linkage between stylistic innovation and sociopolitical activism in the remainder of his study. I would suggest that the disturbance and rejection of restraint that he notes among a younger generation of American writers is intended very much as an agitation, not simply of the literary world but potentially of the whole world.

What Tanner metaphorically calls "contours" were very palpable aspects of language choices for Russian writers during the cold war. Although Socialist Realism was (in principle, at least) not so comprehensively prescriptive after 1953 as it had been during Stalin's time, it still exerted a powerful influence over literature. In *Inside the Soviet Writers' Union* (1990), John Garrard and Carol Garrard discuss the objections to *sotsrealizm* raised at the 1954 Writers' Congress by Konstantin Simonov, then vice general secretary of the Writers' Union and editor of *Novy mir* (*New World*), one of the most influential official Soviet literary journals:

> The Party had its loyal supporters at the same 1954 Congress argue
> that Socialist Realism was not a straitjacket, but could expand to accommodate almost any theme or approach to reality. Konstantin Simonov
> charged that some of his comrades viewed Soviet society through rose-tinted glasses due to a "misunderstanding of the essence of Socialist
> Realism.". . . As a result, instead of remaining faithful to a true Socialist

Realist approach, much Soviet prose had been damaged by the "varnishing of reality" (*lakirovka*). Simonov perceived a distinct threat to Soviet literature in a "vulgarizing" tendency which he identified with specific critics—the tendency to approach Socialist Realism as a "single, unified style" that must be adopted by all writers, and to condemn anything written outside this style as "wicked and evil." (168)

The tendency of Socialist Realism to "varnish reality" is, as many dissident writers repeatedly pointed out, an inevitable result of requiring literature to give preference to *partiinost'* (roughly, "party spirit" or "party discipline") over empirical or even more abstract philosophical truths.

Aksyonov uses the notion of *lakirovka* ironically in a 1964 short story, "Malen'kii Kit, lakirovshchik deistvitel'nosti" ("Little Whale, Varnisher of Reality"). In its pejorative sense, *lakirovka* carries a meaning similar to "whitewashing" in English. Aksyonov's story inverts this meaning somewhat, since it is the protagonist's young son (nicknamed "Little Whale") whose innocent fantasies provide a welcome release from the tedium and deprivations of daily existence, not only for himself but also for his father. Although no more realistic than the distortions of Socialist Realism, Little Whale's form of childish *lakirovka* at least provides some relief from the harsh conditions of Soviet life rather than trying to cover them up. While Simonov stopped short of condemning the Communist Party's ideological dominance, Garrard and Garrard note that any such openly expressed criticism of Socialist Realism by a party leader was "the literary equivalent of Khrushchev's later attack on Stalin—the end of infallibility" (169).

Nevertheless the expansion of Socialist Realism that Simonov proposed was far from universally endorsed, even during the most liberal periods of state control over literature. Official means of publication in the Soviet Union remained firmly bound by ideological strictures: "Executives at Goskomizdat [the State Committee for Publishing Houses, Printing Plants, and the Book Trade] in the Brezhnev period naturally believed that their job was not to produce an economically viable product, but rather to market an ideology. Soviet centralized planning had always stressed production rather than consumption. . . . As long as ideological purity meant more than financial profit, they would continue to receive good reports from their superiors" (Garrard and Garrard 173). This system of publication based on ideological purity helped create the cultural *zastoi* of the 1970s, since it encouraged a lack of creativity in authors hoping to be published through official channels.[1] Few publishers would risk sending a book to Goskomizdat or Glavlit, the official censorship organization, if they were unsure of its ideological worth.

In *The Anti-Soviet Soviet Union*, Voinovich cites the massive influx of party officials into the ranks of the Writers' Union after the Thaw as one of the prime absurdities of such a system. Since members of the party hierarchy were presumed to be ideologically correct, ostensibly literary works written by such individuals were relatively safe to publish, regardless of their artistic value:

> [Policemen], KGB men, managers of stores and saunas, building managers, and the chairmen of dacha coops have all entered the field of literature.
>
> The corruption of literature has gone so far as to have obliterated all the boundary lines between the professional writer and those who are published because they have pull. A KGB general writes no worse than a professional writer, and the professional writes no better than a store manager. (256)[2]

Voinovich states that such a self-perpetuating system results in ideologically consistent but artistically moribund literature: "Living literature was the enemy of the new system, and now that enemy has been laid low, trampled, and nearly wiped out" (258).

Voinovich notes that the emphasis on *partiinost'* over literary merit extended to the highest echelon of Soviet society, helping to bolster Brezhnev's image even in the midst of the *zastoi*: "When Marshal Brezhnev began to publish his three-volume book of mythology, all the leading lights of Soviet literature, the secretaries of the Writers' Union, the heroes of Socialist labor, and all the other prize winners were unanimous in declaring, both verbally and in print, that these books were inimitable masterpieces, comparable only to the best (not just any) pages of *War and Peace*" (256). The "book of mythology" Voinovich mentions is a three-part memoir in which Brezhnev—or more likely his unacknowledged ghostwriter—rather artlessly "varnished" the history of the Soviet Union. Despite (or perhaps because of) rumors of his advancing senility, Brezhnev was awarded the Lenin Prize in Literature for this work in 1979. Voinovich does not hide his low opinion of this award: "When experts now calculate how much damage drunkenness and absenteeism do to the Soviet economy, they should also include the damage done to the economy by Brezhnev's literary indulgences" (322).

Dovlatov also sardonically comments on the sorry state of the Soviet publication system in a chapter of his semiautobiographical *Nevidimaia kniga* (1978; *The Invisible Book*) titled "A Nest of Vipers":

> I am convinced that editorial principles are invariable. . . . There are those who know how to write. And there are those whose vocation is to give orders. Those who write earn less. But they smile more, drink more, and pay alimony. Those in command consist for the most part of former proofreaders, typists, Pioneer leaders, and local trade union activists.
>
> Sensing their creative impotence, these people follow the safe administrative path their whole lives. Their perfect loyalty makes up for their lack of professional skills. (108–9)

Elsewhere he describes the ineptitude of a certain V. Kozlov, head of the prose section at the Leningrad journal *Avrora* (*Aurora*), as a discrepancy between intellectual and physical potency: "At that time manuscripts were piling up fast and furious on his desk—a whole mountain of them! So he, who is physically a very strong man, picked up the whole pile and took it to the dump. After all, how could one be expected to read through such a mountain?!" (103). Given such a glaring lack of literary sophistication among professional editors, stylistic innovation or linguistic experimentalism was often automatically assumed to be concealing ideological divergences.[3] "Avant-gardism" supplanted "cosmopolitanism" and "formalism" as a defamatory buzzword meaning "anti-Soviet" in the parlance of the Writers' Union; most of the Russian satirists included in this study suffered professional (and in some cases physical) castigation for the content and/or form of their works.

Thus the Soviet "city of words" was an even more exclusive environment than that of the United States in the post–World War II years. The "structuring of reality of the available language [was] imprisoning or iniquitous" in the Soviet Union not only in aesthetic terms but also in literal ones, often requiring physical risk or complete departure (on the part of the text, the author, or both) as a precondition to the dissemination of work that wished to critique the established ideology. Tanner's claims concerning the paradox of language facing American writers of the post–World War II period are equally if not more applicable to those writers' Russian counterparts, even though their respective societies are posited as diametrically opposed to one another within the public aspect of cold war rhetoric.

Since Tanner repeatedly couches his discussion of stylistic innovation in terms of freedom and individual identity within a society, extending his ideas to encompass Russian literature naturally requires some examination of how and why the metaphorical confinement of American authors resembles the symbolically and literally confining Russian situation. Tanner states that an identity crisis arose among American authors because of the binary relationship between "utter formlessness" and an "adopted armature [that] is at the same time felt to be an imprisoning deathly constriction" (18–19). He again uses this metaphor of incarceration to formulate one of his principal theses: "The dilemma and quest of the hero are often analogous to those of the author. Can he find a *stylistic* freedom which is not simply a meaningless incoherence, and can he find a stylistic form which will not trap him inside the existing forms of previous literature?" (19). But if Tanner is unwilling to say that this phenomenon is either unique to the period he is treating or out of keeping with general trends in American literature, why should this development be of particular interest, much less a large portion of his thesis? One answer is that cold war society and language presented such an objectionable "rubric" for some authors that they invited or perhaps demanded not just a

Pound-like call for transgressive innovation ("Make it new!") but a form of genuinely subversive resistance and disturbance.

The same can be said for Russian literature of the cold war that protested the status quo. Andrei Sinyavsky (writing as Abram Tertz) launched the post-Stalin era of satirical subversion in 1956 by sending his essay *Chto takoe sotsialisticheskii realizm?* (1959; *What Is Socialist Realism?*) and the accompanying novel *Sud idet* (1959; *The Trial Begins*) to France for publication. Catharine Theimer Nepomnyashchy's assessment of these two works closely parallels, albeit in a more explicitly political context, Tanner's claims about a reaction among post–World War II American writers against the "rubricizing tendency" of inherited language: "They . . . mark the beginning of Sinyavsky's unofficial writing activities in that they constitute an exorcism of sorts, a confrontation with and attempt to overcome the then-prevailing hegemony of Socialist Realism through an exposure of its formal incoherence. The two works thus may be viewed conjointly as the writer's declaration of independence, his escape from the Soviet canon. In each of them Tertz begins by ostensibly positioning his narrator within the conventions of Socialist Realism in order, ultimately, to subvert those conventions from within by calling into question the existence of a single defining center and thus the authority of authorial voice" (40). Sinyavsky, along with most of the dissident satirists that follow in his wake, engages in "resist[ance] and . . . disturb[ance]" of established Soviet language, using this to denigrate by extension the social and political constructs that are supported by such language. As Nepomnyashchy (echoing Tanner and Weisenburger) notes, the "crime committed [from the viewpoint of the Soviet authorities] by *What Is Socialist Realism?* and *The Trial Begins*—and by all of Tertz's other works—consists in posing a challenge to claims to linguistic authority, to the right to define and therefore judge, including those staked by the literary text" (63). During the cold war, such official claims to linguistic authority are more overt in the Soviet Union than in the United States—that is, there is no American governmental organ that corresponds to the Writers' Union or Glavlit. Nevertheless the impulse to undermine the existing language was extensive in both countries, thanks to the abuses brought about by the cold war rivalry between them.

As the cold war progressed, a substantial body of both fictional and critical work emerged that strengthened the proposition that American language after World War II had become semantically impoverished and was therefore less useful as the raw material for literary creation. Although such an assertion may be couched in aesthetic and linguistic terms (as was the case with John Barth's 1967 essay "The Literature of Exhaustion"), the underlying polemical motivation is often more sociopolitical in nature. For example, in the conclusion to *Fables of Subversion,* Weisenburger discusses what he sees as a prominent misconception of the role of literature in "late capitalist"

American culture: "To a number of critics . . . the work of postmodernism consists in an oppositional politics involving the generation and consumption of signs. The problem with [this] argument, however, is that it repeatedly tropes this potential in terms of aesthetic transgression" (258). Weisenburger rejects this strictly transgressive model because it creates a situation in which art voluntarily limits itself to mimicking rather than critiquing the dominant strains of American culture: "Such a reading fails to make a necessary distinction between transgressing and more properly resisting or dissenting practices. There can be no question that transgressing only serves to recuperate the culture of late capitalism. Disrupting all boundaries or conceptions of the subject and its community, art replicates and thus situates us still more comfortably amid the hyperreality of instant pleasures encouraged by Madison Avenue, Hollywood, and the White House" (258).

Weisenburger quotes Charles Altieri in reaffirming the subversive social function of art, in the process echoing the idiom of limits and resistance that Tanner uses in *City of Words*: "As Altieri puts the case, 'It is necessary to posit an explicitly oppositional art devoted to resisting dominant social interests. This art would not so much escape limits as make compelling the pain which those limits create and the interests that thrive on such pain, including interests in the myths of taste and sensibility fostered by the ideals of transgression'" (259). Altieri's (and by extension Weisenburger's) concept accentuates the sociopolitical ramifications of Tanner's dilemma of linguistic imprisonment. The subversive satires of the cold war wish not simply to disassociate themselves (that is, to "escape limits") from the cultural forces that created the cold war world, but actually to undermine their influence or, in the most optimistic cases, to undo the damage they have caused.

Fictionality and the Ultimate Purpose of Subversive Satire

In his *Dissident Postmodernists* (1991), Paul Maltby argues that recognition of a "dissident tendency" is essential to full understanding of the social intentions of a subset of "postmodernist writers, [for whom] the problem of meaning has a contextual dimension insofar as they perceive language as bearing the imprints of the institutions, projects, and conflicts in which it is imbricated" (39). Maltby's explicitly politicized thesis—that much of postmodern play with narrative form contains overtones of social protest—and his choice of words in his title suggest an intentional connection between the American authors such as Barthelme, Coover, and Pynchon that he discusses and such stylistically avant-garde Russian satirists as Aksyonov, Aleshkovsky, and Sokolov.

Whether discussed in the context of Aesopian language, dialogism, polyphony, textual parody, or sociopolitical satire, the notion that the language of fiction can surreptitiously subvert the Soviet "institutions, projects, and conflicts in which it is imbricated" is hardly an innovative one.[4] Maltby's identification of the "dissident" strain in postmodernist *American* literature, however, is an attempt to answer a question that he claims is unanswerable using the established critical models: "Why should the fictionality of meaning become a major issue at a particular time, in a particular place (i.e., in late-capitalist America)? . . . No coherent model of postmodern culture underpins neo-formalist studies of postmodernist fiction. In these studies, the fictionality of meaning is an issue rarely examined beyond its aesthetic and epistemological implications. And yet our very idea of fictionality has been enlarged and enriched by sociological inquiries into the nature of postmodern culture. . . . An explanation of the postmodernist writer's preoccupation with fictionality requires, *inter alia*, acknowledgement of his/her situation in a culture pervaded by illusory use-values and simulacra" (21). My argument throughout this study is not only that such an acknowledgment is integral to comparative examination of Russian and American satirical fiction but also that the sources of this "fictionality of meaning" are directly related to the cultural mindset that allowed the cold war to exist in the first place.

Wolfgang Iser's 1997 essay "The Significance of Fictionalizing" cogently outlines how and why this issue of fictionality is relevant when examining the cultural effects of textual language. Iser's tripartite definition of a "fiction" includes each of the following "acts" on the part of an author:

1) a selection from a variety of social, historical, cultural and literary systems that exist as referential fields outside the text
2) the organization of specific semantic demarcations within the text [that] give rise to intratextual fields of reference
3) the self-disclosure of its fictionality, . . . [which] places the world organized in the text under the sign of the "as if" [and signals to readers] that they must bracket off their natural attitudes toward what they are reading. (Iser 2–3)

Although Iser does not treat satire specifically, his model for literary fictions in general serves an invaluable function in discussing the nature of cold war satire because of the distinction Iser makes between literary and nonliterary fictions. He suggests that the foundations of a wide variety of nonliterary modes are predicated on fiction: "With epistemological positing, it is a premise; with the hypothesis, it is a test; with world-pictures, it is a dogma whose fictional nature must remain concealed if the foundation is not to be impaired; and with our actions, it is anticipation" (2). For my purposes, the next to last of these is the most important form of nonliterary fiction, since the competing "world-pictures" of the United States and the Soviet Union were the primary factors in the continuation of the cold war.

While contending that literary fictions necessarily disclose their own fictionality, Iser points out that nonliterary fictions are not governed by any such requirement. In fact just the opposite is true; nonliterary fictions are required to "mask" their fictionality for a number of reasons: "The masking, of course, need not necessarily occur with the intention to deceive; it occurs because the fiction [within the nonfiction] is meant to provide an explanation, or even a foundation, and would not do so if its fictive nature were to be exposed. The concealment of fictionality endows an explanation with an appearance of reality, which is vital, because fiction—as explanation—functions as the constitutive basis of this reality" (3). Although Iser rightly allows for potentially innocent motivations behind social fictions, the kind of grand-scale fictionalizing that underpins the cold war invites criticism (and thus satire) both because of the high stakes involved and because of the suspicion that these fictions are not intended as forthright explanations but as elaborately constructed and assiduously maintained distortions of reality.[5]

Given Iser's claim that "literary genres are the most obvious and durable signs" for the fictionality of literary fictions, it comes as no surprise that the satires of the cold war often include parodies of the nonliterary "genres" through which social and political fictions were sustained: denunciations, loyalty oaths, political speeches, economic reports, court proceedings, official government documents, and so on.[6] Hutcheon's assertion that "historiographic metafiction appears to be willing to draw upon any signifying practices it can find operative in a society" (133) becomes especially relevant to understanding how textual parody functions in cold war satire. Parody is an inherently fictive literary form, deriving its efficacy from the reader's recognition of the extant text being parodied. Satire takes this process one step further by affirming the absurdity of its object, in this case by uncovering the counterfeit "truths" of which cold war world-pictures consist (and by extension the "dominant social interests" [Weisenburger 259] that created them in the first place). Such overt and explicit proclamation of fictionality is absolutely essential to these satires' effectiveness, since it makes clear the ontological similarities between themselves and the social constructs they deride. The self-evident fictionality of cold war satires thus becomes an integral part of their authors' "acknowledgement of [their] situation in a culture pervaded by illusory use-values and simulacra" (Maltby 21).

The subversive satirical model also helps resolve a philosophical issue that Tanner raises in *City of Words*, since fictions that satirize other fictions for claiming to be truths cannot then turn around and claim such a status for themselves. Weisenburger provides one possible solution for this problem when he states that subversive satire "functions to subvert hierarchies of value and to reflect suspiciously on all ways of making meaning, including its own" (3). His framework neither implies that subversive satirists are seeking a more perfect language of expression to replace the ones they are undermining, nor limits itself to textual transgressions of the extratextual realm. Weisenburger's concept allows one to read subversive satires as categorical denials of the validity of cold war social fictions as the "constitutive basis of [a] reality" that includes both the threat of total nuclear destruction and a pair of relatively small power elites who are the principal beneficiaries of the status quo.

The Cognitive Conception of the Cold War

Matthew S. Hirshberg's *Perpetuating Patriotic Perceptions: The Cognitive Function of the Cold War* (1993) provides a compelling summary of both how that status quo came into being and how it maintains itself. Hirshberg extensively scrutinizes American attitudes (in public opinion, official governmental policy, and academe) about the cold war in the context of cognitive science. In doing so he argues that "patriotic cold war preconceptions affect perceptions of the 'reality' of world affairs" and that these often inaccurate perceptions were in turn used "in perpetuating patriotic support in the face of the many twists, turns, tumbles, and triumphs of U.S. foreign policy" (4). Moreover, Hirshberg's book persuasively outlines the ways in which systematic linguistic associations with certain values formed the basis of a series of complex cognitive schemata that allowed the cold war to continue, often despite evidence that invalidated the dichotomies intrinsic to a binary moral conflict. In doing so Hirshberg creates an invaluable frame of reference for discussing how and why the (de)formation of various forms of public discourse, and subsequent exposures of those discursive processes, are potentially political acts.

Hirshberg begins by outlining what he calls the "American patriotic schema" (39). He remarks that this self-image is "the most important, most salient, and most stable political schema in American culture, and it forms the core of international relations schemata such as the cold war schema" (38). This schema "consists of five concepts (the United States, the self, good, democracy, and freedom) and ten positive relationships among those concepts" (38). In essence it represents a concise summation of the national ideals articulated in the Declaration of Independence and the Constitution. The importance of this schema for Hirshberg lies in its consistent application in shaping policy: "The same American patriotic schema structures mainstream American thinking about both domestic and international politics, providing a stable cognitive basis for patriotic perceptions in both arenas" (39). Thus the logical/rhetorical cycle is established—the schema guides the policy, which reinforces the schema (either in reality or by manipulation of the perception of the policy), which guides the policy, and so on, potentially ad infinitum. As Hirshberg notes, the "American patriotic schema is self-perpetuating: its use reinforces its cultural dominance, which increases its use" (41).

American historians and politicians alike were able to use repeated military triumphs to bolster the patriotic schema and all its constituent associations:

"As we move this patriotic schema into the world of international conflict, we see that at various times in history, the United States, freedom, and democracy have had to do battle with opposing forces. . . . Images of these enemies served to bolster and perpetuate the patriotic national self-image by providing the evils against which the nation could favorably compare itself and the threats in terms of which it could justify questionable policies and actions" (39). Hirshberg argues that the three most important such conflicts in terms of their fortifying potency toward the American patriotic schema are the American Revolution, the American Civil War, and World War II.[7] These three conflicts provide a simplified conception of American history as a process of repeated military vindication of the core values that allegedly define the society. From the conflict that originally liberated the United States from British domination, through an internal challenge by a segment of the population that explicitly opposed individual freedom, right up to an external challenge by an enemy who threatened to force the world to submit to its will, the basic American values *always* triumph over their opposition. This worldview creates the cold war schema, in which international Communism, embodied by the Soviet Union, becomes the new enemy.

Hirshberg does not subject the premises behind these historical perceptions to extensive criticism, but their ideological and logical simplicity hints at the ample covert influence that a binary point of view on politics and history can contain. The American Revolution, the American Civil War, and World War II are obviously all more complex historical events than can be explained by the "we are good, they are bad" formula to which Hirshberg's schemata reduce. Nevertheless demonstrations of the efficacy of such unsophisticated "psychic guides for systematic, selective perceptual omissions and additions" abound (27). For example the degree to which China persisted as a close ally and even a puppet of the Soviet Union in the American popular imagination from the 1960s through the1980s (when Sino-American relations were in many ways considerably better than Sino-Soviet relations) suggests the degree to which such a concept resists change.

Hirshberg notes that American policy toward the Soviet Union since the end of World War II was always more complex than such a tidy framework logically explains. This intricacy arose not only from the memory of the uneasy impromptu alliance brought on by the threat of fascism during the war but also by a postwar containment strategy that "consisted of two tracks, one aggressive, the other accommodative" (46). By the mid-1970s, despite nearly three decades of nuclear stockpiling, regional conflicts, and antagonistic rhetoric, the Soviet Union had become a major trade partner of the United States, meaning that policy needed to strike a balance between economic and ideological concerns that were often seemingly at odds. Extant scholarship on the sociopolitical functions of cognitive schemata suggests how and why such a balance might be achieved through careful message control.

Andrew Rojecki's *Silencing the Opposition: Antinuclear Movements and the Media in the Cold War* (1999) contains an insightful, succinct summary of the sociopolitical effects of cognitive schemata. Rojecki divides the function of cognitive schemata into four interrelated parts that help explain how such concepts "structure memory and associate cognition with affective valences [that are] stored in long term memory after repeated mental connections":

1. People appear less variable when categorized as outsiders—for example, as deviants or minorities—and thus cue less complex conceptualizations. . . .
2. People's perceptions are polarized on members of these *out-groups*: the best are seen in some ways as better than the best in the in-group, but the worst are seen as worse than comparable insiders. . . .
3. When schemas are first developing, we notice complicating inconsistencies provided we are *continually* presented with this information. That is, we can develop suitably complex representations of the world—we are capable of getting beyond stereotypes—provided there is some basis for it. Such information is critical in early stages.
4. People *consistently* presented with credible, persuasive schema-inconsistent information abandon the schema in favor of the incoming information. . . . This is a corollary to the finding in the previous point. A continuous stream of news coverage that shows variety and complexity among movement participants is thus less likely to produce stereotyped thinking in the public mind. (20–21)

All four of these points are important facets of the formation, maintenance, and application of the ideologies that helped divide the world into two antagonistic armed camps during the cold war. Whereas Rojecki focuses mainly on the role of the professional media in performing propagandistic tasks on behalf of the government, his framework can be expanded to include any form of rhetoric that participates in the geopolitics of the cold war.

Rojecki's first two points are easily assimilated into existing perceptions of the cold war. The myriad two-sided divisions that permeate cold war rhetoric—East versus West, Soviet Union versus United States, Communism versus capitalism, good versus evil, right versus wrong, freedom versus enslavement, democracy versus totalitarianism—correspond readily with the spatial metaphor of preferred "insiders" and banished "outsiders." The near-sanctification of dissidents (actual or perceived) by the rival society, furthermore, is a common feature of the cold war, although not exclusive to it. Figures such as Pasternak, Solzhenitsyn, Sinyavsky, Brodsky, and Sakharov, who opposed the Soviet system in some visible way, were almost uniformly hailed in the United States not only as victims of Soviet repression (which each, to differing degrees, clearly was) but also as ideologically sympathetic individuals who yearned to live in a Western-style democracy (which many of them, Solzhenitsyn perhaps most strikingly, were not). Likewise Soviet propaganda of the 1960s and 1970s often used images of American policemen squelching strikes, student demonstrations, or civil rights marches as evidence that capitalist societies brutally repressed their nonelite classes. Additionally, outspoken Marxist sympathizers such as Paul Robeson, Howard Fast, W. E. B. DuBois, and Angela Davis were awarded the International Stalin (later Lenin) Peace Prize, in no small measure because of the extent to which each was marginalized and/or persecuted in the United States.

Rojecki's latter two points concern what Hirshberg terms "counter-schematic information" (45) and the need for vigilant and unswerving corroboration of the values that make up a particular schema. Hirshberg's discussion converges with Rojecki's when the former describes the functioning of the "cold war schema" during the Vietnam War: "American politicians and policymakers justified the Vietnam War by framing it in terms of the cold war schema. Mainstream public discourse and news coverage did not tend to stray from this interpretation, even to criticize policy. Most Americans accepted and used the cold war schema, and this made them susceptible to cold war appeals. It also made them resistant both to criticism of U.S. policy in Vietnam and to evidence that the United States was not supporting freedom, democracy, or good. In the end, the war was rejected, but not because it was not generally seen as a noble cause" (45). Hirshberg's analysis points out the complex and dynamic process required to maintain what is essentially a static construct. According to the patriotic schema, U.S. virtues and enemy evils are not meant to change, even if the specific enemy identity is subject to change. The purpose of propaganda, whether directly issued by members of the government or indirectly disseminated by an accommodating media, is thus to preserve the status quo, in terms of both the power structure ("U.S. policy in Vietnam") and the ideology behind that power structure ("the United States . . . support[s] freedom, democracy, [and] good").

Pynchon's *Gravity's Rainbow* collapses the reality of such tidy moral categorizations. It does so by satirically envisioning a nebulous and sinister network of interests—referred to simply as "Them"—that surreptitiously seeks to control the immediate post–World War II world. He depicts a bewildering multitude of British, American, German, and Russian governmental and financial interests alternately in conflict or in concert with one another, often in total disregard of the overarching military/political situation. Near the end of the third section of the novel, Major Marvy (an American military officer of questionable sanity), Clayton "Bloody" Chiclitz ("one of the American industrialists out here with the T-Force, scouting German engineering, secret weaponry in particular" [558]), and Vaslav Tchitcherine (a Soviet intelligence officer with past connections to the mammoth German IG Farben cartel) discuss their respective progress in locating a secret German rocket prototype *before* Oberst Enzian's Schwarzkommando, a renegade group outside "Their" influence. Their exchange lays bare not only the economic forces behind the ostensibly military business at hand but also the long-standing connections between companies based in countries on opposite sides of the war:

> [Marvy to Tchitcherine] "You ain't got General Electric breathin' over your shoulder, fella. Dillon, Reed . . . Standard Awl . . . shit . . . ."
>
> "But that's just what you folks *need*," Bloody Chiclitz interjects. "Get some business people in there to run it right, instead of having the government run everything. Your left hand doesn't know what your *right* hand's *doing!* You know *that?*" . . .
>
> "A-and what about Herbert Hoover?" Chiclitz is screaming. "He came over here and *fed* you people, when you were starving! They *love* Hoover over here—"
>
> "Yes—" Tchitcherine breaks in: "what *is* General Electric doing out here, by the way?"
>
> A friendly wink from Major Marvy. "Mister Swope was ace buddies with old FDR, you see. Electric Charlie's in there now, but Swope, he was one-thim Brain Trusters. Jews, most of 'm. But Swope's O.K. Now G.E. has connections with Siemens over here, they worked on the V-2 guidance, remember—" (565)

Throughout *Gravity's Rainbow* Pynchon insinuates that the clandestine network of connections among national governments (represented by politicians, statesmen, military leaders, and so on) and corporations such as General Electric, Standard Oil, Siemens, and IG Farben supersedes the supposedly dominant ideological division between the Axis and the Allies. The novel describes and decries these companies' mutually beneficial profiteering before, during, and in the immediate aftermath of the war and brands as contemptible those governmental officials who suborned and supported it.

One of the major subplots of the novel, in fact—Slothrop's quest to discover why he gets erections that appear to foretell German rocket strikes—proves to be wholly intertwined with corporate scheming that ran contrary to the stated policies of the U.S. government. In *The Style of Connectedness* (1987), Thomas Moore traces the intricate design behind Slothrop's conditioning both through historically authentic players as IG Farben, General Electric and its president Gerard Swope, Reichsbank director Hjalmar Schacht, and German tycoon Hugo Stinnes and through fictional characters such as Lyle Bland, Laszlo Jamf, and the Slothrop family.[8] According to Thomas Moore, the interests and influences of this network supercede those of the geopolitical entities at war with one another: "[Tyrone] Slothrop is enabled to discover that he has been 'sold to IG Farben like a side of beef,' and has been under surveillance since the original Jamf experiment. His facility for predicting rocket strikes is somehow bound as a strand in a web of international corporate plotting to which World War II itself may be only incidental" (73).

Such interconnections become commonplace in the second half of the novel, serving to reinforce what Theodore Kharpertian identifies as one of its dominant themes, namely, how "history becomes propaganda so that 'They' can maintain control": "In short, the They-System is seen by *Gravity's Rainbow*'s characters and narrator as an unceasing and universal venture for which the war serves as subterfuge and camouflage. . . . [A] complex overlay of perspectives is used to create a version of World War II that attacks the customary historical explanation as a delusion and affirms a countertheory of 'the real movements of the war' as commercial" (120–21).

While I agree with Kharpertian's assertion, I would add that Pynchon's satire goes beyond stating that the existing historical perspective on the war is simply a "delusion" by criticizing it for its fictionalized and self-serving nature. Not only was the "customary historical explanation" used to distract from the commercial motives that Pynchon sees as driving World War II, but, as Hirshberg's schemata show, it was employed in formulating the ideological premise for the cold war, a conflict in whose continuance "They" had vested financial and political interests. The war, as Pynchon writes, "provides raw material to be recorded into History, so that children may be taught History as sequences of violence, battle after battle, and be more prepared for the adult world" (*Gravity's Rainbow* 105). This preparation essentially consists of being acculturated into the patriotic schema and having it reinforced by "sequences of violence" that have been recast as righteous moral struggles.

The strength of the cold war schema allowed it not only to survive despite counterschematic information but also to be immediately recoverable in time of political expediency:

> Long-term support for this dual approach to dealing with the Soviet threat depended on the ability of Americans both to rally behind their leaders against the evil empire, and to celebrate superpower summits and improved U.S.-Soviet relations.
> . . . If the Soviet Union was always viewed as a hated enemy, then accommodation would have appeared as immoral and unwise as making deals with the devil. Had anti-Soviet sentiments entirely dissolved, however, then U.S. leaders would have been unable to justify aggressive acts as necessary responses to the evil empire. The Soviet Union, communism, and the oppression associated with them served again and again to justify questionable American behavior, and to provide an unsavory image against which a flawed America could be favorably compared in times of doubt and discontent. (Hirshberg 46)

It proved to be a continual political tightrope for both American and Soviet leaders to walk, but from the mid-1960s onward, cold war international relations were based on a bifurcated logic combining both "peaceful coexistence" and dire antagonism.

The cold war schema, thus, was an important tool for the American political, military, and economic elite, as it provided a flexible framework in which to achieve several goals that ideological absolutism would not have allowed: "Positive perceptions of the United States were the immobile anchor of the cold war schema. Perceptions of the Soviet Union varied as the tides of aggression and accommodation changed. Through this mix of rigidity and flexibility, the cold war schema functioned to perpetuate patriotism and public support for U.S. foreign policy throughout the cold war era" (46). Almost the same statement can be used to explain a cold war schema from the Soviet Union's perspective.[9] Important deviations from the American schema include the replacement of the "self" with "the working class" or "the proletariat" as the positive social unit, replacement of "democracy" with "capitalism" as the dominant societal impulse in the United States, and recasting the humanistic dichotomy of "Freedom vs. Oppression" in terms of socioeconomic class struggle (that is, "Power vs. Oppression"). Like the American cold war schema, the Soviet version did not originate during the cold war—class conflict on a global scale was, after all, the driving philosophical force behind the Bolshevik Revolution—but adapted existing sentiments to fit the two-sided balance of power that arose after World War II.

The Soviet model is both as oversimplified and as potentially persuasive as its American counterpart. Both sides, as Hirshberg notes, used an inherently fictitious (or at least knowingly exaggerated) ideological division as the basis for their international and domestic policies: "On both the American and Soviet sides ideologically grounded conceptions of international relations defined and structured cold war antagonisms and made them relevant to domestic politics. . . . The result . . . was that cold war policy and rhetoric served a political legitimation function. In fact, the 'normative frameworks' that served to define the cold war emerged from legitimation processes in both superpowers" (55). Subversive satirists of the cold war on both sides found fertile ground for subject matter thanks to the "normative frameworks" engendered by the respective cold war schemata of the two societies. These satirists subvert these frameworks both by pointing out the wide variety of intentional linguistic and logical distortions required to maintain the cold war and by remarking that such continuation is desirable only to the select economic and/or political elite that benefits from it.

Such distortions occur in wide range of situations: in defense of the sociological, philosophical, and/or political premises ("Americans value individual freedom" or "Communism empowers the working class") on which the cold war schemata are based; as palliative explanations for "counterschematic information" (the Watergate break-in or the spectacular failures of Soviet economic policy during the 1970s); as rhetorical flourishes used to further political ambitions (Ronald Reagan's fervent anti-Communism during the 1980 presidential campaign or Gorbachev's glasnost); as cover for activity that violates the putative principles of the nation (Oliver North's defense of American sales of arms to Iran on the pretext of using the money to support anti-Communist rebels in Nicaragua or the Soviet persecution of political dissidents as "enemies of the state"); and so on.

Both the American and Soviet cold war schemata are, to use Iser's terminology, essentially "dogma whose fictional nature must remain concealed if [their] foundation is not to be impaired" (3). If any of the positive associations (such as "the United States is an advocate of freedom") that comprise these schemata were to be compellingly disproved, the entire structure would become vulnerable. These associations can be invalidated either by presenting counterexamples or by revealing the fictive nature behind them. Because the cognitive schemata of the cold war are reinforced (either by repeated practical vindication or by tight control over information) to withstand contrary evidence, the potential for subversion contained within the former option is limited. Revelation of the fictions behind the dogma, however, offers a more promising alternative, just as exposure of the "man behind the curtain" undermined the fictive image of the "great and powerful Oz."

Sites and Sources of Linguistic Deformation

Numerous scholars of cold war culture have attempted to isolate some of the specific individuals and entities responsible for the persistence of constructs like the cold war schema. Maltby, for example, refers to language as "a medium of social integration" and claims that such a status "calls for attention not only to the ideological inflection of everyday and socially privileged forms of language, but also to other components of the 'discursive field' like the ensemble of institutions and apparatuses that regulate the use of language" (30). Among the components he mentions are "the erosion of the public sphere; the enlargement of the state's propaganda agencies; the impact of technical rationality on language; and the spread of conceptually impoverished discourses that impede critical reflection on society" (30). Maltby explicitly states that these four factors "have all been explained in the context of the restructuring and growth of capitalist economies in their postwar phase" (30), but all of these factors are equally and sometimes more prevalent in Soviet society in *its* postwar phase.

One may apply these claims about American language to Russian language in the cold war era if one accounts for the idiosyncrasies of Soviet culture, and satirists from both countries directly address each of the developments he notes in their works.[10] Taking his cues from Jürgen Habermas, Maltby defines the public sphere as "a domain in which established forms of power and authority (ecclesiastical, aristocratic, and so on) could be subjected to the critical scrutiny and judgment of the public" (30–31). He proceeds to note the mass media's deleterious effects: "Today, the mass media are the main source of public information. This in itself need not damage the health of the public sphere if media provision included critical inquiry and commentary from a standpoint outside the spectrum of the consensus. However, under the prevailing structure of monopolistic ownership and control, the presentation of events from genuinely alternative perspectives is a rare and marginal practice. Mass-media conglomerates are generally united on viewpoint and news values, with proprietors often exercising their prerogative of 'private censorship' to affirm or exclude views as suits their own political prejudices (which are normally biased toward support of the established order). . . . There is, simply, no public sphere" (31). Soviet control of the media was legendary in its restrictiveness, whether in the form of the state-controlled news agency (TASS) or leading newspapers like *Pravda* (*Truth*) and *Izvestiia* (*News*). As Thomas F. Remington writes in his *The Truth of Authority: Ideology and Communication in the Soviet Union* (1988), "The view that the job of gathering and reporting information must be justified by service to the collective good rather than a diffuse civil right to know is integral to Soviet doctrine" (134). When this principle was contravened, the results were usually problematic for the regime. Many historians, for example, have identified the outraged public reaction to the revelation of deliberate misinformation surrounding the nuclear accident at Chernobyl in April 1986 as the beginning of the end for the Soviet Union, since it suggested that Gorbachev's glasnost reforms were essentially hollow when it came to important matters.[11] Suffice it to say, if "private censorship" of the kind that Maltby describes can result in "erosion of the public sphere," then systematic and far-reaching Soviet control over information produced even more pronounced effects.

The mass media's abdication of its power to critique the "established order" is a theme that shows up prominently in Fazil Iskander's *Sozvezdiye kozlotura* (1966; *The Goatibex Constellation*), Robert Coover's *The Public Burning* (1977), Vassily Aksyonov's *Ostrov Krym* (1981; *The Island of Crimea*), and Don DeLillo's *White Noise* (1984), among others. It is Dovlatov, however, who most directly covers this ground. His *The Invisible Book* and *Kompromiss* (1981; *The Compromise*) are based on his experiences as a professional writer in the Soviet Union. Both of these works demonstrate the range of absurdities present in Soviet mass media. In *The Compromise* Dovlatov exposes the falsity of Soviet journalism by quoting verbatim articles he wrote for an Estonian newspaper, each followed by a somewhat fictionalized explanatory anecdote that uncovers the omnipresent ideological filter. In the chapter "The Fifth Compromise," Dovlatov reproduces an article that heralds the birth of the four hundred thousandth inhabitant of the city of Tallinn:

In Tallinn Hospital No. 4, a baby has been born to Maya and Grigori Kuzin—their long-awaited first-born. It's this little boy who is fated to be the four-hundred-thousandth inhabitant of the city. . . .

The happy father awkwardly tries to hide his callused hands. "We'll call our son Lembit," he says. "Let him grow like the folk-hero of that name!" . . .

I do not know what you will grow up to be, Lembit! A lathe operator or a miner, an officer or a scientist. Only one thing is clear: a man has been born! A man condemned to happiness! (25)

In the story that follows, Dovlatov lays bare the series of inaccuracies and outright fabrications that pervade the entire article. To begin with his editor assigns him the specific task of finding a baby appropriate[12] for use in a propaganda piece that celebrates the anniversary of the liberation of Tallinn from the occupying Nazis during World War II. Dovlatov first suggests the infant son of an Estonian woman and an Ethiopian student at the Soviet Merchant Marine Academy and is angrily rebuffed by his editor, who tells him to find a "*normal* human baby" (35), implying that the child's national and racial characteristics make him abnormal and/or inhuman.

Dovlatov's next attempt is equally unsuccessful, as the child he chooses is the son of Jewish—and thus tacitly unacceptable—parents. Even the father's status as a renowned official poet is not enough to merit the baby's selection, although the father's poem to his newborn son is recast in ideologically correct language for use in the eventual article. The only seeming positive characteristic of the father whose child *is* eventually chosen is his Russian last name. Other than that he is an obnoxious and politically unenlightened drunkard, characteristics that are, of course, excluded from the eventual article. The parents want to name the child Volodya and agree to the editor's suggestion of Lembit—a name taken from Estonian folklore—only after a paltry bribe of twenty-five rubles. The editor also contributes the awkward and clearly inappropriate catch phrase that concludes the article. By the time Dovlatov is finished telling his tale about the article's production, practically every word of it has been discredited. Dovlatov repeats this process eleven times within *The Compromise,* in the process explaining why he "said farewell to journalism" (147). On the final page Dovlatov recounts a conversation that drives home with grotesquely dark irony his point about the debasement of Soviet journalism:

My first cousin, who has been convicted twice (once for unpremeditated manslaughter), often says to me:

"Take up some useful kind of work. Aren't you ashamed of what you do?"

"You're a fine one to lecture me!"

"All I did was kill a man," my cousin says, "and try to burn his body. But you!" (148)

Throughout *The Compromise* Dovlatov demonstrates that the credibility of Soviet journalism has been, as his book's title suggests, fundamentally compromised by the absurd distortions and fabrications required to produce ideologically palatable articles. Nevertheless, Dovlatov also insists that recovery is possible, even though "it's a hard road from the reported facts to the truth": "You can never step into the same river twice. But looking down through the thickness of the water you can make out the river bottom covered with tin cans. And behind magnificent theatrical decorations you can learn to see the brick wall, the ropes, the fire extinguisher, and the drunken stagehands. All this is well-known to anyone who has been behind the scenes, even if only once" (4). The metaphors that Dovlatov uses in this passage reverberate with the necessity of exposing polluted and illusory fictions masquerading as objective truths.

Maltby's second point concerns the expanding organs of state propaganda, which are deeply implicated in the erosion of the public sphere. Propaganda is inextricably associated with totalitarian states in the American popular imagination, perhaps because of the word's undemocratic and dishonest associations, both of which run counter to the American patriotic schema.[13] Nevertheless Maltby argues that "U.S. administrations . . . justified the excessive cost, risks, and secrecy of its armament program by deploying its primary propaganda strategy—the Cold War" (33). And this strategy worked because "deliberately raising the level of confrontation with the U.S.S.R." was the means by which "successive U.S. administrations have mobilized public support for their high level of military expenditure" (33).

Chris Hables Gray goes one step further in *Postmodern War: The New Politics of Conflict* (1997), implicitly linking the propaganda of the nuclear arms race with the concomitant desire for political power and economic gain: "Using systems analysis, Albert Wohlstetter claimed he had proven that the Soviets could 'Pearl Harbor' the U.S. nuclear bombers. This threat and a parade of others usually labeled 'gaps,' as in the bomber gap and the missile gap, have all been shown to be nonexistent—after the election was won or the new weapons were built. But before being proven fallacious, they helped create and elaborate the nuclear arsenal of the United States" (152). For both Maltby and Gray, the logic of American cold war propaganda is a cycle of self-fulfilling and self-enriching prophecy that creates a seemingly public justification through deliberate obfuscation or even outright fabrication of the threat posed by the Soviet enemy. Maltby characterizes the strategy of such propaganda as "a kind of ideological/rhetorical process one might call 'dichotomization,' whereby political issues are simplified into emotionally charged pairs of opposing terms; superpower rivalry translated into a conflict between Good and Evil, Light and Darkness, God and Godlessness, Freedom and Slavery" (101).

Coover personifies and satirizes these particular pairs in *The Public Burning*, imagining Richard Nixon as a buffoon caught out of his depth in the midst of an epic battle between the "Sons of Darkness" and the "Sons of Light." Barth's *Giles Goat-Boy*, Percy's *Love in the Ruins*, and DeLillo's *End Zone* perform similar satirical functions, albeit by dislocating the propagandistic dichotomies of the cold war into new contexts. Barth does so by recasting the cold war as a rivalry between two colleges, Nikolayan and New Tammany, and their respective supercomputers, EASCAC and WESCAC, for supremacy in a larger university. Percy's novel involves a psychologist who has diagnosed a pervasive schism within Americans' individual and collective psyche resulting in large measure from a proxy war in Ecuador that strongly resembles the Vietnam War. DeLillo parallels the quasi-martial language of American football with the national political discourse of the early 1970s, making clear the satirical intention of the fact that coach Emmett Creed's constant enjoinders—"Hit somebody, Hit somebody. Hit somebody" (10)— result in players whose "thoughts are wholesomely commonplace, [whose] actions uncomplicated by history, enigma, holocaust or dream" (4). In each case a pervasive and calculated us-versus-them mentality cultivates ignorance and propagates violent conflict.

The Soviet Union under Brezhnev's rule presented a similar situation. The government sought to create public support for military spending through massive anti-American propaganda campaigns even as the populace suffered from endemic shortages of food and other necessities. The massive political education system in the Soviet Union that had existed since the 1920s had always sought not only to shape public opinion but to assure its conformity with Marxist-Leninist philosophy. As Remington observes, it was "not understanding or belief that the propaganda system aspire[d] to achieve in its audience but the standardization of public discourse" (86). However, Sinyavsky points out in *Soviet Civilization* that a new set of potential cognitive dissonances demanded a refinement of this goal during the early years of the cold war: "Everything pointed toward chauvinism: the Soviet Union's aggressive policy, the cold war with the West, the abrupt increase in anti-Western sentiment. Propaganda's job was to present yesterday's allies—the British and the Americans—as accomplices of fascism. . . . It was necessary to compensate ideologically and psychologically for the terrible losses incurred during the war and camouflage with extravagant phraseology the low standard of living. . . . Thus the patriotic hysteria began, the limitless self-glorification" (251–52). As relations with China worsened during the 1960s, the economy sputtered in the 1970s, and the Red Army became bogged down in Afghanistan in the 1980s, the need for such rhetorical smokescreens only intensified.

Given its ubiquity in Soviet culture, it is not surprising to see propaganda crop up frequently as a theme in subversive satire, including almost all of the Russian works mentioned in this study. For example, the satire of official Soviet language in Alexander Zinoviev's work is encyclopedic and blunt. *Ziiaiushchie vysoty* (1976; *The Yawning Heights*), whose title puns on a stock phrase of Soviet propaganda,[14] is a mock sociology of Ibansk ("Fucktown"), a society governed largely through constant repetition of the utterly irrational tenets of "soc-ism." In *Svetloe budushchee* (1978; *The Radiant Future*), Zinoviev makes an elaborate physical grotesque out of another stock phrase of Soviet propaganda by depicting the decay of a metallic monument that spells out the words "Long Live Communism—The Radiant Future of All Mankind!" (7). Aleshkovsky's novels focus more on the producers than the products of propaganda. In *Ruka* (1980; *The Hand*) he creates a protagonist whose cleverness allows him to turn the duplicitous power of official language against the same Soviet system that killed his father and destroyed his childhood village, while *Kengeru* (1981; *Kangaroo*) tells the absurd story of a two-bit criminal and the elaborately managed, hyperpropagandistic show trial in which he is charged with raping and murdering a kangaroo.

Iskander's *Kroliki i udavy* (1982; *Rabbits and Boa Constrictors*) is a complex animal fable that examines how propaganda enables the kind of chauvinism that Sinyavsky describes. The novel concerns a society of rabbits beginning to realize that the hypnotic power exerted upon them by preying boa constrictors is a myth. Finally Voinovich's *Moskva 2042* (1987; *Moscow 2042*) satirically envisions what the Soviet Union's "radiant future" might look like, in the process illustrating Sinyavsky's claim about propaganda serving to "camouflage" Soviet society's flaws. Voinovich depicts a Potemkin village of a state in which propaganda is so far-reaching that individuals have ceased to discriminate between food and excrement. Taken together these works form a comprehensive satirical critique of both the Soviet propaganda organs and their products.

Maltby identifies a third source of negative influence on cold war American language in what he calls the "technologist-rationalist ideology [that] is understood to acclaim the benefits of systematization, 'cybernetization,' . . . and global planning, the goal being the technical-bureaucratic organization of production and consumption" (34). Essential to this ideology is "the tendency to think of all social practices in systemic terms—wholes to which all parts ('subsystems') must be adapted or adjusted in order to optimize the system's 'performance'" (34). Systemic thinking was the organizing principle of the state-controlled Soviet economy, especially the intricate five-year plans that guided most aspects of production until the dissolution of the Soviet Union. In fact Maltby's notion of "parts" being "adapted or adjusted in order to optimize the system's 'performance'" recalls the "from each according to his ability" portion of the familiar Marxist-Leninist dictum. Mikhail Epstein discusses what he calls the "hyperreality" of Soviet economic reports, stating that "no one knows . . . whether the harvests reported in Stalin's or Brezhnev's Russia were actually reaped, but the fact that the number of tilled hectares or tons of milled grain was always reported down to the tenth of a percent gave these simulacra the character of hyperreality" ("Postmodernism, Communism and Sots-Art" 5). This hyperreality is created in part because the government needs harvest reports for the abstract purpose of validating the systemic thinking behind Soviet economic policy than for the "real" purpose of feeding the populace. In this way even the most mundane economic statistic became a possible source of linguistic distortion in the service of ideology.

In *Zhizn' i neobychainye prikliucheniia soldata Ivana Chonkina* (1977; *The Life and Extraordinary Adventures of Private Ivan Chonkin*), Voinovich uses forged harvest figures in his satire on the insubstantiality of Soviet life. From the first Voinovich shows how the bureaucratic state system has tacitly agreed to cooperate in obscuring the dismal failure of agricultural collectivization. Ivan Golubev, chairman of the *kolkhoz* (collective farm) in the town of Krasnoye,[15] is introduced in a drunken stupor, as a result of "questioning Granny Dunya on the subject of her home brew" (9). The narrator, who frequently intrudes into the narrative frame to add folksy asides or tangential anecdotes, immediately begins the process of confusing reality by pointing out that "things at the kolkhoz were going poorly. Not what you would call very poorly, you could even say things were going well, except that they were getting worse and worse every year" (10). The narrator states that Golubev, as would be expected in a system that putatively abhors corruption and slackness, "lived in constant expectation of the arrival of some committee of inspection—then he'd pay for everything, and in full" (10). In fact, although Golubev still fears that "someday a Maximum Responsibility Committee of Inspection would suddenly appear and have final say in the matter," his experience with the "various district inspectors, and examiners" who have inquired after the affairs of the kolkhoz invariably involve nothing more than "drink[ing] vodka with him while munching on lard and eggs, [after which] they'd sign the documents of certification and drive off, everything still in one piece" (10–11).

Later in the novel, Voinovich presents Golubev in the act of composing one of his falsely rosy crop reports; the narrator adds a commentary that again discloses the complicity of the entire hierarchy of power in maintaining this illusory productivity and prosperity:

> Ivan Timofeyevich Golubev was sitting in his office, toiling over the composition of a report concerning haymaking in the last ten-day period. Needless to say, the report was a fraud, since there had been practically no haymaking at all during the last ten-day period. The men were leaving for the front, the women were getting them ready, some harvest that was! The District Committee, however, did not consider such reasons

valid. Borisov cursed him out on the telephone and demanded that the plan be fulfilled. Naturally, he knew that, in times like these, he was demanding the impossible, but the paper signifying work completed was more important to him than the work itself—Borisov was also being cursed out by those over him. And so Borisov collected papers from all the kolkhozes, compiled the figures, and sent them off to the province, where further reports were compiled on the basis of the district reports, and so it went, all the way to the top. (218)

In a development that recalls Gogol's play *Revizor* (1836; *The Government Inspector*), Golubev originally mistakes Private Ivan Chonkin, a rather inept and simple-minded Red Army soldier sent to Krasnoye to guard a malfunctioning plane, for the authority figure who will finally call him to task for failing in his duties as chairman. Golubev even goes so far as to confess to Chonkin and consequently prepares himself to be shipped off to prison.

Golubev's fate turns out differently, though. He is arrested much later (in the sequel, *Pretendent na prestol* [1979; *Pretender to the Throne*]) on totally unrelated charges, when all of Krasnoye is accused of aiding and abetting Chonkin, himself suspected of being both a Nazi collaborator and the illegitimate son of a prerevolutionary prince. Even on this occasion, though, Golubev mistakenly believes his detention to be related to his bogus reports:

The phone rang every now and again, and representatives of various organizations requested information about the delivery of milk and meat, about the requisitioning of supplementary horses for the army, the preparation of the seed fund; they asked about the livestock, farrows, the number of laying hens and the fodder supply.

"Everything's going according to plan," Golubev would answer and hang up.

They'd call back. "What do you mean according to plan, when this isn't being done and there's none of that and that's not happening?"

"All according to plan," Golubev would repeat and hang up. (283)

The vindication of the plan ultimately is more important (and feasible) in this system than the inconvenient but necessary business of actually procuring and distributing food. Although the two Chonkin books are set before the cold war, the food shortages of the 1970s provide contemporary relevance for Voinovich's satire on the inept system of Soviet agriculture.

The incongruity between the physical truth and the ideological fiction of collective farming was just one aspect of Soviet systemic thinking that satirists exposed, though. Tertz/Sinyavsky's *Liubimov* (1963; *The Makepeace Experiment*) and Aksyonov's *Zolotaia nasha zhelezka* (1980; *Our Golden Ironburg*) likewise address the topic along somewhat different vectors. *The Makepeace Experiment* details the rise and fall of Lenya Tikhomirov ("Lenny Makepeace" in the English translation), a would-be enlightened despot who rules a nondescript village through a combination of pseudoscience, marvelous gadgetry, and dynamic personality (literalized in the novel as a form of psychic power). Tikhomirov calamitously transforms the entire town of Liubimov ("Lovetown") into a proving ground for his oxymoronically rational-yet-mystical political philosophy, ostensibly an improvement on Soviet Communism. His "experiment" fails despite the superficial appearance of having created a utopia. Like Brezhnev, Tikhomirov cannot provide enough food for his subjects, a problem that Sinyavsky satirically implies will plague *any* social system that conceals rather than addresses its inherent contradictions. On the surface *Our Golden Ironburg* parodies the form of the relentlessly positivist Soviet "industrial novel" in telling the story of a group of scientists searching for a new subatomic particle. Through metafictional destabilization of a narrative form whose sole purpose is to glorify Soviet industry and science, Aksyonov exposes the vapidity of both the literary subgenre and the politicized (and often dubious) scientific knowledge described therein.

Systematization in American cold war culture takes on a variety of forms as well, but none was more prominent than the development of the military-industrial complex against which Eisenhower warned in his farewell address. As early as 1952, Kurt Vonnegut's *Player Piano* questioned the ways in which the postwar industrial economy was routinizing and degrading life. The novel depicts a thoroughly mechanized United States that has arisen after a war won by technology: "It was the miracle that won the war—production with almost no manpower" (1). The outwardly tranquil society of the novel's early pages was achieved only after "the men and women had come home, after the riots had been put down [and] after thousands had been jailed under the anti-sabotage laws," a wholesale abandonment of the individualist and humanist values upon which the country was founded (1). The novel's hero, Paul Proteus, manages a giant mechanized factory, the Ilium Works. As the novel progresses, he gradually rejects the values that have made him "the most important, the most brilliant man in Ilium" (1). The best apparent alternative to the vast controlling technocracy is the Ghost Shirt Movement, a group of neo-Luddite saboteurs whose goal is the destruction of the machines that produce and run everything.[16] Proteus is ordered by his superiors to infiltrate and inform on this group, but instead joins them and is eventually proclaimed to be (and sacrificed as) their messiah. They begin a rebellion, which collapses after a few minor successes; by the novel's end, Proteus is disillusioned by the complete undesirability of either system.

Not only does the dream of individuality prove to be impossible in this world, but the competition between equally undesirable modes of living also leads to violence without improvement; to paraphrase Walter Duranty's famous apologia for Stalin's methods, the eggs are broken, but no omelet results. Vonnegut's vision in *Player Piano* is more bleak even than conventional dystopia, in which the power of the state is so durable and far-reaching that all efforts at revolution are doomed to fail. Vonnegut suggests that the failed revolution depicted in *Player Piano* would change only the outward appearance of the status quo, not the dystopian system behind it. Such criticism of the uselessness and destructiveness of counterforces that do not fundamentally subvert the established power structure is a central theme of later a new, distinct mode of cold war anti-utopianism that I call serial or systemic dystopianism.[17]

Whereas *Player Piano* focuses on the industrial element of the military-industrial complex, a host of other works satirize the military component thereof, including Heller's *Catch-22* (1961), Eugene Burdick and Harvey Wheeler's *Fail-Safe* (1962), Kubrick's *Dr. Strangelove* (1963), Vonnegut's *Cat's Cradle* (1963), and Pynchon's *Gravity's Rainbow*. Whereas *Fail-Safe* and *Dr. Strangelove* both satirically refute the underlying rationales for nuclear deterrence policies, *Catch-22*, *Cat's Cradle*, and *Gravity's Rainbow* decry the logical, ethical and rhetorical deformations created and sustained by the constant militarism of the cold war. In different ways each of these novels point out that military, political, and economic interests were intertwined out of necessity during World War II, while also warning that this process has continued unabated, often clandestinely, with deleterious implications not only for democracy but potentially for the entire planet.

Finally, "conceptually impoverished discourses that impede critical reflection on society" are perhaps *the* overarching subject matter for subversive cold war satire and appear in some form or another in every work of fiction mentioned in this study. Maltby bases his discussion on the ideas of Herbert Marcuse and thus creates a model applicable to both sides of the cold war ideological divide: "[Marcuse] identifies a public discourse notable for its use of 'syntactical abridgement,' as in the propensity for acronyms and catchphrases. It is a syntax which erodes the critical space between the parts of a sentence by condensing subject and predicate. . . . This results in propositions such as 'the Free World' or 'the clean bomb' which come across as 'self-validating, hypnotic formulas.' It is . . . an 'irreconcilably anti-critical and anti-dialectical language,' which 'absorbs . . . the negative oppositional elements of Reason.' Evidently, for Marcuse, this (perceived) deadening of the critical impulse in language facilitates the integration of the subject into the social order" (35–36). Whether articulated as Tanner's "imprisoning or iniquitous" languages, as Hirshberg's cognitive schemata, or as Iser's "masked" fictions, intentionally debased modes of expression become a potent tool for maintaining the cold war status quo, both within the respective superpowers and from a geopolitical standpoint. As Sinyavsky notes above, such intentional limitation of critical reflection (that is, "deadening of the critical impulse in language") is an intrinsic element of official Soviet language from Stalin onward.

While Maltby blames the "phenomenal profit-motivated expansion of mass-media broadcasting and publishing" in the United States for spawning modes of expression that "inhibit reflection and lack the perspectives necessary for critical analysis of the social order" (36), governmental control of the media and cultural production in general led to a similar situation in the Soviet Union. Arguably such "syntactical abridgements" form the core of *all* cold war satires given that both parties involved in the ideological conflict relied on a cultural mindset that did not waver, much less collapse, in the face of glaring absurdities and other cognitively untenable positions. Among the Russian works that explore such themes most fully are Aksyonov's *Say Cheese!*, Iskander's *The Goatibex Constellation*, Zinoviev's *The Yawning Heights* and *Gomo Sovietikus* (1980; *Homo Sovieticus*), and many of the shorter pieces collected in Voinovich's *Putiom vzaimnoi perepiski* (1979; *In Plain Russian*) and *The Anti-Soviet Soviet Union*. Thematically similar American works include Vonnegut's *Cat's Cradle* and *Galápagos* (1985), Barth's *Giles Goat-Boy*, Ishmael Reed's *The Free-lance Pallbearers* (1966), DeLillo's *White Noise*, and Tim O'Brien's *The Nuclear Age* (1985).

The narrator of Zinoviev's *Homo Sovieticus* examines the issue of "deadened" language metanarratively by musing at length about the nature of the book he is writing. Unable to settle on a single representative genre, he decides to classify the work as a "novel-denunciation-Report-tract" and discusses how each of these constituent parts is a sham under the Soviet system. He notes that "Soviet people are trained to write Reports about everything [as] . . . an indispensable element of the Communist organization of work" (14). This work proves to be as empty an exercise as Golubev's agricultural reports, since these reports are guided not by the desire to "do a summing-up or extract lessons, but by virtue of certain higher, mystical considerations" (15). These satirically exaggerated considerations turn out to be simply the length of the report, wholly exclusive of the ludicrous content of the subject matter:

> In my Quarterly Report I once wrote that I had discovered ten new elementary particles. I did this with the purely cognitive intention of checking my theory of Reports. The director of the section sent for me. I was on the point of thinking that my theory was mistaken, but I needn't have worried. My Report, Director said, was too short. Would I add a couple of pages? I made a demagogic declaration: the value, I said, of a Report lay not in the number of pages but in what, according to the Report, had been done. "Read what I have done," I said, "and compare it with what the others did." "Don't try and fool me," said Director calmly. "Do you think the others have done less than you?" And so I added a couple of pages to the Report in which I communicated that I had discovered a method of converting the contents of Moscow's rubbish-bins into first-class foodstuffs. "Well done!" said Director,

filing my Report in a bundle of other unread Reports by my colleagues. "The man who can write a good Report is a good worker" (15–16)

The narrator provides the same sort of deflating explanation for the other "genres" in his formula, ultimately making his own work a paragon of meaninglessness since it is representative of four distinct yet ultimately "impoverished discourses."

Zinoviev savagely mocks the emptiness of Soviet Russian thought and language from the beginning of *Homo Sovieticus*. In the second of the hundred-plus chapters that make up the book, the narrator states, "I have a wish to get something done; but I rarely have the wish actually to do what I want to get done." He cautions the reader not to mistake this for "a piece of dead sophistry," claiming instead that it is "living dialectics" (9). He simplifies his problem: "I want to do something, but I don't want to make the effort to accomplish what I want" (9). This predicament frames the discussion of the absurdity of Soviet life—and its supposedly dialectical and inevitable advancement toward Communism—that takes up the remainder of the book. The narrator claims that the paradox within his malaise points out the inability of this mode of thinking to deal with "the deepest and most complex" philosophical problems: "For instance, take the eternal Problem Number One: 'to be or not to be?' For the Russian it comes out in the form: 'to b[ooz]e or not to b[ooz]e?' And there can't be two opinions about that: of course, b[ooz]e. And seriously, by God! Then start boozing again. Then some more. And then begin all over again. In the Russian language one can also formulate this Problem Number One in another way: 'to be[at] or not to be[at]?' And again there are no two ways about that: be[at]. Of course one must beat. And above all, in the face! In the West, of course, they don't understand this, because you can't translate Russian problems into Western languages. If you try to do that, all the romantic nuances disappear, and all the psychological profundity" (9–10; brackets in original).[18] This section closes with the narrator's disclosure that the "wish to do nothing arises in me even more often," causing him to "make titanic efforts to accomplish my wish" (10). The propagandistic hyperbole of this passage provides the satirical contrast to the narrator's claim that "Western thinkers see in this 'typical Russian laziness.' And they are wrong, as always" (10). He is right; this is not "typical Russian laziness" but the "titanic" uselessness that Zinoviev sees as endemic to Soviet society and its modes of thinking.

A gloomier satire of such cultural hollowness can be found in Vonnegut's *Cat's Cradle,* which repeatedly invokes a mysterious holy man named Bokonon as an antithetical voice to balance out the passionate positivism expressed by other characters including scientists working for the defense industry, businessmen, and banana republic dictators. Bokonon freely admits that his philosophy is a necessarily limited construct—in Iser's terms, he "discloses the fictionality" of his words—in the opening line of his quasi gospel, *The Books of Bokonon*: "All of the true things I am about to tell you are shameless lies" (5). He also asserts that even though the quest for understanding is noble and proper, it is also folly to believe that such understanding is perfectible: "Nowhere does Bokonon warn against a person's trying to discover the limits of his *karass* and the nature of the work God Almighty has had it do. Bokonon simply observes that such investigations are bound to be incomplete" (4). The invented notion of the *karass*—a "free-form" grouping of humans "that [does] God's Will without ever discovering what they are doing" (2)—is central to the novel, both because of the term's ultimate incomprehensibility and because of Bokonon's claim that humans invariably and consciously order themselves into other groups (*granfalloons*) that are "meaningless in terms of the way God gets things done" (91). Among the *granfalloons* that Bokonon singles out are "the Communist Party, the Daughters of the American Revolution, the General Electric Company, the International Order of Odd Fellows—and any nation, anytime, anywhere" (91–92).

Vonnegut's satire places blame for the novel's concluding apocalypse on those characters guided by inflexible adherence to one or more such constructs, but especially on those who follow "the secular Antichrist figure that relentlessly hounds humanity toward species destruction: a two headed-beast, government and science" (Dewey 55). Bokonon does not intend his philosophy to serve as a simple solution to the world's problems, since positing it as such would inherently make it just another *granfalloon*. As in many of Vonnegut's other works (such as *God Bless You, Mr. Rosewater* and *Slaughterhouse-Five*), the advice offered to the reader is an exhortation not only to be more discerning about one's surroundings but also to make love for humanity as a whole the core principle of one's personal philosophy.[19]

Although both the causes for and the nature of social, political, and economic problems found in the United States and the Soviet Union during the cold war differ greatly, the essential approach of subversive satirists is remarkably similar in terms of their uses of language. Parodying official modes of discourse devalues these modes by asserting meaninglessness in ideas where meanings important enough to risk nuclear destruction supposedly reside: militarism, scientific rationalism, technology, utopianism, and grossly simplified ethical binaries such as "good" versus "evil" or "us" versus "them." Satirical subversion is achieved by first making the language itself seem absurd, then by rejecting as false the ideology that creates the system from which such instances of meaningless language spring. Various examples of this twofold technique occupy the remainder of this study.

Civil Defense: *A Manhattan Project for Subversive Satirists*

Before setting out on a broad thematic survey of cold war satire, I wish briefly to trace the gradual infusion of satire into one of the first sustained topoi of the cold war: civil defense. Emergent artistic responses to official civil defense rhetoric in Great Britain and the United States served as a microcosm of cold war literature in general. In particular the chain of increasingly satirical commentaries on the effectiveness of civil defense eventually culminates in one of the iconic exemplars of cold war satire, *Dr. Strangelove,* thus retrospectively making it a sort of countercultural Manhattan Project for the development of a satirical approach to the cold war. A short summary of the subversion of civil defense rhetoric serves both as a model for the remainder of this study and a point of entry into the more detailed discussion of primary texts.

The civil defense movement in the United States from the late 1940s through the early 1960s powerfully exemplified how old "modes of thinking" that Einstein referred to in 1946 were both inadequate and intentionally misinformed. Predicated first on mass evacuation, "duck and cover" techniques (such as those taught to schoolchildren via "Bert the Turtle" movies), and then fallout shelters, these tactics were essential to large-scale government propaganda efforts to quell fears about atomic warfare. Even as officials privately acknowledged that civil defense was increasingly irrelevant in light of technological innovations such as the hydrogen bomb and the neutron bomb, they publicly conducted vigorous campaigns encouraging citizens to believe that American society and values could survive even a full-scale nuclear war. Along with local governments, the Federal Civil Defense Administration, established in 1950, supplied willing print and television media with plentiful information reinforcing the notion that nuclear war was not so different from conventional bombing and eminently survivable, provided one prepared for it properly. Historian Allan Winkler notes that civil defense produced few substantive results in terms of physical national security, but it did do "a good deal of cajoling of the American public" (quoted in Boyer, *Bomb's Early Light* 322).[20]

Published testimony by knowledgeable scientists largely discredited civil defense, but fictionalized works also contributed by offering less idealistic speculations about the potential behavior of the survivors of a nuclear exchange. The epitome of such works is *The War Game,* a film produced in 1965 by Peter Watkins for BBC television, which refused to air it on the grounds that it was overly dismal.[21] Using a documentary style, the film simulated the hypothetical (and by many estimates understated) effects of an atomic blast on Kent, effectively functioning as a noncomic satire that shattered the rose-colored glasses through which civil defense encouraged citizens to view nuclear warfare. *The War Game* dramatized the effects of a nuclear explosion and, more shockingly, the resulting firestorm, fallout, radiation sickness, and deprivations, topics that official civil defense documents of the 1950s tended to downplay.[22] It also suggested the vaunted spirit of cooperation, regularly invoked in optimistic British civil defense pamphlets as the reason for the country's survival during the Blitz, would prove an untenable fantasy in the harsh reality of a nuclear war. For example, even before the bomb explodes, some white citizens are shown refusing to admit "colored" evacuees from the city into their homes. The inherent chaos of a plausible postnuclear scenario repeatedly thwarts the civil defense policies designed to maintain order. The film unambiguously insisted that the familiar nuclear adage about the living envying the dead would become true in the aftermath of even a relatively minor nuclear war.

But even before *The War Game,* British and American popular culture had already begun to point out the inherent fallacies of the civil defense campaign. Both the 1957 novel and the 1959 movie version of *On the Beach* question of the effectiveness of civil defense. Its plot revolves around the lives of several characters awaiting the inevitable arrival of a deadly radioactive cloud in Australia after a nuclear war confined entirely to the Northern Hemisphere. Some characters, mainly the women and the somewhat emasculated British scientist Julian (played by Fred Astaire in the film version), express mild horror at the situation. The remainder of the country goes on living life as normally as possible[23] until "the time" (of the cloud's arrival) comes, and then they commit mass suicide rather than wait to die of radiation sickness. Despite the legitimate criticism that it "made world extinction a romantic condition" (Weart 219),[24] *On the Beach* is not simply a conventionally lachrymose tale of tragically doomed love. Admittedly the extensive development of the romantic relationships served to obscure the real message for much of the reading and viewing audience: "Nearly everyone [in *On the Beach*] was already accepting the gradual approach of what the film called 'the time,' the nuclear midnight. In ignoring this peril, was not the world public like the fictional Australians who refused to acknowledge imminent death?" (Weart 219). Nevertheless both the movie and the book implicitly ask how survival of a nuclear war could be possible in a warring nation, if no one can survive in a country where bombs and missiles do not even fall.

The Eisenhower administration was sufficiently apprehensive of public reaction in the wake of the film's release that it declared in a special State Department report that *On the Beach* "grossly misconstrues the basic nature of man" and that it "is inconceivable that even in the event of a nuclear war, mankind would not have the strength and ingenuity to take all possible steps toward self-preservation" (quoted in Boyer, *Fallout* 110). On the other hand, chroniclers such as John Hersey, whose *Hiroshima* was published barely a year after the use of the atomic bomb against Japan, and psychologists such as Robert Jay Lifton argued that strength and ingenuity become irrelevant when one feels there is no reason to survive. *On the Beach,* like *The War Game,* clearly follows this latter line of reasoning—albeit with a markedly different cinematic aesthetic—in denying the substance of civil defense rhetoric.

In a somewhat different vein, Rod Serling's *Twilight Zone* television series aired an episode titled "The Shelter" on September 29, 1961. In this episode all cooperation between a previously congenial group of neighbors erodes in the wake of a CONELRAD warning.[25] A family retreats into its shelter and refuses admittance to neighbors who have not prepared shelters of their own; they refuse on the perfectly reasonable grounds that the shelter is stocked with food, water, and air for only three people. The neighbors grovel pitifully for admittance then attempt to break into the shelter; a scene of panicked violence threatens just as the all-clear sounds. As Boyer writes in *By the Bomb's Early Light*, the "shaken neighbors recognize that they have been destroyed as a community almost as surely as if the bomb had actually fallen" (354). Civil defense materials and novels like Pat Frank's 1959 postapocalyptic best seller *Alas, Babylon* suggested that Americans' willingness to help each other out in times of adversity would get the country through even the toughest postnuclear times.[26] Serling's fiction speculated that the actual response would be considerably less hopeful.

Released less than two years after "The Shelter" aired, Stanley Kubrick's film *Dr. Strangelove* also contained a critique of civil defense, thereby setting an example of wholesale satirical subversion of one of the central policies of the American government during the cold war. First a poster featuring the slogan "Civil Defense is Your Business!" and a drawing of a smiling family in a shelter, saying "Gee Dad! Thanks for thinking of us!" is visible in a pivotal scene three-quarters of the way through the film. The poster continues the film's satirical use of conspicuously self-contradictory language. The ubiquitous billboards around Burpelson Air Force Base proclaiming "Peace Is Our Profession" establish this pattern, and President Merkin Muffley picks up this theme later when he tells the Russian ambassador and General Buck Turgidson that they are not allowed to fight in the "War Room." The poster also provides a satirical commentary on the ineffectuality of civil defense, since Group Captain Lionel Mandrake (behind whom the poster appears) is thwarted at every turn in his efforts to perform the ultimate act of civil defense, namely, providing the president with a code required to call back a bomb wing that has been sent to attack Russia by an insane American general. The satire is especially poignant since Mandrake is temporarily prevented from fulfilling his mission by a putative ally, an American colonel named "Bat" Guano. Instead of assisting Mandrake in making his important phone call to Washington, Colonel Guano semiliterately accuses him of being a "prevert" (largely because he fails to recognize Mandrake's RAF uniform as that of an ally) and seems more worried about the sanctity of the Coca-Cola company's property (a soft-drink machine containing change that Mandrake needs to place a phone call to the White House) than the imminent threat of a nuclear war. As with Milo Minderbinder's decidedly unfriendly "friendly fire" in *Catch-22*, the greatest danger in this situation comes from the sheer irrationality of one's own putative allies.

The film satirizes civil defense again in its final scene, as the activation of the Soviet "doomsday machine" has become inevitable. Doctor Strangelove, a former Nazi scientist now in charge of the American nuclear weapons program, outlines his plan for the "future of the human race," much of which resembles, albeit in grotesquely deformed ways, American civil defense strategy of the early 1960s. Strangelove urges the president not to "rule out the chance to preserve a nucleus of human specimens . . . at the bottom of some of our deeper mine shafts." As he continues his speech, he struggles with his left arm, hitherto paralyzed but now dangerously animated and independent. It tries alternately to strangle him and to extend itself in a Nazi salute, thereby implying a connection between Strangelove's survival scheme and the eugenics of the Third Reich. Strangelove's explanation of how American society could persist in mine shafts combines civil defense rhetoric with a scathing parody of the kind of jingoistic "Golden Age" language used by R. W. Langer and other advocates of nuclear power in the 1940s and 1950s:[27]

Strangelove: It would not be difficult, Mein Führer! Nuclear reactors could . . . I'm sorry, Mr. President. . . . Nuclear reactors could provide power almost indefinitely. Greenhouses could maintain plant life, animals could be bred and slaughtered! A quick survey would have to be made of all the available mine sites in the country, but I would guess that dwelling space for several hundred thousands of our people could easily be provided.

Muffley: Well I would hate to have to decide who stays up and who goes down.

Strangelove: Well, that would not be necessary, Mr. President. It could be easily accomplished with a computer. A computer could be programmed to accept factors from youth, health, sexual fertility, intelligence and a cross-section of necessary skills. Of course, it would be absolutely vital that our top government and military men be included to foster and impart the required principles of leadership and tradition. [His arm, seemingly against his will, gives a "Heil Hitler" salute.] Naturally, they would breed prodigiously. There would be much time and little to do. But with the proper breeding techniques and a ratio of, say, ten females to each male, I would guess that they then could work their way back to the present gross national product within, say, twenty years.

Muffley: But look here, doctor. Wouldn't this nucleus of survivors be so grief-stricken and anguished that they would . . . well . . . envy the dead and not want to go on living?

Strangelove: No, sir . . . excuse me [fights with arm]. . . . Also when they go down into the mine, everyone would still be alive. There would be no shocking memories and the prevailing emotion will be one of nostalgia for those left behind, combined with a spirit of bold curiosity for the adventure ahead!

Their patriotism and sexuality equally aroused, the audience in the War Room leans closer to hear Dr. Strangelove's ideas, at which point General Turgidson suddenly jumps onto a bench to give an impassioned speech that threatens to extend the arms race into the bomb shelters: "I think it would be extremely, uh, naive of us to imagine that these new developments are going to cause any change in Soviet expansionist policy. I mean, we must be increasingly on the alert to prevent them from taking over other mine shaft space in order to breed more prodigiously than we do, thus knocking us out through superior numbers when we emerge! Mr. President, we must not allow . . . a mineshaft gap!" Turgidson's absurd reasoning that the cold war will continue even after the eradication of all life from the planet's surface rests on the unshakable belief that elaborate civil defense strategies like Dr. Strangelove's can actually work to preserve societies (and their values) intact regardless of their near-total destruction.[28] Any remaining sympathy among the audience for such a sentiment is erased by Kubrick's immediate jump cut at the end of Turgidson's oration to stock footage of nuclear explosions, implying that the Doomsday Machine has been triggered and that the end is truly near.

Despite the refrain playing over the closing scene of burgeoning mushroom clouds ("We'll meet again / Don't know where, don't know when"), Kubrick chooses not to end his film with the kind of pointed direct address to the audience that Stanley Kramer uses at the end of *On the Beach*. That film closes with a wide shot of a banner hanging over a deserted Melbourne square. As a dramatic orchestral chord sounds, the camera zooms in on the banner so that we can read its cautionary warning: "There Is Still Time . . . Brother." Kubrick seems less certain, but the ambiguous optimism of the ironically juxtaposed final song does allow the audience a brief moment of comic relief from the film's satiric indignation. The ending also restores some sense that avoiding a scenario like that depicted in the film is both desirable and necessary if "we" are actually to "meet again some sunny day." The satire shows that Russian and American secrecy, militarism, conspiracy, bureaucracy, warhead diplomacy, and emphasis on technology over humanity have created a nightmarish, self-destructive world in which love, especially when directed (as the subtitle states) toward the bomb, is indeed strange. As such it provides a suitable starting point for the discussion of the works of fiction that use satire in an attempt to subvert the cultures that spawned these various characteristics.

"The Bind of the Digital" and Other Oversimplified Logic

"Bad shit, to be avoided": *The Pathology of Cold War Dichotomies in the United States*

In his *The Making of a Counter Culture* (1969), Theodore Roszak, encapsulated the nascent resistance to the amorphous entity/mindset he named "technocracy": "Understood . . . as the mature product of technological progress and the scientific ethos, the technocracy easily eludes all traditional political categories. Indeed, it is characteristic of the technocracy to render itself ideologically invisible. Its assumptions about reality and its values become as unobtrusively pervasive as the air we breathe. While daily political argument continues within and between the capitalist and collectivist societies of the world, the technocracy increases and consolidates its power in both as a transpolitical phenomenon following the dictates of industrial efficiency, rationality, and necessity" (8). Roszak's formulation of the technocracy as "an umpire . . . the man who stands above the contest and who simply interprets and enforces the rules" (8) prefigures Pynchon's notion of the overarching "Them" from *Gravity's Rainbow* and echoes succeeding critics' observations.[1] As the next three chapters will corroborate, Roszak not only identifies the ultimate target of almost all the subversive satires of the cold war but also precisely articulates the reason why it must be subverted: "The angry debates of conservative and liberal, radical and reactionary touch everything except the technocracy, because the technocracy is not generally perceived as a political phenomenon in our advanced industrial societies. It holds the place, rather, of *a grand cultural imperative which is beyond question, beyond discussion.* . . . While possessing ample power to coerce, it prefers to charm conformity from us by exploiting our deep-seated commitment to the scientific world-view and by manipulating the securities and creature comforts of the industrial affluence which science has given us" (9; emphasis added). As a totalized system or "a grand cultural imperative" impervious to criticism (or even dialogue), Roszak's technocracy is a "disease" and his book unhesitatingly sides with the young "centaurs" opposing it. He does so because of the high stakes involved if the disease is allowed to progress: "The prime symptom of that disease is the shadow of thermonuclear annihilation beneath which we cower. The counter culture takes its stand against the background of this absolute evil, an evil which is not defined by the sheer *fact* of the bomb, but by the total *ethos* of the bomb, in which our politics, our public morality, our economic life, our intellectual endeavor are now embedded with a wealth of ingenious rationalization. . . . Whenever we feel inclined to qualify, to modify, to offer a cautious 'yes . . . *but*' to the protests of the young, let us return to this fact as the decisive measure of the technocracy's essential criminality: the extent to which it insists, in the name of progress, in the name of reason, that the unthinkable become thinkable and the intolerable become tolerable" (47). The subversive satirists of the cold war collectively undertook the twofold process of diagnosing this "disease" and exposing of the "essential criminality" behind it.

Any social order predicated on simple absolutes such as those that constitute Hirshberg's schemata or the "antiquated categories" (8) that Roszak claims are superficially operative in late 1960s politics is open to question by even fairly moderate skeptics, given the constant potential for cognitive dissonance. The oversimplified good/bad relationships that informed the official rhetoric of the cold war in the United States may have made good sound bites for domestic politics—President Reagan's famous characterization of the Soviet Union as the "evil empire" springs immediately to mind—but they were hardly based on honest appraisals of geopolitics, a fact that had become evident to a number of American satirists by the mid-1960s. After the Cuban Missile Crisis, the Kennedy assassination, and the intensification of the undeclared war in Southeast Asia, dissatisfaction with or even outright hostility toward government had intensified, most prominently (as would perhaps be expected) among individuals and groups associated with the broadly defined counterculture.

With satires such as *Catch-22* and *Dr. Strangelove* still fresh in American cultural memory, the period from 1965 to 1977 witnessed an explosion of satirical fictions that attempted to pierce the veil of the binary oppositions underlying the dominant cold war social fictions, both domestic and international. Two of the most compelling of such satires, Pynchon's *The Crying of Lot 49* and Barth's *Giles Goat-Boy,* were published within months of each other in 1966. Anticipating the dramatic expansion of digital culture that took place in the decades after its release, Pynchon introduces the concept of "excluded middles" to the literary scene as an undesirable ordering principle for 1960s American society. Borrowing his metaphor from the fundamental language of computer programming, Pynchon creates a divided society that largely functions along the lines of the ultrarational digital logic of ones and zeroes, thus marginalizing the excluded middles (in mathematical terms, the infinite range of nonwhole numbers in between these two integers).

Oedipa Maas, the heroine of the novel, is forced to undergo a bizarre and unnerving quest for reliable information in the wake of the death of her former lover, an eccentric millionaire named Pierce Inverarity. The more Oedipa becomes embroiled in the secretive and mind-bogglingly complex world in which Inverarity operated while alive, the less she can trust the various polarized concepts that previously shaped her thinking. Using either/or logic, she tries to make sense of the bewildering array of details she learns concerning the shadowy, seemingly countercultural Tristero organization: "She had heard all about excluded middles; they were bad shit, to be avoided. . . . For it was now like walking among matrices of a great digital computer, the zeroes and ones twinned above, hanging like balanced mobiles right and left, ahead, thick, maybe endless. Behind the hieroglyphic streets there would either be a transcendent meaning, or only the earth" (Pynchon, *Crying* 181). As the phrasing of the final sentence above shows, Oedipa's attempts to determine nature of the Tristero's existence do *not* avoid excluded middles, in this case the range between "transcendence" and ordinariness. In fact her retention of strict either/or reasoning is even more limiting, forcing her to assert that the only possible explanations for what she has experienced are either paranoid delusion or an alternate reality that remains impenetrable to her: "Another mode of meaning behind the obvious or none. Either Oedipa in the orbiting ecstasy of a true paranoia, or a real Tristero. For either there was some Tristero beyond the appearance of the legacy of America, or there was just America and if there was just America then it seemed the only way she could continue, and manage to be at all relevant to it, was as an alien, unfurrowed, assumed full circle into some paranoia" (182).

Thus Oedipa discovers the paradox of using binary logic to make sense of something that seems to exist beyond its means of explanation. Her situation is comparable to that of a dissenter against the political logic of the cold war, since the only readily acceptable stances in such an unqualified framework are those of friend or foe, plus or minus, for or against, us or them, one or zero. In the eyes of a system founded on a binary model, one cannot dissent against it in toto, only against one part of its constituent pairs.[2] The individual who claims to reject *everything* in a system implicitly rejects that which the system deems to be "good." If the only options for classification are "good" or "bad," then any form of dissenter becomes simply another enemy.[3]

Therefore Oedipa's potential for salvation lies precisely in the "middle" that is excluded by the closed binary system of San Narciso, which symbolizes the United States as a self-venerating whole, as the two parts of the town's name make clear. Neither the familiar version of America ("only the earth" or "just America") nor the inscrutable alternative mail system of the Tristero presents her a viable option, seemingly suggesting that a third option that supersedes both of these is necessary if she is to break out of what Alec McHoul and David Wills term "the bind of the digital, the binary of the either/or, all or nothing" (75). As a sort of American everywoman caught in the cogwheels of social machinery that she finds difficult if not impossible to comprehend, Oedipa symbolically signifies the United States in a state of societal and cultural crisis because of its logical inflexibility. As Frank D. McConnell writes in *Four Postwar American Novelists* (1977), "Pynchon's metaphor, however relevant it might be to its time and place, is deeply involved with the viability of human speech; for in the daylight, public society has produced a language whose prefabricated assurances do not admit the possibility of dissent, then society refuses to admit the possibility of the individual moral will—the will to say 'No!' if not in thunder then at least in a still, small voice. . . . The subversive communications network of Tristero, the language of the lost, becomes at once an escape from the tyranny of the daylight culture and an admission that the only human alternatives remaining are silence and apocalypse. For what can Tristero's elaborate networks carry, except the word that the word is, indeed, totally lost?" (172–73). Although McConnell's identification of the Tristero as "subversive" is accurate, he also succumbs to the same logical trap as Oedipa (and Rorty, for that matter). He retains the biases of the binary status quo by asserting that the Tristero suggests only two possible "human alternatives." His options of "silence" or "apocalypse" are analogues of Oedipa's choices ("orbiting ecstasy of a true paranoia, or a real Tristero"), but the Tristero would only be apocalyptic to a culture that is threatened by the very existence of nonoppositional alternatives, as is any rigidly binary system. The Tristero is properly understood (and perhaps only participated in) by individuals who abandon the binary perspective that governs American technocratic society.

The Tristero's motley collection of users includes representatives from myriad groups that are pushed to the edges of American life, whether for political, economic, sexual, intellectual, or other reasons. The Tristero's radical diversity marks it conspicuously as an alternative to the more homogeneous America suggested by San Narciso's suburban landscape. Moreover its unconventional pluralism reflects the Tristero's inclination and ability to accept and even to incorporate paradoxes. As Maltby writes, "Pynchon indicates that the Tristero System is not a mirror image of that which it opposes by representing its communicants (real or imagined) in ways which *conflate* contradictory alternatives" (149). Oedipa's investigation uncovers a wide range of apparent Tristero users: Mike Fallopian, a member of the zealously pro-American Peter Pinguid Society who scoffingly refers to members of the John Birch Society as "our more left-leaning friends" (50); Stanley Koteks, a somewhat bohemian engineer and disaffected employee of Yoyodyne, Inc.; Emory Bortz, a vaguely Dionysian literature professor; Winthrop Tremaine, who manufactures and sells swastika armbands and plans to market reproductions of SS uniforms "in teenage kid sizes" and perhaps "a modified version for the ladies" (149); and Jésus Arrabal, who quotes nineteenth-century Russian anarchist Mikhail Bakunin and preaches anarchic (that is, *wholly* subversive) revolution. These members' seeming incompatibility is reconciled by our recognition that such incongruities hold true only within the existing binary American value system, divided as it is into left and right, liberal and conservative, radical and reactionary, and so on.

Thus the Tristero *could* be a model for an alternative social order; however, Oedipa never definitively discovers its ontological status and therefore cannot free herself from the binary trap. Near the novel's conclusion, she formulates four potential explanations—still configured in an extended either/or binary—for the nature of the Tristero: "Either you have stumbled indeed, without the aid of LSD or other indole alkaloids, onto a secret richness and concealed density of a dream; onto a network by which X number of Americans are truly communicating whilst reserving their lies, recitations of routine, arid betrayals of spiritual poverty, for the official government system. . . . Or you are hallucinating it. Or a plot has been mounted against you, so expensive and elaborate . . . , so labyrinthine that it must have meaning beyond just a practical joke. Or you are fantasying some such plot, in which case you are a nut, Oedipa, out of your skull" (170). Oedipa claims that "she didn't like any of them," which is hardly surprising since they all still leave her with only the options of irrelevancy (she has only observed, not yet been allowed entry into the Tristero) or one of three forms of misapprehension. In the final scene of the novel, she refines her options further into the simple either/or proposition ("Either Oedipa in the orbiting ecstasy of a true paranoia, or a real Tristero") noted above and continues her quest for "her target, her enemy, perhaps her proof" (183). Pynchon does not resolve this binary dilemma, however, ending the novel without a denouement—in fact, the event for which the book is named is still incipient as the novel closes. In doing so he gives the reader a metafictional dose of Oedipa's medicine. Considering the pessimistic tone that pervades Pynchon's next work (*Gravity's Rainbow*), he may have despaired of finding such a solution on a larger social scale in time to avoid either complete acquiescent silence (irrelevance, or the *effective* state of nonexistence) or global apocalypse (the very *real* state of nonexistence).

Each of Pynchon's first three novels involves characters engaged in a quest. Herbert Stencil, the closest thing to a protagonist *V.* has, is on a quest that resembles Oedipa's in attempting to solve a mystery left behind in a vague posthumous document. Stencil pursues and attempts to narratively reconstruct a nebulous figure identified only as "V." in his dead father's notebooks. *Gravity's Rainbow* deals with a multitude of different searches, chiefly Tyrone Slothrop's desire to discover the reasons for his unusual erections, several parties' hunt for the missing V-2 rocket, and Tchitcherine's pursuit of Enzian.

Rarely, if ever, do these quests reach a conclusion, and such conclusions that we do get are usually either unsatisfactory, as is the case with the "Counterforce" in *Gravity's Rainbow,* or knowingly ignored in order to continue the search, as in Stencil's apparent discovery of the identity of his eponymous bounty in *V.* Pynchon's myriad loose endings imply not only that "the bind of the digital" is extremely strong in the late twentieth century but also that it perpetuates itself through individuals' willingness to maintain convenient fictions rather than to recognize potentially obscure or unpleasant truths. As Maltby writes, such recognition would involve subversion of the systems in which these characters find themselves, rather than simple opposition to them: "Pynchon denies the subversive value of opposition based on binary alternatives such as Left/Right or religious/secular. He suggests that a truly revolutionary movement would not be a reversal or inversion of the prevailing order of things because such options remain within the orbit of established oppositions; rather, the revolutionary movement must be radically discontinuous from the prevailing order" (148). Pynchon suggests in *The Crying of Lot 49,* however, that such a "radically discontinuous" movement is possible, and has Oedipa express this as she observes the W.A.S.T.E. mail system in action: "Here were God knew how many citizens, deliberately choosing not to communicate by U.S. Mail. It was not an act of treason, nor possibly even of defiance. But it was a calculated act of withdrawal from the life of the Republic, from its machinery. Whatever else was being denied them out of hate, indifference to the power of their vote, loopholes, simple ignorance, this withdrawal was their own, unpublicized, private. Since they could not have withdrawn into a vacuum (could they?), there had to exist the separate, silent unsuspected world" (124–25). Whether or not the malcontents that make up the Tristero are themselves a *desirable* alternative is another question altogether, one that implicitly demands examination of the groups whose desires are preeminent in a society (that is, whose will is empowered). Their mere existence, however, represents a subversive challenge to the established order, since it reaffirms the legitimacy of an "excluded middle" independent of *any* official recognition, positive or negative.

I believe that Pynchon intends the Tristero not to be an idealized or utopian system in reaction to the status quo but rather a philosophical construct that at least allows a more polyvocal culture to exist entirely separate from it. The Tristero certainly stands in opposition to the status quo from the postal system's perspective, but the Tristero users do not wish to take over the postal system's role, as the typical power-based dynamic of binary logic would dictate. Instead they seek to deny the postal system's authority to transmit (and thus to exert a measure of control over) the sort of socially marginalized communication in which they are engaging. In this way the Tristero also undermines the idea of dialectical advance from thesis and antithesis to synthesis, since becoming just an antipostal system would bolster the validity of the original binary thesis/antithesis opposition (given that synthesis can *only* result from the existence of an antithesis). The Tristero is fundamentally *alternative* rather than *oppositional*.

Pynchon harbors no illusions that achieving or even envisioning such an alternative system is a simple proposition. Oedipa's inability to arrive at a satisfactory conclusion for her either/or propositions indicates that such solutions cannot be envisioned without breaking free from the "orbit of established oppositions." Like any "typical" American, Oedipa will have to work still harder to overcome the culturally and logically undemanding[4] background of Tupperware parties, television, and the Young Republicans in which she exists at the novel's opening and that is even more pervasive in the fictional versions of California that Pynchon depicts in *Vineland* (1990) and *Inherent Vice* (2009). In essence both of those novels show (*Inherent Vice* in the Nixonian 1970s and *Vineland* in the Reagan-era 1980s) the adverse effects of remaining within the "digital" ground rules. At best one can hope (as in Don DeLillo's *White Noise*)[5] for the mediated bliss of consumerist sedation, and at worst incarceration or outright extermination is one's fate.

At virtually the same time that *The Crying of Lot 49* was suggesting the subversive necessity of reintegrating marginalized values, John Barth's *Giles Goat-Boy* considered similar topics in an even more metaphysical (and metafictional) context. Although the extent of its direct political dissent is debatable,[6] *Giles Goat-Boy* is one of the most thorough satires of the fundamental cold war worldview. Within the copious space of eight hundred pages, Barth presents a thinly veiled allegory of the cold war, recast as an ideological conflict (the "Quiet Riot") between two dominant colleges (Nikolayan and New Tammany) within a global university and the computers (EASCAC and WESCAC) that both control and threaten the lives of individuals there. Barth simultaneously weaves a bildungsroman into this allegorized setting, telling the story of Billy Bocksfuss / George Giles and his quest to redeem the novel's dangerously divided world by becoming a "Grand Tutor," a messianic archetype corresponding closely to Joseph Campbell's monomythic hero. Barth's refiguring of the cold war as an academic rivalry allows him to play out a number of arguments predicated on antithetical, flawed, and/or intentionally vague premises to their belabored and irrational conclusions.

At the chronological start of the narrative,[7] Billy is a human child being raised as a goat in an artificial state of pastoral innocence by his mentor Max Spielman, one of the original developers of WESCAC. Spielman has exiled himself to a goat farm at the edge of campus as a protest against the way the computer is being used as a weapon in the Quiet Riot, making him a clear analogue for J. Robert Oppenheimer (among others).[8] After a series of incidents that make Billy aware of his human nature, he begins unsteadily walking upright instead of on all fours and asks Spielman to treat him henceforth as a normal human being. Spielman's faith in humanity has been so thoroughly shaken that he attempts to dissuade Billy from this course of action, and his justification for raising Billy as a goat instead of as a human demonstrates that this loss of faith stems from his belief that humans are unable to reconcile potentially contradictory aspects of their nature: "I'd watch you frisking with Mary's [a nanny on the goat farm] kids, that were never going to hear what *true* and *false* is, and then I'd look at the wretchedest man on campus [Spielman himself], that wrote *The Theory of the University* and loves every student in it, but killed ten thousand with a single brainwave! So! Well! I decided my Bill had better be a goat for his own good, he should never have to wonder who he is" (107).

Spielman represents a viewpoint that, despite its seemingly good intentions, succumbs entirely to binary logic, especially an ostensibly absolute innate distinction between humans and animals. Suffering the emotional aftereffects of his role in creating WESCAC, Spielman ceases to wrestle with the ambiguities that fall between oversimplified binaries such as truth and falsehood or good and evil, and he tries to insulate Billy from them as well. Because the Quiet Riot as a whole is nominally predicated on such constructs, his self-exile from the New Tammany power structure is wholly consistent with this attitude. Spielman's solution differs from that of the Tristero by doing precisely that which Oedipa can still question, if only parenthetically; he withdraws, but he withdraws into a vacuum that negates the possibility of an authentic alternative, since remaining there would force Billy to exist as something he is decidedly not, a nonhuman animal.

Spielman is not the only voice exerting formative pressure on young Billy, though. He is also visited by a woman he calls Lady Creamhair, who entreats him to rediscover his humanity, albeit by invoking the kind of binary logic that the novel's overall structure eventually subverts. She tells Billy, "I want you to be a human being and Dr. Spielman wants you to be a goat, and you're caught in between. . . . Here's what I think: you've got to be one or the other, and Dr. Spielman and I must go along with your decision." When Billy asks her why he must choose, she replies in terms that echo the inflexible concept of the excluded middle: "You just can't, my dear: if you try to be both, you'll end up being neither" (60). Both of Billy's early mentors thus reinforce the notion that the world functions along exclusively dualistic lines, even if the particular dualisms (or the sides they take in any given opposition) do not always correspond to one another. In the case of the goat-versus-human dichotomy, Lady Creamhair's argument ultimately proves more persuasive to the impressionable young goat-boy, and he insists on becoming human.

Despite his reservations Spielman eventually gives in to Billy's wishes. He agrees to provide Billy with an introduction to the ways of the university, from which the young goat-boy has been shielded to this point. In the course of this education, Spielman tells his protégé the story of how Billy came to be his surrogate son. Billy was brought to the farm by G. Herrold, a janitor who discovered the infant Billy inside an elevator used to transport reels of tape containing data into WESCAC's "Belly" (its core). How he came to be there is unclear, although Spielman surmises that he was the result of an artificial intelligence experiment gone awry and was left there to die for some reason by "someone high in the administrative hierarchy of the campus" (104). Finding the answer to this mystery becomes one of Billy's chief concerns through the remainder of the novel. The mystery surrounding his origins is further complicated by the presence of a strangely configured and anonymous Prenatal Aptitude Test (PAT) card—WESCAC issues such a card for all newborns indicating what vocation their intelligence indicates they are best suited for—that bears the words "Pass All Fail All" (104). Given that the concepts of passage and failure are roughly equivalent to salvation and damnation, respectively, within the novel's metaphorical setting, their obscure and paradoxical appearance on his card seemingly marks him for some higher purpose. Again displaying his inherently dualistic worldview, Spielman vigorously rejects such a metaphysical significance: "It don't make sense how one student could pass everything and flunk everything too" (104).

Nevertheless the correspondences between the details of Billy's peculiar beginnings and the stories Spielman and Lady Creamhair have told him about mythological heroes and religious figures such as Enos Enoch (the novel's analogue for Jesus) ultimately convince Billy that he is indeed destined for something more than simple existence as either a goat or a human; he becomes certain that he is meant to be a Grand Tutor. In short, Billy uses fictions, or at least fictionalized versions of reality, in his attempts to define himself. This point is driven home by the fact that he literally devours (as befits a goat) the pages of the books of mythology from which Lady Creamhair—who later turns out to be his biological mother—reads to him.

Early in the book Billy realizes the difficulties of becoming a unifying messiah in a world that steadfastly chooses to define itself in terms of irreconcilable and oppositional differences. Spielman tells Billy of his erstwhile belief in "Student-Unionism" (that is, Communism), with which Spielman "like many intellectual Moishians [Jews] . . . had sympathized whole-heartedly . . . during Campus Riot I," but goes on to explain to his young protégé that it ultimately differed very little from its sworn enemy, "Informationalism" (that is, capitalism): "'It wasn't until later,' he declared sadly 'we saw that the "Sovereignty of the Bottom Percentile" was just another absolute chancellorship, with some pastry-cook or industrial-arts teacher in charge. The great failing of Informationalism is selfishness; but what the Student-Unionists do, they exchange the selfish student for a selfish college. This *College Self* they're always lecturing about—it's just as greedy and grasping as Ira Hector, the richest Informationalist in New Tammany'" (93).

As Douglas Robinson suggests, Barth's novel is a call for a new kind of hero who understands the irony of the cold war / Quiet Riot and who can accordingly help the world avert its potential self-destruction: "For Barth, the *threat* of apocalypse and the resultant societal anxiety are undeniable cultural realities that possess considerable potential for fiction. . . . Anxiety creates need, and need motivation; and the need felt by modern society for salvation from imminent apocalypse motivates the parody of the hero myth" (178). The novel is at once a parody of the mythic coming-of-age story and a recalibration of this genre and its attendant cultural goals—a state in which "life no longer suffers hopelessly under the terrible mutilations of ubiquitous disaster, battered by time, hideous throughout space" (Campbell 29)—to the specific conditions of the nuclear age.

In accordance with the archetypal mythic-heroic pattern that Billy has chosen to emulate,[9] Spielman takes on the role of the mentor, giving him a new name (George Giles) and reciting the history of the college, WESCAC, and the Quiet Riot for him, simultaneously explicating this complicated allegorical structure for the reader. When Billy/George sets out to enroll in classes seven years later, he almost immediately meets Maurice Stoker, a demonic figure who controls New Tammany College's energy supply and its police force. He also meets Stoker's beautiful and sexually promiscuous wife Anastasia, with whom he immediately falls in love, like any good Campbellian hero in search of a "mother goddess" who will facilitate his mythic resurrection (in Greek, *anastasis*). The antagonism between Maurice's egotism and Anastasia's selflessness develops into George's guiding metaphor in his quest to become a Grand Tutor. Anastasia becomes his symbolic ideal, and he divides the world cleanly into two classes of people based on how he perceives the couple's respective natures. In essence he wishes to save Anastasia and people like her from Maurice and people like him. Having inherited the practice of dividing the world into neat halves from his two main mentors, he now applies it in his quest to become a Grand Tutor.

George matriculates and begins working toward enlightenment (refigured as "commencement" in this academic setting). He believes that achievement of this goal, which involves correctly answering a series of questions put to him by the omnipotent WESCAC, will affirm his status as a Grand Tutor, thereby affording him the rarefied messianic status he seeks and allowing him to overthrow entirely the established system of New Tammany College. His motivation for wanting to topple the status quo stems both from having absorbed much of Spielman's resentment against the administration for the perversion of WESCAC and from his desire to save Anastasia from the evil he perceives in Maurice and, by extension, the "state" he serves.

A significant problem arises, however, in that a rival aspirant has arrived on the scene, a man named Harold Bray. He steals George's thunder at a performance of a play, *Taliped Decanus,* by announcing himself to be the Grand Tutor. Specifically he claims to be the GILES ("Grand-tutorial Ideal, Laboratory Eugenical Specimen" [143]) that WESCAC's programmers had wanted it to produce as part of the project that Max believes may have created George. Just as the play before the characters is a parody (for Barth's reader, not for the characters themselves) of Sophocles's *Oedipus Rex*, Bray functions as a parody of the idealized heroic identity that George has conceived as his own destiny. The assembled crowd enthusiastically accepts Bray at his word, and he usurps the authoritative position George had planned to claim for himself.

Robinson claims that "as antigiles, Bray's task is to thwart George at any cost; and in addition to linguistic tricks and direct violence, one of the ways he seeks to complete his nefarious task is by tempting George to give up his quest altogether" (225). Although Bray is not the genuine GILES, Robinson points out that he "is apparently an emanation of WESCAC" (225), making him the physical manifestation of a technological innovation designed to carry out a binary ideological conflict and thus the literal and metaphorical embodiment of the rhetoric that defends the power elites of New Tammany College against internal and external challenges. In the terms of the overriding historical allegory, Bray becomes the mouthpiece of American authority, which, like New Tammany College, is backed up by lethal technology. Because he couches his opposition to George in explicitly binary terms (that is, he is the "antigiles"), he essentially serves as a normative tool for suppressing dissent. This parallel is further enhanced by Robinson's list of the three strategies Bray uses to confound George, since disinformation and euphemism ("linguistic tricks"), imprisonment or other material consequences ("direct violence"), and threats of ostracism ("tempting [him] to give up the quest altogether") were at one time or another important components of U.S. domestic policy during the cold war.[10] Undeterred by the presence of an unexpected rival, George continues with his plan to graduate, hopefully also exposing Bray as a fake along the way.

Upon matriculating George receives a list of seven "assignments" from WESCAC, and the latter half of the novel treats the two successive philosophical positions that George develops in response to his assigned tasks. Both of these schemata represent attempts to reconcile the ambiguous message ("Pass All Fail All") previously noted on his PAT card and reappearing on his assignment sheet. This paradoxical "PAT-phrase" (Barth, *Giles* 383) and the list of assignments represent exactly the sort of logically problematic language from which Spielman hoped to isolate Billy/George. George's initial reaction to his assignments shows, he only vaguely comprehends what he is being asked to do, much less how to do it: "Founder! Founder! Those I thought I grasped, I gasped at; most signified not a thing to me. . . . Fist to brow I told them over, faintful list, and struck at each" (384). As Robinson points out, George's first proposed strategy for approaching his assignment does not arise from understanding it but instead from intentionally altering it: "Because paradoxical thinking does not come easy to George at first, the phrase seems like a contradiction in terms, and so he unconsciously amends it to make it easier to handle: he tends to think of the phrase with an 'or' in the middle . . . , and faced with a choice to Pass All *or* Fail All, George knows he must cleave to Passage. This tiny addition to the PAT-phrase distorts and simplifies its import, and helps George formulate his first position: Passage, he says is always Passage, and Failure is always Failure, and the two should be kept as far apart as possible" (287). To George the simple binary division defining the world is thus the product of a "tiny addition" that "distorts and simplifies" ambiguity by reducing it to an "either/or" construction. George applies this absolutist philosophy to the completion of all his assigned tasks, including answering a series of questions in WESCAC's Belly as part of his "Finals." Some of these questions do not seem to lend themselves to the "yes or no" answers to which George is limited (*"ARE YOU MALE OR FEMALE?"*) or even to be questions at all (*"GILES, SON OF WESCAC"*), yet George answers them all in the affirmative. He briefly believes himself to have passed, but Bray has concocted an elaborate ruse that reinforces the public's belief that Bray is the true GILES. Rather than exposing his rival via his passage, George is himself accused of being an impostor and is about to be hanged when an alarm sounds, signifying an attack by the Nikolayans. Unaware that the alarm is false, the angry mob scatters and George is spared execution.

Disheartened by his failure and imprisoned under Maurice Stoker's super-vision, George overcompensates, swinging to the opposite pole. His new position argues that Passage and Failure, indeed all oppositions, are mean-ingless: "The way to salvation, he says, is to embrace all the opposites within yourself, and to give full reign to the innate and fruitful chaos of good and evil, order and disorder, wisdom and madness in the human soul" (McConnell 149). George again takes his Finals in WESCAC's Belly, this time answering all questions negatively. The results are much the same as before, with the campus thrown into a state of chaos after it adopts his nihilistic principles.

These two antithetical positions prove equally unsatisfying; each, in fact, nearly results in the destruction of the college. The novel's positive resolu-tion occurs only after George rejects altogether the binary thinking upon which the adversarial world of the Quiet Riot is founded. As McConnell puts it, George "discovers the most nebulous of alternative positions to his earlier premises. In fact, it is not an alternative at all, but rather a resignation of alternatives . . . , a declaration that both rationalism and nihilism, order and disorder, are equally true, equally valid imaginations of the human condi-tions" (149). This reconciliation of philosophical opposites is embodied by the final scene of the main narrative, in which both thesis and antithesis are simultaneously dispelled: George "at once vanquishes Harold Bray forever and witnesses the execution of his old teacher, Max—a moment, that is, when the living forces of mockery and wisdom, negativity and culture are held in a precarious balance of mutual destruction" (149). Spielman's death signifies that existence within a true state of paradox requires the sacrifice of some-thing dear, specifically the tenuous security that comes from adherence to simple binary logic. Although Spielman rejects the dualistic thinking of New Tammany College after his retreat to the goat barns, his refusal echoes Weisenburger's distinction between "transgressing and more properly resist-ing or dissenting practices" (*Fables* 258). Spielman does not subvert the struc-ture as much as ignore it out of frustration at being unable to reconcile the existence of opposites. He still believes the world is divided into good and evil (or true and false) but feels oppressed by the existence or perhaps even the dominance of values that oppose his own, and he regresses into a sort of nihilism by default. The simultaneous disappearances of Bray and Spielman keep New Tammany in equilibrium by not allowing either the former's ratio-nalism or the latter's nihilism to overwhelm the other.

Barth's combination of cold war allegory and mythopoetic/philosophical inquiry results in a work that directs critical evaluation and, ultimately, satiri-cal subversion toward all narratives (broadly defined) that claim absolute veracity, including the synthetic philosophical solution that finally allows George to achieve his goal in *Giles Goat-Boy*.[11] Barth undercuts any sense of prescriptive truth telling via the series of three brief framing devices that conclude the book. First George himself contributes a "Posttape" in which he appears to disown the precepts laid forth in his autobiographical tale. This is followed by a "Postscript to the Posttape" in which "J. B." (the ostensible caretaker of George's manuscript and himself a follower of its teachings) claims that the "Posttape" is a bogus document and should not have been included. Finally a "Footnote to the Postscript to the Posttape" is appended by the book's fictional editor, in which he questions the authenticity of J. B.'s "Postscript to the Posttape."

Barth's intention is *af*firmation, rather than *con*firmation, of the exis-tential paradox.[12] After all, placing an ethical value on what is ultimately a philosophical given—and paradox is still the status quo at the end of both George's framed parodic hagiography and the framing postscripts of *Giles Goat-Boy*—would repeat the mistake of a fiction that claims itself to be true. Iser's explanation for the differences in the intentions of "literary fictions" and "fictions of our ordinary world" is valuable in accounting for Barth's seemingly self-negating ending: "The [fictions of our ordinary world] are assumptions, hypotheses, presuppositions and, more often than not, the basis of world views, and may be said to complement reality. . . . Fictionalizing in literature, however, appears to have a different aim . . . , [for literary fictions] are always accompanied by convention-governed signs that signalize the 'as if' nature of all the possibilities they adumbrate. Consequently, such a staged compensation for what is missing in reality never conceals the fact that in the final analysis it is nothing but make-believe, and so ultimately all the possi-bilities opened up must be lacking in authenticity" (Iser 5). The concatenated postscripts serve as the "convention-governed signs" that clearly and indelibly mark the fictionality of George's story even as they comically purport to establish its veracity through a simulated editorial (that is, nonfictional) correspondence. In doing so they also help subvert the possible interpretation of George's solution as a dialectic synthesis, and therefore a philosophical truth, since they destabilize or perhaps even destroy the reader's faith in the authenticity of the entire narrative.[13]

Thus *Giles Goat-Boy* is not truly intended as a surrogate gospel, as its subtitle "The Revised New Syllabus" might imply. Rather it seeks, as Charles B. Harris argues, to subvert altogether the power of social fictions: "George has not answered WESCAC's questions, he has invalidated them, denied their legitimacy. He solves his problem, which is finally linguistic in nature, by transcending it" (100). The "linguistic" root of George's problem is specifically the rhetoric of binary logic, whether progressive dialectics or divisive antagonism. The novel's "solution" is so complete that it even calls its own ability to tell the truth into question and, therefore, does what Harris sees as the next (and only) best thing it can: it "faces an ultimacy, an artistic dead end, turns it back upon itself, and produces art" (102).

The kind of "life-and-death anomalies" that McConnell claims are raised in *Giles Goat-Boy* lie at the very heart of the cold war, which represented the most grievously threatening either/or choice ever put before the world. Neither *Giles Goat-Boy* nor *The Crying of Lot 49* offer any palliatives for the "bind of the digital" that retain its basic reasoning, whether out of fear, naïveté, habit, or some combination thereof. Instead both novels subvert the validity of such binary constructs by showing the violence and self-negation that necessarily results from them. Both present alternatives that offer the temperate redemption of continued and more genuine existence, if not the elusive paradise of utopia.

"But you're one of ours, aren't you?": *Russian Subversions of Binary Logic*

Satirical subversion of binary cold war logic is not limited to American fiction. If anything the wide-ranging influence of such thinking in Russian history makes it an even more prominent theme in Russian literature and not just during this time period. Soviet rhetoric of the cold war has deep roots in several sets of cultural opposites that have persisted in Russian culture for centuries, some of the most important of which are East versus West, old versus new, and native versus foreigner, each of which serves to define who "we" are as Russians as compared to who "they" are as non-Russians. Yuri Lotman and Boris Uspensky note that these dichotomies arise from a cyclical process that can be traced back at least as far as the Christianization of Russia in the year 988: "The history of Russian culture in the period that we have selected [that is, before the nineteenth century] provides convincing evidence of the culture's clear-cut division into stages that replace one another dynamically." However, this dynamic replacement takes place within a system that is fundamentally polarized, which results in "new historical structures in pre-nineteenth-century Russia [that] invariably regenerate the culture of the past." They argue that this process arises from the worldview of medieval Russia: "The basic cultural values (ideological, political, and religious) of medieval Russia were distributed in a bipolar field and divided by a sharp boundary without an axiologically neutral zone. . . . The Russian medieval system was constructed on an accentuated duality . . . , the division of the other world into heaven and hell. Intermediate neutral spheres were not envisaged. Behavior in earthly life could, correspondingly, be either sinful or holy. This situation spread into extra-ecclesiastical conceptions; thus secular power could be interpreted as divine or diabolical, but never as neutral" (32).

This "accentuated duality" repeatedly creates a "new" state out of ideological remnants of a past at least one step removed from the present: "Duality and the absence of a neutral axiological sphere led to a conception of the new not as a continuation, but as a total eschatological change. . . . Under such conditions, the dynamic process of change has a fundamentally different character [from the West]: change occurs as a radical negation of the preceding state. The new does not arise out of a structurally 'unused' reserve, but results from a transformation of the old, a process of turning it inside out. Thus repeated transformations can in fact lead to the *regeneration* of archaic forms" (32–33). Lotman and Uspensky argue that the result of this "consistently and cyclically repeated 'negation of negation'" (33) is that genuinely contemporary variants (that is, not simple "remnants of receding cultural periods" [31]) of traditional value systems shape Russian history and culture in a way that is revolutionary in the short term but homeostatic in the broader historical context.

Among the most illustrative examples of this simultaneously subversive and normative dualism in Russian history are the Old Believers (*starovery*), who played a leading role in the mid-seventeenth-century schism (*raskol*) within the Russian Orthodox Church and later led the resistance to Peter the Great's societal reforms (themselves an inversion of the most immediate "old" state). In the nineteenth century, the Slavophile movement partially took up the mantle of the Old Believers by vociferously opposing the introduction (past, present, or future) into Russian culture of any foreign ideas or values, among which they naturally included most of Peter's innovations. Russian history of the past ten centuries is filled with violent clashes that center upon these kinds of seemingly irreconcilable dichotomies. Lotman and Uspensky emphasize the mutability of these binaries in Russian history, a factor that contributes to their longevity: "The activity and significance of [the opposition between 'the old and the new'] is so great that from the subjective position of the 'native speaker' of the culture, it has at various stages included or subsumed other singularly important contrasts, such as: 'Russia versus the West,' 'Christianity versus paganism,' 'true faith versus false faith,' 'knowledge versus ignorance,' 'upper classes versus lower classes,' and so on" (33). The crucial innovation regarding the use of this dichotomy and others like it during the Soviet period is that the ideological conflict is predominantly focused outward on a global scale (as befits both a theoretically internationalist movement and a paranoid state that feels "encircled" by class enemies) rather than inward onto Russian society. Lenin's pronouncement that "as long as capitalism and socialism remain, we cannot live in peace" (Lenin 398) makes clear the inflexibly binary *philosophical* basis of the Soviet state, even if the practical reality (during, for example, the NEP period or détente) was occasionally less absolute.

In *Soviet Civilization,* Sinyavsky discusses the exclusively dichotomous and chauvinistic mindset of the Soviet state: "The distinction between ours and not ours is part of the psychology and the official language. When interrogating a dissident at the KGB, they often begin by saying: 'You're not one of ours!' Then, to push him to repent: 'But you're one of ours, aren't you? Answer? Are you or aren't you?' One wants to ask: 'Why do I have to be one or the other?' But that is forbidden. Because humanity is divided into ours and not ours. And this is rooted deep in the subconscious in the form of that disjunctive question: 'Russian or non-Russian?'" (261). Sinyavsky repeatedly points out that this binary approach is merely *exaggerated* by the Soviet system rather than *created* by it. He sardonically points out that the Russian language itself contains a number of words or phrases that subtly reinforce the ours / not ours split: "'Ours' [*nashi*] can only mean Russians. Whereas the German spirit is alien, inhuman. The Russian word for Germans (*nemtsy*) has the same root as the word dumb (*nemy*): the Germans are those who can't speak Russian, 'nonpersons,' sometimes evil spirits. 'Tatars' are those who come from Tartar, from Hell. But we Russians, we are bright, we are good, we are Orthodox, we are Slavs" (260). Even though centuries of usage and the aggressive recontextualizations of Soviet idiom have largely effaced these etymological connections, Sinyavsky claims that the "distinction between ours and not ours persists, in a more diffuse, less precise form." Ultimately, he contends, the "nuances tied to a specific historical period" (260) are not as important as the fact that binary logic is consistent in its presence throughout Russian history, even if the identities of the opposing sides tend to change. Such logic then serves as the foundation for a cognitive schema that is extremely resistant to counterschematic information, just as a collective sense of virtuous exceptionalism with its roots in the nation's ostensibly Puritan origins (and the attendant Calvinist binary of election and preterition) fortified the patriotic schemata of the United States during the cold war.

In 1934 the strength of this dichotomous logic shaped the infamous Article 58 of the Criminal Code of the RSFSR (Sektsiia 58 Ugolovnyi Kodeks RSFSR).[14] This law was used to convict large numbers of political prisoners during the Stalinist terrors, especially during the purges of 1937–38. Although less frequently invoked after Khrushchev's 1956 criticism of Stalin's "excesses," it fostered a simple pro-Soviet / anti-Soviet division used as legal justification for the imprisonment of such noted dissidents as Sakharov, Sinyavsky, and Daniel. Article 58 deals specifically with "Counter-revolutionary crimes" (*Kontrrevoliutsionnye prestupleniia*) and defines such activity: "'Counter-revolutionary' is understood as any action directed toward the overthrow, subversion, or weakening of the power of worker-peasant councils or of their chosen (according to the Constitution of the USSR and constitutions of union republics) worker-peasant government of the USSR, union and autonomous republics, or toward the subversion or weakening of the external security of the USSR and the fundamental economic, political, and national gains of the proletarian revolution." Especially in cases involving writers and other members of the intelligentsia, paragraph 10 of this article proved to be the most useful tool of repression. This paragraph specifically treated published or otherwise explicitly stated counterrevolutionary thought: "Propaganda, or agitation, containing a call for the overthrow, subversion, or weakening of Soviet authority or for the carrying out of other counter-revolutionary crimes . . . , and likewise the distribution or preparation or keeping of literature of this nature shall be punishable by deprivation of liberty for a term not less than six months. The same actions during mass disturbances, or with the use of religious or nationalist prejudices of the masses, or in a war situation, or in areas proclaimed to be in a war situation shall be punishable by measures of social defense, indicated in article 58.2 of this code." These "measures of social defense" included "shooting, or the proclamation as an enemy of the workers, with confiscation of property and with deprivation of citizenship of the union republic, and likewise of citizenship of the Soviet Union and perpetual expulsion beyond the borders of the USSR." Paragraph 10 also allows for the punishment to be reduced "to deprivation of liberty for a term of no less than three years," but only "under extenuating circumstances" (Cunningham, *Article 58*).

Article 58 thus codified the ours / not ours binary into the Soviet legal system, first by defining ideological dissenters as enemies of the state and consequently by deeming them unworthy to be a part of Soviet society by depriving them of physical freedom, citizenship, or life. Hundreds of thousands of Soviet citizens were indicted under this article and the extent to which this law was spuriously used to control and/or exterminate members of the Soviet population, especially those actively opposing Stalinist totalitarianism, indelibly etched its rhetorical structure into the memory of Soviet dissidents.

Although the terrible significance of Article 58 in the post-Stalin Soviet cultural conscience does not automatically transform *any* criticism of Stalinism or the Soviet legal system into a condemnation of ours / not ours logic, such criticisms usually contained a strong thematic undercurrent of this sort, especially since "enemy of the state" or "enemy of the workers" rhetoric remained a salient feature of official attempts to control dissent well into the glasnost era. In describing various pathways to dissidence among his generation, Sinyavsky singles out the labor camps as the most important: "The Soviet camps and prisons exercised the strongest influence. Primarily through the prisoners themselves, amnestied or rehabilitated after Stalin's death. These were people of another generation, mostly old men, returning home after long terms to tell their own and other people's stories, life experience that the young intelligentsia greedily consumed. . . . Very often these were old Communists or distinguished people once devoted to the Soviet power. But time in camp had forced them to change, to reconsider their ideals" (234–35).

Sinyavsky claims that these experiences propagated a subculture of opposition and became something of a dissident's litmus test, ironically based on yet another version of the ours / not ours distinction: "Their hard experience had the advantage of pushing the younger generation into action. These older people were coming back from camp, to which they had been sent for no real offense, while the younger ones were about to be sent off: it is in this context that a sort of nostalgia for camp emerged: 'Can I consider myself a man, an honest intellectual, if I've never been in prison? Can I judge life if I myself have never been through life's chief experience, that of prison?'" (235). The bitter divisions among many émigrés of the post-Stalin era often reflect this attitude that credible dissidence stems primarily from personal hardships suffered at Soviet hands, a theme expressed in much of the period's satirical fiction.[15] In view of the degree to which domestic Soviet rhetoric was dominated by the struggle of "heroes of socialist labor" against "enemies of the state" (a binary opposition rife with social fictions designed to uphold the patriotic schemata of the state) it was perhaps inevitable, if also lamentable, that the supposed enemies would employ such binaries in their own processes of self-definition.

The real enemy in theoretically class-oriented Soviet binary logic, though, is neither simply the ideas and values of the West nor someone, internal or external, who actually or allegedly espouses them, as was generally the case in the nineteenth-century Slavophile worldview.[16] Rather the countries of the West themselves—the United States foremost—also became the Soviets' enemies, since they represented territories ruled by bourgeois, empire-minded (and thus physically as well as ideologically threatening) capitalists. Despite the prominent role that proxies and satellites played in its actual conduct, numerous propagandists on both sides imagined the cold war pitting Misha the Russian Bear against Uncle Sam.

Although official Soviet authors used this dichotomy extensively during the Cold War (as they had during the 1920s and early 1930s)[17] to satirize the United States as the ideological enemy against which the Soviet people virtuously struggled, many dissident writers produced works that satirically engaged the ours / not ours mentality instead. The official anticapitalist, anti-Western, and anti-American position was expressed in such works as Vadim Kozhevnikov's *Znakom'tes', Baluev* (1960; *Introduce Yourself, Baluev!*), Vsevolod Kochetov's *Sekretar' obkoma* (1961; *Regional Party Secretary*), and Alexander Chakovsky's *Pobeda* (1980–82; *Victory*) in rigidly formulaic terms that adhere closely to the requirements of Socialist Realism from before the cold war.[18] In contrast works such as Zinoviev's *Yawning Heights*, Aksyonov's *Our Golden Ironburg* and *The Island of Crimea*, Iskander's *Rabbits and Boa Constrictors*, Dovlatov's *Nashi* (1983; *Ours*), and Voinovich's *The Life and Extraordinary Adventures of Private Ivan Chonkin* (hereafter referred to simply as *Chonkin*), *Pretender to the Throne*, and *Moscow 2042* all use satire to subvert the validity of the Soviet binary worldview as well as *any* system of thinking based on simple black-and-white divisions. Like their American counterparts, these Russian authors do not wish simply to ally themselves with the "other side" within the existing framework of conflict but to step outside that framework and discredit it altogether by pointing out its inherent contradictions, oversimplifications, and distortions.

Most of these texts achieve their satirical effect at least in part by parodying genres of fiction formerly used in Russian literary history to uphold some portion of the cultural philosophy informing the ours / not ours binary. For example Ryan-Hayes argues that *Ours* is essentially a parody of the family chronicle, a genre dating back to Sergei Aksakov's novel *Semeinaia khronika* (1856; *A Family Chronicle*). She also argues that *Rabbits and Boa Constrictors* can be read as a parody of the traditional Russian allegorical fairy tale and that *Moscow 2042* is simultaneously a parody of both utopian and dystopian fiction, especially in its science fictional variant.[19] Clowes similarly asserts that *The Island of Crimea* is "framed in the popular genre of the international thriller combining adventure, romance, and intrigue" (177) even as it serves as a dark, often uncomic dystopian satire.[20] Nina Kolesnikoff argues that *Our Golden Ironburg* parodies the "so-called 'industrial novel,' which . . . offers accounts of work at construction projects, factories or research institutes" (195). Furthermore, Voinovich's two *Chonkin* novels can be read as parodies of the host of novels, songs, poems, and so on that glorified the intelligence, bravery, and resourcefulness of the simple Soviet soldier during the "Great Patriotic War" (World War II).[21] The parodic-satiric tendency is widespread in post-Stalin dissident literature and has been extensively documented in the extant criticism.

As the writers mentioned above began their careers in the late 1950s and early 1960s, however, these genres were either entirely absent from or only gradually reemerging onto the Soviet literary scene after more than thirty years of neglect stemming from the governmentally enforced emphasis on Socialist Realist writing during Stalin's rule. The subversive potential contained within these novels is thus two-tiered, a trait that helps delineate their peculiarity as specifically cold war satires. First, the original genres being parodied in these works (with the exception of the *Chonkin* novels and *Our Golden Ironburg,* both of which parody the most dogmatic subgenres of *sotsrealizm*) are themselves already reactions against what Katerina Clark calls the "master plot [of Socialist Realism] that stitches together several significant layers of culture, including its history, its philosophical anthropology, and its literary presuppositions" (252). Many if not most of these "layers of culture" still appeared in official Soviet literature even after the Thaw, during which the variety of the Soviet novel slowly expanded from Clark's catalogue of the six subgenres[22] of Socialist Realism. Each of the genres parodied thus already represents a form of protest against the withering of Russian fiction under Stalin, either by rehabilitating a pre-Soviet genre (the family chronicle or the beast fable) or by imitating a Western, and thus ideologically proscribed, model (such as the "international thriller").

The second and more significant form of subversion resides not in the parodic but in the *satirical* nature of these novels. As noted before the reforms of the Thaw had stopped well short of creating a literary atmosphere in the Soviet Union in which most forms of explicit dissent were possible.[23] The genres that resurfaced after the loosening of Socialist Realism's strictures during the Thaw quickly took on the ideological tenor of the state, especially after Brezhnev replaced Khrushchev. Clark explains this phenomenon: "Although it is, de facto, no longer mandatory to use the conventions of Socialist Realism that were standard under Stalin, fiction [of the Brezhnev era] is not entirely independent of them. Even when writers advocate values they believe to be opposed to Stalinist values, they often articulate them against the old patterns. Thus those patterns still have some currency as a code through which meaning can be conveyed symbolically" (236). Later she explains these "patterns" and "codes" in terms of myth making, linking her analysis back to Iser's concepts of literary and social fictionality: "Instead of doing what we have come to think of as the work of literature, Socialist Realism performs an essentially mythological task. It is mythic in the degree to which it supports and explains the main thrust of the politically dominant forces in its society" (252). She claims, furthermore, that the literary myths expressed in Socialist Realism and the societal practice reinforced each other cyclically, thereby assuring the durability of the system: "In the Soviet Union, the story in myth . . . informs the rituals of the culture in which it exists. There is a mutual interdependence between myth and ritual, and it operates dialectically" (253).

Clark's argument echoes Iser's notion of "masked" social fictions, especially his assertion that "the concealment of fictionality endows an explanation with an appearance of reality, which is vital, because fiction—as explanation—functions as the constitutive basis of this reality" (3). Socialist Realism—and the subsequent fiction that unironically retained elements of its system of patterns, codes, and/or myths—adopts a nominally objective and mimetic perspective on Soviet reality, as well as an oracular quality, given the inevitable future dictated by Marxist-Leninist dialectics. Yet such a perspective can only be achieved through dissimulation, thereby ironically creating an *inherently* fictive reality. It is this fictiveness that the four satirists treated in this section wish to expose, as doing so also undermines the validity of official Soviet reality. This course of action entails unraveling the rhetoric of the cultural context from which these novels arose, specifically the fallacies in the traditional ours / not ours division on which that rhetoric is based. In this way, their novels serve not only to satirize the Soviet Union, but the intrinsic pitfalls of binary thinking in general.

Written between 1974 and 1976, Zinoviev's dense and fragmented satire *The Yawning Heights* was among the first cold war satires that explicitly attacked the language and logic of the Soviet Union. Zinoviev does not limit himself to parodying Soviet literary genres; rather, the wide-ranging satirical scope of the book creates the parallel society of "Ibansk,"[24] a parody of the Brezhnev-era Soviet Union in toto. The mixture of vernacular and official language spoken by (and frequently commented upon, dissected, or otherwise metafictionally addressed by) Zinoviev's huge cast of simultaneously allegorized and particularized characters[25] allows Zinoviev to satirize the Soviet system from a linguistic perspective. As Wolf Moskovich writes, "The real Russian language of Zinoviev's understanding is that of Russian people (ordinary ones and intellectuals) as opposed to the wooden official Russian language. A liberal use of the resources of Russian argot, without official limitations, is a sign of protest against the official Soviet order of things. Used in such an unrestricted way, Russian becomes an anti-language showing protest against official Soviet norms" (91). Official Soviet language for Zinoviev is not only "wooden," as Moskovich asserts, but also rife with logical inconsistencies and has become semiotically diminished by its constant attempts to mask reality (as the pun in the title makes clear). As Edward J. Brown notes, Ibansk is governed by an "official ideology that numbs the mind . . . [with] perverted logic" and Zinoviev's status as a professional logician "magnificently equip[s him] to expose such perversion by linguistic mimicry." The novel thus satirically tears down "the intellectual edifice built in Ibansk to domicile and legitimize the complex family of lies that govern Ibanskian life" (314).

The sarcastic "Author's Note" preceding the novel suggests that Zinoviev's goal is not simply oppositional protest but a more subversive invalidation of the illogic of Soviet society. The narrator introduces the novel as "fragments of a manuscript which were found accidentally—that is, without the leadership's knowledge—on a newly opened rubbish dump which was soon abandoned thereafter" (n.p. [9]).[26] He notes that the dump's opening was commemorated with "an historic speech in which [the Leader] said that the age-old dream of mankind would soon be realised, as on the horizon we could already see the yawning heights of soc-ism" (n.p. [9]). The narrator's explanation of "soc-ism" (referred to also simply as "the Ism") frames Zinoviev's subsequent narrative in terms of the inherent irrationality of the society it describes:

> Soc-ism is an imaginary social order which would come into being if individuals were to behave to one another within society in complete accordance with the social laws. It can in fact never be attained because of the falsity of the premises on which it is based. Like every extra-historical absurdity, soc-ism has its own erroneous theory and incorrect practice, but it is almost impossible to establish either in theory or in practice what the theory and practice of soc-ism actually are, and to distinguish between them. Ibansk is a populated area inhabited by no-one, and which has no existence in reality. And if by sheer chance it did exist it would be a pure figment of the imagination. At all events, if its existence were possible it is anywhere but here, in Ibansk. Although the events and ideas described in the manuscript are, all things considered, imaginary, they have a certain interest as evidence of the erroneous ideas of mankind and human society held by the remote ancestors of the people of Ibansk. (n.p. [9])

The fact that the narrator gives the dateline "Ibansk 1974" to this introductory section leaves little doubt as to Zinoviev's satirical intent, since the parodic analogues to soc-ism and the various residents of Ibansk are readily apparent to readers familiar with the Soviet Union of the early to mid-1970s.

Once the novel itself begins, Zinoviev continues to present immediately recognizable examples of Soviet language that completely frustrate readers' attempts to make sense out of them. In other words Zinoviev shows how the forms of official language lack content. In the novel's opening chapter, the people of Ibansk are described as exceptional in ways that echo the Soviet self-image conveyed first by Marxist-Leninist theory and then by decades of monological reinforcement by the Soviet leadership: "[The inhabitants of Ibansk] are taller, not by reason of any reactionary biological superiority . . . , but because of the progressive historic conditions in which they live and the correctness of the theory for which they have been the guinea pigs; and thanks too to the wisdom of the leadership that has guided them so brilliantly." This exceptionalism extends to their very lives, described as "epoch-making experiments" that Ibanskians carry out "even when they know nothing about them and take no part in them, and even when the experiments are not taking place at all." The whole text is circumscribed by the curiously self-negating statement that "this book is dedicated to the examination of one such experiment" (13). The description of both the name and methodology of the experiment reveal the satirical intention unmistakably, even as the language continues to use the "codes" (for example, acronyms and references to Marxist-Leninist theory) of official Soviet language:

> The experiment under consideration is called STACMLFTC, from the initial letters of the names of its principal participants. The name was composed by Colleague and was first used in the scientific literature by Thinker, who took this opportunity to publish a series of articles on another and more compelling theme. The articles were written on a high dialectical level, with the result that no-one read them, but everyone applauded them. . . . Two groups of people took part in the experiment; the experimenter group and the guinea-pig group. These groups were composed of one and the same people. . . . Thanks to the principles which have been set out there was an increase in the flow of useless information . . . and, like every well thought out and logically conducted experiment, it ended in nothing. (13–14)

The apophatic nature of Zinoviev's satirical parody essentially reproduces the strategy of Soviet rhetoric by ascribing sociological and historic significance to a narrative about an idealized society. The main difference is that Zinoviev's narrator openly acknowledges that his narrative is "imaginary," set in a place with "no existence in reality," and he recounts a potentially nonexistent experiment that "ended in nothing." The irony, of course, lies in the fact that Zinoviev's admittedly fictionalized text is more rhetorically valid than the supposedly truthful official Soviet version. As Zinoviev and his readers are well aware, the place he describes by parodic association unmistakably *does* exist, neither "by chance" nor "as a pure figment of the imagination" but because of the deliberate fictionalization of history by the Soviet power elites.[27] As a satirical parody, *The Yawning Heights* unmasks the social fiction behind Soviet logic as it unmasks its own status as a literary fiction.

Although it is problematic to assert that binary logic in particular is a primary target of Zinoviev's satire in *The Yawning Heights*—if anything, the novel's fragmentary complexity[28] deliberately routs any attempts to make comprehensive thematic pronouncements about it—the novel does contain numerous sections in which Zinoviev discusses the relationship between Ibanskian ideology and its opponents, both internal and external. The characters divide (as is the case with their real-life analogues) into such officially acceptable figures as Artist and others such as Dauber, who either proclaim themselves to be dissidents or are considered such for lack of alternative categories. They engage in extensive discussions about the nature of the

Ibanskian state and the social logic that informs it. This technique accentuates Zinoviev's metalinguistic commentary by offering him opportunities to engage in a complex parody of certain official Soviet rhetorical styles. The second section of the novel, for example, opens with a chapter heading that grandly promises a "Treatise on fate, freedom, truth, morality, and so on" but almost immediately undermines its own coherence and credibility through a series of logical contradictions and by acknowledging its lack of significance: "In this treatise which aims to be both exhaustively incomplete and rigorously unsystematic, it is my intention to set down everything which I do not know on good authority about the emergence of the guardhouse in the Ibansk School of Military Aviation (ISMA) and about its early period of development which was omitted from the official history because it had no consequences" (24).

Zinoviev's views on the disguised authoritarian nature of Soviet language are made clear in an exchange between Member, a devotee of the state, and Chatterer, a dissident: "Member said that language was given to man for the purpose of expressing his thoughts. Chatterer remarked that Member said this rather as if language were handed out by the government in the same way as they hand out work, accommodation, bread, and trousers" (104). Although Member's comment suggests freedom of expression, Chatterer's rejoinder, especially when viewed in the historical context of the food shortages of the mid-1970s *zastoi* period, suggests that the reality is that language has become simply another poorly made government-issue commodity.

Nearly 350 pages later, Zinoviev illustrates the innate folly of such language. In a chapter titled "A page of heroic history,"[29] Zinoviev satirizes the rigidity of Soviet society by refiguring the conformist policies of Socialist Realism under Stalin as a standardization of pants under "the Boss": "During the era of the Boss a pan-Ibanskian standard was laid down for trousers. There was to be one type of trouser for all ages and sizes, for all professions and all circumferences. They were wide at the waist, at the knees and below. The crotch hung down to the knees. They had well delineated flies and pockets down to the heels. They were ideologically consistent trousers. Ibanskians were unfailingly recognised by their trousers throughout the world. Even today on the streets of Ibansk one can still sometimes see examples of these living memorials to the glorious epoch of the Boss" (464). The origins of these ridiculous pants are explained by the narrator in terms that are distinctly binary in nature and directly parody Soviet rhetoric of the early 1930s: "The pan-Ibanskian trouser was developed in the context of the bitter struggle against deviationists and class enemies. Leftist deviationists wanted to make the trousers even wider waisted and bring the crotch down to the ankles. They were counting on realising the total Ism in the next six months and stuffing the starving workers with food. . . . The leftist deviationists were liquidated by the rightist deviationists. These wanted rather to widen the trousers at the knees and eliminate the flies. They had no faith in the creative potential of the masses and put all their hopes in the bourgeoisie. . . . The rightist deviationists were liquidated by the left" (465). In both instances the Boss steps in to correct the ideological positions of the "deviationists" (presumably those left after the internecine warfare mentioned by the narrator). His pronouncements are not only presented in dialect that marks them as the product of a provincial hick but also with farcically facile logic: "'T'leftists,' he said, ''av made wun ov them theer typickle errors. They've coot'emselves off from t'masses and gon' agate rushin' ahead o'theer selves.' . . . 'T'reight deviationists 'av made a typickle error. They've coot'emselves off from t'masses and gon' agate rushin' back'ards'" (465).[30] In short, the Boss's Ibansk is absurd not only because it tries to foster "ideological consisten[cy]" among its citizens by requiring everyone to don utterly impractical pants, but because the rationale for such a policy is formulated by and debated over by dimwits.

Zinoviev's satire does not end with the Boss's demise. He continues by extending his metaphor of the pants into "the Period of Perplexity," his analogue for the Thaw: "When the Boss had died and the Ibanskians had got over their drunken rejoicing, rather narrow trousers began to appear. They were followed by really tight drainpipe trousers. A merciless battle was launched against the drainpipers. Their trousers were hacked to pieces in public, they were expelled from the universities, fired from their jobs, fined and denounced in the press. But on the other hand they were no longer shot. . . . It wasn't the narrowness of the trousers themselves which caused such terror. Indeed, the fashion was advantageous, since it led to an immediate doubling in the country's textile output. But narrow trousers were a sign and symbol of a growing intolerance of authority, of self-assertion and cynicism" (465).[31] Zinoviev's satirical metaphor has a clear nonmetaphorical analogue in Soviet history. Soviet industry often made absurd adjustments to meet production quotas that were pegged either to gross weight or units produced. Marshall Goldman's *The Soviet Economy: Myth and Reality* (1968) cites instances when overly pragmatic responses to nail and shoe production quotas flooded Soviet markets with nothing but Lilliputian or gargantuan units, depending on whether those quotas were based on quantity or weight (92–95). Thus the "immediate doubling in the country's textile output" that is touted by the narrator as a positive side effect of the new style of trousers is an unambiguously ironic reference to Soviet reality for readers familiar with the sight of nothing but ludicrously sized commodities. However, the reaction against the trousers by the "drainpipers" extends this from a simple economic joke to a broader political and metaphorical satire of the philosophy behind this absurd production system.

Zinoviev thus reinscribes the revolt against political orthodoxy in literature by such prominent writers of the late 1950s and early 1960s as Aksyonov,

Solzhenitsyn, Yuri Bondarev, or Viktor Rozov as a change in sartorial style. Rather than belittling their intentions, this technique heightens the sense of incompatibility between rigid ideology and aesthetic fashion. As Clark notes, style and content were both potential sites of dissent in Soviet literature. Zinoviev's argument does not reduce the dissident works of the Thaw to simply stylistic revolts, either. The fact that the ideological rebels' narrow pants actually serve the purpose of pants more effectively than the state's grotesque garments speaks to their superior "content" as well. Style essentially becomes content. Not only does Zinoviev imply that the state has bad taste in such matters—the official pants, like Socialist Realism, are aesthetic disasters and are wholly impractical for any purpose other than marking ideological uniformity—but he also insists that their attempts to control self-expression will ultimately be unsuccessful anyway, since creative minds will always be a step ahead of dull minds who attempt to legislate style: "In the end, however, narrow trousers, like cybernetics, were purged of all ideological deviationism and recognised officially as corresponding with all the ideas of the Ism. By which time, they had already passed out of fashion" (465). As with attempts to reassert control over literature after the Thaw, Zinoviev argues that co-opting the outward forms of dissidence in the service of the state is bound to be unsuccessful since genuine dissent will find new means of expression.

A point perhaps lost on the majority of Western readers is that Communism is not in and of itself the target of Zinoviev's satire. Rather it is the unquestioned status of ideology of any form that draws his ire, whether in the form of fictional satire or nonfictional invective, and Soviet Communism is, for obvious reasons, his most familiar example. Indeed, since his 1978 emigration Zinoviev has stated that "Western ideology, like Soviet ideology, is destroying the bulwarks of civilization built up over the centuries which were designed to, and did in fact, constrain the spontaneous forces of people's social environment." He has singled out "the propagation of sexual depravity, the propagation of matrimonial infidelity, coercion, gangsterism, [and] parisitism" (quoted in Kirkwood 56) as mores inherent in contemporary Western culture that have resulted from unexamined adherence to ideology (that is, belief in the innate superiority of Western culture). While Zinoviev's pronouncements in this regard are admittedly somewhat overgeneralized and occasionally even shrill, they remain logically consistent with his satirical treatment of the simplistic philosophy of Ibansk. Soviet Communism is abhorrent to him in large measure because it seeks to obscure its patently absurd reasoning beneath an intentionally hollow rhetorical façade, a figurative metaphor that Zinoviev literalizes in his next novel, *The Radiant Future*.[32]

Iskander's *Rabbits and Boa Constrictors* similarly exposes fraudulent utterances but widens its satirical scope by directing its opprobrium toward the *producers* of such social fictions as well as to their willfully ignorant *receivers*. As Clowes persuasively argues, the book "alludes to the tradition of the revolutionary fable, while more broadly addressing habits of reading and thinking that have been fostered in the Soviet era." Despite a number of intentionally superficial correspondences, Clowes asserts that the overall structure of the book and the narrative tone serve to undermine the "Aesopian approach to interpretation assumed by Iskander's implied reader [that] seeks out simple, one-to-one correspondences between the characters . . . and real people and conditions in Soviet society and politics. . . . [*Rabbits and Boa Constrictors*] tackles readerly habits such as simplistic allegorical thinking and an unexamined didactic response, that is, an expectation that the text will furnish a simple and concrete moral. The kind of mentality that Iskander's story supports in its implied reader is specifically meta-utopian. It encourages an ability to weigh several kinds of ideology, among them that of the realized utopia, to see ideological structures individually and together in their relationship to sources of political power" (184). Iskander's technique in the novel involves suggesting analogous symbolic associations and then invalidating them, either by casting doubt on his narrator's veracity, by including contradictory associations within the same character, or by parceling out associations with one historical figure among several characters. Thus he exposes and undermines glaringly simplistic interpretive rubrics and challenges the readers to exercise their mental capacity more vigorously.

The rabbits who follow the advice of Ponderer and his young protégé Yearner attempt to transgress the system established—apparently in concert with the Great Python, leader of the rabbits' sworn enemies, the boas—by the king of the rabbits. They ultimately (and perhaps inevitably) fail to subvert it because their vision is limited to improving their lot *within* the established system instead of fundamentally altering it. In doing so they submit to the rules of the status quo without recognizing that these rules are heavily skewed toward self-perpetuation rather than progress. Iskander's metaparody involves his readers by making them complicit in this process, since acceptance of the text's simple allegorical interpretation duplicates acceptance of the deceptively simple social fictions that the leaders of both the rabbits and the boas use to maintain their power. The novel thus points out how unscrupulous rulers exploit their subjects' credulity, thereby accomplishing Iskander's stated goal of "trying to analyse the way that power works in general, and the way that those subject to it—whatever nation they belong to—connive in their powerlessness" (quoted in Laird 20).

The interactions within and between the societies of the rabbits and the boas (they are technically not yet boa *constrictors* at the start of the novel, since the plot ostensibly explains how boas developed the technique of strangling their prey) provide Iskander with numerous opportunities to demonstrate how the ours / not ours division produces absurdities. For example, in the opening chapter of the book, a boa named Squinter recalls an incident in which he swallowed a rabbit who, unlike all the other rabbits that boas had ever swallowed, refused to be digested. The rabbit stood up inside Squinter's stomach and hurled insults at Squinter and his whole species, a fact that got Squinter into trouble when the Great Python arrived on the scene. From his first appearance, the Great Python's character suggests associations with Stalin. As a different species of snake, he is an outsider ruling over the boas, just as Stalin was a Georgian ruling a predominantly Russian country. Furthermore he is an inveterate self-aggrandizer, using language filled with the kind of nationalistic bombast that marked Stalin's reign. The narrator informs the reader that "when the Great Python appeared among the boa constrictors, he uttered the battle hymn, to which all the boas listened, their heads raised as a sign of loyalty":

> Descendants of the Dragon,
> Glory's heirs, victors,
> Disciples of the Python,
> Young Boa Constrictors,
> Bear the sweet burden of rabbit ingested,
> This the future hath requested. (11)[33]

In six short lines, this battle hymn parodies several of the most prominent tropes of Stalinist propaganda (linkage to a glorious distant past and a more glorious near future, the cult of youth, militarism, and fealty to a single leader) as well as making the destruction of the rabbits a necessary duty for collective advancement of the species.

After the pomp and circumstance die down, the rabbit inside Squinter directs his ridicule toward the Great Python, which causes the Great Python to accuse Squinter of being a traitor because of his supposed ideological complicity with the rabbit inside him:

> "Your stomach has become a rabbit's soapbox," he said ominously, "but you'll pay for this, you miserable invalid."
> "Oh, my Lord," poor Squinter pleaded.
> "I'm not your Lord or your Tsar," the Great Python replied severely. "Any boa who harbors a talking rabbit is not the kind of boa we need."
> (19)

Squinter is dragged off to be trampled by elephants, a punishment that (like being sent to the Soviet labor camps) is not explicitly intended to kill him but to squash the rabbit inside him. Squinter appeals to the guards who are leading him away, saying, "Brothers, . . . have mercy, you know that the elephants will trample me along with the rabbit." They refuse him mercy, though, gruffly replying that he has "no brothers but the rabbits" (20). Every aspect of Squinter's treatment parodies the ways in which Article 58 was used in the 1930s to ostracize or even eliminate anyone suspected of dissent against the state.

Following Squinter's removal, the Great Python tells the assembled boas a riddle/joke that puts the relationship between boas and rabbits into the kind of materialist, quasi-scientific terms that marked Stalinist rhetoric as well. He asks, "When can a rabbit become a boa?"[34] It is a question that, like its allegorical analogue ("When can the enemy of a communist become a communist?"), has no possible answer in a binary logical framework. Many of the boas refuse to answer, suspecting that "the Tsar was trying to ferret out future traitors with the aid of this riddle," and instead demand the answer emphatically from their leader. The Great Python replies with logic that clearly prefers ideology over either biology or ontology: "A rabbit that has been swallowed by a boa can become a boa . . . [because] a rabbit processed and digested by a boa is thus transformed into the boa. That means boas are actually rabbits at their highest stage of development. In other words, we are former rabbits and they are future boa constrictors" (21). To lend further credence to this assertion, the Great Python states that it is "all according to science," a shibboleth that he invokes repeatedly in the novel to persuade the credulous boas, just as Stalin and other Soviet leaders pointed to the "science" of Marxist dialectics as support for their policies. The boas' society under the leadership of the Great Python is thus presented in the early sections of the novel as unmistakably Stalinist.

As Ryan-Hayes points out, Iskander almost immediately begins to undermine the seemingly tidy interpretation that his "allegory that is subject to instant decoding" (25) invites. He presents the reader with a society of rabbits that considers itself opposed to that of the boas, but, as Clowes points out, "both boas' and rabbits' states are recognizably Stalinist": "The rabbits think of their state as a kind of elective monarchy, with the king 'democratically' chosen. In fact, the tenor of political life is conditioned by the rather Byzantine court of the Rabbit King, which functions on a system of favors and rewards for service to the throne and increasingly caves into [sic] the paranoia of the king and his army of surveillance operatives and informers" (184). The parallel between the rabbit king and Stalin is made most clear through the king's constant invocation of the future happiness that will be the rabbits' lot upon the completion of experiments that will allow them to cultivate cauliflower. The language of his utopian promises parodies the general tenor of Soviet propaganda about the "radiant future" under Communism, but the somewhat sinister manner in which the "great dream of having cauliflower helped the King to keep his multitude of rabbits in fairly compliant submission" is decidedly more sinister and Stalinist in tone:

> If the rabbits had any aspirations or yearnings that the King found
> objectionable, and if he couldn't put a stop to those yearnings in the
> usual way, the King in the last resort relied on his favorite means, and
> that of course meant invoking the name of cauliflower.

"Yes, yes," he would say to his rabbits in such situations, when he thought their ideas were unacceptable, "your aspirations are justified, but they're inopportune, because precisely at this moment, when the efforts to grow cauliflower are so close to fulfillment. . . ."

If the rabbit who had the yearnings continued to be stubborn about them, he disappeared unexpectedly, and then the other rabbits came to the conclusion that he had been spirited away to the secret plantation. This was quite natural, since some of the best and smartest rabbits exhibited these tendencies, and these intelligent ones were of course needed most of all for the work on growing the cauliflower. (29)

Mirroring the ways in which Marxism-Leninism served as a corrective (or bludgeon, depending upon circumstances) to divergent "aspirations or yearnings" in Stalin's Soviet Union, the king appeals to the universal ideology that motivates the society in order to suppress any potential threats to his power.

The last sentence in the preceding quote illustrates how subtly Iskander begins to undercut his direct parody of historical allegory, because the members of the intelligentsia targeted by Stalin's purges were often publicly vilified as counterrevolutionary enemies of the state rather than simply being removed from society without any clear pretext (although simple "disappearings" became more common as the purges progressed). The gullible response of the rabbits demonstrates the totality of their belief in propaganda in much the same manner as the majority of the Soviet population accepted (or at least *appeared* to accept) the accusations leveled against those purged in the late 1930s. Because Iskander's narrative departs from direct historical correlation here (as elsewhere), the satirical critique is directed not only at the rabbit king for using propagandistic language to control his subjects as Stalin did, but also at the ordinary rabbits for acceding to this control so willingly. As Iskander introduces his various potential dissidents into the novel—Ponderer, Yearner, and the upstart boa named Hermit—he subjects them, as symbolic representatives of an educated class that *should* know better, to an even greater measure of criticism for being unwilling and/or unable to engage in genuinely dissenting practices.

When Ponderer discovers that the boas' supposed power of hypnosis over the rabbits—the means they have used to catch and devour their much quicker prey—is a sham and announces this fact to the entire rabbit citizenry in the Royal Meadow, a genuine change in the order of the rabbits' society seems possible. Ponderer announces that the boas' hypnosis is simply the result of the rabbits' self-instilled fear of the boas, a conditioned response reinforced by lifetimes of identical deadly interactions with the predatory snakes. However, when Ponderer overhears Squinter telling the story of the rabbit who actively and successfully resisted being swallowed, he learns what Hirshberg would identify as "counter-schematic information" and attempts to impart it to his initially jubilant fellow rabbits.[35] What Ponderer does not seem to realize is the extent to which the king is complicit in maintaining the myth of hypnosis. The narrator, though, with insight into the king's thoughts during the celebration that follows Ponderer's oration, explains the extent to which this fear is the result of the king's largely rhetorical manipulations:

> Yes, the King was right when he sensed the tremendous danger inherent in Ponderer's words. All of the King's activities were tied to the fact that, together with his aides among the courtiers, he personally decided how much fear and caution the rabbits should experience when facing a boa, depending on the season, the atmospheric conditions in the jungle and many other factors.
>
> And suddenly this cunning system for controlling the rabbits, which had been worked out over the course of years, was on the verge of collapse, because the rabbits, you see, didn't have to fear hypnosis.
>
> The King knew that by using hope (the cauliflower) and fear (the boa constrictors), he could direct the rabbits' lives in an orderly way. But you can't stay alive for long on cauliflower alone. (31–32)

The hope/fear combination that the king employs closely resembles the dichotomous cognitive schema that governed both U.S. and Soviet society for much of the cold war, in which the ruling classes sought to retain power through a balance of utopian domestic hopes and fear of the ideological enemy. The "tremendous danger" that the king senses is oriented toward neither his person nor his subjects but toward the perceptions that allow him to remain in power. The king goes so far as to collaborate with the boas in order to keep the system (and himself) in place, a detail reflecting how U.S. and Soviet power elites reaped mutual benefits by conducting the cold war as they did. Like McCarthy and Stalin, the king has directed "paranoiac fear of the enemy" (Clowes 185) at his own society, making the absurdity of the existing situation even more apparent. As in Sinclair Lewis's *It Can't Happen Here* (1935), this detail emphasizes that ideological differences, including ostensible oppositions, do not necessarily manifest themselves in social realities.

The king, however, has a strategy for dealing with Ponderer's introduction of counterschematic information and puts this into motion immediately. First he asks whether Ponderer would require the rabbits to give up the practice of "remov[ing] the excess produce" (33–34) from the gardens of the local humans, since from the humans' point of view that is an injustice as great as the swallowing of rabbits by boas is from the rabbits' perspective. Then, with the help of a rabbit named Sharpie, the king twists Ponderer's meaning in order to question his patriotism. In response to the king's leading line of rhetorical questioning, Sharpie asserts that "if Ponderer's right, then it turns out that all our ancestors who perished heroically in the jaws of boa constrictors were simply fools and cowards, it means they perished because of their stupidity!" (37). Ponderer parries the king's rhetorical thrusts at first—so successfully, in fact, that one rabbit "thumped his forehead with his paw, and fell dead" because "his poor mind couldn't face the thought" (40) that the hypnosis is a fabrication. The narrator, in fact, states that all the rabbits sensed that "there was something tempting in Ponderer's words, an inordinately alarming truth, but that the King's message contained the boring, but comforting truth" (40).[36] Their unwillingness to break free from this "boring, but comforting" fiction masquerading as truth ultimately allows the King to dupe them into reaffirming his control, and thus the predatory influence of the boas, over them. As Iskander says in his interview with Laird, "[The rabbits] have to bear a great part of the blame themselves. That's what the book's about. They've adapted to their situation and don't want to change" (quoted in Laird 20).

Despite his rhetorical victory over Ponderer, the king still feels himself threatened by the potential for insurrection that his rival represents and arranges for the rabidly loyal Sharpie to betray Ponderer to the boas. Sharpie is an ambitious functionary desiring little more than entrance into the elite society of courtiers known as those "Admitted to the Table," a group whose sycophantic behavior throughout the novel parodies the Soviet party cadres. The king orders Sharpie to go to the forest and read aloud a poem whose thinly disguised symbolism will disclose Ponderer's whereabouts to the boas, who are equally, if not more, interested in suppressing any knowledge about the nature of their hypnosis. Sharpie, as the king notes, "has a conscience" (57) and understands the consequences of his appointed task. He tries to change the wording of the poem to make its symbolic meaning less apparent, but ultimately sublimates his conscientious objections to his ambition and does the king's bidding. Rather than simply ordering Ponderer's death, an action that belies his benevolent reputation and contradicts the rabbits' law against capital punishment, the king sets up a situation that will not only allow him to remove his political adversary but also to enhance his own standing in the eyes of his constituency, for his plan is to expose Sharpie as the sole orchestrator of the treacherous betrayal of Ponderer to the enemy. This episode echoes Stalin's behavior in eliminating potential rivals such as Leningrad party leader Sergei Kirov in 1934[37] as well as the complicity of the intelligentsia, especially the literary intelligentsia, in carrying out the wishes of the leadership, since Sharpie only wishes only to disguise the text carrying Ponderer's betrayal rather than to condemn it genuinely.

The numerous instances of the king's paranoid behavior satirize the extent to which the distrust inherent in the ours / not ours division makes life logically absurd and practically unworkable. For example the king makes an elaborate sequence of adjustments to his royal guard that illustrates the illogic of power based on adversarial distrust. Initially he decides to "augment the royal guard, in order to free up some time and strength for those matters which were the goal of his striving for power" (60). Before long, though, this noble goal recedes because of his paranoid fear of losing power to an overly large and powerful guard. Accordingly the king "made the guard even larger, and he gave these new guards the secret assignment of protecting the King from the older guards" (60). The fact that this new guard would become an alternate and potentially unchecked power of its own because of its authority over the old guard leads the king to issue a secret order to the old guard to maintain surveillance of the new guard as well. This process continues, ultimately resulting in a situation that not only makes the king devote considerably more time to maintaining his power than before, but also results in a ridiculous state in which everyone is under surveillance by someone else:

> "I don't even exclude myself," the King said to the Chief of the Guards. "If you discover that I have joined a conspiracy against my own legitimate power, then punish me, as you do with the others."
> "Just try and get involved in such a conspiracy," the Chief of the Guards replied threateningly, and this calmed the King. (61)

The king's suspicion thus becomes a self-justifying sentiment that spins out of control, just as Stalin's unpredictably paranoid behavior helped instigate and maintain the purges and terrors of the late 1930s.

In keeping with Iskander's feeling that the rabbits are still partly culpable for their plight, the narrator claims that the rabbits' nature allows this system to thrive. In fact, he argues, their psychology readily allows them to concoct and to accept outrageous charges, especially against the most innocent rabbits: "By not giving any real details of enmity, he forces the rabbit checking up on him to ascribe to him, sooner or later, a certain baseness. And not just a little villainy. But why 'not just a little?' That's how the rabbits' psychology is structured. Ascribing to a rabbit who must be informed on, the concealment of an extra carrot from the royal storehouse? That would be silly! In order to justify somewhat the baseness of a report, the informing rabbit makes the imagined villainy sufficiently significant, and that helps him to preserve a feeling of his own dignity" (63). This mindset is so ingrained in the rabbits' psychology that the narrator argues "that it's simpler for the informer to demonstrate that an innocent rabbit has formed a conspiracy against the King than it is to show that an innocent rabbit is pilfering a royal carrot from the storehouse." The reason for this apparent contradiction lies in the reluctance to ask for evidence in the case of an accusation of conspiracy against the king. Such a question would be considered indiscreet, exposing the questioner to "an outburst of patriotic rage" that might implicate him or her by association with the conspiracy: "In the rabbits' kingdom, the most frightening thing of all was to be under fire because of patriotic rage. According to the rabbits' customs, patriotic rage had to be always and everywhere encouraged. Every rabbit in the kingdom, at the moment when he displays his patriotic rage, instantaneously occupies a rank higher than the rabbits against whom his patriotic rage is directed" (64).

The narrator's comment that the only "weapon against patriotic rage" was "to become superpatriotic and rage even more than one's opponent" (64)[38] underlines the facile nature of the rabbits' worldview and links Iskander's satire with *any* society in which patriotic discourse substitutes for reason. Despite the fact that the rabbits' society on the whole is clearly modeled on the Soviet Union, such an accusation can be directed at the United States and the Soviet Union, especially during the most intense periods of the cold war. The rabbits' willingness to believe fabricated charges works satirically in the context of the House Committee on Un-American Activities much as it does for the Stalinist show trials, even if the punishment was more severe in the latter. Exact verisimilitude with a particular historical analogue is not Iskander's goal; rather, he intends to demonstrate the flaws of *any* voluntarily oblivious society.

Returning to the society of the boas after the chapter in which Sharpie is tried and banished for his betrayal of Ponderer, Iskander once again confounds the reader looking for a perfect allegorical parallel between the rabbits and the Stalinist Soviet Union. First Iskander describes the luxurious underground palace in which the Great Python lives. In addition to the plentiful reserve of live rabbits stored there for the Great Python's nourishment (he no longer hunts), there was also a sculpture gallery commemorating some of the noteworthy animals swallowed by boas in history. The narrator's comments about this gallery echo the workings of the cult of personality that surrounded Stalin, and to a lesser degree Brezhnev:

> It must be said that certain of these outstanding swallowings, the sculpted commemorations of which were exhibited here, had been performed by other notable boas. But when the Great Python was named Tsar of the Boas, for some reason he quarreled with these notable boas, after which they disappeared, though the exhibits remained. And lest an outstanding feat in this area, which had educational significance, be lost, it became necessary to attribute them to the Great Python.
>
> More precisely, it wasn't even necessary to attribute these outstanding swallows to him. His closest aides and advisors ascribed these feats to him directly. (118)

The history of the boas is thus distorted because of its "educational significance," that is, its utility in maintaining the ideological and political status quo, a process that the boas are so conditioned to carry out willingly that their leader no longer even needs to prod them to do so.

Things begin to change somewhat, though, after a messenger from the king of the rabbits arrives with a message for the Great Python. Among other news, he informs the Great Python that the king is upset because the boa who responded to Sharpie's summons and swallowed Ponderer had "violated the inter-species agreement about the humane swallowing of a rabbit, had conducted mocking conversations with his prey, had applied torture in the form of caprice and uncertainty, and had finally refused to swallow the mortally tormented rabbit" (121). The Great Python is so enraged at this breach of protocol that he gathers all the boas and relates the "shameful behavior" of the boa who swallowed Ponderer. The boa, who will soon take on the name Hermit, tries to defend himself by using a version of the Great Python's materialist logic, claiming that he had "deprived the rabbits of their wisest member, [and thus] he had removed a leader and at the same time acquired that rabbit's wisdom" (123). The Great Python denies the validity of this defense, invoking inflexibly binary logic in claiming that "all wisdom has an intraspecific sense. . . . Wisdom for the rabbits is stupidity for [boas]" (123–124). No one among the gathered crowd seems to care or mind that this contradicts the Great Python's earlier pronouncements—the boas are as conditioned to accept the truths given them by their leaders as the rabbits are—and the boa is sentenced to be banished to the same desert to which the rabbits exiled Sharpie.

While in exile Hermit meets Sharpie, who engages in a verbose and intricate attempt to justify his betrayal of Ponderer. Hermit listens but fails to understand any of Sharpie's elaborate rationalizations, finally losing his temper and lambasting Sharpie: "'Oh, you're just talking nonsense!' the Hermit Boa interrupted him. 'Even before I swallowed the wisest rabbit, I could have told you what stupid things you were saying. Who could have stopped you if you'd never told anyone about your treachery? Still, you're a real bastard! You've woven all these words in order to hide their true substance'" (130). After exposing Sharpie's linguistic fabrication, Hermit expresses the desire to swallow Sharpie, who immediately points out that he believes Ponderer's revelation that the boas' hypnosis is a fraud. Denied his usual technique of hunting, Hermit becomes enraged and involuntarily feels his muscles contract, which leads him to state that he feels "that [his] hatred is giving birth to some rather fruitful thoughts" (130). He encircles Sharpie and suffocates him, thereby "discovering" the boas' new, more deadly means of killing their prey. Hermit returns to the boas' society and regains the favor of the Great Python because his new technique promises to put an end to the famine that has afflicted the boas ever since Ponderer's revelation diminished the myth of hypnosis. The Great Python is so impressed with Hermit that he names him his successor and puts him in charge of teaching the new method of killing to all the boas. Eventually the Great Python dies and Hermit announces that "his body would be eternally on display beside his hunting trophies, since the sculptor was going to make him a mummy" (169). Enshrining the Great Python's corpse in the museum parody the Soviets' use of Lenin's body as a source of posthumous propaganda, and it suggests that Hermit will continue the Great Python's policies of distorting history in the service of power.

The very transfer of power from the Great Python to Hermit is a constant reminder of the way power tends to perpetuate itself. Hermit succeeds largely by promising a different order but quickly falls into his predecessor's ruling habits. He announces that his ascension to the leadership is "in accordance with the Great Python's wish [that] a boa shall rule over the boas." He also makes the purely cosmetic linguistic gesture of announcing that "from now on, there will be no more palaces. . . . The Great Python's palace will now be known as the Hermit's Cell" (169). Like his predecessor he acquires the honorific sobriquet "Great" before his name when a toadying boa asks him, "Is it possible to address you as the Great Hermit, in honor of all your deeds?" He "modestly and accurately" answers that it is not necessary but also not unwelcome. The Great Hermit begins acting even more like Stalin than either the Great Python or the king of the rabbits, even giving a speech, "Smothering Is Not an End in Itself," whose content is, as Ryan-Hayes points out, deliberately reminiscent of Stalin's 1930 address, "Dizzy with Success" (Ryan-Hayes 31). Iskander again associates the Great Hermit with Stalin when the narrator describes the way in which the trophies in the museum have been recontextualized to fit Hermit's wishes: "Instead of the former pieces, the collection had been enlarged, starting with the display of a stuffed rabbit who was the first to be dealt with in the new way. And a number of old trophies had been restored according to the Great Hermit's recollections. The Great Hermit's personal trophies concluded with the mummy of the Great Python with his eyes open, which created an awesome ambiguity and hinted rather frighteningly that the Python had been the Great Hermit's most brilliant kill. And what's more, there had been dark rumors among the boas that not long before the Great Python's death, he had either been deprived of the right to have a say, or deprived of the gift of speech" (*Rabbits* 170).[39] Those "dark rumors" correspond with ones regarding Stalin's conduct while Lenin was on his deathbed in 1923 and early 1924. Likewise the Great Hermit's alteration of the trophies to fit his "recollections" fits with Stalinism's succession of Leninism as the guiding principle of the Soviet Union (not to mention Stalin's practice of having purged party members airbrushed out of historical photographs). Ultimately the Great Hermit's main distinction from the Great Python is his substantially heightened affinity for and efficiency at killing, as symbolized by his ostentatious and sinister display of the Great Python's mummy.

Having endowed three ostensibly distinct regimes with unambiguously Stalinist characteristics, Iskander makes the satirical point that *any* society that voluntarily acquiesces to despotic rule in the ways that the boas and the rabbits do, whether or not they acknowledge their acquiescence, is bound to descend into absurdity and be subject to abuse by its own leaders. Iskander's satirical technique of laying bare the methods various leaders used to create and maintain the social fictions that help them extend their rule is familiar.

His metafictional technique of frustrating (or even penalizing) his readers' attempts at easy interpretation of the narrative is more innovative, though, and drives home the point that the target of the satire is not the Soviet people but any logically unsophisticated recipients of information, especially ones like the Soviet intelligentsia, who (in Iskander's view) should have known better than to be conned by the social fictions of the Soviets. The ominous fate of both the boas and the rabbits in light of Hermit's new method of killing and his assumption of power bolsters Iskander's contention that any action that does not genuinely resist despotic power ultimately serves, perpetuates, and even exacerbates it. As he has no specific historical target in mind for his satire, he also does not advocate a prescriptive solution to his readers beyond thinking more analytically than the menagerie of animals that populates his mock fable.

"Backwards fly, my locomotive!": *Two Moralistic Subversions of Cold War Logic*

While many influential satires from the cold war subvert simplistic logic without substituting a specific moral philosophy of their own, there are also instances in both U.S. and Russian literature of more didactic satire that can still be classed as subversive. Yuz Aleshkovsky's novel *Ruka: Povestvovanie palacha* (1980; *The Hand, or, The Confession of an Executioner*), for example, uses satire to comprehensively reject the fictionalizing impulse behind Soviet language; it also offers a specific moral vision for the future to replace the system it casts off. Like so many of his peers, Aleshkovsky's anger at the Soviet system comes in large part from having been personally abused by it. He spent the years from 1950 to 1953 in prison for violating military discipline and suffered professional reprisals for most of his career as a writer for refusing to conform to official demands. Outside of a few collections of children's stories, Aleshkovsky's publication history in the Soviet Union was confined to *samizdat*. After contributing three songs about life in the Siberian camps to the illegally produced literary almanac *Metropol'* (1979), Aleshkovsky emigrated from the Soviet Union, first to Vienna and then to Connecticut. Within three years of arriving in the West, he published five fictional works, including *The Hand*.

The novel consists almost entirely of a monologue delivered by a KGB colonel known as "the Hand." He gains this nickname by virtue of his oversized hand, which he uses to punish those he interrogates (and once used to kill a mad dog attacking Stalin, thereby gaining his seemingly undying favor). His name is given within the novel as Vasily Vasilievich Bashov, but in telling his tale he relates that both his name and his biography were altered during his youth in order to make him more appealing to Stalin as a potential member of the Cheka (114). His father's name is Ivan Abramych—which would make his patronymic Ivanovich, not Vasilievich—and his "real" first name is never revealed.[40] His adopted name is made even more important by the fact that Gurov, the prisoner he is interrogating throughout the novel (by telling him, rather than asking for, the details of his crimes), is also named Vasily Vasilievich. Like Bashov, Gurov's name is subject to frequent change in the novel, making this correlation both coincidental and artificial. Gurov was born as Conceptiev[41] and takes the surname Brutnikov only after denouncing his father and being adopted by a Communist Party loyalist tellingly named Collectiva L'vovna Brutnikova. He changes this to Gurov after murdering Brutnikova[42] and marrying her daughter, Electra (whose last name is presumably Gurova).[43] Thus neither man's name is a stable signifier of his identity, making the resemblance between their names and patronymics semantically meaningful—inasmuch as it hints at their mutual participation in the Soviet system—only in a fictional context. Finally the mutable naming of Bashov and Gurov recalls the new names that Stalin (Dzhugashvili), Lenin (Ulianov), and Trotsky (Bronshtein) took for themselves after beginning their involvement with Communism. The indeterminacy and artificiality of names in the novel is just part of Aleshkovsky's critique of Communism's adverse effects on language.

Bashov explicitly points out early in his monologue that he fervently opposes Communism despite his rank in the KGB. Only four pages into his astonishingly profane harangue, Bashov explains his striking choice of language to Gurov: "I gather you're wondering why I use thieves' jargon and obscenities so often. At one time I did have an assignment working with criminals. As for the obscenities, I use them because dirty words, Russian mother-oaths, are my personal salvation in the fetid prison cell that is now the home of our mighty, free, great, etcetera, etcetera language. Poor sucker, it gets chased under the bunks by every thug in the cell: propagandists from the Central Committee, stinking newsmen, scabby literati, pulp writers, censors, even our proud technocrats. They chase it into editorials, resolutions, interrogation reports, the lifeless speeches at meetings, congresses, rallies, and conferences, where it has gradually lost its dignity and health—it's a goner! They're beating it to death!" (7). As M. Keith Booker and Dubravka Juraga note in *Bakhtin, Stalin, and Modern Russian Fiction* (1995), Bashov's "speaking style results precisely from an attempt to inject new life into a language that Stalinism has left deadened and impoverished." Furthermore they argue that Aleshkovsky is using Bashov's extreme departure from officially sanctioned Russian to satirize the inherently mendacious character of Soviet language: "It has been used to tell so many lies that it no longer has any real meaning. Far from containing the mystical force of meaning described by Gogol [in *Dead Souls*] in relation to the Russian language, the 'dead word' of Stalinism has no connection to reality at all: it represents nothing but the fictional constructions of official power" (109). Like Aleshkovsky himself, Bashov chooses to set himself apart from the Soviet system by the words he uses, claiming that all the various manifestations of Soviet language are corrupt and meaningless.

Bashov demonstrates that this corruption is the result of the Soviets' attempts to hide their colossal failures. He reconciles the potential paradox of serving the regime he loathes by pointing out that he reviles its deceitfulness (that is, its unacknowledged fictionality) and associates its propaganda with all manner of infernal refuse:

> We pups, we punks, before all the other kids our age and before a
> lot of the old farts, had guessed right: underneath the sheep's clothing,
> underneath the flittering of philanthropic Party slogans, underneath the
> sweet promises, underneath the invitation to the housewarming at the
> World Commune was the wolf-toothed grin of diabolical forces.
>
> With our puppy-dog eyes, not yet clogged by the rainbow puke of
> Soviet illusions, we saw how our well-to-do country had become hungry
> and ill clad. Under the banner of building a new life, chaos had pene-
> trated trade, daily living, the economy, justice, culture, and art. . . .
>
> Despite the demonic orgy of agitation and propaganda that en-
> meshed soul and reason, we punks sensed what was hidden behind
> the slogans and fine words: a deathly abyss or a latrine barrel full of
> shit. The words hid us from a monstrous tyranny, bloody carnage, the
> collapse of the five-year plans, the bankruptcy of the routine propa-
> ganda campaigns, the abuse of power, all-out thievery, moral degener-
> acy, the mockery of faith.
>
> The Forces, in their high-handed attack on what was human, used
> the Word, they used Language, and at the same time tried to destroy its
> essence. (100–101)

This recognition allows Bashov to formulate his revenge against the group of Communists who murdered his father and destroyed his village during the collectivization of 1929. He tells Gurov that he decided to emulate the Count of Monte Cristo, whose story he had read while at an orphanage, and subvert the power structure from within:

> I came to hate utopians, Marxes, Engelses, Lenins, revolutionaries,
> socialists, Dantons, Robespierres, Chernyshevskys, and other demons. I
> came to hate the promises of alleged friends of the people, who assured
> the nervous and skeptical that it was possible to create a new order on
> earth. I wasn't thinking philosophically, of course, or even politically.
> This was all stewing and baking in my heart. But even then, my feeble
> little mind could not help correlating the glaring reality of the Soviet
> hell, or the hell of the French Revolution, with its ideological and
> moral sources. . . .
>
> And after my horrors, which occurred almost nightly, I would imag-
> ine that my nook in the hole was the count's island cave. I was the

count, trying on the coat of my Chekist uniform before setting off
with a rapid-firing cannon and a detachment of trusty friends on a
vengeful crusade against Stalin, Fourier, Kamenev, Saint-Simon, Trotsky, Voroshilov, Zinoviev, Karl Marx, Pyotr Verkhovensky, Yagoda, Campanella, Bukharin and the rest of the gang. . . . I daydreamed; in my
dreams I wrought retribution; and I did so, purely for reasons of camouflage, in the Chekist uniform that I hated. (103–4)

Bashov learns the linguistic tricks of the trade so well as a Chekist that he
gradually avenges his father's death by employing the very fictionalizing that
he deplores. He ensnares Gurov's father, for example, a close confidant of
Stalin and thus a difficult target to bring down,[44] by composing and then
filming two elaborate scenarios in which Conceptiev and several of his colleagues act out a pair of wholly fictionalized plots to kill first Lenin and later
Stalin.[45] Bashov ironically presents these fabrications to Conceptiev as a possible means of refuting charges that his son has made against him in a denunciation. Every step of Bashov's elaborate plan to hoist Conceptiev upon his
own petard involves intentional confusion of the fictive and nonfictive.

To spring his trap on Conceptiev and his cohort, Bashov sets loose the
Cheka's vast disinformation network. Earlier in the novel he ironically refers
to these individuals as the "'poets' of their profession" at work in various
"Palaces of Literature" (that is, prisons) with the "same goal: to create, with
the aid of one or more unhappy prisoners, a literary work of a piofuckineer-
ing new genre: the Case" (28–29). They first begin turning out falsified newspapers that Bashov shows the detainees in order to convince them that their
reputations are being sullied: "Our printing house immediately began turning out Moscow newspapers with personal data on the arrestees and all sorts
of fantastic blooey about their double-dealing: their links with foreign intelligence, the Trotskyite opposition, and domestic reactionaries. We had a
couple of novelists and a certain now-deceased mammoth of journalism, the
vile David Zaslavsky, who all did a glorious job on it. They found a gruesome
satisfaction in the work, and I also convinced them that their discovery of
new literary and journalistic genres would certainly be followed by medals,
honor, and national fame" (165). Once Bashov has convinced Conceptiev
and the others that their situation is grim, he steps in to offer them an apparent escape that in fact irrevocably seals their doom: "There is, however, a
remedy. . . . The charges brought against you are provocative and ridiculous.
The more ridiculous the charges, the more absurd they are, the more im-
probable your confession will necessarily seem to Stalin. He will have to
doubt the reality of the case, the circumstances of it, and the moral probity
of the informers and false witnesses. The remedy is dialectics. Your salvation
is to confess to something that could not, objectively, have happened. Think
about it. We'll continue our conversation tomorrow. We must demolish the

two main charges dialectically. The rest will wither away of themselves" (167). Invoking the supposedly inviolable logic of Soviet dialectics even as he presents a wholly fictionalized and admittedly absurd scenario involving Lenin's death, Bashov persuades Conceptiev to cooperate in the filming of the ridiculously "fabricated phantasmagorias" (168).

Simply "shooting the episodes of the 'investigation'" (170) does not suffice for Bashov, though, since he wants to make sure his fictions have the desired effect. Ironically invoking Lenin's politico-aesthetic pronouncement about the importance of film as a tool for Soviet propaganda—"I was the director, and at that moment, for me, the cinema was truly 'the most important of the arts'"—Bashov brings in a variety of film professionals to polish the product: "In the end, the materials were edited by a leading documentary filmmaker. We dubbed the testimony, which I personally had written on a sleepless night. Dunaevsky composed a marvellously expressive score, which the sound technicians synchronized with Lenin's hoarse breathing, the groans of his flesh being tortured by Communist labor" (171). In sum Bashov employs nearly every means at his disposal of fictionalizing the "case" against Conceptiev, eventually creating a document so compellingly perfidious (albeit utterly nonsensical) that Stalin, of course, orders Bashov to execute the whole supposedly treacherous lot immediately.

The irony of this judgment is compounded by yet another fraudulent document that Gurov mentions in denouncing his father. Gurov repudiates Conceptiev—in the process unwittingly initiating Bashov's revenge on both of them—in part because Conceptiev fabricated a note purportedly from Stalin as part of his strategy to coerce Bashov's father's village into collectivizing. Gurov informs on Conceptiev not out of loyalty to Stalin or to the principles of the revolution but to further his own literal and figurative fortunes within the party. On the other hand, Conceptiev's "crime" of impersonating Stalin was actually part of an attempt to ruthlessly enact Stalin's will, and this act is exposed not by those who were victimized by it but by one who originally abetted it and gained from it. The supposed exoneration for that crime, cunningly set up by Bashov through his elaborately staged fictions, ultimately becomes a "real" crime that gets Conceptiev executed. The entire fabric of the intertwined stories of Bashov and Gurov's lives is woven from a long string of forgeries and dirty tricks.

Bashov exposes the entire system of justice as nothing more than the "most elaborate works of Socialist Realism" and completely fictionalized, like a stage play: "The trials, whether open or closed, were perceived by our leaders, and by spectators temporarily remaining at large, as mighty pageants where any deficiency in Shakespearean passion or depth of artistic thought was compensated for by the real-world setting of the opener, the real denials of guilt, the real pressure from the prosecutor, the forced confessions, and the details of the epic crime as reconstructed in the soul-freezing dialogues between the judges and defendants. Then the culmination and finale" (29). Aleshkovsky's satire repeatedly demonstrates that the moral corruption he sees as an inescapable aspect of the Soviet Union results from fictions having been misrepresented as reality. This process is so advanced that "our leaders" up to and including Stalin himself can no longer discriminate between reality and a patently absurd imitation, despite having presided over the creation of a state dependent on unacknowledged fabrication.

Even though much of the recollected action of the novel takes place in the 1920s and 1930s, the narrative present in the days leading up to the sixtieth anniversary of the Bolshevik Revolution,[46] placing it in autumn of 1977, squarely in the middle of the *zastoi* and thus the cold war. Aleshkovsky uses Bashov's recollections, not just from the Stalinist era but throughout Soviet history, to uncover the roots of the wholly empty promise that Communism has become by the time of Brezhnev. Bashov recalls a lengthy anecdote, for example, about Khrushchev nearly allowing a single deputy of the Supreme Soviet to vote in opposition to an issue[47] rather than having a unanimous vote on the question. Bashov claims that this gesture was intended to demonstrate to Western Communist parties specifically how Stalinism had been replaced by enlightened government. All of the party cadres begin suffering horrible health problems as a result of the stress that this "historic step" causes them. As Bashov tells it, Khrushchev reneges on the deal after the delegate, a certain Fyodor Boronkov, declares his *actual* ideological opposition to every facet of Soviet policy in a private conversation with Khrushchev. Khrushchev's angry abandonment of the plan, complete with thoroughly formulaic condemnatory sobriquets, shows the shallowness of the Thaw's much-lauded open-mindedness: "No, Fyodor . . . Kulak, White Guard modernist kike-face, you will not go vote. You will abstain. We will simply inform the comrades privately, 'He abstained.' One can't be opposed right off. Liberalization is an endlessly lengthy process, like the path to absolute truth. There's no hurry. Stay put. Here's the key to the bar. Drink anything you want, listen to some music. . . . Then you'll go home. We'll defend our fundamentals. For the life of me, I just can't understand it: how did you agree, organically, to be opposed? Shut up, son of a bitch, and say thank you that we aren't liquidating you like we did Beria!" (93–94). Instead of making even a token gesture toward openness, Khrushchev offers Boronkov stupefaction (liquor), empty propagandistic clichés ("Liberalization is an endlessly lengthy process"), and threats of reprisal, which is essentially the bargain that Bashov, and by extension Aleshkovsky, claim that the Communists concluded with the Soviet Union's populace.

In addition to repeatedly identifying Communism as a Satanic invention, Bashov explicitly links nuclear war (and Soviet rhetoric of ideological conflict) with the fact that "Soviet Fascism is metastasizing successfully" under the devil's guiding hand: "Civilization, which Satan has been nurturing for several dozen centuries now . . . has at last begun to bear fruit for him. Darkened skies. Rivers puking shit and Moloch's undigested grub into the seas and oceans. An all-out undeclared war being waged on man by things, which occupy the Time and Space of his existence. Hundreds of millions of souls already taken captive. . . . And Satan keeps perfecting weapons of mass destruction to use on souls. 'Just wait, you fuckheads,' he must be thinking, this Supreme Con of all times and peoples, 'I'll exterminate your souls, every last one of them. And I'll be goddamned if I expect any trouble with your bodies. I've got everything ready for the "last decisive battle"—the annihilation of life on earth'" (52–53).[48] Subverting Soviet ideology thus means subverting the devil's work, an especially virtuous task in light of Aleshkovsky's own Orthodox Christian values, embodied in the character of Frol Vlasych Gusev, "the protector of people and animals" (150).

Gusev, alternately portrayed as a saintly fool and a dissident savant, represents Russian values wholly outside (and thus antagonistic to) the Soviet notions of social history, and his influence over Bashov eventually leads to the latter's radical abandonment of the system (via a staged suicide) in favor of a morality rooted in a religious worldview. Bashov uses religious terminology in connecting power over language and power over people when he asserts, "The soul of a word, like that of a man, is easy to kill" (102). This principle permeates the novel, with all forms of corruption resulting from attempts to construct an artificial philosophy of "reason" to supercede or even to destroy the innate "soul" of Russian language and society. Gusev represents Aleshkovsky's suggestion of how this damage might be undone. Even Gusev's rather archaic-sounding name hearkens back to a distant Russian past the Soviets intentionally effaced. The first name Frol is not only uncommon for the time but also suggests a connection with the seventeenth-century stories about the Russian *picaro* Frol Skobeev. These tales were among the first secular literary writings produced in Russia and as such occupy a prominent place in the nation's cultural history. The patronymic Vlasych is derived from the name Vlas, which is itself taken from an archaic Russian word meaning "slow" (in modern Russian, the most common word for "slow" is *medlennyi*). Finally the surname Gusev, derived from the noun *gus* (goose),[49] is appropriate to his self-designation as "protector of . . . animals," but it also serves metaphorically as an animate and pastoral counterpoint to the inanimate and industrial name Stalin (derived from *stal'*, or "steel").

Gusev and Bashov originally come into contact partly because of Gusev's name. His wife denounces him for his anti-Soviet attitude, citing as evidence the fact that he "refused to exchange his religious name and patronymic for the progressive Vladlenst Marxenglich" (149). Bashov is assigned to investigate the case and naturally rejects this denunciation as mindless ideology, allowing Gusev to write his self-exonerating testimony while "ensconced . . . comfortably at [Bashov's] desk, smoking occasionally and sipping strong tea"

(150). In his rambling statement, Gusev unambiguously rejects the Soviet doctrine of social and historical progress, a fact most clearly demonstrated by his supposed conversations with "Outraged Reason" (199), the Soviet Zeitgeist personified. Reason alternately abhors, abuses, pines for, and weeps over his mate, Soul, who has abandoned him because of his preference for Communist ideology.

As Gusev recalls his alleged actions of February 28, 1935,[50] he literalizes a common metaphorical association taken from early Soviet propaganda. Gusev claims that he commandeered the locomotive of Soviet historical progress and turned it around so that it actually ran backward. His immediate reaction to this is a parody of the language of prerevolutionary writers like Mayakovsky or Valentin Kataev:[51] "I was having a modest snack, as it were, with my first gulp of space: quivering at the delicious, unearthly sensation of history moving backward, I stuck my head out the window so that the wind would spark tears in my eyes and not let them fall from my cheeks, so that it would carry away from my lips, to the rumbling accompaniment of the wheels, the words of an absurd little ditty: Backwards fly, my locomotive! Make stops! Halt at each for hours please. I'll cherries buy in paper sacks, made from *Pravda* and *Izvestia*. And at the kiosk I shall drink a soda pop, a soda pop . . . I love, I so-o-o-o love any stop. Except the commune. Heigh-ho, fireman, come poke up the coal in the furnace" (199). The "fireman" who turns up in response to this call is none other than Outraged Reason himself, and the remainder of this testimony consists of a conversation between Gusev and Outraged Reason in which they weigh the benefits and costs of Communism.

Using the rhetoric of Soviet propaganda, Outraged Reason initially claims that the Faustian bargain (in his case, the literal loss of his "Soul-mate") has been worth it because of current progress and future achievements: "Look at the view from our locomotive! You won't deny our achievements will you? Look! The foundation for new social relations has essentially been laid. Our own world we have built, a new world, and planes on duty in the sky continuously renew the motto that stretches from horizon to horizon but whose author has not yet had the honor to be born: 'Communism is history that has gone into eternal retirement.' Tremendous!" (200).[52] Gusev counters that Reason's willful abandonment of Soul was a foolish gamble based on false premises, and his reply sarcastically invokes an oft-repeated catch phrase of Soviet propaganda: "I refer to your participating in the game 'Communism is the radiant future of all mankind.' That is the extreme case when you consider it permissible to choose the tactic of limitless sacrifice, throwing colossal resources and millions of human pawns into the battle. The incorrectness of your gambit is excused (this you impress on both yourself and the pawns, to the applause of foreign fans who crave exciting spectacles), by the same old goal—a showy ending to the big game, the world-history experiment, the building of Communism" (212). Gusev's rejoinder essentially restates both

Maltby's and Hirshberg's points about the ways in which justifying the "old goal" overrides the fundamental "incorrectness" of a situation that consumes enormous quantities of resources, both human and financial. Even though Gusev's discussion ostensibly dates to the 1930s, its later influence on Bashov, after forty more years of the locomotive's progress, extends its applicability to the novel's (and novelist's) cold war present.

Gusev's philosophy influences Bashov so greatly that his lecture to Gurov cites Gusev as an authority. Gusev's legal deposition transforms into a religious testimony that finally causes Bashov to seek repentance for his lifelong pursuit of bloody vengeance. Gusev becomes for Bashov what the simple soldier Platon Karataev was for Pierre Bezukhov in Tolstoy's *War and Peace,* a kind of informal spiritual mentor whose direct connection with an earthy and honest (if also romanticized) sense of Russianness helps his misguided pupil see the error of his prior ways.

Bashov decides to forego his planned retribution against Gurov; he reverses himself entirely, in fact, asking Gurov to kill him instead. Aleshkovsky presents this conversion as a religious redemption akin to Raskolnikov's in *Crime and Punishment.* Bashov states that the chief motivation for his contrition is the desire to see his father again in the afterlife. In his final moments Bashov even identifies himself both with Christ and with Gusev's rejection of the soul-versus-reason model of Soviet-style Manichaeanism. As Gurov readies himself to shoot Bashov, the latter exclaims, "Receive me, Father. . . . Understand the darkness of the wanderings of my reason, and the fury of my ruinous passion. . . . Understand, Father, and receive my poor sinless soul. . . . It bears no blame for my deeds, for my falsehood, dissembling and executions. None!" (260). This speech evokes Christ's dying words from Luke 23:46 ("Father, into Thy hands I commit my spirit!") while it also reinforces Aleshkovsky's belief that resistance to the Soviet system—and the redemption that ultimately results from such resistance—is not properly achieved by adopting its methods but by returning to a life in which soul and reason are not sundered.

When considered in the broad context of Russian social history from 988 onward, Aleshkovsky's satire is normative, since it espouses a return to values similar to those that were predominant in Russia centuries before (and on numerous different occasions). However, within the context of Soviet society, his satire is clearly subversive. It thoroughly overthrows the value system on which that society is based, exposing its unacknowledged fictionality at every turn. As such it participates in the process of cultural homeostasis that Lotman and Uspensky identified as characteristic of pre-nineteenth-century Russia (and that others like Sinyavsky have carried forward into recent times) by attempting to make a contemporary version of traditional values into a "new" prescription for the ills of "old" Soviet society.

Not all American subversive satires eschew prescriptive moralism either. Walker Percy's *Love in the Ruins: The Adventures of a Bad Catholic at a Time*

Near the End of the World (1971), resembles several of the aforementioned Soviet satires in blending anti-utopian characteristics, scathing criticism of technocratic thought/language, and antibinary satire. Like Aleshkovsky, Percy produces a satire that explores the potential for religion to come to the aid of a perishing cold war society. The dire situation of the "old violent beloved U.S.A. and the Christ-forgetting Christ-haunted death-dealing Western world" (3) is clear from the book's outset (set on the afternoon of July 4, 1983), at which Percy's protagonist, a psychiatrist and inventor named Dr. Thomas More, states, "I have reason to believe that within the next two hours an unprecedented fallout of noxious particles will settle hereabouts and perhaps in other places as well. It is a catastrophe whose cause and effects—and prevention—are known only to me. The effects of the evil particles are psychic rather than physical. They do not burn the skin and rot the marrow; rather do they inflame and worsen the secret ills of the spirit and rive the very self from itself" (5).

More uses the now-familiar language of nuclear warfare in forecasting a "fallout," yet the novel's central metaphor of a spiritual disease is established when the symptoms of this fallout are described in terms that make radiation poisoning seems benign by comparison. As is the case in San Narciso and New Tammany, More's ironically named community of Paradise Estates is noteworthy for being a house divided against itself: "The scientists, who are mostly liberals and unbelievers, and the businessmen, who are mostly conservative and Christian, live side by side in Paradise Estates. Though the two make much of their differences—one speaking of 'outworn dogmas and creeds,' the other of 'atheism and immorality,' etcetera etcetera—to tell the truth, I do not notice a great deal of difference between the two. . . . There are minor differences. When conservative Christian housewives drive to town to pick up their maids in the Hollow, the latter ride on the back seat in the old style. Liberal housewives make their maids ride on the front seat" (15). Although More's comments suggest the differences between the conservatives and liberals are more rhetorical than ontological, his example of the "minor differences" also points out that he is missing or perhaps discounting more genuine social divisions of race and class, both of which contribute heavily to the upheaval that looms as the novel opens.

Outside this mirage of an "oasis of concord in a troubled land" exists a thoroughly divided society, strongly reminiscent of the schism between San Narciso's well-heeled insiders (such as Inverarity) and the motley outsiders of the Tristero:

> Yonder in the fastness of the swamp dwell the dropouts from and
> castoffs of and rebels against our society . . . Bantu guerillas, dropouts
> from Tulane and Vanderbilt, M.I.T. and Loyola; draft dodgers, deserters
> from the Swedish army, psychopaths and pederasts from Memphis and

New Orleans, whose practices were not even to be tolerated in New Orleans; antipapal Catholics, malcontented Methodists, ESPers, UFO-ers, Aquarians, ex–Ayn Randers, Choctaw Zionists, who have returned from their ancestral hunting grounds, and even a few old graybeard Kerouac beats. . . .

By contrast with the swamp, the town has become a refuge for all manner of conservative folk, graduates of Bob Jones University, retired Air Force colonels, passed-over Navy commanders, ex–Washington, D.C., policemen, patriotic chiropractors, two officials of the National Rifle Association, and six conservative proctologists. (15–16)

The situation beyond More's locality is no better, with the country cloven into polarized "Leftist" and "Knothead" (formerly Democratic and Republican) political factions. Religion is likewise divided, Catholicism having undergone another schism, this time into conservative and radical factions with only superficial links to the old church hierarchy. Only a small and wholly inconsequential—until the novel's conclusion—group remains loyal to the pope, who has relocated from Rome to Cicero, Illinois. A race war is clearly impending between black (called "Bantu" in the novel) and white groups. Finally the relationship between More and Art Immelman, a sinister figure who identifies himself as a liaison between governmental and private interests, takes on parodic overtones of an apocalyptic struggle between Christ and Antichrist in regard to More's invention (see below). As Gary M. Ciuba writes in *Walker Percy: Books of Revelations* (1991), in the United States of the novel "all institutions and individuals lack that selfsame integrity whereby opposites complement and correct reach other, the whole cohering as a harmony of mutually sustaining contradictions. Rather, each has become divided into pairs of absolute and incompatible extremes" (133). Within this diametrically divided environment, Percy unleashes a social and, in part, religious satire that strikes at the very root of postwar America's self-definition. With the American landscape reduced to a three-part microcosm of either extreme dichotomization or willful ignorance, hope for avoiding More's prediction of a psychic catastrophe seems scant.

The broader geopolitical situation further exacerbates the country's divisions, with "the war in Ecuador [that] has been going on for fifteen years" clearly functioning as an analogue to Vietnam.[53] More comments that this conflict was "not exactly our best war" and proceeds to describe a situation wholly contingent on a good-versus-evil mentality, even as its underlying reality (like that in Vietnam) belies the futility of such a simple binary conception: "The U.S.A. sided with South Ecuador, which is largely Christian, believing in God and the sacredness of the individual, etcetera, etcetera. The only trouble is that South Ecuador is owned by ninety-eight Catholic families with Swiss bank accounts, is governed by a general, and so is not what you would call an ideal democracy. North Ecuador, on the other hand, which many U.S. liberals support, is Maoist-Communist, and has so far murdered two hundred thousand civilians, including liberals, who did not welcome Communism with open arms" (19–20).

American governmental support for South Ecuador is thus based on criteria ("sacredness of the individual") in line with Hirshberg's American patriotic schema. Similarly the support More mentions among "U.S. liberals" for North Ecuador, despite also being presented as an unsavory nation, mirrors the purely oppositional support that North Vietnam received from some on the American Left in the late 1960s. The reality of the South Ecuadoran government exposes these criteria as fallacious, just as the corruption of the South Vietnamese government, whether under Ngo Dinh Diem or Nguyen Van Thieu, fomented doubts about the American moral imperative in that conflict.[54]

Nevertheless, despite the general concurrence among Pynchon, Barth, and Percy in their diagnoses of America's social malaise in the post–World War II era, a significant difference arises in that Percy is willing to propose a potential (if admittedly idealistic) means for transcending the self-destructive binary system. More's dismissive (and habitual) repetition of "etcetera, etcetera" in the quotes above suggest a healthy skepticism toward binary thinking such as that separating liberals from conservatives or South Ecuadorians from North Ecuadorians, but throughout most of the book, he nevertheless insists that his invention, the "Qualitative-Quantitative Ontological Lapsometer" (30), is "the very means for inoculating persons against" the worsening spiritual sickness. More retains his bipolar diagnosis of this epidemic largely because he himself has developed psychological and physiological ailments that, according to his clinical observations, should not coexist because of their innate political tendencies:

> Conservatives have begun to fall victim to unseasonable rages, delusions of conspiracies, high blood pressure, and large-bowel complaints.
> Liberals are more apt to contract sexual impotence, morning terror, and a feeling of abstraction of the self from itself. . . .
> It is my misfortune—and blessing—that I suffer from both liberal and conservative complaints, e.g., both morning terror and large-bowel disorders, excessive abstraction and unseasonable rages, alternating impotence and satyriasis.

More suggests that his invention "can diagnose and treat with equal success the morning terror or liberals and the apoplexy of conservatives" and thereby "save the U.S.A." (20), but Percy gives his readers plentiful opportunities to doubt More's reasoning.

For starters the lapsometer is based partly on observations that More made while observing an accident that occurs during an experiment involving significant satirical allusions to Enrico Fermi's groundbreaking experiments with atomic energy beneath the football stadium at the University of Chicago: "Do you recall the Heavy Sodium experiments that were conducted years ago in New Orleans under the stands of the Sugar Bowl stadium? . . . The physicists were tinkering with a Heavy Sodium pile by means of which they hoped to hit on a better source of anticancer radiation than the old cobalt treatment. . . . The long and short of it is that the reactor got loose, killed a brace of physicists, sent up an odd yellow cloud" (25). In the wake of this cloud, More begins to notice that "something peculiar happened in the Tulane Psychiatric Hospital, where I was based. . . . Some of the patients got better and some of the psychiatrists got worse" (26). He discovers that all the affected individuals have "significant levels" of the chemicals involved in the experiment in their blood and publishes an article in *JAMA* on "More's Paradoxical Sodium Radiation Syndrome" (26). He also notes that it took him "twenty years to figure out why some got better and some got worse" and, in turn, to develop the lapsometer to deal with the condition whose name reveals its rigidly binary perspective: "Heavy Sodium radiation stimulates Brodmann Area 32, the center of abstractive activity or tendencies toward angelism, while Heavy Chloride stimulates the thalamus, which promotes adjustment to the environment, or, as I call it without prejudice, bestialism. The two conditions are not mutually exclusive. It is not uncommon nowadays to see patients suffering from angelism-beastialism" (27).

More's device thus proposes to cure the "manifold woes of the Western world, with its terrors, and rages and murderous impulses" (28), and he so steadfastly believes in his vocation as a healer that he appears to invalidate the very binarism that his invention purports to resolve: "Don't tell me the U.S.A. went down the drain because of Leftism, Knotheadism, apostasy, pornography, polarization, etcetera etcetera. All these things may have happened, but what finally tore it apart was that things stopped working and nobody wanted to be a repairman" (62–63). More's belief that he can heal the angelism-beastialism binary because he has now ostensibly risen above it parallels the oversimplified and hence flawed solution that Paradise Estates represents in respect to the divided society in which it is embedded.

The unwillingness to abandon this model leads to his inability to "get it right," even in the more hopeful epilogue that takes place five years after the abortive apocalypse of the Bantu uprising. More begins the epilogue by reflecting on the ways in which his life has stabilized in the intervening period: "Despite the setbacks of the past, particularly the fiasco five years ago, I still believe my lapsometer can save the world—if I can get it right. For the world is sundered, busted down the middle, self ripped from self and man pasted back together as mythical monster, half man, half beast, but no man. Even now I can diagnose and shall one day cure: cure the new plague, the modern Black Death, the current hermaphroditism of the spirit, . . . chronic angelism-bestialism that rives the soul from body" (382–83).

Ultimately More's solution to angelism-bestialism (and by extension that of the entire society) is a withdrawal from it, withdrawal back into a heavily revised version of loyal Catholicism. More attends a Christmas mass and goes to confession, at which he penitently renounces his adulterous and alcoholic past, behavior closely tied to his philosophical perspective throughout the novel. Ironically his renunciation triggers what seems to be yet another binary reaction in his new wife as well as a recurrence of his "etcetera" tic: "Ellen's cheek radiates complex rays of approval-disapproval. Approval that I will now 'do right,' be a better husband, cultivate respectable patients, remain abstemtious, etcetera. . . . What bothers her is an ancient Presbyterian mistrust of *things,* things getting mixed up in religion. . . . For she mistrusts the Old Church's traffic in things, sacraments, articles, bread, wine, salt, oil, water ashes" (400).

This time, however, the binary is not (to use Ciuba's language) a pair of "absolute and incompatible extremes" but a "harmony of mutually sustaining contradictions" since More's new ecumenical faith incorporates Catholic virtues but without relying too heavily on "things," a comment that both indicts More's earlier faith in the lapsometer and alludes to Protestant critiques of Catholic ritual. More imagines Ellen telling him to "Watch out!" against falling back into the kinds of practices she distrusts, to which he responds (albeit inwardly), "I will. We will" (400). The love they have found is, as the title implies, a love "in the ruins" of American society, but Percy seems to suggest this love contains some measure of real promise—and not just cold comfort—after having been refined through a trial by fire. In this regard Percy's ending bears some similarity to the (oft-derided) tempered optimism of Pat Frank's postapocalyptic *Alas, Babylon,* in which the survivors in Fort Repose, Florida, have created new and deeper bonds of kinship and community as a result of their survival process.

Critics have not necessarily agreed as to how and why Percy's conclusion relates to his overall satirical intentions in *Love in the Ruins.* Ciuba asserts that More's partaking of the Eucharist represents the moment at which he has definitively "forsaken the self-divisive angelism-bestialism, . . . once again feed[ing] on God rather than 'feasting on death'" (169). On the other hand, in her *American Dream, American Nightmare* (2000), Kathryn Hume insists that Percy's ending is not meant as an absolute prognosis. Her reading thus departs (correctly, in my view) from the widespread interpretation of the book as a normative satire intended to preach resumed religious (specifically Catholic) devotion in the manner of Flannery O'Connor's comic-satirical works. Hume maintains that More's persistent belief in the efficacy of the lapsometer demonstrates his continuing lack of true enlightenment: "Right up to the end, however, More still thinks that this machine could somehow save humanity, and readers are given no clue that he understands the error of this attitude, though we are clearly meant to see the futility of such scientific materialism" (97). Hume's negative interpretation is somewhat problematic, though. More's confession takes place during a time in which Jewish, Protestant, and Catholic services are overlapping, thus making the scene not simply one of normative retrogression into traditional religious values but rather what she herself calls a "'new [paradigm] of man's authentic existence in community' . . . [and] one of the best hopes for America" (168). Hume is correct in stating that Percy's solution is not didactically definitive, but it does also involve a complete subversion of the discordant binaries that afflict his fictionalized version of cold war America. As such, it is an improvement that suggests (if perhaps gingerly) that the next lapsometer may offer real healing, just as More's new hybrid religious belief is an improvement on the fragmented, isolating forms that preceded it.

In a larger historical sense, Percy's satire in *Love in the Ruins* works much like Aleshkovsky's satire in *The Hand* in seeking to renew connections with a spiritual realm that has largely been forgotten. Unlike Aleshkovsky, though, the spiritual solution that Percy puts forth is not hearkening back to a particular past (that is, Gusev's old-style Orthodoxy and traditionalist sense of Russianness) but moving toward a more inclusive version of an older system of belief in order to transcend the multitudinous traps of binarism. Although both visions are normative in a broader historical sense, both also clearly run contrary to the dominant cultures of their time, making them at least locally—in time *and* place—subversive.

4

Cold War Critiques of Utopia

Series and Systems: *The Chronic Nature of Cold War Dystopia*

One of the most common and most exhaustively studied aspects of cold war literature is the prevalence of dystopian and/or anti-utopian themes. As the prefixes of both terms imply, the genres that attempt to discredit utopias have generally been perceived in opposition to their model texts, that is, utopias posit an ideal society, whereas dystopias posit a terrible society resulting from specific utopian premises. Although numerous contemporary critics[1] have explained the relationship between utopian fiction and dystopian fiction in terms that transcend such straightforward divisions, the dystopian fiction of the cold war suggests that there is still some utility in considering (though not adopting) the more simplistic definition. This value arises from two sources: (1) utopian language, and thus utopian fiction, generally contains a simple good/bad dichotomy,[2] and (2) the predominant public discourses of both the Soviet Union and the United States during the cold war frequently relied on such simple binary utopian sentiments. In my view the prevalence of dystopian and anti-utopian sentiment in Russian and American fiction is a parodic-satirical response intended to subvert the utopianism rampant in both superpower cultures during the cold war.[3] The authors of the works examined here do not support either side in this bilaterally utopian ideological struggle but attempt to invalidate the conflict's overarching logical context.

In *The Boundaries of Genre* (1981), Gary Saul Morson broadly defines "anti-utopia" as an "anti-genre" that parodies utopian thinking and classifies dystopia as a subset therein. He maintains that antigenres are distinct because the "set of conventions governing the interpretation of [anti-generic] works . . . establish a *parodic* relation between the anti-generic work and the works and traditions of another genre" (115). Morson's concept of the anti-genre resembles Leon Guilhamet's notion of generic satire as a borrower/deformer of other forms, although Morson's scheme sets up a more specifically contradictory relationship between a genre and its parodic foil. Morson further delineates a subclass of parodic texts as "metaparodies . . . [that]

exploit [a] dialogue between parody and counterparody (or . . . between genre and anti-genre)" (142) in order to confound any attempts at definitive inter-pretation. The "meta-utopian" form "allows [the author] to entertain utopian or anti-utopian arguments, but does not ultimately commit [him or her] to them" (146). Two meta-utopian approaches that recur frequently in cold war satire are what might be termed "serial dystopia" and "systemic dystopia." In the serial mode society is caught in a loop of equally undesirable revolutions and restorations; in the systemic mode *all* parties in a given ideological strug-gle are presented as dystopian, thereby undermining any claim of moral supe-riority. Such works attempt to extract social reasoning from the panoply of false binaries that result from competition between mutually exclusive utopian philosophies.

Morson also asserts that antigenres, unlike genres, "do not necessarily have exemplars—that is, acknowledged originating works—because the broader tradition of literary parody may provide models" (115). To wit, he notes that *Don Quixote* is an exemplary text for many anti-utopian works, despite not being an anti-utopia itself, because of its innovative use of parody (115). The models for anti-utopian literature do not even need to be literary in charac-ter since both utopian and anti-utopian scenarios can be found in historical, philosophical, political, and scientific texts: "Anti-generic motifs may also be drawn from a body of nonliterary texts, a knowledge of which is part of the competence the anti-genre presumes and encourages in its readers" (116). Several cold war anti-utopias (such as Orwell's *Nineteen Eighty-Four,* Coover's *Public Burning,* Aleshkovsky's *Hand,* and Voinovich's *Moscow 2042*) are predi-cated on the notion that distinctions between literary, historical, and politi-cal texts are tenuous and even fraudulent because of undue influence exerted upon them by governmental or other external forces.

In *The Scientific World View in Dystopia* (1984), Alexandra Aldridge fur-ther distinguishes utopia from dystopia in terms of their respective temporal orientations: "It should be recalled that satire is always implicit in utopian literature in the sense that the utopian state serves as a standard against which the author's contemporaneous society can be measured. . . . If utopia has a plus sign, dystopia has a minus sign in the same area—that is, the pres-entation of a non-ideal outweighs the attack on contemporary trends. . . . In dystopia our fuller attention is directed to the alternative structure itself as a 'possible impossible' . . . future world and our lesser attention to the ongoing present; the opposite is true of utopian satire" (6). Because of this "alterna-tive structure," dystopian fiction tends to emphasize the ideological premises of the dystopian state. Since these premises generally stem from the author's own time, this tendency almost inevitably returns dystopia's focus to the present more significantly than Aldridge's "lesser attention" indicates. The satirical thrust of utopia generally moves backward in time from the future utopian state to the present (presumably inferior) state, stopping there and suggesting modifications that will effect the utopian transformation, whereas dystopia satirizes by showing how much worse a future plausibly derived from the present could be. Keith Booker echoes this in *The Dystopian Impulse in Modern Literature* (1994) by stating that "dystopian societies are generally more or less thinly veiled refigurations of a situation that already exists in reality" (15). Finally I agree with David Sisk's claim in *Transformations of Language in Modern Dystopias* (1997) that "dystopian fiction is fundamentally concerned with the writer's present society and builds its horrific power on extrapolating current trends to what the writer considers their logically fearsome conclusions" (Sisk 7), although I would also add the qualification that the temporal focus of dystopia is less fixed than either its utopian or anti-utopian cousins. It allows authors not only to project perceived flaws of the present into the future[4] but also to look backward to point out the origins of dystopias that, in their view, have already arrived. Writers sympathetic to the notion that the "doomsday clock" was rapidly approaching midnight could certainly find admonitory value in either of these approaches.

Gravity's Rainbow, for example, depicts a dystopian world in a temporal setting that actually predates the book's publication by almost thirty years. Although the catastrophic ending moves into the present, the vast majority of the novel is set at in the final days of World War II. In this novel, as in several others from the period,[5] the dystopia is already well underway, and it may be impossible to do anything about it except to make some small, final gesture of compassion: "There is still time, if you need the comfort, to touch the person next to you, or to reach between your own cold legs" (760).

The Cultural Context of Cold War Utopianism

David M. Bethea argues in *The Shape of Apocalypse in Modern Russian Fiction* (1989) that "the binary oppositions by which Russians have tended to define themselves from their first steps into literacy have had . . . a profound impact on the eschatological view of national history passed down through the centuries" (12).[6] He further asserts that "none are more important than the fundamental temporal distinction between 'old' and 'new' and the fundamental spatial distinction between 'east' and 'west'" (13). From these Bethea derives a further dualism—apocalypticists versus utopians: "The apocalypticist tends to interpret the old/new opposition by making the first element positive (the original pristine faith) and the second element negative (contemporary impiety and desecration), while the utopian tends to do the reverse, making a fetish of what is new, 'enlightened,' 'advanced,' such as technology (usually seen in Russia's case as coming from the West), and denigrating what is old, 'superstitious,' and 'ignorant,' such as religious tradition (usually seen in Russia's case as indigenous)" (14–15). He argues that these oppositional categories are the most powerful determinants of the social and intellectual divisions in Russian culture from the early 1600s onward.

Bethea uses this binary framework to interpret Soviet-era works such as Bulgakov's *The Master and Margarita,* Pasternak's *Doctor Zhivago,* and Andrei Platonov's *Chevengur,* each of which he claims "look[s] back on [the Bolshevik Revolution] with the wisdom of disconfirming hindsight" (37), thereby taking on an anti-utopian character. Bethea contends that Platonov is "a *failed utopian,* not a confirmed apocalypticist . . . [who nevertheless] uses many of the same space-time symbols found in other works of apocalyptic fiction" (163). Furthermore he asserts that Platonov's "experience as a failed utopian during the years of NEP had taught him that the use of aesthetic shape . . . to suggest that personal and national histories have coherent and meaningful beginnings, middles, *and* ends was dishonest" (165). To reinforce this argument, Bethea quotes Joseph Brodsky's claim that "like no other Russian writer before or after him, Platonov was able to reveal a self-destructive, eschatological element within language itself, and that, in turn, was of extremely revealing consequence to the revolutionary eschatology with which history supplied him as his subject matter" (quoted in Bethea 165). Whether or not one agrees that Platonov was "uniquely" attuned to the nuances of Soviet rhetoric, the technique of interpreting perceived flaws in language as manifestations and/or causes of flaws in society is consistent not only in anti-utopian writing but also in subversive satire in general.

With moderate qualification Bethea's thesis is applicable to the subversive satires that were written *after* Stalin's death. Bethea describes Bulgakov, Pasternak, and Platonov as anti-utopian largely because they had lost faith that a Soviet utopia could or should be achieved, and he suggests that each reverted to a form of retrospective apocalypticism in response.[7] I claim that the Russian satirists of the cold war era were anti-utopian (but only rarely apocalypticist)[8] because—like Bulgakov, Platonov, and Pasternak—they decried not only the utopian language and philosophy of the Soviets but also their cynical exploitation of the deep-seated old/new, East/West, religion/technology, and faith/reason schisms. The difference for the writers who began their careers during or after the Thaw was that the dystopian character of the Soviet Union (that is, the *inverted* utopia, not simply the failed utopia) had already been made clear through three decades of intentional misuse of the binary foundations of Russian cultural logic. Rather than simply reversing the polarity of such binaries to their pre-Bolshevik settings, a strategy with a track record of bloody failure over centuries of Russian history, the cold war satirists instead called for a closer examination and eventual abandonment of the logic upon which such binaries are founded.

The Soviet Union was not the only superpower involved in the cold war to have utopian foundations, though, and the proliferation of anti-utopian literature in the United States from 1950 onward demonstrates the degree to which American utopianism was also being subjected to more rigorous examination. Kathryn Hume singles out the "American Dream" as the central utopian concept of in the post–World War II United States and attributes the rise of subversive novels in the 1960s and 1970s to a growing disillusionment: "The American Dream had promised an expansive future, and what we now find is a melancholy loss of faith in America's exceptionalism, a sense of tarnished morality at odds with the official propaganda upholding America's innocence and good will. . . . The more liberal writers are obsessed with America's loss of goodness and righteousness, a claim that had stemmed from the promise of liberty and justice for all and that had always seemed to justify America's prosperity. Many of these writers were children in the 1950s . . . and were bombarded in grade school with statements that our national fairness, honesty, prosperity, and good will made America the best nation in the world, a utopian state realized rather than something needing to be striven for" (288–89). Hume goes on to stress that this is not the first time that the American left's utopian dreams had been shattered in the twentieth century: "Whereas political leftists from before the war gave up on utopian dreams when they rejected Stalin and communism, the later generation of liberals invested some of their utopian hopes in America. With the economic shifts of the 1970s, people all around the political compass felt their hope and faith diminish" (289). In failing to find utopia in the nominal exemplars of both Communism and capitalism, American dissidents turned their attention away from finding yet another potential utopian model and toward a general criticism of the harmful effects of centuries of utopianism on American culture.

America had, of course, been associated with a perfect (or, at least perfectible) society in a number of pre–cold war sources, both literary[9] and nonliterary. Perhaps the most influential (and longest lasting) of such associations date back such sixteenth-century Spanish explorers as Juan Ponce de León and Hernando de Soto, who searched the Americas for the "golden illusion" of El Dorado, and the neo-Calvinist Puritans, whose voyage to New England to escape persecution was frequently cast, both by themselves and by outsiders, in utopian terms. Other groups such as the Quakers (whose leader, William Penn, referred to Pennsylvania as his "Holy Experiment"), the Latter-day Saints, and the Oneida Colony contributed in smaller ways to the United States' sense of exceptional and potentially utopian status among nations, despite the fact that most of these groups were also well outside the mainstream of American life and often ostracized. Furthermore the putative core values of the nation are delineated in documents that use rhetoric (the desire to establish a "more perfect union" in which "all men are created equal" and that is devoted to "life, liberty, and the pursuit of happiness") that is at least strongly idealistic, if not downright utopian. These various factors added up, as numerous cultural historians have demonstrated, to create a society highly inclined toward utopianism.

Such inclinations created fertile ground for the development and entrenchment of what would become the American cold war schema in the early
years of the atomic age. The combination of postwar triumphalism, burgeoning prosperity (especially in relation to the other victorious but war-ravaged
Allies), and a rampantly optimistic extant rhetoric surrounding atomic power
facilitated a utopian worldview that blunted or even wholly effaced the grim
realities of life in a world with nuclear weapons. Henriksen notes: "Throughout its history America has always been resistant to admitting an end to that
fresh innocence first proclaimed in the Puritan vision of a shining city upon
a hill. At the end of World War II Americans were especially reluctant to yield
to such suspicions because their nation was tantalizingly close to realizing all
the promise embodied in that vision" (9). This belief in the imminent achievement of the "American dream" was not something that arose organically from
within the culture, though, but rather was in significant measure stimulated
by a wide-ranging advertising campaign that fused governmental, commercial,
and military[10] desires. Tom Engelhardt recalls this period in his memoir-
cum-cultural history, *The End of Victory Culture* (1995): "The worlds of the
warrior and of abundance were, to my gaze, no more antithetical than they
were to the corporate executives, university research scientists, and military
officers who were using a rising military budget and the fear of communism
to create a new national security economy. An alliance between big industry,
big science, and the military had been forged during World War II. This
alliance had blurred the boundaries between the military and civilian by fus-
ing a double set of desires: for technological breakthroughs leading to ever
more instant weapons of destruction and to ever easier living" (77). One of
the strategies to offset the inherent difficulties of maintaining this alliance—
the exclusivity and elitism of which run contrary to many of the values
(democracy, equality, freedom) embodied in Americans' self-image—was to
appeal to a new form of atomic-powered utopianism that had been developing since the late nineteenth century.

Henry Adams's claim that the discovery of radioactivity was an event that
"wakened men" to a "fact, long since evident" (Adams 494) shrewdly frames
the manner in which science, politics, and militarism can effectively collaborate in propagating an insidious utopian vision in American culture. Only a
select few individuals had a practical understanding of radioactivity in 1896
or nuclear fission in 1945. Thanks both to their innate complexity and the rigorous governmental control over information deemed potentially dangerous,
these concepts remained mysterious to most Americans and Russians during
the cold war. Nevertheless the rippling effect of such discoveries on the culture at large was heightened by the increasing presence, direct or indirect, of
science and technology in daily life, a process abetted by utopian prognostica-
tions that frequently accompanied scientific and technological developments.

Such exceedingly rosy forecasts are generally the work of individuals or groups who stand to benefit most, deepening skepticism about the integrity of such language. Abusers of this sort range from unscrupulous purveyors of patent medicines that masquerade as "miracle drugs" to government officials intentionally underestimating and obscuring the dangers of nuclear energy and weapons testing.[11]

As Stephen Hilgartner, Richard Bell, and Rory O'Connor point out in their *Nukespeak: Nuclear Language, Visions and Mindset* (1982), the dawning of the atomic age was already heralded with "euphoric visions" of a "Golden Age" (2, 18) that would be produced through the use of nuclear power. They open the book with a discussion of the profound effect that the roughly contemporaneous discoveries of X-rays and radioactivity had on American culture. They report that within four months of being discovered by Wilhelm Roentgen, "X-rays had been used to test welds, to locate bullets in gunshot wounds, to set broken bones, to kill diphtheria microbes, to diagnose tuberculosis, pneumonia, and enlarged hearts and spleens and to treat cancer" (2). Furthermore they report that "by 1898, personal X-rays had become a popular status symbol in New York" and that in 1911 "experimenters at the University of Pennsylvania made plans to use X-rays to take a photograph of the human soul" (2–3). Radium enjoyed a similar wide-ranging popularity immediately after the recognition of its radioactivity. The respected scientist Sir William Ramsay was even led to speculate on radium's importance in the *New York Times*, writing that the *"philosopher's stone* will have been discovered, and it is not beyond the bounds of possibility that it may lead to that other goal of the philosophers of the Dark Age—*the elixir vitae*" (quoted in Hilgartner, Bell, and O'Connor 4).

Such grandiose language continued almost unabated for several decades, reinforcing utopian visions of nuclear energy's transformative potential even before Enrico Fermi actually split the atom. Spencer Weart claims that "[by the 1930s] it was a cliché that atomic energy might bring someday bring about an industrial revolution, a golden age of plenty" and that any corollary fear of atomic weapons was neutralized by the belief that their massive power would mean that "the human race would have to foreswear war" ("Heyday" 85). An article by physicist R. W. Langer in the July 6, 1940, edition[12] of *Collier's* demonstrates both of these lines of argumentation:

> [There will be] unparalleled richness and opportunities for all. Privilege and class distinctions and the other sources of social uneasiness and bitterness will become relics because things that make up *the good life* will be so abundant and inexpensive. War itself will become obsolete because of the disappearance of those economic stresses that immemorially have caused it. Industrious, powerful nations and clever, aggressive races can win at peace far more than could ever be won at war.

. . . This is not visionary. The foundations of the *happy era* have already been laid. The driving force is within our grasp. Reality is about to be handed from the scientists in their laboratories to the engineers in their factories for application to your daily life. It is a new form of power—atomic power. (quoted in Hilgartner, Bell, and O'Connor 18)

Langer's words echo Weart's contention that what he calls the "heyday of myth and cliché" underpinned Americans' conviction that "the atomic golden age would enjoy not only prosperity but peace" ("Heyday" 85). After the war this utopian belief served not only to soften the potential psychic guilt of using the bomb but also to prepare the way for acceptance of grotesques like Mutual Assured Destruction: "Atomic bombs themselves mightily strengthened the old idea that nuclear energy could solve every social problem, including war. . . . In mid-1945 most people had expected the fighting to go on for many more bloody months, and now atomic bombs seemed to have forestalled that as if by a stroke of magic" (87).

The central theme of *Nukespeak* is the revelation, still generally unacknowledged at the time of the book's publication, that the linguistic gyrations required to "sell" atomic power and the atomic bomb had a notably Orwellian effect on American culture:

In Nukespeak, atrocities are rendered invisible by sterile words like *megadeaths*; nuclear war is called a *nuclear exchange*. Nuclear weapons accidents are called *broken arrows* and *bent spears*. . . .

Nukespeak is the language of the nuclear mindset—the world view, or system of beliefs—of nuclear developers. . . . A mindset acts like a filter, sorting information and perceptions, allowing it to be processed and some to be ignored, consciously or unconsciously. Nukespeak encodes the beliefs and assumptions of the nuclear mindset; the language and the mindset continuously reinforce each other. (xiii)

The authors connect this new language and mindset—a concept whose function is described in terms similar to Hirshberg's cognitive schemata—directly to "euphoric visions of nuclear technologies" stemming from the discovery of X-rays and radium as well as the achievement of nuclear fission in 1938 (xiii–xiv). The barrage of official propaganda extolling the virtues of "the sunny side of the atom" (xiv), taken to the seemingly absurd length of measuring fallout in "Sunshine Units" (219), created an atmosphere in which those in power use language to distort reality in their favor.

The efficacy of such strategies is readily demonstrable, not just anecdotally but also empirically: "In October 1957 the National Association of Science Writers commissioned the first major postwar survey of U.S. public views of science. . . . The survey revealed a nearly spiritual reverence for science and technology. Nearly 90 percent of those polled agreed that the world was 'better off because of science'—for its contributions to medicine, to rapidly rising living standards, to American economic dominance, and for winning the Second World War. . . . Only 12 years after atom bombs vaporized Japanese cities, during an increasingly frenetic nuclear arms race, 90 percent of the sample could not name a single negative consequence of science" (Piller 5). In their *The Genocidal Mentality* (1990), Robert Jay Lifton and Eric Markusen suggest that such forms of "reverence" result from intentional and often obfuscating processes. They describe in detail the officially sanctioned efforts to create "nuclear normality," which they describe as "a generally perceived obligation to view [nuclear] weapons in certain ways because it is morally right, politically necessary, and personally mature to do so." Furthermore they note that the rationale for such an obligation is not solely the result of experts' honest explanation; it is "also influenced by the fear, mystery, and technological claims surrounding the weapons." As the survey results above illustrate, "nuclear normality . . . becomes a cultural assumption, partly manipulated and at times so urgently put forward and embraced as to obscure the bizarre ideological and psychological assumptions contained in it" (38).

Cold war satire does not limit itself to criticizing deformation of language in the service of absurdity or corrupt power, however; it also casts aspersion on cultural forces that allowed "nuclear normality" to occur in the first place. Margot Henriksen discusses this theme as part of a broader cultural movement in *Dr. Strangelove's America: Society and Culture in the Atomic Age* (1997): "In the wake of the Cuban missile crisis a more radical and diverse rebellion grew in response to the menace of American power and to the menace of an American system that had absorbed the debased values associated with the bomb and the cold war. . . . The revolt expanded to encompass a broad range of issues that mirrored the larger concerns raised in the civil defense debate: the morality and sanity of America, the reliability and responsibility of the government, the fear of extinction and extermination, the quest for peace and a new society, with a regenerated sense of human history and of community and individual ethics" (241). With only marginal qualification, these same characteristics can be ascribed to many of the Russian satirists who used their ideologically unacceptable fictions to defy the Soviet state in the 1960s, 1970s, and 1980s. The Russian "sense of human history[,] . . . community and individual ethics" was understandably less "regenerated" than that of their American counterparts, having undergone not only the cultural stresses of the cold war, but also of World War II, the Stalinist "great terror," and the Russian Revolution and Civil War before that. Weart notes that "total war was an abstraction to most Americans, but most Russian families had personal memories of a wretched life amid rubble at some point during the years between 1914 and 1945, and the memories were kept alive by a ceaseless barrage of patriotic films, stories and ceremonies" (240). If anything, Russian writers were much more personally familiar with violence in the defense of "debased values," whether an actual defense, as in World War II, or a putative one, as in the purges of 1937 and 1938. Therefore they reacted against these values with greater skepticism.

Resulting partly from the rise of a dissenting subculture, a great number of cold war satires view the world from a distinctly anti-utopian and/or dystopian perspective. Drawing primarily on Zamyatin's *We* (1924), Huxley's *Brave New World* (1932), and Orwell's *Nineteen Eighty-Four* (1949), these works argue that the destructive political climate of the cold war grew from bogus utopian promises gone astray. Unlike their predecessors, however, most of these later works do not focus primarily on one aspect of utopianism in the way that Orwell condemns totalitarianism or Zamyatin and Huxley criticize the technologization (and concurrent dehumanization) of society. Taking the dichotomous paradigm of the cold war as their model, the cold war subversive satirists instead present as inherently flawed *any* competition between social models containing utopian premises. They argue that such situations inevitably lead not to progress but to one dystopian society succeeding another.

Although arguably more prevalent after the nuclear showdown in Cuba, serialized and systemic dystopias are not unique to the late cold war era. Kurt Vonnegut's first novel *Player Piano* (1952), published only three years after Orwell's *Nineteen Eighty-Four,* starts out resembling an archetypal dystopia but ends up blurring the line between the proponents and opponents of the status quo. Likewise, many novels written between the world wars showed the deleterious effects of competing dystopian systems. Lewis's *It Can't Happen Here* (1935) presented a society in which the actions of rabid American anti-Communists (perhaps) inadvertently mirror those of their ostensible adversaries. Booker writes that "Lewis shows these anti-Stalinist zealots employing brutal methods that are virtually indistinguishable from those used by Stalin himself" (98). Lewis's earlier novel *Babbitt* (1922) also evokes such a seesawing dystopian attitude in focusing on the life of George Babbitt, a sort of middle-class American everyman. Lewis shows the grave errors his protagonist makes in replacing the utopian boosterist ideals of "Zenith the Zip City—Zeal, Zest, and Zowie" (133) first with the hedonism espoused by Tanis Judique's circle and then with the reactionary fervor of the "Good Citizens' League" (290, passim). James Branch Cabell's *Jurgen* (1919), a novel extensively informed by Russian folkloric traditions, reads in part as a satire on the ineffectuality of each of the idealistic systems in which its protagonist takes part. All of the social structures Jurgen encounters during his yearlong Wednesday—the chivalric feudalism of Camelard, the carefree eroticism of Cockaigne, the romanticism of Leukê, the totalitarianism of Philistia, or the patriotic traditionalism of Noumaria—prove ultimately to be less desirable than the somewhat pedestrian reality of his life in Poictesme.

In additional to these potential literary precursors, nonliterary models of all kinds (that is, "social fictions" of the sort Iser discusses) were also plentiful after World War II, as the cold war itself inverted the promise of a better world that was a conceivable, and publicly projected, result of the defeat of global fascism in 1945. The United Nations, an organization with a distinctly utopian albeit noble mandate,[13] was rendered largely powerless for much of the cold war era because of the tension between the two superpowers that was deemed strategically necessary to avoid global destruction. Furthermore, given the high-mindedness (and the correspondingly high-flown rhetoric) upon which both were founded, the United States and the Soviet Union in their cold war manifestations are both at least partially dystopian societies.[14] I base this contention on the simple premise that any society whose survival or supremacy is predicated on the destruction of its enemy in a time when such destruction *inevitably* leads to total mutual annihilation is dystopian by the very nature of its self-negating illogic.

"It's much more difficult to convince one individual of an idiotic idea than an entire people": *Undoing the Damage of Utopianism*

In light of such a cultural context, Henriksen asserts a redemptive function for novels such as *Catch-22* that "attack the internal security bureaucracy and its various by-products, like informing and loyalty-oaths" (242). She contends that these works are ultimately intended to point out how American culture had deviated from its original idealistic path even as it continued to invoke it: "At a point near the end of the novel Milo lectures Yossarian on the dangers of his rebellion against the system: 'Morale was deteriorating and it was all Yossarian's fault. The country was in peril; he was jeopardizing his traditional rights of freedom and independence by exercising them.' Daring to exercise these rights—thus the right of dissent—fed into the moral and ethical code of the 1960s and it was the fictional Yossarian's kind of example that illustrated the possibilities of opposition and alternative states of mind" (256). Henriksen maintains that Heller is constructing a radically contradictory, subversive means of interpreting historical events by calling attention to the patent absurdity of statements like Milo's. This new perspective *might* avert a terrible future like that Yossarian glimpses during his Dante-esque journey through Rome in the later stages of the novel, because it reinstates human individuality (and mortality) in a position of invariable and primary importance: "It was possible by the early sixties to exercise imagination and the right to dissent, to see a different version of history, a version that transformed cold war rationality into all-encompassing malignant American arrogance. Heller's anti-heroic and darkly humorous reinterpretation of World War II and its legacies promoted an appreciation both for this acknowledgment of American arrogance and for the necessity of eluding and renouncing the dangerous future that such arrogance promised. A more human and moral vision of the meaning of life and history in the atomic age appeared:

Man is perishable matter" (256). Western critics regularly attributed this kind of positive countercultural influence to anti-Soviet Russian authors (often misinterpreting "anti-Soviet" as "pro-Western" in the process), but it is equally applicable to many American satirists from Heller onward.

Although it is only sporadically identified as a dystopian novel, *Catch-22* became the prime cold war exemplar of an ostensibly utopian order leading instead to dystopian chaos. The destructive repercussions of such an inversion are more pervasive, more irrational, and more complete in *Catch-22* than in *Jurgen, Babbitt,* or *Player Piano.* Milo Minderbinder's hypercapitalist syndicate, which will drop bombs on or for anyone for a price, regardless of political affiliation (except, ironically, the Soviets, who do not respect his value system), is no improvement over the demonstrably inept and dangerously stupid bureaucratic power structure of the military, especially for those who cannot afford Milo's prices. He even goes so far as to bomb his brothers-in-arms with their own planes (and presumably their own munitions). When this act results in a simultaneous upsurge of business and expression of outrage, Milo feels compelled to clarify his new profit-oriented reasoning: "'In a democracy, the government is the people,' Milo explained. 'We're the people, aren't we? So we might as well just keep the money and eliminate the middleman. Frankly, I'd like to see the government get out of war altogether and leave the whole field to private industry. If we pay the government everything we owe it, we'll only be encouraging government control and discouraging other individuals from bombing their own men and planes. We'll be taking away their incentive'" (254).

By looking back at World War II with the hindsight of eighteen years' experience, Heller retroactively lays bare the ways early 1960s American society, dominated by a milder form of the capitalism that Milo represents, was already well on its way to becoming a dystopia. In *American Fictions, 1940–1980,* Frederick Karl refers to Milo as "our [the United States's] own I. G. Farben, the element that holds everything together and, at the same time, makes war desirable" (311). This reference helps link *Catch-22* to *Gravity's Rainbow,* another novel that looks backward in time for the sources of negative, potentially dystopian conditions in the present. Heller himself made the associative symbolic meaning of *Catch-22* clear in an interview more than a decade after the novel was published: "I wrote it during the Korean War and aimed it for the one after that. . . . The Cold War is what I was truly talking about" (quoted in Weart, *Nuclear* 395).

Catch-22 combines the darkly comic satire of Lewis and Vonnegut with the grim inevitability of a dystopian society's victory over the individual found in *We* or *Nineteen Eighty-Four.* As Weisenburger writes, "*Catch-22* is . . . quite clearly satirical in fulfilling [the] intent to mime the degeneration of a human culture absurdly devoted to everything nonhuman, mechanical, dead" (173). Heller's technique accomplishes Weisenburger's goal for subversive satire, "to pull off the vest shielding us in convention and conformity, so to reveal the deadly chaos underneath" (172); it also makes the dystopian nature of the world he describes apparent. Everything that Yossarian believes should create a positive effect instead results in a negative one, and vice versa. Heller creates a Chinese finger-trap-like world in which Yossarian's rational attempts to overcome the irrational adversities around him only aggravate his situation. Not only is the one-eyed man not king in this land of the blind, it seems everyone is out to deprive him of his last eye. The insanity of this situation is encapsulated in the paradox for which the book is named and against which Yossarian ultimately rebels: "There was only one catch and that was Catch-22, which specified that a concern for one's safety in the face of dangers that were real and immediate was the process of a rational mind. Orr was crazy and could be grounded. All he had to do was ask; and as soon as he did, he would no longer be crazy and would have to fly more missions. Orr would be crazy to fly more missions and sane if he didn't, but if he was sane he had to fly them. If he flew them he was crazy and didn't have to; but if he didn't want to he was sane and had to. Yossarian was moved very deeply by the simplicity of this clause of Catch-22 and let out a respectful whistle" (Heller 46). Almost every action in the novel triggers an irrational reaction, a situation that renders cause and effect largely meaningless and creates a paradoxical and increasingly lethal world from which escape is nearly impossible.

The kind of circular logic contained in this explanation of Catch-22 permeates the whole novel, from Milo's validation of his actions to the Glorious Loyalty Oath Crusade, in which Captain Black attempts to demonize Major Major, a rival officer who has received an appointment that Black coveted, through simplistic anti-Communist logic: "When fellow administrative officers expressed astonishment at Colonel Cathcart's choice of Major Major, Captain Black muttered that there was something funny going on; when they speculated on the political value of Major Major's resemblance to Henry Fonda, Captain Black asserted that Major Major really *was* Henry Fonda; and when they remarked that Major Major was somewhat odd, Captain Black announced that he was a Communist" (111). Captain Black begins a practice of requiring loyalty oaths with the intention of producing evidence of Major Major's Communist sympathies. His system is rigged to ensure that Major Major cannot possibly defend himself: "'From now on, I'm going to make every son of a bitch who comes to my intelligence tent sign a loyalty oath. And I'm not going to let that bastard Major Major sign one even if he wants to" (111).

As in *Rabbits and Boa Constrictors,* Captain Black's self-righteous invocation of patriotism touches off a wave of hyperpatriotism in which various officers on the base attempt to outdo each other in expressions of devotion to the United States. Captain Black even has one of his aides "sign hundreds of [loyalty oaths] with [Captain Black's] name each day so that he could always prove he was more loyal than anyone else" (112). Captain Black even admits the meaninglessness of this gesture, saying, "The important thing is to keep them pledging. . . . It doesn't matter if they mean it or not. That's why they make little kids pledge allegiance before they know what 'pledge' and 'allegiance' mean" (112). Heller's satire condemns conspicuous, routinized patriotism as empty rhetoric, a stance that destabilizes the validity of both its practitioners and its message. As Peter G. Jones notes in *War and the Novelist*, the military system of *Catch-22* "is no respecter of persons; its machine-logic takes words only at face-value" (49–50). Thus it serves as a paradigm of Maltby's "conceptually impoverished discourses that impede critical reflection" (30). Throughout the course of the novel, Heller exposes several varieties of such semantically "dead" language, thereby revealing that the "probability of death and an insane bureaucratic and moral corruption were the true legacies and meaning of World War II" (Henriksen 247). As such *Catch-22* merits a dystopian designation, since the conventional cultural wisdom of the United States regarding World War II posited a society rescued from (rather than afflicted with) characteristics such as death, insanity, and corruption that could be readily associated—through the use of social fictions like Hirshberg's patriotic schema—with the enemy.

Catch-22 thus marks a distinct shift in tone that remains fairly consistent in later cold war satire. Criticism of the irrational and innately dangerous nature of the status quo—interpreted in political, literary, scientific, historical, and mythological terms—shows up frequently in both American and Russian literature, most often in works that borrow heavily from both science fiction and dystopian conventions.[15]

Vonnegut's *Cat's Cradle* is one of the most prominent American examples of dystopian cold war satire, in part because its author managed to bridge the gap between "popular" and "literary" fiction in conveying his "urgent sense of history speeding toward an end" (Dewey 55). Published less than a year after the Cuban Missile Crisis, *Cat's Cradle* presents a gloomy vision of humanity's near future if it continues its unchecked faith in the progressive capabilities of science. As Max F. Schulz writes, "*Cat's Cradle* is a novel about the varieties of truth available to man" (57) that simultaneously argues against reliance on any one of them, especially those that most ardently stake a claim to veracity.

Vonnegut explicitly associates the end of the world with the atomic bomb, even though it is a hybrid water molecule called "ice-nine" rather than nuclear war that causes its ultimate demise. Dr. Felix Hoenniker, the inventor of ice-nine, is introduced by John/Jonah, Vonnegut's authorial stand-in, as one of the so-called Fathers of the first atomic bomb. In a letter to Jonah, who is conducting research on a book about the use of the atomic bomb on Hiroshima, Hoenniker's son Newt says that "people couldn't get to him because he just wasn't interested in people" (13–14). He also relates Hoenniker's reaction to witnessing the Trinity test at Alamogordo, New Mexico: "After the thing went off, after it was a sure thing that America could wipe out a city with just one bomb, a scientist turned to Father and said, 'Science has now known sin.' And do you know what Father said? He said 'What is sin?'" (17). Hoenniker's attitude parodies several of Oppenheimer's self-critical comments in the immediate aftermath of the bomb's development and use.[16] It also demonstrates how Hoenniker's simultaneous lack of reflection and foresight, coupled with his lack of interest in humanity, makes him a dangerous figure. Rather than being a "harmless and gentle and dreamy" (67) innocent who simply exists on a different intellectual plane than most people, Hoenniker becomes a symbolic analogue for the nation, and perhaps mankind as a whole. Vonnegut's satire exposes Hoenniker's innocence as willful ignorance of the consequences of his actions, a trait that ultimately results in the eradication of all life on earth. As Marvin Breed, the brother of Hoenniker's former employer, rhetorically asks Jonah, "How the hell innocent is a man who helps make a thing like an atomic bomb?" (68).

In undermining Hoenniker's innocence, Vonnegut draws on the March 1948 issue of the *Bulletin of the Atomic Scientists* in which Oppenheimer asserts that "the physicists have known sin, and this is a knowledge which they cannot lose" (66), a position that resulted in part from his reflection on the idealism that accompanied a prior development in the science of explosives: "When it went off . . . that first atomic bomb, we thought of Alfred Nobel, and his hope, his vain hope, that dynamite would put an end to all wars" (quoted in Henriksen 6). In the opinion of many historians, the atomic bomb helped speed the end of World War II and thus saved many times more lives than it took at Hiroshima and Nagasaki. Nevertheless it also precipitated the cold war and unleashed the kind of grave anxieties that Vonnegut must have felt quite keenly in the immediate aftermath of the nuclear showdown in Cuba. Far from achieving the utopian goal of ending all wars peacefully, an aim echoed in Langer's rosy predictions for the atomic age, in 1963 nuclear weapons seemed much more likely (in the popular imagination, if not necessarily that of statesmen) to end all wars by ending all human life. Henriksen argues that Hoenniker's indifferent attitude toward his scientific creation, both the bomb and ice-nine, "represent[s] the depraved nexus of scientific and military values . . . [and] suggests the general qualities needed for the promotion of Armageddon" (310). More important, Vonnegut's use of Hoenniker's comment as near-verbatim satirical foil for Oppenheimer's postwar attitude implies that the disastrous outcome of *Cat's Cradle* is what awaits a world that adopts Hoenniker's blissful moral ignorance instead of Oppenheimer's more repentant reflection.[17]

Ice-nine's creation, like that of the atomic bomb, stemmed from extensively intermingled military and commercial concerns.[18] Hoenniker develops ice-nine in response to a request by a Marine general who "felt that one of the aspects of progress should be that Marines no longer had to fight in mud" (42–43). Having stumbled on the secret of how to make the water crystals lock by observing a large chemical manufacturing operation, Hoenniker devises his substance in the secrecy of the Research Laboratory of the General Forge and Foundry Company,[19] an institution that Newt explains was co-opted at Hoenniker's insistence for governmental military research during the Manhattan Project. Hoenniker's military research is classified (as was automatically the case with any such work), and his research for the company would presumably have been confidential in order to conceal any potentially profitable company secrets. It is this secrecy that allows Hoenniker to create the single chip of ice-nine without "anyone's realizing what he was doing [or] leaving records of what he'd done" (50). Hoenniker creates what is essentially a Doomsday Machine every bit as powerful as that in *Dr. Strangelove,* and like the device in Kubrick's film, ice-nine causes the accidental end of the world in part because its existence was a secret.

Hoenniker's astonishingly irresponsible offspring are responsible for the actual dissemination of ice-nine, although it is Hoenniker's lack of care with his dangerous discovery that allows them to blunder into apocalypse. Hoenniker takes the glass vial containing the fateful chip with him on the family's Christmas vacation to Cape Cod and goes about "teasing his children with hints about *ice-nine,* showing it to them in a little bottle on whose label he had drawn a skull and crossbones, and written: 'Danger! *Ice-nine!* Keep away from moisture!'" (247). While his children are out playing on the beach with a dog on Christmas Eve, Hoenniker "play[s] puddly games in the kitchen with water and pots and pans and *ice-nine*" (247), during which he takes a break and dies unexplainedly, leaving a saucepan full of ice-nine behind. The children return and accidentally freeze their dog solid while cleaning up the water in the kitchen, after which they discover that their father has died. The three Hoenniker children make three chips out of the ice-nine remaining in the saucepan, place the chips into individual thermos bottles, and take possession of one each. As Henriksen points out, each of the Hoenniker children eventually abuses his or her terrible inheritance, in the process bringing it into some aspect of cold war geopolitics: "Angela bought her husband with it, and his secret government research for America was based on ice-nine; Newt had enticed an Eastern-bloc dancer with his ice-nine, and when she deserted him, she took the ice-nine secret to the Soviet sphere of influence; and Frank had gained his position of power in San Lorenzo through his knowledge of science and ice-nine. Given this cold war scenario, it seems just a matter of time before catastrophe strikes" (314).

Vonnegut suggests that the irresponsibly cavalier and capitalistic attitude of the Hoenniker children toward the ice-nine is quintessentially American by including characters such as Dr. Asa Breed, Hoenniker's boss at the Research Laboratory, or bicycle manufacturer H. Lowe Crosby. Breed proudly claims that "new knowledge is the most valuable commodity on earth" (Vonnegut, *Cat's* 41) but is ironically ignorant of Hoenniker's success in creating ice-nine. Crosby is an ardent patriot who is nevertheless moving his factory (at Frank Hoenniker's invitation) to the Caribbean island of San Lorenzo from Chicago, complaining that his business has suffered in the United States because the "eggheads sit around trying to figure out new ways for everybody to be happy" (89). With few exceptions Vonnegut's Americans are individuals willfully incapable of either foresight or dealing with contradictions. They inevitably fall back on the easy answers of a *granfalloon* such as patriotism, positivism, or capitalism, a condition that renders them blind to the dangers in their midst. Even Horlick Minton, the newly appointed U.S. ambassador to San Lorenzo, who gives a decidedly humanistic ("Never mind with countries. Think of people." [256]) speech just before the onset of the ice-nine apocalypse, seems resigned to the dreary, suicidal fate of the world.

Predictably the catastrophe that Henriksen forecasts does strike once Jonah and all the Hoenniker children gather on San Lorenzo for Frank's installation as leader. Frank purchased his status as successor to "Papa" Monzano, the island's ruthless military dictator, by giving him his chip of ice-nine, which Monzano uses dramatically to commit suicide on his deathbed. After a string of calamitous blunders, similar to the unlikely but plausible circumstances leading to an accidental nuclear attack in *Fail-Safe* and *Dr. Strangelove,* Monzano's frozen body ends up plummeting into the sea, setting off a chain reaction that irrevocably freezes all the water on earth. Jonah and a few others survive for several months, an interval during which Jonah composes the book (titled *The Day the World Ended*) the reader is ostensibly paging through. The seeming inevitability of this destruction is what makes *Cat's Cradle* dystopian. In some ways repeating the story of the Fall, humanity again loses its place in the world by acquiring and using knowledge for whose moral / ethical dimensions it neither is, nor was intended to be, prepared.[20] Far from living up to Breed's utopian assertion that "new knowledge is the most valuable commodity on earth," it actually proves to be *least* valuable, since it causes the end of the world. *Cat's Cradle* upends the idealistic, and perhaps naive, hopes of scientists such as Nobel and Oppenheimer through a fictional invention that recalls their own destructive offspring. Ostensible enlightenment has resulted in eternal darkening of the world's skies, and Vonnegut's dystopia closes without much hope that humanity on its current course will survive much longer.

Although R. W. Langer's forecast in *Collier's* was intended specifically for an American audience, many of the rhetorical elements of his vast atomic utopia are just as readily found in Soviet propaganda about the egalitarian state that would exist once true Communism and the dictatorship of the proletariat had been achieved. Zinoviev, Aksyonov, and Voinovich (among others) show how the collective consciousness of both groups and individuals can be swayed by a language/mindset cycle of reinforcement that functions much like Nukespeak did in the United States. Sinyavsky writes in *Soviet Civilization* that the utopianism of the Soviet Union (and, to some extent, utopianism in general) was predicated on an inherent contradiction: "This utopia is in an ambiguous situation vis-à-vis the world (in space) and history (in time). On the one hand, it proposes itself and imposes itself on the rest of humanity, as if with open arms, beckoning it into the great, victorious idea. On the other hand, it divorces itself in every possible way from the outside world as from an alien and dangerous environment. The idea of capitalist encirclement, even if no such thing exists any longer, plays the part of the sea to this island utopia. . . . Extreme expansionism goes hand-in-hand with extreme isolationism. Given the nature of this ideal State or the victorious idea, this is understandable. For real-life utopia conceives of itself as a universal system and doctrine; at the same time, it is singular and will brook no other idea" (28). The cognitive dissonance engendered by constant exaltation of this "universal system" within a politically xenophobic and rhetorically monological society provides the impetus for a number of exemplary cold war satires, including two that explicitly literalize Sinyavsky's metaphor of an encircled island.

Picking up where his debut left off, Zinoviev's *Radiant Future* sets its sights directly on exposing fatal flaws in the "great, victorious idea" being imposed upon the Soviet citizenry. Whereas *The Yawning Heights* achieved its satire mostly by parodically impersonating various forms of Soviet propagandistic language, *The Radiant Future* ironically deflates such language by demonstrating the glaring disparity between its idealism and the actual situation it purports to describe. The phrase *svetloe budushchee* (radiant future) is a cliché lifted intact from official Soviet language, and Sinyavsky demonstrates its role in Soviet historical dogmatism by sardonically outlining the potentially pejorative meaning of "utopia": "Utopians only fantasize about the radiant future, having no idea how to get there in fact, whereas we [Soviets] already know and are getting there" (*Soviet Civilization* 29). Laying the foundation for his critiques in *The Radiant Future*, Zinoviev echoes and simultaeously subverts such a view of utopianism through the character of Chatterer in *The Yawning Heights*. When told by the morally ambiguous[21] character of Brother that Ibansk is "developing towards utopia" and "putting forward radiant ideals towards which men aspire in one way or another," Chatterer derides Brother's naïveté by noting that utopia requires deliberate misperception: "What is utopia?. . . It is an abstraction based on a given reality. Utopia is built in the following way. You take the positive and negative aspects of this reality. The positive aspects are either implicitly admitted or deliberately exaggerated. The negative aspects are erased. . . . If you try to construct a utopia which offers us radiant ideals, you will arrive at Ibanskian society but without careerists, informers, parasites, and so on. All the inventors of utopias make the same mistake. They ignore the fact that both the positive and negative aspects of reality which play their part in the formation of a utopia are both engendered by the same society" (531–32). Chatterer goes on to say that "only one kind of utopia can produce radiant ideals . . . a degenerate form of utopia consisting of a multitude of the negative aspects of our reality" (532). *The Radiant Future* is precisely such a "degenerate" utopia, one that deflates the "sense of superiority" that saturates Soviet notions of emergent Communist society.

The Radiant Future announces its satirical intent on the first page with a literally decrepit and decaying "permanent slogan" (*statsionarnyi lozung*), a large metallic piece of propagandistic public art bearing the phrase "Long Live Communism—The Radiant Future of All Mankind!" (7). The public disregards "the Slogan" except to adorn it with vulgar graffiti. The government refurbishes the slogan at least three times a year, all of which are occasions for propagandizing Communism: "once for the May-day celebrations, once for the November celebrations, and on every occasion when Moscow entered for the All-Union contest for the model Communist city, and the multimillion army of Moscow office workers was driven out onto the streets to clean up the rubbish" (7). Nevertheless, despite the fact that a "huge amount of money was poured into it—no less (it is rumored) than was invested in the whole of our agriculture during the first five-year plan," the slogan is so poorly constructed that this maintenance costs "several times more than its initial construction" (7). Given that the First Five-Year Plan (1928–32) was marked mostly by massive expenditures on industry rather than agriculture and that the most noteworthy agricultural policies of the period—the collectivization and elimination of the *kulaks*—contributed to a major famine in 1932–33, Zinoviev's reference here manages to damn both the alleged grandiosity of the Slogan's expense and a key moment Soviet history with one instance of faint praise.

Much like *The Yawning Heights,* the bulk of *The Radiant Future* consists of conversations among characters belonging to the intelligentsia. Chief among these characters is the novel's unnamed protagonist/narrator, who introduces himself: "I'm the Head of the Department of Theoretical Problems of the Methodology of Scientific Communism. . . . I am a doctor of philosophy, a professor, a member of the editorial board of our leading philosophical journal, a member of countless Scientific councils, committees, commissions, societies, the author of six monographs and a hundred articles" (10–11). In short he is utterly embedded within the ideological and social structure of the state via his position as an approved commentator on and producer of official Soviet language. By reifying such language in the form of the Slogan and then demonstrating the thorough debasement of this corporeal symbol, Zinoviev undercuts both the myths of Soviet society and the means by which they are transmitted and perpetuated. A simultaneous albeit less literal process of revelation, triggered in large measure by his dissident friend Anton, who is struggling to publish a book that gives "an objective description of communism as it really is" (286), takes place within the narrator as he comes to recognize the hollowness and corruption of the ideas he has propagated through his position.[22] The Slogan acts as a linguistic Potemkin village in that it attempts to disguise an unpleasant reality with an idealized façade.

The Slogan is renovated with great pomp and circumstance in honor of the Twenty-fifth Party Congress, with new materials that had, in a cliché of Soviet propaganda, been "saved up by the construction workers of Moscow in honor of the coming Congress" (8). This ostensible thrift saves the builders of the slogan ten million rubles, which they in turn spend on "permanent reinforced concrete frames to carry the portraits of the members of the Politburo, thus putting the crowning glory (as the newspapers said) to the splendid architectural ensemble of Cosmonaut Square and the wasteground adjoining it" (8). Thus materials presumably diverted from other, potentially necessary construction projects are diverted for a self-aggrandizing monument that also serves, as its architect argues, "to conceal the ugliness of the wasteground from the eyes of the foreigners [visiting the city for the Congress]" (8). So in every aspect the Slogan embodies for Zinoviev a Soviet rhetoric whose dual purposes are the obscuration of one undesirable reality (the wasteground in the middle of the city "where the Avenue of Marxism-Leninism meets Cosmonaut Square") and ostentatious superimposition of another (the "glory" of the Politburo).

As might be expected, the refurbished Slogan becomes almost immediately a "seat of debauchery twenty-four hours a day." Initially there is some official indignation to this development and a group of Komsomol "vigilantes" is dispatched "with great enthusiasm" to prevent its further desecration. This effort soon fails because "those who stood guard duty were students and junior research assistants who, on account of their youth, were inclined to drunkenness. And since the Slogan was close to the 'Youth' café and a supermarket with a well-stocked wine and spirits department, the vigilantes didn't waste their time." The students eventually get so drunk that they accost passersby and all but one are "carted off to the cooler," the exception being "a lad who had fallen into the gap between two letters and was not discovered." The Komsomol institutes a "considerable education program" following these events, but it consists solely of a senior member teaching his younger charges "how to hold [their] liquor" more effectively (45–46). Within weeks, the Slogan ironically seems "destined to become a kind of international salon" that represents everything *but* the superiority of Communism: "The spaces between the letters proved to be very convenient places for the trysts of the lovelorn young. That was on the side reading 'Long Live Communism.' The other side ('The Radiant Future of All Mankind') which was closer to the 'Youth' café and the wine shop, provided a home for the drinking bouts of the local alcoholics. . . . Next, a particular sort of young woman began to frequent the area around the Slogan. The word 'Radiant' became a center for drug-trafficking. And the word 'Communism' was soon taken over completely by homosexuals" (58–59). Party cadres attempt to solve this problem by destroying several buildings (including a fifteenth-century church) to facilitate the transformation of "the Avenue of the Construction Workers into a route for government use only (it led directly to the suburban palaces of the highest leadership)" (93). The street is named after the workers who ostensibly donated time and materials to refurbish the Slogan, but these very workers would be prohibited from using the street commemorating their contributions. This irony proves largely irrelevant because the heedless nature of the construction work causes the Slogan to be buried beneath a heap of rubble from the demolished buildings, during which time "everyone [except for some "pensioners" who complain to the newspapers] forgot about it" (93). The Slogan is eventually exhumed but becomes "very difficult to get to," causing the "morally unstable elements of society" to gather elsewhere and giving "citizens and visitors . . . the opportunity to admire the marvelous spectacle of the Slogan," which they predictably do not do (93).

As Cosmonaut Square is reconstructed (again) in preparation for the Party Congress, the Slogan becomes "a place to be shown off to foreigners" when its letters are recast in titanium instead of stainless steel, which had "first of all turned black and then come out in brown blotches." Zinoviev satirizes the false and crude construction of Soviet rhetoric when his narrator suggests that "someone had made a nice little profit for himself by supplying ordinary cast iron instead of the intended stainless steel" (144). The new glory of the Slogan is short lived, though, because "some scrounger from the Ministry of Foreign Trade . . . had decided to cover the roof of his three-(!!)story villa (with its own swimming pool!!) in nothing less than titanium" and had "hired some crooks, who for a healthy fee delivered the first three letters of the slogan ('LON') to his villa" (181). Like the seizure of the Avenue of the Construction Workers, the cadres have cannibalized another monument to the proletariat and again no one notices until "one age-old pensioner . . . had taken his great-great-great-granddaughter for a walk and noticed that something was not quite right." He recalls "stroll[ing] around this square with Ilyich [Lenin?]" but only knows that "something sort of communist" is missing. An investigation is mounted and allegedly resolves when cosmonauts spot the "gleaming roof of the villain's villa" from space, thus also conveniently providing "incontrovertible proof of the practical value of space flight" for the regime. Unfortunately a lack of titanium mandates that the missing letters be replaced with wooden planks painted gray, which the narrator laments "wasn't quite the same" (182).

Immediately after recalling a conversation in which Anton insists that "the slogan 'Live for a Radiant Future' is nothing but a badly camouflaged demand to live with an eye on the privileges of the topmost ranks of society" (224), a claim repeatedly demonstrated by the physical Slogan's treatment to that point, the narrator decides to walk past the Slogan on a beautiful spring day to reinforce his faith that "life is good even in our radiant communist society." There he finds that the statue of Lenin erected next to the Slogan lost an eye lost an eye, changing his expression from one of "arch joviality" into one of "sheer ill temper," while the Slogan itself is in terrible disrepair: "Some of the letters of the Slogan had disappeared altogether to some unknown destination. Others had fallen down, and the rest had been so bespattered by the pigeons that not even mathematical linguists could decipher them" (225–26). He hails a taxi home with a driver who curses "the idiots who cluttered up the road with all this rubbish [the Slogan]," and eventually the narrator joins him in "attack[ing] our way of life in chorus and with redoubled strength" (226). His disillusionment is nearly complete and, not surprisingly, he soon finds himself marginalized from the corridors of power than he had previously inhabited. He ends up in "a miserable little faculty" but retains mild hope that he "will be able to turn it into something decent" (286). As the book ends, he is walking past the Slogan and notes that it is covered in scaffolding awaiting yet another renovation. He ruefully laments that this event will be hailed in the usual ways by his old institute, rhetorically asking, "When will someone decide to get rid of all these idiots and replace them with some worthwhile people?" His final thought still asserts that "we will build communism," but the book's final line echoes Gogol's famous question to Russia in *Dead Souls*, as he is not even sure where he is headed in the final line of the book, much less where his country will go. He worries that "passersby would look at [him] and laugh" (287), but like the Slogan he is largely ignored and left to head into his ambiguous, decidedly nonutopian (although not necessarily dystopian) future.

Like his character Anton, Zinoviev is no adherent of a simple anti-Communism in his critiques of the absurdity of the Soviet system. Zinoviev finds the idealistic official language of the Soviet Union, whether verbalized, published, or monumentalized, to be an empty and absurd cipher, regardless of its political content. He repeatedly claims that Soviet citizens had long since ceased to believe in (or even to notice) the ideas underlying Soviet rhetoric, just as the townspeople in his book continually disregard or controvert the Slogan's message. As Brown notes, "Zinoviev has an affinity with Gogol in his exposure of linguistic idiocies; both writers exhibit the linguistic forms of logical statement in an automatized state and empty of content" (314). The direct correlation between the "automatized state" of his fictional societies' logic and its lack of substance is not only one of Zinoviev's primary concerns, but a recurrent theme in cold war satire in general.

Sinyavsky's metaphorical conception of a utopian Russian "island" state is the central metaphor of Aksyonov's dystopian novel *The Island of Crimea*

(1981). In this novel the island is not the entire Soviet Union but just the Crimea. Separated from the Russian mainland, rather than being connected to it by a small strip of land, Aksyonov's fictional Crimea is an independent bastion of democratic capitalism populated largely by the descendants of former "Whites" (non-Bolshevik Communists) who fled there during the Russian Civil War. Andrei Luchnikov, the novel's protagonist, is a well-known Crimean newspaper editor who also heads a movement called the Common Fate League (Soiuz obshchei sud'by, or SOS) that idealistically seeks reunification with the Soviet Union. With a fervent belief in enlightened Communism that hearkens back to their revolutionary ancestors, Luchnikov and his associates naively believe that the Soviets will bring order to the island's tempestuous political climate, while still retaining certain of the more progressive policies that have allowed Crimeans to thrive economically and culturally. Although Aksyonov's Crimea at times resembles both Taiwan and Hong Kong in terms of its historical and cultural relation to a neighboring Communist giant, the situation is more complex than that. The novel depicts the complicated fragmentation of the island nation's outwardly idyllic society— in large measure due to the Common Fate League's influence—prior to being forcibly absorbed by its northern cousin.

In a preface written especially for the novel's 1983 English translation, Aksyonov frames *The Island of Crimea* with reference to a seminal cold war dystopia:

> Every Russian schoolboy knows that Crimea is connected to mainland Russia by an isthmus, but not even every adult knows how flimsy an isthmus it is. When a Russian rides along it for the first time and sees it for its narrow, swampy self, he can't quite suppress a seditious "what if."
>
> What if Crimea were really an island? What if, as a result, the White Army had been able to defend Crimea from the Reds in 1920? What if Crimea had developed as a Russian, yet Western, democracy alongside the totalitarian mainland?
>
> The southern coast of Crimea is a subtropic zone protected from the fierce Russian winter by a range of mountains. During that winter the mountains are covered with black clouds seemingly fixed in time, while down below the sun is shining. If those isolating, doomful black clouds remind the Westerner of Stanley Kramer's film of *On the Beach,* the Russian can't help thinking that selfsame seditious "what if." (ix).

In this novel Aksyonov plays out a scenario markedly different from *On the Beach* in that the catastrophe befalling the sun-drenched island society is not the result of external conflict, but a consequence of the Crimeans' own actions, especially those of Luchnikov and his "Common Fate" colleagues in attempting to unify Russia. As Booker points out, the novel's approach is simultaneously anti-utopian and dystopian, in essence refuting the potential value contained in Aksyonov's "what if": "The Capitalist 'utopia' on the island of Crimea casts the Soviet Union in a dystopian light, though the eventual end of the book calls into question the utopian pretensions of capitalism. The book's outcome indicates that, within the oppressive context of the Soviet Union, transgressive behavior generally leads not to emancipation but to swift and brutal retribution. Moreover there is a suggestion that the material wealth and carefree Western lifestyle of the island (and perhaps of the West in general) lead to a political naiveté and complacency that make it easy prey for Soviet conquest" (*Dystopian* 129). Aksyonov denies the credibility of both the Communist and capitalist versions of utopia, claiming that the hindrance to critical thinking that they both represent can lead—one directly, the other indirectly—to the same end, namely, ruthless totalitarian subjugation. The recklessly blasé attitude of the Crimeans (reminiscent of the Australians in *On the Beach* as the end of the world approaches)[23] contributes greatly to their own demise as an independent and free nation.

Clowes notes that Luchnikov's desire to reunite the Crimea with the Soviet Union is based on his "nostalgic, semi-Slavophile attachment to an ideal of mythical national unity." This ideal echoes both Sinyavsky's ours / not ours formulation and the division between apocalypticists and utopians central to Bethea's vision of Russian history. Clowes adds a further dimension to this comparison, claiming that the most important variance between Aksyonov's imaginary Crimea and the Soviet Union occurs in the context of ideological pluralism versus monologism: "Cosmopolitan playground, center of world trade and diplomacy, and technological miracle, this hypermodern Crimean meta-utopia is based on a multiplicity, one might even say a 'cacophony,' of ideological voices—all coexisting in provisional and constantly fluctuating forms of consensus and compromise. [It] is striking for its proximity to a geographical entity, the Soviet Union, that represents its ideological opposite—monological, ideologically fixed, stagnant, in short, a traditional utopia."

She continues by making nearly the same assertion as Sinyavsky about the paradox inherent in such a traditional utopia: "In its structure [the Soviet Union] contains the unresolved oppositions of a utopia: it is isolated, yet claims international influence, drab and egalitarian yet hierarchically regimented, oppressive yet proclaiming liberationist policies" (178). Because of his traditionalist Russian views, Luchnikov fails to recognize both the value of Crimea's extant pluralism and the degree to which the Soviet system *demands* a single-voiced ideology, and Clowes argues that this ignorance reflects the main target of Aksyonov's satirical criticism: "Implicit . . . is the thought that historical determinism is a mask for an intellectually lazy and politically ruinous nostalgia for some *Gemeinschaft,* some easy social harmony and unity that never has existed and never will exist. In the case of Luchnikov, the dream is certainly more appealing than reality" (180). As Iskander did in

Rabbits and Boa Constrictors, Aksyonov satirizes practitioners of overly simplistic logic along with those who aid and abet it by settling for the uncomplicated truths of tradition rather than the dangerous reality before their eyes.[24]

From the earliest pages of the novel, Aksyonov presents Luchnikov as a
man who has difficulty breaking away from traditional Russian patterns of
behavior. As he drives around Simferopol, the Crimea's ultramodern capital,
Luchnikov crosses himself "out of habit" at an intersection where an Orthodox church formerly stood. Not only does Luchnikov himself question this
seemingly instinctive behavior, but the narrator explains that this habit "was
the subject of great glee among his new friends in Moscow," that is, the Soviets with whom he has been in contact in his efforts for reunification: "The
brightest of them, Marlen Kuzenkov, would even lecture him about it: 'You're
almost a Marxist, Andrei, and even from a purely existential standpoint it's
ridiculous to indulge in such naïve symbols.' Luchnikov's standard response
was a slight and slightly ironic smile, and every time he saw a golden cruci-
fix in the sky, he continued to make a quick cross 'as a mere formality.' But
he'd been troubled lately by the formalities, the vanities of his life style, his
distance from the Church, and here he was, to his horror, crossing himself
at a traffic light" (4).[25] Although Luchnikov's religious habit is no vestige of
Soviet thinking, it does reflect his tendency to sidestep potential contradictions. Despite living in a Crimean society that allows ideologies with disparate
and even conflicting tenets, Luchnikov attempts to think in the single-minded
fashion of his Soviet associates and their Slavophile forebears (with mixed
success, as his conflicted reactions to his residual religious habit demonstrate). By incompletely but fervently adopting the logic of the Soviets, he
marginalizes himself from both societies and fails to comprehend the world
around him.

Even on occasions when Luchnikov endeavors to strengthen his convic-
tions and transcend the simplistic logic of his Soviet collaborators, he unwittingly plays into their hands. For example, while Luchnikov is on a visit to
Moscow, his paper, the *Russian Courier,* becomes an uncritical mouthpiece
for the Common Fate League and its articles use rhetoric as empty as that
of the ubiquitous slogans that shout out Communist propaganda from every
corner of Moscow: "The Idea of the Common Fate had appeared on every
page, but that was the problem: it had merely put in an appearance, sat
there, instead of pulsating like a live artery. Soviet features and all Soviet
themes had grown stiff and formulaic, almost bureaucratic in style" (237). To
remedy this Luchnikov writes an article called "The Nonentity: On the Hun-
dredth Anniversary of Stalin's Birth" (238), in which he vigorously attacks neo-
Stalinist elements in the Soviet Union for lying to the Russian people and
"spread[ing] havoc throughout the land" (243). Luchnikov argues that Russia
can achieve a form of utopian existence if it can manage to throw off Stalinist remnants and become a truly democratic *and* socialist society: "Russia has

the opportunity to blossom into a great creative community of people communicating directly with God, yet always mindful of its own sufferings and the sufferings of others" (243).[26]

The article creates an understandable stir among the Soviet leadership but Kuzenkov, the KGB operative in charge of overseeing the Crimea, explains the perceived shift of the *Courier's* politics in terms they understand: "A passing fancy for the silly ideas of our dissidents or the new emigration, perhaps, a typically idealistic reflex" (268). Kuzenkov points out that, despite its occasional departures from strict Soviet ideology, the Common Fate League presents the best opportunity for the Soviet Union to acquire the Crimea because it stimulates "sympathy toward the Soviet Union and even the desire to merge with us" (266). The Common Fate League thus indirectly serves the ideological purposes of the Soviets, who have no intentions of allowing Crimeans to continue their way of life after reunification, as the comments of the "*portrety*" (that is, members of the politburo featured in Soviet propagandistic portraits) demonstrate:

> "Whoa, hold on a minute. . . . Isn't this reunification going to be more trouble than it's worth? Where will we put them all, anyway? Forty parties and nearly as many different nations. . . . "
>
> "The Party has amassed a good deal of experience in these matters. . . . The multiparty system, of course, can be done away with in days. The nationality issue is more complicated, though as I see it, the Greeks belong in Greece, the Italians in Italy, the Russians in Russia, and so forth." (264)

Luchnikov's attempt at backtracking, whether genuine or not, is thus rendered ineffectual. Not only does his rhetoric of reunification retain the utopian dream of "easy social harmony and unity that never has existed" that Clowes mentions, but Luchnikov's monological political stance undermines his ability to condemn selected aspects of Soviet Communism. As Clowes states, Luchnikov's "alarmist, even apocalyptic attitude toward serious open disagreement and debate" (a trait she labels as "peculiarly Russian") makes him incapable of "tread[ing] the difficult middle realm—to be tolerant, perceive a variety of ideologies, and still act with moral integrity" (179, 181).

The novel closes with Luchnikov attending the burial of his wife, killed by the invading Soviets. Luchnikov regards his watch "in great anguish" (369) as its hands appear to spin rapidly forward, a twofold symbol that suggests both the heavy psychological price that Luchnikov's politics have exacted from him and the fact that the Crimea is now a part of the Soviet Union, whose self-aggrandizing rhetoric frequently features the idea of accelerating progress toward the "radiant future." Since the future of the Crimea will now presumably resemble the drab and stifling atmosphere of Aksyonov's fictionalized Soviet Union, the symbol of time whirling out of Luchnikov's control heightens the dissonance between reality and Luchnikov's romantic vision of a unified and symbiotic Russian state.

As an intellectual and a political liberal (in spite of his pro-unification stance) who should seemingly know better than to hand his country over to the voraciously predatory Soviets, Luchnikov is only one in a series of Aksyonov heroes—including the Samopalov brothers of "The Steel Bird," the five protagonists of *The Burn,* and Maxim Ogorodnikov of *Say Cheese!*—who embody a dystopian sentiment peculiar to the Russian intelligentsia of the cold war. As Ellendea Proffer writes, much of Aksyonov's work from the 1970s and 1980s deals with "the subject of the sins and expiations of the Russian intelligentsia, the intelligentsia which created the monster [of Soviet Communism] and then was devoured by it" (133). She argues that Luchnikov is motivated by a sense of guilt for the actions of his class: "His reasoning is [that] . . . the Russian intelligentsia let the genie out of the bottle, caused the Revolution, then let its people suffer. It is the duty of the intelligentsia, particularly the free intelligentsia, to accept responsibility for this, rejoin the main culture, and soften as much as possible the existing regime" (136). I concur with Proffer except on the matter of "soften[ing] . . . the existing regime," as Luchnikov's rhetoric in the newspaper piece clearly shows a continuing tendency not to "soften" Soviet Communism but to correct it and put it back on the track to a paradisiacal society "communicating directly with God." Utopianism remains a salient component of Luchnikov's philosophy and provides the means by which the Soviets can manipulate him into doing their will.

Featuring an even more comprehensive catalogue of manipulative rhetorical practices, Voinovich's *Moscow 2042* is the most direct satire by a Russian writer of the forms and effects of utopian thinking during the cold war. The novel's overall rhetorical structure principally works to undercut two intertwined notions: the utopian exceptionalism of the Soviet Union and the purely dystopian idea that *anything* is better than the Soviet system. Moreover, although Voinovich's narrator/protagonist Vitaly Kartsev (biographically similar to his creator) is at times a keen observer of folly, he is also ultimately something of a dupe in his own right. Any sense that Kartsev will be a trustworthy narrator is destroyed on page one, when (after announcing that he has lost all of his notes except for an incomprehensible scribble) he tries to convince the reader of his story's reliability: "What I describe here is only what I saw with my own eyes. Or heard with my own ears. Or what was told to me by someone I trust greatly. Or not that greatly. In any case, what I write is always based on something. Sometimes it's even based on nothing. But anyone with even a nodding acquaintance with the theory of relativity knows that nothing is a variety of something and so you can always make a little something out of nothing. . . . I think this is sufficient reason for you to have complete confidence in this story" (4).

Although Kartsev does not appear to be attempting consciously to deceive the reader, the combination of his pseudoscientific rationalization and the unacknowledged yet self-evident contradictions in his introduction do anything but create "complete confidence." Similar blind spots in Kartsev's objectivity recur throughout the opening pages of the book, placing him among the pantheon of voices ultimately discredited. In this way, Voinovich achieves a meta-utopian rather than strictly dystopian tone; his novel calls into question both simple pro-Soviet and simple anti-Soviet attitudes.

The novel's plot concerns Kartsev's fantastic journey to Moscow sixty years in the future. A relatively unheralded Russian émigré writer living, like Voinovich himself, in West Germany, Kartsev's tale begins with a discussion about technology and literature with his enigmatic German friend, Rudi. When Rudi claims that Kartsev's relative obscurity as a writer is due to his dedication to realism, Kartsev replies that Rudi's beloved science fiction is "not literature but tomfoolery like the electronic games that induce mass idiocy." Rudi replies that science fiction writers have proven their value by predicting dystopian social developments: "Take Orwell, for example. Didn't he predict in detail the system that exists in Russia today?" Kartsev scoffingly rejects this notion, claiming that "Orwell wrote a parody of what already existed at the time" and that he "described a totalitarian machine that worked perfectly and could simply never exist in a real society" (6–7). Both the tenor and content of their discussion help establish Voinovich's meta-utopian tone, as his own novel will serve both as a genre-parody of works like Orwell's but also as a satire of Kartsev's dismissive rejoinder, given that the dystopian society depicted in the novel is perhaps more banal than Orwell's perfect "totalitarian machine" but is also, like *Nineteen Eighty-Four,* a "parody of what already existed" circa 1980 in the Soviet Union.

After their conversation begins to wane, Rudi tells Kartsev about a travel agency that can book him passage on a Lufthansa flight that moves both in space and time, traveling from Munich to Moscow and from 1982 to 2042. Kartsev initially rejects this as more science fictional claptrap, but his interest increases after visiting the travel agent Rudi recommends, especially when he learns that "there's no limit on the amount of drinks passengers can be served on this flight, plus they're all free of charge" (13). His enthusiasm increases still further after an American journalist named John offers to pay the nearly two million dollars that the ticket will cost as well as another million as a fee in exchange for an exhaustive article describing his journey. Kartsev briefly suspects John is a CIA agent but blithely sets aside his legitimate concerns (how does John know of Kartsev's plans?) after John strokes Kartsev's writerly ego by telling him that this article will be "the sensation of the century" (17).

Kartsev's last source of reticence concerns the uncertainty about the political situation he will find in the year 2042—the travel agency can only get him to a given year, not predict the situation upon arrival—but he accepts John's offer after the quintessentially Gogolian development of a conversation with "the devil who dwells within me . . . [whose] only thought has been to incite me to go on adventures" (18). Kartsev accedes to this devil's wishes after asking whether he loves the Soviets: "'Do I!' cried the devil. 'What's not to like? They're devils in their own way too, they're always coming up with some jolly idea'" (19). Voinovich thus begins the book with two explicit levels of metafictional framing: a critique of the value of both science fiction and dystopian literature and the *mise en abîme* device of Kartsev's ostensibly journalistic article that is both inspired by an adventure-seeking "devil" and quite possibly bankrolled by an organization in diametrical opposition to the "devils in their own way" that make up the Communist government of the Soviet Union. These overt frames are designed not just to remind the reader of the full range of genre models being parodied (and thereby continually unmasking the text's fictionality) but also to set up Voinovich's larger satire of the overly simplistic and serially dystopian Soviet / anti-Soviet dichotomy.

This latter theme especially is reinforced in the chapters leading up to Kartsev's departure. In the days before he boards the plane, Kartsev encounters representatives from a variety of factions who like John have mysteriously learned about his travel plans and seek to benefit from his trip. First he is briefly abducted by a group of Arabs who want Kartsev to "bring back a detailed plan for an ordinary nuclear bomb, which they wanted solely for peaceful purposes" (25). They give him a small bag of gold for his troubles and promise him fifty times more if he succeeds. Next, while shopping for gifts to take into the future, he has a "surprise encounter" (27) with Lyoshka Bukashev, a former journalism school classmate and current KGB major general. Kartsev and Bukashev converse over beers at a café in Munich that is apparently staffed by incognito but somewhat inept KGB agents. Bukashev implies to Kartsev that he has been following him and knows all about his planned trip. After admitting that he thinks the current Soviet system is "perfectly idiotic" (33), Bukashev intimates that he would find information from the future very beneficial for making improvements to the present-day Soviet system: "It's almost impossible not to make mistakes in such a complex operation. Now, if you could only look into the future, say, fifty or sixty years, and find out what the results would be" (36). Kartsev lies and tells Bukashev that his planned trip is to Honolulu, but harbors no illusion that Bukashev believes him.

After this Kartsev is summoned to Toronto to meet with Sim Simych Karnavalov, a reclusive, neo-Slavophile exile from the Soviet Union who bears more than a passing resemblance to Solzhenitsyn.[27] Karnavalov lives with his faithful entourage on an estate in the countryside named "Solace" (*Otradnoe*), where he constantly rehearses his triumphant reentry into Russia astride a white horse named Logos and works on the remaining twenty-four of a projected sixty "slabs" of his gigantic novel *The Greater Zone*.[28] Kartsev is appalled by Karnavalov's dictatorial behavior around the estate as well as the reactionary anti-Soviet but pro-Russian nationalism he spouts for an obliging American television crew suspiciously headed by John, his alleged contact from the *New Times*. Despite his reservations Kartsev meets with Karnavalov, who arrogantly informs Kartsev that he will be taking with him on his journey to the future Moscow a floppy disk containing the existing thirty-six slabs of *The Greater Zone*, along with a wax-sealed letter addressed "TO THE FUTURE RULERS OF RUSSIA" (93). Karnavalov haughtily instructs Kartsev to use the version of *The Greater Zone* on the disk to proofread and correct the version he is sure will have been published (albeit with distortion) in the future Moscow and then to "turn the disk in to the Karnavalov Museum" (92) as an invaluable historical artifact. When Kartsev asks Karnavalov "with guarded malice" what he is to do if the book has not been published or if there is no such museum, Karnavalov instructs him to "print as many copies as possible. Then distribute them, the more widely the better. Just hand them out right and left. Let people discover what their voracious rulers are really like" (92). Kartsev protests that this activity would potentially prove dangerous, and Karnavalov berates him for his lack of willingness to sacrifice himself in order to save Russia from the "voracious predators" (92). Karnavalov unceremoniously calls for one of his assistants to escort Kartsev to the highway, secure in his belief that Kartsev will do his bidding. Kartsev tosses the letter in the trash upon arriving back in Munich but keeps the disk, "without knowing why myself" (93).

The inherently *textual* nature of Kartsev's preflight encounters is, in my view, central to Voinovich's satirical intent. Among the existing critics, only Clowes has examined the way in which Voinovich uses the interplay between the various implied and intrusive readers of his transparently metafictional novel to extend the satirical reach of his work: "As he plans his trip to Moscow, Kartsev runs into trouble with the intrusive reader. He is not permitted simply to appeal to and play epistemological games with a mass audience. All of the figures of the intrusive reader type in *Moscow 2042* are Russian writers and political leaders of the type familiar to anyone who knows the long history of Russian literary politics" (194).

Clowes is correct in noting the existence of familiar intrusive readers such as the ubiquitous and relatively omniscient government agent that Bukashev appears to be, the "self-righteous, moralistic writer" (194) Karnavalov astride Logos ("the word" and, of course, "the Word") or the various party functionaries that Kartsev meets in the Moscowrep[29] of 2042. Nevertheless her analysis also overlooks the presence of such non-Russians as John and the mysterious Arabs among their number, thereby largely missing Voinovich's complication of Kartsev's metafictional conundrum. Admittedly these non-Russians are minor characters in terms of the plot of the novel, but their influence over the metanovel (and thus the satire) is considerably more extensive. Not only is Kartsev's text[30] subjected to the conventional Russian/Soviet pressures, but it is simultaneously in danger of becoming a tool of Western anti-Soviet propaganda because it was bankrolled by U.S. intelligence at a high point of the cold war. The Arabs introduce an additional wrinkle by being largely uninterested in his primary text (the story of how the Soviet Union has or has not developed in sixty years) in favor of their own text (the plans for a nuclear weapon), which is wholly peripheral to the binary geopolitics of the cold war. In short Kartsev is faced with a number of readers competing for control over the interpretation and/or content of his text even before it exists.

Communists and anti-Communists are irreconcilable enemies according to the rigid ideological and political logic of the cold war, but Voinovich repeatedly points out the absurdities of this supposedly antagonistic relationship in *Moscow 2042*. During their Biergarten conversation, Bukashev expresses reservations to Kartsev about the Soviet system, thereby departing from the norm for his character type in the official literature. When Bukashev surprisingly reappears late in the novel as the "Genialissimo,"[31] the Stalin-like leader of the Moscowrep in 2042, his status as a representative of Soviet ideology is not merely invalidated but satirically inverted. Having been arrested and deposed as leader in the final days before a coup d'état led by Karnavalov, Bukashev reveals to Kartsev that he has actually been working to sabotage Communism irreparably from within even as he appeared to be its foremost practitioner:[32]

> "Do you remember our conversation in the English Garden?" asked my cell-mate.
> "Do I ever!" I said. "I remember it very well. I even remember you saying you intended to build communism, but like your predecessors, you turned out to be a real utopian, a dreamer."
> "You're mistaken, you little fool!" he said, quite merry all of a sudden. "I didn't turn out to be a utopian. I *did* build communism." (400)[33]

When Kartsev incredulously replies that the intellectually and materially impoverished Moscowrep hardly embodies the ideal Communism he had envisioned, Bukashev replies that "when people start realizing their dreams in real life, when they start moving en masse towards a single goal, something like what you've seen here [in the Moscowrep] is always the result" (401). Kartsev points out that Bukashev is "speaking like a total anticommunist" to which he merely replies, "At last, you've guessed" (401). Even though Bukashev's dissent is phrased in terms of a binary relationship (in which every anti- needs its corollary pro-), the paradox in which the most devoted Communist is simultaneously the most devoted anti-Communist ultimately renders the cold war's ideological distinctions absurd.

The Moscowrep's institutional structure itself confounds the division between allies and enemies; in fact, its language and rituals serve to render almost all potentially significant distinctions meaningless. Upon his arrival in the Moscowrep, Kartsev makes a discovery while reading *Pravda* that demonstrates what passes for ideological refinement in the Moscowrep: "Under the name of the newspaper was a line to the effect that the paper was the organ of the Communist Party of State Security. Now I understood the abbreviation I had seen on one of the banners: KPGB. The Party had merged with the KGB" (137).[34] Although the party and the KGB are presumably already ideologically consistent with one another, such a merger blurs the distinction between a tool of the state and the state itself. If security is not only a responsibility of the state but also its raison d'être, the instinct for self-preservation at all costs will invariably override all state decisions, a common conclusion in dystopian fiction from *We* onward. In essence, this combination makes *explicit* what had been an *implicit* symbiotic relationship since the early years of the Soviet Union: the party used the KGB (and earlier the NKVD) to solidify its hold on power, and the KGB assured its own survival, individually and collectively, by doing the party's bidding.

The party's absorption of the KGB is somewhat irrelevant, in fact, since the oppositional framework of the CIA/KGB split has also become irrevocably muddled by 2042. Dzerzhin Gavrilovich Siromakhin, a major general in SECO,[35] the state security organ of the Moscowrep, explains the situation to a disbelieving Kartsev:

> "It's hard for you to make sense of it all. You're still new here. The thing is that SECO is entirely staffed by CIA agents."
>
> "Now listen," I said with anger, "why are you handing me that crap, if you'll pardon the expression. I'm aware that hostile agents could infiltrate SECO, but, if you want my opinion, saying SECO is CIA through-and-through is utter nonsense."
>
> "Alas, you're still so naïve," said Dzerzhin, cunningly narrowing his eyes. "Unfortunately, what I just told you is not utter nonsense but the whole sad truth of it."
>
> The sad truth, in Siromakhin's telling, was that over the course of many years, the CIA had infiltrated SECO step by step. "It's like a cancer, you see," said Dzerzhin, adopting a scientific and instructional tone. "First the cells accumulate slowly. But when their number reaches a critical mass, they seize control of everything. It's the same with CIA agents. At first, they infiltrated one by one. But later on, when they were a majority in leadership, they seized control of everything. Now their impudence has reached a point where a cleaning woman can't be hired by SECO without Washington's permission." (296–97)

When a still-confused Kartsev asks Siromakhin why the army of the Moscow-rep has not simply expelled the CIA agents, Siromakhin's answer further confounds the binary logic: "Don't you see? If our army smashed SECO, the Americans would respond by smashing their CIA, which is entirely staffed by SECO people, and that wouldn't serve any purpose of ours" (297). Kartsev remains puzzled and finally asks Siromakhin, "If SECO is staffed with nothing but CIA, then which one are you with?" (297). His answer is simultaneously threatening and indicative of the paradoxes that such a question threatens to unleash: "Alright, my darling, let's get things straight once and for all. To avoid any possible problems, you are never to ask me any more questions like that, OK?" (298).[36]

The complete cross-infiltration of the two security apparatuses renders the Moscowrep's xenophobic geopolitical perspective even more nonsensical. Not long after his arrival, Kartsev is informed that "the communism which had been built in the greater Moscow area naturally elicited not only admiration, but also the envy of various elements of the population living outside of its bounds" (142). What results from this supposed envy is a tripartite system of "Rings of Hostility" that describe the world in terms of a slightly more elaborate us/them construction. Communi Ivanovich Smerchev, one of the government officials assigned to help Kartsev assimilate to his new surroundings, explains the system to him:

> Relations between the Communites and those living outside the
> boundaries of the Moscowrep were marked by a certain tension and
> even hostility, one which, as the Genialissimo had correctly observed,
> was ringlike in structure. The First Ring of Hostility was formed by
> the Soviet republics which the Communites called the filial republics,
> the Second Ring was composed of the fraternal socialist countries,
> and the Third by the Capitalist enemy.
>   "In formal parlance," explained Smerchev, "we call them the Filial
> Ring of Hostility, the Fraternal Ring of Hostility, and, of course, the
> Enemy Ring of Hostility. But most of the time we just say the First
> Ring, the Second, and the Third." (142)

The logical incongruity of phrases such as "Filial Ring of Hostility" reveals the absurdity of the isolationist position the Moscowrep has assumed, and again illustrates Sinyavsky's point about the ambiguity, if not outright paradox, of the Soviets' universalizing yet xenopohobic rhetoric. The contradictions also echo the rhetoric the Soviets used in "offering fraternal aid" while suppressing dissidence (and independence) in Eastern European satellite countries such as Hungary or Czechoslovakia. In essence, Voinovich's depiction of the Moscowrep's foreign relations is only a parodically exaggerated form of Soviet us/them logic. Even the supposedly "filial" and "fraternal" nations are also officially perceived as hostile simply because they lie outside the Moscowrep. The difference between the "filial republics" and the "capitalist enemy" has been reduced to a mere matter of degree.

Voinovich's satire is not just conducted on a geopolitical scale, however. He also consistently parodies everyday Soviet administrative language, both for its extensive use of needlessly bureaucratic euphemism (a toilet, for example, has become a "natfunctbur,"[37] short for "Bureau of Natural Functions" [135]) and for its necessary role in masking the flaws in the system. All citizens of the Moscowrep are required to turn in their "secondary matter" (feces) in order to receive governmental coupons redeemable for proportional amounts of "primary matter" (food), including the oxymoronically named "vegetarian pork." Although Kartsev's description of the food he is served makes distinguishing between it and "secondary matter" difficult,[38] the system is inherently ridiculous because of the need for "primary matter" in the production of "secondary matter" (and vice versa) in the first place. As Clowes points out, the causal distinction between "primary" and "secondary" is rendered irrelevant, as in the relationship between chicken and egg (52). Voinovich engages in a Rabelaisian parody of the "From each according to his ability, to each according to his need" credo of Soviet socialism, since need and ability in this context refer solely to excretory function rather than labor productivity. Ultimately the entire novel illustrates Bukashev's assertion that "it's much more difficult to convince one individual of an idiotic idea than an entire people" (403). Communism's utopian goal of achieving a seemingly perfect society, represented in the comically idyllic dream that Kartsev has shortly after arriving in the Moscowrep, is that "idiotic idea."

The conclusion to Kartsev's journey undermines any notion that Voinovich's satire is suggesting a normative solution that would simply return Russia to its prerevolutionary state. When Karnavalov triumphantly returns to the city and assumes power, he wastes little time instituting a neo-tsarist regime that becomes as socially repressive as the Moscowrep. He issues edicts (*ukazy*) that seek to control nearly every aspect of life, many of which hearken all the way back to the conservative society of pre-Petrine Russia (an edict "making it mandatory for all men forty and over to have beards" [407]).[39] Ironically many of his decrees echo policies enacted by the Bolsheviks in the early years of the Soviet Union. For example, like the Communists in 1917, he refuses to honor foreign debts incurred by the prior regime. Likewise his demand for universal conversion to Russian Orthodoxy is every bit as inflexible as the Soviet demands for total ideological uniformity from the late 1920s and 1930s. Finally, in a clear linguistic and historical parody of Soviet practice, Karnavalov decrees that all property now belongs to "His Majesty" and is "to be distributed free of charge by social committees to individuals capable of productive labor and who had avoided collaborating with the predatory communists" (407).

Karnavalov, though, does not limit himself to adopting the language and policies of the Moscowrep (even as he anathematizes them) but even adapts certain portions of the old regime's infrastructure to meet his needs, as stated in his "Imperial Proclamation": "The former organ of state security (SECO) is to be transformed into the Committee on National Peace (CNP)" (405). Like the Cheka, the political police in the early years of the Soviet Union, the CNP also has an "emergency board"[40] that carries out its most repressive actions, apparently including copious executions. The transformation from SECO to CNP is in reality little more than a name change, since this committee's primary task is to enforce ruthlessly Karnavalov's dictatorial edicts under the euphemistic guise of providing national peace. Although Karnavalov's minions are rounding up and summarily executing other former Moscowrep officials, Siromakhin is allowed to keep his position in the secret police because he claims "they need specialists like me. Any regime does. No matter what kind of revolution you make, you have to have something to protect it with after. And who's going to do that? We are. Any individual can be replaced but you can't replace all of us at the same time" (409).[41] Despite the allegedly new political situation, Siromakhin coyly refuses to answer Kartsev's question of whether or not he is still working for the CIA, thereby implying that the larger geopolitical status quo will continue unchanged as well.

Like the essentially cosmetic transition from the Great Python to Hermit in *Rabbits and Boa Constrictors*, the lack of substantive difference between the Moscowrep and Karnavalov's neo-tsarist state reinforces the notion that nothing has really changed except the superficial form and language of the rulers. The underlying rhetoric of the state remains suffused with exclusionary binaries and thus bodes another cycle of repression and violence for its citizens. *Moscow 2042* thus presents a serially dystopian society that will never truly change for the better until it discovers a genuinely subversive alternative. Voinovich's satirical depiction of nearly *all* the competing societal models of the cold war implies that he believes such an alternative has not yet been formulated. In some ways, Voinovich is like Bukashev in that he has exposed the absurdity of the system but cannot (or will not) provide a definitive model of his own with which to replace it. The narrative and ontological instability of the novel itself hints both at his reluctance to unequivocally propose such an alternative—perhaps wanting not to resemble Karnavalov—and at the difficulty of doing so.

Other roughly contemporary anti-utopian works, such as Iskander's *Goatibex Constellation*, Tertz's *Makepeace Experiment*, and the Strugatskys' *Skazka o troike* (1968; *Tale of a Troika*) and *Gadkie lebedi* (1972; *The Ugly Swans*), similarly treat the theme of utopianism as a weakness that can and will be exploited by those seeking to impose their will on others.[42] The recurrent subversion of various forms of grandiosely idealistic rhetoric indicates the degree to which official language during the cold war was subject to cynicism or outright disbelief. As the cold war progressed and the nuclear arms race augmented humanity's ability to destroy itself, this cynicism manifested itself with increasing regularity in works that fused satire, parody, antiutopianism, and apocalypticism to depict societies that were fundamentally diseased and deformed by the deliberate use of fabricated and fallacious language.

5

Totalized Distortions
and Fabrications

"Is It O.K. to Be a Luddite?": *Technology,*
Dehumanization, and Resistance

In late October 1984, Pynchon published a brief piece in the *New York Times Book Review* titled "Is It O.K. to Be a Luddite?" in which he discusses (among other things) his misgivings about the influence of the military-industrial complex on the society and government of the United States. This essay marked Pynchon's first public commentary on the state of the world since the publication of *Gravity's Rainbow,* his controversial magnum opus, in 1973. His essay appeared as a number of historians and journalists were declaring the arrival of "the second Cold War," a position premised on the notion that détente was a fundamental departure from the geopolitical dynamics of the cold war. Pynchon disputes this view, arguing that the social, economic, and governmental forces that created the cold war in the first place had been consistently functioning ever since.

The ostensible occasion for Pynchon's essay is the twenty-fifth anniversary of C. P. Snow's lecture "The Two Cultures and the Scientific Revolution." For Pynchon this address was "notable for its warning that intellectual life in the West was becoming increasingly polarized into 'literary' and 'scientific' factions, each doomed not to understand or appreciate the other." Although Pynchon claims that the ubiquity of technology and "information" had, for better or worse, rendered this distinction largely meaningless by 1984, he felt compelled to address Snow's "immoderate, and thus celebrated, assertion" that "literary intellectuals" were both resistant to and incapable of understanding the Industrial Revolution and were thus "natural Luddites" (Pynchon, "Is It O.K.?" 1). Pynchon wryly recites the origins and history of the Luddite movement and argues that Mary Shelley's *Frankenstein* is a quintessentially Luddite novel because it attempts, "through literary means which are nocturnal and deal in disguise, to deny the machine" (41).

While Pynchon never directly refers to his own fictions in answering the rhetorical question that appears in the essay's title, he discusses a series of themes that recur in his three prior novels. He also replies to his critics by defending the right to disapprove of and even to subvert the existing social system. He argues that those who stand to gain the most from the status quo are the same ones who attempt to use their attendant control over language to marginalize those "literary intellectuals" who oppose it: "The idea of a tech-nosocial 'revolution,' in which the same people came out on top as in France and America, has proven of use to many over the years, not least to those who, like C. P. Snow, have thought that in 'Luddite' they have discovered a way to call those with whom they disagree both politically reactionary and anti-capitalist at the same time" (41). Pynchon's reclamation of the Luddite moniker directly enters literary discourse when he argues against the ways in which those "people who came out on top" deprecate literary dissidence: "But if we do insist upon fictional violations of the laws of nature—of space, time, thermodynamics, and the big one, mortality itself—then we risk being judged by the literary mainstream as Insufficiently Serious. . . . The Gothic attitude in general, because it used images of death and ghostly survival toward no more responsible end than special effects and cheap thrills, was judged not Serious enough and confined to its own part of town. It is not the only neighborhood in the great City of Literature so, let us say, closely defined. In westerns, the good people always win. In romance novels, love conquers all. In whodunitsses we know better. We say, 'But the world isn't like that.' These genres, by insisting on what is contrary to fact, fail to be Serious enough, and so they get redlined under the label 'escapist fare'" (41). Pynchon not only endorses a quasi-Luddite sensibility but also challenges the belief that opposing "fact" is either irrational or irrelevant, mostly because he doubts the origins of such presumed truths.

Pynchon explicitly connects such critically disregarded genres with politi-cal opposition during the cold war: "This is especially unfortunate in the case of science fiction, in which the decade after Hiroshima saw one of the most remarkable flowerings of literary talent and, quite often, genius, in our his-tory. It was just as important as the Beat movement going on at the same time, certainly more important than mainstream fiction, which with only a few exceptions had been paralyzed by the political climate of the cold war and McCarthy years" (41). He avers that science fiction, which he defines expan-sively enough to presumably encompass his own works, represents a syn-thesis of the two cultures that Snow counterposed. As such it became "one of the principal refuges, in our time, for those of Luddite persuasion" (41). Pynchon views science fiction as an ideal medium for writers in an anxious age to express their concerns with and, more important, their dissent against the governing values of such an age.

He does not equivocate in identifying the source of cold war anxiety, link-ing it with the cultural milieu that spawned the original Luddites: "By 1945, the factory system—which, more than any piece of machinery, was the real and major result of the Industrial Revolution—had been extended to include the Manhattan Project, the German long-range rocket program and the death camps, such as Auschwitz. It has taken no major gift of prophecy to see how these three curves of development might plausibly converge, and before too long" (41). Each of "these three curves of development" appears either implicitly or explicitly in Pynchon's early novels. *Gravity's Rainbow* focuses on the Nazi V-2 rocket program, which Pynchon associates with both the atomic bomb and the Holocaust. The bombing of Hiroshima is mentioned in the course of the search for the mysterious Schwarzgerät, a secret Nazi rocket prototype that seems to promise near-mythic power to its wielder, thereby strengthening the leitmotif associating the V-2 rocket with an ICBM: "We must also never forget famous Missouri Mason Harry Truman: sitting by virtue of death in office, this very August 1945, with his control finger poised right on Miss Enola Gay's atomic clit, ready to tickle 100,000 little yellow folks into what will come down as a fine vapor-deposit of fat-cracklings wrinkled into the fused rubble of their city on the Inland Sea" (Pynchon, *Gravity's Rainbow* 588).

The Holocaust figures prominently in the novel's background, both through the omnipresence of IG Farben (whose well-documented use of slave labor and production of poison gas inextricably link it with the Holocaust) and through the setting of the Dora forced-labor camp infamously attached to the rocket production complex at Nordhausen. Pynchon alludes to the Holocaust in *V.* as well. Herbert Stencil, the narrator of the section titled "Mondaugen's Story," points out that German troops attempting to subjugate the native Herero population of Südwestafrika in 1904 claimed sixty thousand lives.[1] Being aware of later German atrocities, Stencil blithely notes that this is "only 1 per cent of six million, but still pretty good" (*V.* 245).

To Pynchon the cold war and its accompanying threat of nuclear annihilation are a clear signal that the convergence of the three curves is ongoing, perhaps even accelerating: "Since Hiroshima, we have watched nuclear weapons multiply out of control, and delivery systems acquire, for global purposes, unlimited range and accuracy. An unblinking acceptance of a holocaust running to seven- and eight-figure body counts has become—among those who, particularly since 1980, have been guiding our military policies—conventional wisdom" (41). He believes this "conventional wisdom" was opposed by "the people who were writing science fiction in the 50's" and ascribes a neo-Luddite worldview to such authors: "In the science fiction of the Atomic Age and the cold war, we see the Luddite impulse to deny the machine taking a different direction. The hardware angle got de-emphasized in favor of more humanistic concerns—exotic cultural evolutions and social scenarios, paradoxes and games with space/time, wild philosophical questions—most of it sharing, as the critical literature has amply discussed, a definition of 'human' as particularly distinguished from 'machine'" (41).

The list of themes he enumerates practically summarizes Vonnegut's oeuvre dating back to *Player Piano,* one of the quintessential post–World War II "Luddite" novels. Pynchon's own fiction, and that of many of his fellow subversive satirists of the 1960s and 1970s, clearly treats these kinds of "more humanistic concerns" as well. Although all Pynchon's works touch on themes of dehumanization and inanimacy, *V.* engages them most explicitly. The plot loosely centers around the gradual mechanization of the mysterious figure—an amalgamation of Virginia Woolf's *Orlando* and the Grim Reaper in her uncanny knack for appearing at scenes of violence and political intrigue—whose pseudonym gives the novel its title. Individual episodes further blur the line between humans and machines. The novel's ineffectual protagonist Benny Profane imagines having a conversation with a glorified crash-test dummy named SHROUD ("synthetic human, radiation output determined" [284]), during which the latter explains that there is little difference between the two of them (286).

Noting that the "word 'Luddite' continues to be applied with contempt to anyone with doubts about technology, especially the nuclear kind," Pynchon puts the question in his essay's title into the cultural context of 1984 by hearkening back once more to the cold war's early years: "As well-known President and unintentional Luddite D. D. Eisenhower prophesied when he left office, there is now a permanent power establishment of admirals, generals and corporate CEO's, up against whom us average poor bastards are completely outclassed, although Ike didn't put it quite that way" (41).[2] He claims that the tremendous power of what Eisenhower called the military-industrial complex had created a situation in which the only form of dissent possible is the kind of subversion symbolized by the historical Luddites and expressed by the kind of literature he describes in his essay. Although Pynchon limits the scope of his article to American society, his treatment of similar issues in *Gravity's Rainbow* suggests that he fully understands their global nature. Soviet government was, if anything, even more fully dominated by a military-industrial complex of a different nature (socialist rather than capitalist) but one that still siphoned off vast, and ultimately unaffordable, quantities of the nation's economic resources to fight both military and ideological wars. In the face of such a situation, Pynchon argues that not only is it "O.K." to be a Luddite, but it may even be vital to surviving the nuclear age.

"Peace Is Our Profession": *Science, Industry, and the Military Working Together*

Published only months before "Is It O.K. to Be a Luddite?," Jacques Derrida's article "No Apocalypse, Not Now" examines the relationship between language and nuclear war. He claims that "the growing multiplication of the discourse—indeed, of the literature, on this subject" has created a world in which nuclear war can be perceived as "a pure invention: in the sense in which it is said that a myth, an image, a fiction, a utopia, a rhetorical figure, a fantasy, a phantasm, are inventions" (23). In likening the potential annihilation of humanity with literary creations, Derrida does not intend to diminish the gravity of the nuclear threat; rather, he hopes to expose the immense power contained within the language used to defend the policies the cold war. Referring to the contemporary linguistic landscape as a site of "fearful domestication, the anticipatory assimilation of that entirely unanticipatable entirely-other,"[3] he repeatedly identifies nuclear discourse as a quasi-literary construct: "You will perhaps find it shocking to find the nuclear issue reduced to a fable, but then I haven't simply said that. I have recalled that a nuclear war is for the time being a fable, that is, something one can only talk about. But who can fail to recognize the massive 'reality' of nuclear weaponry and of the terrible forces of destruction that are being stockpiled and capitalized everywhere, that are coming to constitute the very movement of capitalization. One has to distinguish between this 'reality' of the nuclear age and the fiction of war" (23).

J. Fisher Solomon's gloss of Derrida provides a useful starting point for discussing the ways in which cold war authors criticize the scientific and pseudoscientific rhetoric that promoted the political and economic goals of the cold war. Solomon writes: "Derrida presents us with two peculiarly interrelated phenomena. . . . On the one hand, we have the historical 'reality' of a nuclear arms race; on the other we have a 'fabulous' representation of a war that has never happened. But the two are difficult to separate from each other, for the 'reality' of the arms race has itself been predicated upon the 'fiction' of the war. Our nuclear stockpile has been stockpiled in the *name* of the war, and in the name of deterring that war" (22–23). This interpretation resonates with Chris Hables Gray's contention that "fallacious ['gaps'] . . . helped to create and elaborate the nuclear arsenal of the United States" (152), a subject satirized at the end of *Dr. Strangelove* by General Turgidson's wildly patriotic and absurdly self-serving warning against the possibility of "a mine shaft gap." It also informs Stephen Miller's argument that the "military-industrial complex was able to re-use the dire good-versus-evil confrontation of World War II . . . [to create] a prevalent illusory world outlook that, with the Soviet Union's explosion of its first atomic bomb in 1949, was paradoxically predicated on the 'bottom line' need to prevent the world's nuclear destruction through the stockpiling of thermonuclear devices and the unacknowledged public works project of defense spending" (44). Each of these views suggest that nuclear reality is founded upon "fabulous," "fallacious," and "illusory" language. Gray and Miller explicitly add the concomitant qualification that this manufactured reality specifically benefits a select group of powerful individuals, a situation rife with potential for abuse (and thus also satire).

As Solomon notes, an even greater problem of this deliberate intermingling of fiction and reality is the resultant loss of meaning, especially in the case of scientific knowledge:

> There is nothing but *doxa,* opinion, "belief'" in the face of the nuclear referent, Derrida suggests, because one "can no longer oppose belief and science, *doxa* and *épistémè,* once one has reached the decisive place of the nuclear age. . . ." For in "this critical place, there is no more room for a distinction between belief and science . . . nor even for a truth in that sense." . . .
>
> Perhaps, in the practical pragmatic sense, this is the most disturbing of Derrida's nuclear aporias, because it essentially undermines the objective, scientific claims of every voice in the nuclear debate. Whose "belief" could claim "truth," and upon what basis? How could we test the relative merits of our various speculations? (23)

Satirists like Pynchon answered such questions by insisting that the beliefs of those with a political or economic stake in the immutability[4] of the cold war were the ones afforded the status of truth. This was the case not necessarily because these beliefs were true, but because these powerful stakeholders could impose their truth-values on others, either through overt coercion or through more insidious subterfuge, such as the deliberate distortion of language.

Given the increasingly interconnected nature of government, the military, and science during and after the Manhattan Project, it comes as no surprise that one of the most frequent forms of such linguistic distortion is the use of scientific or scientific-sounding rhetoric to create a semblance of validation for policies beneficial to an existing power structure. Instances in which scientific language was mobilized to provide validation for cold war policy are plentiful, but few are as clear-cut as the development of "deterrence" as the guiding principle of U.S.-Soviet nuclear policy. As both superpowers rapidly expanded their nuclear arsenals throughout the 1950s and early 1960s, the viability of civil defense strategies became increasingly suspect.[5] U.S. policy gradually shifted away from plans for surviving an attack toward maintaining a "balance of terror" (a phrase coined by RAND Corporation strategist Albert Wohlstetter in 1954) that would theoretically prevent attack, since neither side would want to risk touching off a war that led to complete commitment of the other's atomic arsenal.

In *Fallout* Boyer discusses the evolution of "the arcane reassurance of nuclear strategy": "From 1945 to 1950, and continuing into John Foster Dulles's term as secretary of state, atomic strategy as practiced in Washington was a fairly simple (if often unnerving) matter. By the 1960's, however, it had become a highly specialized pursuit dominated by a small group of civilian experts under contract to the military and based at semiautonomous research institutes at larger universities or at such 'think tanks' as the Institute for Defense Analysis, the System Development Corporation, the Center for Naval Analysis, the Research Analysis Corporation, and the RAND Corporation" (117). He goes on to state that "only the dimmest awareness—analogous, perhaps, to a medieval peasant's grasp of the theological concepts with which monastic scholars like St. Thomas Aquinas wrestled—filtered beyond the walls of the institutes and think tanks" (117–18). As Gray notes in *Postmodern War,* the highly specialized forms of knowledge required to comprehend the work of these think tanks included the following: "scenario writing, heuristic programming, computer modeling, linear programming, dynamic programming, problems scheduling, nonlinear programming, [and] the Monte Carlo method" (152). All of these techniques are "borrowed directly or metaphorically from computer science . . . [and] are all ways of simulating (gaming, predicting, calculating) possible futures so as to justify constructing one in particular" (152). Since computer science was a field of inquiry limited to an even smaller set of individuals in the 1960s than today, the direct advisory influence of these modeling techniques on important foreign policy decisions placed an enormous amount of control in the hands of a highly select core group of intellectuals.[6] Their objectivity is called into question not only by Gray's implication that the data these individuals produced were designed to justify a favorable outcome, but also by the staggering amounts of money the government was willing to spend on nuclear weapons research, development, and strategy based on their largely speculative models.

As intellectually inaccessible as the strategists' mathematical projections were to the average citizen, the deliberate *physical* inaccessibility of information prevented even a rudimentary technical understanding of nuclear energy from developing among the populace. Starting with the Atomic Energy Act of 1946, which explicitly classified "any information related to the design, manufacture, or utilization of atomic weapons, the production of enriched uranium or plutonium, or the use of those materials for the production of energy" (Hilgartner, Bell, and O'Connor 62), the actual science behind nuclear energy and weaponry was known to only a handful of experts given security clearance. As David Holloway elaborately details in his *Stalin and the Bomb: The Soviet Union and Atomic Energy, 1939–1956* (1994), the nuclear elite in the Soviet Union was a similarly select and isolated group. Few ordinary citizens in either country understood even the basics of nuclear science, even though its ramifications affected nearly everyone on the planet. This situation enabled propaganda in both the United States and Soviet Union that overplayed the military threat of the enemy's arsenal while simultaneously lauding the merits of nuclear energy, but without fully disclosing possible risks or environmental side effects.[7]

As Boyer notes, the exclusive nature of nuclear knowledge struck many observers as patently undemocratic: "As early as 1959, Robert M. Hutchins questioned whether democratic theory retained much relevance in the new era of strategic planning, and similar questions gained force in succeeding years. In the mid-1960s, the political scientist Hans Morgenthau stated: 'The great issues of nuclear strategy . . . cannot even be the subject of meaningful debate . . . because there can be no competent judgments without meaningful knowledge. Thus, the great national decisions of life or death are rendered by the technological élites, and both Congress and the people retain little more than the illusion of making the decisions which the theory of democracy supposes them to make'" (118).

Morgenthau's comments echo Maltby's point about "conceptually impoverished discourses that impede critical reflection on society."[8] And indeed the un- or perhaps even *anti*democratic nature of this new policy-making process was inherently absurd, since its oft-intoned goal was the defense of democracy from totalitarian Communism. The sense that the strategists, and the military their projections helped support, might have plans for creating a de facto government of their own is echoed in General Ripper's chilling remark in *Dr. Strangelove* that politicians "have neither the time, the training, nor the inclination for strategic thought." The potential for undue influence by the military in national affairs was hardly a paranoid fantasy in a country that at the time of *Dr. Strangelove*'s release had only recently retired a former five-star general as president and was less than a decade removed from a divisive struggle of wills between President Truman and Gen. George MacArthur over military tactics, especially those concerning the use of nuclear weapons, in the Korean War.

Satirical depictions of the undesirable interlacing of the military, big business, and politics are plentiful in cold war fiction. The furious pursuit of the Schwarzgerät in *Gravity's Rainbow*, for example, is used to symbolize and satirize the drive for dominance over the post–World War II environment by forces ranging from the victorious Allied governments, multinational corporations like IG Farben and Standard Oil, and a motley assortment of lesser players (as well as tenuous and mutable coalitions within and among these groups). The narrator even reminds the reader that "the real business of the War is buying and selling," a process that occurs on a number of levels: "The true war is a celebration of markets. Organic markets, carefully styled 'black' by the professionals, spring up everywhere. Scrip, Sterling, Reichsmarks continue to move, severe as classical ballet, inside their antiseptic marble chambers. But out here, down among the people, the truer currencies come into being. So, Jews are negotiable. Every bit as negotiable as cigarettes, cunt, or Hershey bars" (105).

Pynchon's mordant tone serves not only to transmit his sense of outrage, but also to point out the dehumanization inherent in perceiving equivalence among the "currencies" he mentions. Foodstuffs and luxuries are commodified to the same degree as humans, who are described in an exploitative context based either on sexual synecdoche ("cunt") or power imbalance (Jews in Nazi Germany). In *The Fictional Labyrinths of Thomas Pynchon* (1988), David Seed maintains that this reduction of humans "to the same level as information—mere items in business transactions" speaks to Pynchon's larger critique of the interconnection of industry and politics: "Pynchon takes as his prime example of big business in action the German multinational I. G. [*sic*] Farben which he repeatedly links with arms manufacture. We are never allowed to separate the V-rocket from its commercial matrix (supported by I. G.) nor to view I. G. as a non-political institution" (192). By focusing its subversive satire not just on IG Farben but on the philosophy that the company and its collaborators represented, *Gravity's Rainbow* forcefully cautions against allowing the distorted truths of any military, industrial, and political cartels to go unquestioned.

Perhaps more than any other institution in U.S. culture, The RAND Corporation exemplifies such a cartel, and Herman Kahn is among the most noteworthy of its strategists. Because of his high public profile Kahn was the first among what Oak Ridge National Laboratory director Alvin Weinberg called the "technological priesthood" (quoted in Hilgartner, Bell, and O'Connor 58) to be satirized individually. In 1961 Kahn published *On Thermonuclear War*, a work that used extensive statistical modeling to postulate a variety of "Tragic but Distinguishable Postwar States" based on such factors as civilian casualties and the time required for total "economic recuperation" (Kahn 20). Kahn acknowledges that any nuclear war would be a disaster but adds that, in his opinion, "poor [civil defense] planning" could lead to "an additional disaster, an *unnecessary* disaster that is almost as bad as the original disaster" (20–21). He maintains that "normal and happy lives for the majority of survivors and their dependents" are not out of the realm of the possible, despite the increased "amount of human tragedy . . . in the postwar world," provided that the appropriate preparations are made (21).

Kahn also was a leading proponent of what became known as "escalation theory," a concept intended to reduce the potential for all-out nuclear war by interpolating a number of gradual steps by which conflict could be intensified (and presumably settled) prior to full nuclear commitment. Kahn's ideas also helped spur the adoption of Mutual Assured Destruction (MAD), a strategic doctrine that achieves absolute deterrence through the explicit reciprocal threat of massive and complete retaliation for any form of nuclear attack. This doctrine subsequently informed (at least in public announcements) such bilateral nuclear agreements as the Strategic Arms Limitation Treaty (SALT I) and the Anti-Ballistic Missile Treaty (ABM Treaty), both signed in 1972. Thus while not himself an elected or appointed governmental official, Kahn shaped many of the operative concepts of U.S. nuclear diplomacy.

In addition to providing a framework for international relations, deterrence and escalation theory provided good domestic public relations cover for continuing or even accelerating the nuclear arms race. The reality of weapons research and development (a top secret matter in both the United States and Soviet Union) was vastly different than the public language of treaty making, a dissonance that undercuts the perception of two discontinuous cold wars separated by détente. In his outspoken objection to Soviet ABM research (despite their understandable interest in such technology, given an American warhead superiority of six to one as of 1964), Robert McNamara claimed that an effective ABM system would upset the MAD-maintained equilibrium by eliminating the deterrent consequences of launching a preemptive first strike. Despite this public cry of foul, the largely covert U.S. strategic response to Soviet ABM research (in addition to studying the possibility of producing their own ABM system)[9] was to concentrate on developing multiple independently targetable reentry vehicles (MIRVs) that could deliver up to sixteen warheads from one rocket. MIRVs ultimately proved to be a considerably more feasible and unbalancing concept than ABMs and sparked another stage of rapid acceleration in the arms race. The ABM Treaty guaranteed that "each nation must remain vulnerable to the other side's missiles," thus upholding the "mutual suicide pact [that] had become the Golden Rule of deterrence theory" (M. Moore 22). The reality behind this MAD reasoning, though, was that the mere *potential* for destabilization attributed to wholly unrealized ABM systems had resulted in the very real development of MIRVs,[10] in the process illustrating Derrida's notion of the nuclear arms race as a self-actualizing fiction.

Whatever Kahn's original intention, his strategic models, themselves predicated almost entirely on hypothetical statistical modeling and vaguely referenced "objective studies" (21), almost immediately became fodder for satire, first in *Fail-Safe* and not long thereafter in *Dr. Strangelove*. Eugene Burdick and Harvey Wheeler satirize Kahn in a wholly uncomic manner in *Fail-Safe*, putting his ideas almost word for word into the mouth of Professor Groteschele, a presidential adviser. Groteschele is an emotionally frigid demagogue who prides himself on the fact that he has "provided a respectable language and theory within which the 'first strike' or 'preemptive war' could be discussed" (113). From his first appearance Groteschele espouses opinions clearly intended to evoke Kahn; Groteschele's standing as a strategic adviser, for example, is based primarily on a book, *Counter-Escalation*, the thesis of which he summarizes during a meeting with high-ranking Pentagon officials:

> He reviewed alternative theories of modern thermonuclear war and, with all the deliberateness of a machine gunner, shredded them to pieces. . . .
>
> Without smiling, using his new vocabulary, he presented the alternative of the United States striking first. However, he never quite used those words. He took the people around the table to the edge of the

abyss, forced them to look over the edge. Then, his language still cold, he described a situation in which the abyss was not threatening, but was in fact a magnificent and glowing opportunity. (115–16)

His presentation is a rousing success and he quickly becomes a voice of unquestioned authority on matters atomic, both in military circles and in the mass media: "Groteschele knew that he was regarded as a magician. The awesome powers on which he was expert, the facts of life and death and survival, the new cabalistic language of the nuclear philosophers and high scientists, were merely matters of fact. But the layman, the rich socialite, the industrialist, the politician, endowed Groteschele with *control* of the things he described" (118). This passage echoes Boyer in emphasizing the "cabalistic" nature of Groteschele's vocabulary and knowledge, while it also makes explicit the potential for power (that is, control) inherent in creating and manipulating such "respectable" language.

Throughout the novel Groteschele justifies nuclear war through his fervent anti-Communism. When informed of an impending attack (inadvertently triggered by a computer malfunction) on the Soviet Union by a squadron of nuclear bombers, Groteschele urges the president to seize the opportunity to rout Communism: "Group 6, however its accident happened, has provided a God-given opportunity. One of our groups is well launched toward Russia with a reasonable chance for success. I am convinced that the moment the Russians realize that, they will surrender. . . . Group 6 has given us a fantastic historic advantage. By accident, they have forced us into making the first move, the move that we would never have made deliberately" (185). Rejecting Groteschele's entreaties, the president attempts to ward off a full nuclear war by offering to destroy New York to balance the unintended destruction of Moscow, spurring Groteschele to lament the effects this action will have on his prospects for continued employment:

> Groteschele thought of his future. If both Moscow and New York were destroyed it would be the end of his present career. After such a catastrophe . . . the world would not tolerate further discussion and preparation for nuclear war. . . .
>
> For a moment he felt a pang of theoretical regret. He really would have liked to see the thermonuclear war fought out along the lines which he had debated, expounded, and contemplated. It was not true, he told himself, that one fears death more than anything. One might be willing to die to see one's ideas proven. (270–71)

Not just Groteschele's almost mechanical lack of emotion—even his regret is theoretical—but his unwillingness to put the reality of human suffering ahead of his theory ultimately undermines his ideas. Any sense that he might be chastened by this experience, should he survive, is dashed by the final thought attributed to him in the novel: "Then Groteschele swung his attention to what his future work would be. If there were drastic cutbacks in military expenditures many businesses would be seriously affected; some of them would even be ruined. A man who understood government and big political movements could make a comfortable living advising the threatened industries. It was a sound idea, and Groteschele tucked it away in his mind with a sense of reassurance" (271). Confronted with his culpability in the deaths of tens of millions of people, Groteschele comforts himself with the promise of a "comfortable living" (compare Kahn's "normal and happy lives" above), one that seems to be based on his far-reaching personal connections within the military-industrial complex.

In his self-serving willingness to risk everything in opposing Communism, Groteschele becomes a satirical exemplar of the norm in U.S. politics circa 1960. While hardly radical in their opposition to this norm, General Black and the President, the novel's two most likable characters, nevertheless represent a more reasoned and sympathetic position. However, their relative sagacity only limits the destruction rather that forestalling it entirely. They are each ultimately forced to annihilate New York in order to prevent all-out nuclear war. This decision is both personally and societally tragic, as both the president's wife and Black's family are visiting New York the day the city is destroyed by a bomb dropped from a plane that Black pilots. Groteschele, on the other hand, ponders his family's fate in nearby Scarsdale briefly, and only "because he had always heard that in emergencies men thought of their families" (270). This sacrifice emphasizes the great potential for disaster inherent in even the most enlightened nuclear policies, much less those of an unfeeling technocrat like Groteschele.

The novel's resolution presents a best-case scenario for a nuclear engagement within an escalation-based paradigm, largely because the novel's crisis arises not because of an emotionally charged military showdown but because of a mechanical failure, something Groteschele repeatedly asserts "is almost impossible" even as the evidence for it becomes incontrovertible (178). Moreover the president's philosophical depth and the Soviets' trustfulness under duress differ markedly from the brinksmanship displayed by both sides during the Cuban Missile Crisis, which occurred only months after *Fail-Safe* was published. The somber ending suggests that setting the distorted logic of escalation theory into motion inevitably leads to monstrous tragedy, no matter how "limited" its scope of destruction.

Dr. Strangelove satirically treats the intentional obfuscation inherent in cold war rhetoric in a manner simultaneously more grim and more comic than *Fail-Safe*. Kubrick's film adopts a more totalized satirical perspective in subverting some of the same factors that actually limit the catastrophe in *Fail-Safe*—in essence, it parodies the nonsatirical elements of *Fail-Safe*. The mechanism of checks and balances still works well enough to prevent complete destruction in *Fail-Safe,* but the nuclear apocalypse at the end of *Dr. Strange-love* is (to use General Turgidson's euphemism) largely the result of a series of a series of "slip-up[s]" implicating science, politics, and the military in equal measure. These mistakes include the following: General Ripper's insanely extremist anti-Communist politics (which, as the president complains, should have been screened out by the "human reliability tests" required of all nuclear personnel); the loophole in "Attack Plan R" that allows Ripper to order a nuclear attack on the Soviet Union without the usual presidential approval; Premier Kissof's vanity in delaying the revelation of the Doomsday Machine's existence until the more politically expedient occasion of the Party Congress; Kissof's licentious impetuosity at the time of the incident; Colonel "Bat" Guano's dim-witted detainment of Captain Mandrake, which causes a critical delay in transmitting the abort code to the bombers; the disabling of the "CRM 114" encoding device (the sole piece of machinery needed to receive a valid "abort" message) aboard Major Kong's B-52 by a missile intended to shoot the plane down; and even Major Kong's extraordinary and unfortunate resourcefulness in performing his duty to the letter.

President Muffley, General Turgidson, and Premier Kissof, furthermore, are all parodies of their comparatively sagacious counterparts in *Fail-Safe,* and it is largely as a result of their ineptitude, both within and prior to the time frame of the film, that the world ends. To the last both Turgidson and Strangelove espouse strategies derived from Kahn's works,[11] as exemplified by the final dialogue of the film, in which Dr. Strangelove explains to the assembled crowd in the War Room how a small remnant of American society could be preserved in mineshaft shelters.[12] Whereas *Fail-Safe* criticizes the conventional wisdom of the cold war for relying on absolutely optimal conditions to deter complete annihilation, *Dr. Strangelove* exposes the ridiculousness of this logic by setting it in motion. Kubrick depicts a plausible though comically exaggerated scenario that causes the failure of all the supposed safeguards built into a system that insists that "Peace Is Our Profession," as billboards around Burpleson Air Force Base reassuringly state. Both *Fail-Safe* and *Dr. Strangelove* satirize the entire quasi-scientific logical structure of deterrence, especially the ways in which it privileges often ill-conceived and self-serving military concerns over all others to create an inhuman reality.

Although constrained by the dual factors of the backlash that followed in the wake of the Thaw and the high degree of secrecy regarding science in the Soviet Union, Russian writers also found occasion to denounce the deliberate distortion of scientific knowledge in the service of state propaganda. Works such as Tertz's *Makepeace Experiment* and Iskander's *Goatibex Constellation* that engaged in critiques of this sort sporadically appeared during the 1960s, but the former was published only in *tamizdat* in France, and the latter limited itself to a relatively mild mockery of agricultural science. On the other hand, *Our Golden Ironburg*, written in the early 1970s, but unpublished until after Aksyonov's emigration in 1980, is a much more caustic and far-reaching satire of intellectual corruption in Soviet science. Aksyonov parodies the "industrial novel" and "production novel"[13] genres in *Our Golden Ironburg*, but the manner in which he does so expands the scope of the parody to include Soviet governmental rhetoric.

The salient difference between *Our Golden Ironburg* and most of its satirical forerunners is that Aksyonov not only subverts his narrative through conventional literary parody but also metafictionally uses Memozov, a character identified explicitly as an "anti-author," to force Kitousov, the novel's putative "author," to alter his narrative whenever he lapses into the simple formulas of official Soviet literature. Indeed, Memozov nearly wrests control of the story from Kitousov entirely before being forced to flee near the end of the book. Memozov's subversive influence on both the plot details and the narrative style—elements the industrial novel inextricably links—from within the text itself helps call attention to the thorough aesthetic and logical debasement of the genre because of its heavy-handed, often nonsensical, expression of ideology. Much as Zinoviev used the absurdly large pants in *The Yawning Heights* on two levels of satirical signification, the scientific institute and surrounding city constructed in *Our Golden Ironburg* not only serve as satirical grotesques in and of themselves but also parody the historical creation of "towns of science" like Akademogorodok (literally, "Little Academic Town") near Novosibirsk in the 1950s.[14] Aksyonov's simultaneously aesthetic and political satire thus subverts the power of both the literary genre *and* the nonfictional elements of Soviet society that the genre attempts to glorify, namely, science and the industries it supports.

While some critics have interpreted Memozov as a negative presence (a target of Aksyonov's criticism rather than its instrument) because of his power to debilitate the narrative,[15] I concur with the more positive assessment of critics such as Stephan Kessler, Per Dalgård, and Nina Kolesnikoff, who see Memozov's effect on the novel as comparable to Aksyonov's own role within Russian literature. Dalgård contends that Memozov's "aim is to rouse brains by unorthodox means" (93), a task akin to DeLillo's desire to stave off "collective brain fade" in *White Noise* (see below). Kolesnikoff similarly argues that Memozov is an essential part of Aksyonov's parody of the industrial novel because he represents the stock character of the "internal enemy" (196) who must be overcome on the road to completion of the "heroic" feat of labor at hand (see also K. Clark 258). As both an aesthetic dissenter against official forms of literature and a political dissenter against the system that requires these forms, Aksyonov is, by Soviet standards, an "anti-author." Like Memozov, Aksyonov recognizes the patent falsity of the authorial stance required by Socialist Realism (or its somewhat diluted late-Soviet offshoots) and attempts to sabotage it wherever possible.

The "heroic" labor depicted in *Our Golden Ironburg* is the discovery of a mysterious subatomic particle called the "Double-Few,"[16] although none of the five intellectuals gathered together at the state-of-the-art scientific institute that has been built in Siberia especially for this purpose seems fully to comprehend their task. Even Veliky-Salazkin,[17] the leader of the group of scientists and the driving force behind the search for the particle, understands his research only in an abstract and even romanticized sense: "We really need your fairy, this accursed little particle Double-Few, not for admiration's sake, not for tickling our minds, but for the nations of the earth to use; and we'll catch her, this infection, and force her to do something—maybe treat malaria, maybe cut steaks, maybe—I'll let it out—try to inspire the creative act among the elderly population with it—in general, it won't be wasted!" (*Ironburg* 45–46). Even as he acknowledges that it may not exist (by calling it a "fairy") and reveals his ignorance of its nature, Veliky-Salazkin parodically echoes the rhetoric that extolled the "sunny side of the atom" in his complete faith that the Double-Few contains inherently positive power, whether as a cure for disease, as an aphrodisiac, or simply as a handy kitchen tool.

The novel's fragmented and meandering narrative ostensibly recounts the conception and construction of Ironburg (Zhelezka) and the surrounding town of Pikhty (literally, "fir trees"), as well as the collaborative search for the "Double-Few." The institute is named for a small piece of metal (*zhelezka* is a colloquial term for a piece of iron) found on the site—an island oddly covered in fir trees (hence the name of the town)—at the groundbreaking. Without any corroboration other than hearsay and his idiosyncratic interpretation of subsequent events, Kitousov claims that this fragment is the stove damper from an alien spacecraft that crash landed in Siberia in 1909 and was mistakenly declared to have been the mysterious Tunguska meteorite. This fabulous explanation is an important part of Aksyonov's satire, as it shows the absurd lengths to which Kitousov will go as an author to mythologize Ironburg. Memozov's presence disrupts both the work going on at Ironburg and Kitousov's attempts at shaping the accounts of this work in a manner consistent with the ideological genre conventions of the industrial novel.

Kitousov introduces himself anonymously and in the third person ("The author had to spend a lot of money in order to write this novel" [9]) and shows off his supposed ability to control the events of the novel in the prescribed fashion: "It was important for the author to fit a large group of future heroes into one airplane (they were returning from summer vacations), in order to develop a well-composed exposition by all the rules. He now expresses his thanks to Aeroflot because it was possible to do this without any special effort, and the author only had to use a little of his arbitrariness. Using force on a hero always depresses people, even in our (also) humane profession" (9). As soon as he spots Memozov in the airport, though, it rapidly becomes apparent that the author will indeed have to put forth some "special effort" to maintain his "well-composed exposition by all the rules." Describing Memozov as "his recent and unpleasant acquaintance . . . a young member of the 'avant-garde' who in the last few years had managed to breach his creative citadel three times" (10), the author scraps his plans to write a "calm, third-person narration" and instead "show[s] some cowardice, grab[s] for his tried and true weapon, the 'I' and [begins] to drone like the senior scientific worker Vadim Apollinarievich Kitousov, and at the same time in the first person" (10). This reidentified author/narrator then begins telling the story of Ironburg, all the while lapsing in and out of first person into a variety of different characters' perspectives. Aksyonov intentionally destabilizes the degree to which his narrator, primarily associated with Kitousov, can be seen as truly "omniscient." After all Kitousov is an ordinary human character *within* the narrative. This technique immediately begins the process of undermining monological narrative authority, a prerequisite of the industrial novel, indeed of most official Soviet literature.

Critics have tended to see Memozov's narrative intrusion, a process that ultimately results in the destruction of Ironburg entirely, as either a *reflection* of tight Soviet control over literary work or an exemplary rejection of such tight control. Proponents of the former view, such as Konstantin Kustanovich, generally cite Memozov's supposed defeat at the end of the novel[18] as Aksyonov's positive statement about the power of art (in this case, Kitousov's novel about Ironburg) to survive repression. This perspective is logically unsatisfactory because it ignores the parodic/satiric dimension of the novel and trustingly accepts Kitousov's version of reality as that which Aksyonov values. If, as I do, one reads the novel as a quasi-dystopian metafictional satire, Memozov's apparent defeat does not so much discredit his avant-gardism as point out the durability of simplified ideologies (cognitive schemata) that are constantly reinforced and reinscribed.

Taking issue explicitly with Kustanovich's argument, Kessler points out the fallacy in privileging Kitousov's perspective: "The mere existence of a real and dangerously avant-garde opponent—in the eyes of Kitousov—has upset the narrator's intention of maintaining distance and pursuing a quiet narrative. This is an intention that therefore does not seem avant-garde: conventional, ordinary, quiet—a typical production novel. It is therefore not correct that, as Kustanovich sees it, the position of the narrator ('author') contains a positive, affirmative valuation for the reader" (377).[19] Kessler's primary proof for this assertion lies in the fact that the negative depiction of Memozov stems from Kitousov, a narrator whose language is marked not only by frequent and often logically inappropriate recourse to "the language of the official Soviet propaganda as used in the media and in many industrial novels" (Kolesnikoff 199)[20] but also by academic-style footnotes and scientific formulas. Kessler points out that the garbled and seemingly arbitrary inclusion of these elements is merely form without content, since the formulas are incapable of conveying any information: "Footnotes and formulas constitute the novel together with the narrated events as parody, because both paratextual elements are normally characteristic of other genres and, moreover, are included in *Zolotaia nasha zhelezka* in a nonsensical fashion. As far as the formulas are concerned, despite their typographical appearance as potentially stemming from mathematics or physics, they are intrinsically nonsensical" (358). Any faith the reader may have in Kitousov's narration is thus shaken by these superficial attempts to make the novel appear consistent with "the rules" of the genre.

Even though the classic Soviet industrial novel was becoming obsolete by the early 1970s, Aksyonov's parody of its linguistic, logical, and ideological methodology in *Our Golden Ironburg* is so thorough that it becomes a satire of the fundamental values that originally shaped that genre. These values continued to define the Soviet Union up to and even to some extent through Gorbachev's reforms in the mid- to late 1980s, making Aksyonov's satire historically relevant to not only the earlier period when the industrial novel dominated Soviet literature[21] but also his own authorial present. As Clark points out, the neo-Stalinist tendencies of the Brezhnev era were an attempt to "rebuild a sense of pride in the Soviet past and present" and as such reaffirmed a number of "attitudes toward governance that were meant to have been discredited in the Khrushchev era" (237–38). The substantial fluctuation in the official estimation of Stalin in the two decades following his death helped undermine further trust in the pronouncements of the leadership, especially given the limited but nevertheless repugnant details about the "excesses" of his reign that were revealed during the Thaw. Aksyonov's parody of a predominantly Stalinist genre, then, also parodies Brezhnev's policies,[22] arguing that, like Kitousov's narrative, the Soviet Union of the later cold war period is governed through the use of inconsistent, dubious, or even wholly nonsensical logic. Implicit in such a position is the knowledge that this kind of logic has already led the country down a dour, bloody path before and has the potential to do so again.

Although both Khrushchev and Kennedy tempered their public attitudes toward nuclear weapons after the Cuban Missile Crisis, the reality of the arms race remained a highly volatile one that actually worsened despite a flurry of high-profile treaty signings in the ten years after Cuba: "In both the United States and the Soviet Union, nuclear weapons research, construction and deployment went forward rapidly after 1963. Taking advantage of the [1963] test ban treaty's gaping loophole, both sides developed sophisticated techniques of underground testing. The United States conducted more tests in the five years *after* 1963 than in the five years before, some involving weapons fifty times the size of the Hiroshima bomb" (Boyer, *Fallout* 113).

In short, even though the rhetoric of militarism had been scaled back somewhat in favor of "peaceful coexistence," preparation for and even execution of military conflict was still proceeding apace, a dissonance between word and deed that was a common feature of cold war politics in general (and thus a *locus* of subversive satirical potential). The increasing number of conflicts between superpower proxies in Southeast Asia, Africa, Central America, and elsewhere during détente allowed this particular "dissimulation of violence" to develop still further. The majority of these smaller "hot" wars were nominally predicated on the same Communism-versus-capitalism ideological dichotomy that defined the cold war, which the superpowers were allegedly now trying to resolve. The speciousness of this position vis-à-vis militarism was patently obvious to many writers whose faith in the system, American and/or Soviet, was already shaken. They collectively criticize the mindset that psychologist Erich Fromm catalogued in his book *The Anatomy of Human Destructiveness,* which posited that wars are "caused not by dammed-up aggression, but by instrumental aggression of the military and political elites" (quoted in Jones 198). Consequently their satires convey cynicism toward the military-industrial-scientific complexes of authority by identifying the absurdity and duplicity of the language and logic that they used to justify the cold war (and many of its "hot" adjuncts).

"Poetry is the art of subordinating facts to the imagination":
Cold War Pathology in the United States

Deterrence theory, "bad" science, and militarism, however, are not the only self-justifying behaviors that cold war satirists decry as injurious masks for political and economic self-interest. The final group of cold war satires that I will examine below exemplify Hutcheon's notion of historiographic metafiction in that they are "willing to draw upon any signifying practices [they] can find operative in a society. [They want] to challenge those discourses and yet to use them, even to milk them for all they are worth" (137). Whether having their characters perform before comic pantheons of celebrity/importance or trapping them within linguistic environments that are overstuffed to the point of nonsensicality, such works expose how *all* forms of masked fictionality are symptomatic of considerably more pervasive and dire cultural pathologies.

Robert Coover's *Public Burning* is perhaps the most exhaustive subversion of American cold war cultural attitudes. Coover not only accuses the U.S. political and social elite of violent and self-serving distortions of logic and language, he also implies that such behavior is omnipresent throughout the nation's history. Because of Coover's willingness to identify his satirical targets unambiguously, *The Public Burning* supersedes even *Giles Goat-Boy* as an unrestrained satire of cold war American culture. Barth's allegorical transformation of the cold war world into a university campus in *Giles Goat-Boy* allows him to satirize many of the institutional and rhetorical follies of both academic and political life, but his approach ultimately stops short of unambiguously indicting specific historical figures or institutions.[23] Coover retrospectively denounces the anti-Communist rhetoric of American politics during one of the cold war's earlier flashpoints, the execution of Julius and Ethel Rosenberg in June 1953, in order to satirize it in his own time, the mid-1970s. As Maltby notes, though, Coover's intentions are more expansive than simple satire of particular moments in American history: "The adversarial power of the book surely need not depend on a developed political analysis of recent American history. Rather, that power resides primarily in the novel's forceful deconstruction and de-mystification of the ruling historical narratives of cold war America" (100). This "deconstruction and de-mystification" is achieved by demonstrating the corrupting influence of the cold war's binary logic on an exceedingly eager recipient: Richard Milhous Nixon. By linking Nixon with the other "incarnations" of the voraciously nationalistic Uncle Sam, Coover sets up a critique that indicts the principles on which the nation was founded, or, more accurately, he satirizes the historical variance between these principles and the actual practice of the nation's power elites.

Although it was not published until 1977, the bulk of *The Public Burning* was composed while Nixon was still in the Oval Office, which encourages the association between Nixon's thoughts and actions as vice president (and as the narrator of most of the novel) in 1953 and those of Nixon as president in the late 1960s and early 1970s. As vice president Nixon is largely an outsider to the political intrigues that result in the Rosenbergs' executions; consequently his narration remains reportorial for most of the first half of novel. As the novel progresses and Nixon becomes more directly involved with Uncle Sam—Coover's larger-than-life satirical personification of American values and the ideological counterpart of the Phantom, whose name contains overtones of both menace and nonexistence—his role changes from that of observer to active participant and somewhat inept orchestrator of the events going on around him.

For most of the early chapters, Nixon is little more than a bit player in Eisenhower's government. He works diligently in his office and takes part in cabinet meetings, but Eisenhower is clearly in charge, as is made abundantly clear by a scene in which Ike and Nixon play golf. As they walk the course, Uncle Sam materializes physically ("he slipped out of his duffer's disguise" [83]), temporarily supplanting the personality of Eisenhower, into whom he has incarnated himself. As befits his relative omnipotence, Uncle Sam immediately hits a hole in one and asks Nixon's opinion on the Rosenberg case. Nixon's fumbling answer ("Well . . . well, I believe they're, uh, probably guilty" [85]) demonstrates his lack of understanding of the case's political exigencies. Uncle Sam incredulously responds, "Well, hell yes they're guilty!"; but Nixon says that he "resented what seemed like some kind of entrapment" and replies that, from what he's seen of the case transcripts, "the case has not been proven" (85).[24] Uncle Sam immediately attempts to make the reality of the situation clear by explaining that the legal proof against the Rosenbergs is subsidiary to the advantageous fiction their conviction will perpetuate:

"Hell, *all* courtroom testimony about the past is ipso facto and teetotaciously a baldface lie, ain't that so? Moonshine! Chicanery! The ole gum game! Like history itself—all more or less bunk, as Henry Ford liked to say, as saintly and wise a pup as this nation's seen since the Gold Rush—the fatal slantindicular futility of Fact! Appearances, my boy, appearances! Practical politics consists in ignorin' facts! *Opinion* ultimately governs the world!" (86).[25] Uncle Sam essentially asserts the same connection between persuasive public relations and effective governance upon which Hirshberg bases his patriotic schema. The premise that the Rosenbergs' trial is primarily a spectacle to improve American morale in the face of worldwide gains by the forces of the Phantom[26] remains in place throughout the rest of the book.

Retaining his lawyerly mindset, Nixon continues to misapprehend Uncle Sam. He simultaneously struggles with his golf game, a metaphorical association that underscores Nixon's ongoing difficulties in conforming to the values of the American ruling class despite his familiarity with their rhetoric.[27] Nixon's working-class, rural, Quaker upbringing in California did not involve learning how to play golf—an activity associated even more in the 1950s than today with the economic, social, and racial elites—making his lack of skill in the face of Uncle Sam / Eisenhower's prodigious five-iron shots even more of a contrast. As Nixon flails his way around the course, Uncle Sam explains the true nature of the "crime" of which the Rosenbergs are guilty in distinctly biblical, specifically Judaic terms: "They have walked in the spirit of perversity . . . violators of the Covenant, defilers of the sanctuary." Nixon finally takes the bait and finishes Uncle Sam's thought with a stock phrase of anti-Communist rhetoric: "*Sons of Darkness!*" (88). Coupled with Uncle Sam's identification of the "good guys [who] achieve peace and prosperity" as "Sons of Light" two pages later, Coover establishes a biblical/political dichotomy at the center of his cold war milieu and uses it to denounce fraudulent rhetoric that harnesses the power of religious language—but rarely its underlying ethics—to further political goals.

Coover does not limit himself to wholesale inventions of language to accomplish his satirical objectives in this regard. The novel contains three "Intermezzos" that incorporate actual quotes from the documentary record of the time and recasts them into recognizably literary forms. The first of these interstitial sections is laid out on the page as a lengthy poem (presumably an epic, given the grandeur of its title, "The War between the Sons of Light and the Sons of Darkness: The Vision of Dwight David Eisenhower") taken entirely from "*Public Papers of the Presidents,* January 20–June 19, 1953" (149). The latter two "Intermezzos" are even more elaborate recontextualizations of historical primary sources, one being a "Dramatic Dialogue by Ethel Rosenberg and Dwight Eisenhower" (247) and the other a "Last-Act Sing Sing Opera by Julius and Ethel Rosenberg" (381). This technique underscores Coover's belief in the inauthenticity, to use Iser's terminology, of the entire

proceeding against the Rosenbergs (and by extension American political rhetoric in general), while also making his satire even more damning, especially
in the first "Intermezzo," since he uses Eisenhower's own words against him.

In *The Boundaries of Genre*, Morson writes that "a parody can be *verbally
identical* to its original if the parodist uses contextual, rather than textual,
change to indicate the fact and grounds of double-voicing" (112). Coover uses
precisely this technique to parody *and* satirize the histrionic tenor of Eisenhower's appeals to the binary logic of cold war patriotism. As Maltby writes
of the first narrative interruption, "The title, with its Manichaean image of
two fundamentally conflicting principles, gives an indication of what is to
come: a sequence of the reified dualisms which limit popular political thinking in America" (101). Maltby goes on to quote three of the dozens of instances
in this "poem" in which Eisenhower casts the ideological conflict between
the United States and Soviet Union as an apocalyptic battle between armies
representing polar moral opposites. The fact that these are limiting rather
than enlightening comparisons is the relevant issue for Coover. Eisenhower's
"lexicon of totemic words . . . and bogey words" (Maltby 102) simultaneously
draws upon and reinforces the various parts of Hirshberg's patriotic schema.
This rhetorical approach distracts the American public's attention from such
counterschematic information as the Rosenbergs' presumed innocence or
the demonstrably antidemocratic behavior of South Korean leader Syngman
Rhee, the putative defender of American values in the conflict with Communist North Korea. Uncle Sam's influence over the discourse of the Eisenhower
administration is complete (as demonstrated by Uncle Sam's use of several
key phrases prior to their appearance in Eisenhower's speeches) and calculated specifically as a strategic maneuver against the forces of the Phantom.

Having spent two days (and more than half the novel) scrutinizing the
dubious details of the case against the Rosenbergs, Nixon still questions the
validity of Uncle Sam's contention that their deaths are a necessary national
inoculation against the Phantom's expanding influence. His research calls
into question the objectivity of institutions such as *Time* magazine (personified as "the National Poet Laureate" [319 and passim]), the *New York Times*,
and the FBI in perpetuating the political mythology of the cold war. The novel
thus indicts print journalism as simply another tool through which governmental rhetoric is transmitted to the people. The relatively omniscient narrator with whom Nixon's voice alternates writes: "Before *The New York Times*,
if you wished to destroy a man, you inscribed his name on a pot and smashed
it. Or stuck a clay image with a pin. Now you attach his name to a sin and
print it. Such an act is beyond mere insult or information, it is a magical disturbance of History. It is a holy act and an act of defilement at the same time.
It may bring peace and prosperity, it may result in madness and disaster. Is
Alger Hiss a Communist? Is Joe McCarthy a Fascist? Is Justice Douglas a
Traitor? Is Richard Nixon a Farting Quacker who dreams of selling his pajamas

at Coney Island? What matters is: where are such questions being asked?" (194–95). The arcane power of characterization may have been passed from shamanic priests to newspaper editors, but its efficacy in reinforcing dogmatic beliefs remains seemingly undiminished.

Time, on the other hand, is presented as a different kind of anthropomorphized entity, an artist who "frankly acknowledged [the] above-the-board package of prejudices [that were] essential to his genius" (325). Among these "prejudices" are an unquestioning probusiness bias and a "great poetic affinity for War" (323), both of which lead him to disseminate information with a "spin" beneficial to the government's aims: "This is what his art is all about, this is what it means, as his mother says, to be 'called to be the servant of truth.' It is not enough to present facts—something has to *happen* in time and space, observed through the imagination and the heart, something accessible and illuminating to that reader he writes for, the Gentleman from Indiana. Raw data is paralyzing, a nightmare, and there's too much of it and man's mind is quickly engulfed by it. Poetry is the art of subordinating facts to the imagination, of giving them shape and visibility, keeping them *personal*" (320). Having recast journalism into the language of artistic (and thus fictional) creation, *Time* goes on to defend himself against charges of unwarranted subjectivity: "Some would say that such deep personal involvement, such metaphoric compressions and reliance on inner vision and imaginary 'sources' must make objectivity impossible and TIME [*sic*] would agree with them, but he would find simply illiterate anyone who concluded from this that he was not serving Truth. More: he would argue that objectivity is an impossible illusion, a 'fantastic claim' . . . , and as an ideal perhaps even immoral, that *only* through the frankly biased and distorting lens of art is any real grasp of the facts—not to mention Ultimate Truth—even remotely possible" (320). Were *Time* actually an artist, of course, this final claim would resonate closely with the objectives attributed to the postmodernist authors who were subverting the literary "master narratives" esteemed so highly by modernism. The problem, of course, is that *Time* is not an artist and the ideas contained in its articles are not acknowledged as fictive constructions, being presented instead as trustworthy journalistic "facts." The *Times* and *Time* are both shown to have the ability to bring ideologically convenient "truths" into practical (that is, exploitable) existence simply by uttering them publicly.

Coover implies that J. Edgar Hoover has been granted similar power in order to find a scapegoat to justify Nixon's 1949 claim to have evidence of a massive Soviet atomic spy ring.[28] Nixon describes the workings of the FBI under Hoover: "Hoover was in many ways a complete loony, arbitrary in his power and pampered like a Caesar, and if he dreamed up a spy ring one day, then by God it *existed*. Doubt was out. It was an agent's job to increase the Bureau's 'statistical accomplishments' and 'personally ramrod field investigations of "major cases" to successful conclusions,' and never to question the remote wisdom of the Director" (371). Even as he ponders the ramifications of challenging Hoover's version of the truth concerning the Rosenbergs, Nixon understands the potential danger of exposing the agency's fictitious history-manufacturing power: "If we went after the FBI and the Justice Department, what then? Could the American people take it? The incorruptibility of U.S. agencies and institutions—above all, the FBI—was an article of faith in this country: could the people brook an attack on that faith?" (371). Of course Nixon's question is (fictionally) posed more than ten years before Kennedy's assassination spawned a host of conspiracy theories about the "incorruptibility of U.S. agencies and institutions." His phrasing, though, echoes Hirshberg's discussion of the detrimental consequences of overwhelming counter-indicative information to the patriotic cognitive schema (that is, "faith in this country").

Coover's grotesque retelling of the Rosenbergs' trial also contains parallels with Aleshkovsky's novel *The Hand*. Much as Bashov reveals the KGB's extensive resources for fabricating whatever damning materials might be needed to convict a defendant, Nixon relates the importance of potentially manufactured evidence in the case against the Rosenbergs: "Nor did he [Manny Bloch, the Rosenbergs' defense lawyer] challenge any of the physical exhibits, a lot of which were very dubious and should have been exposed to public scrutiny—hell, the FBI has a special section which does nothing but produce fake documents, they have to do this, it's a routine part of police work, the kind of thing I might have enjoyed doing if they'd given me that job I asked for when I left Duke—and much of the stuff that Saypol offered up looked like it might well have come from that factory" (123). Coover implies that this "factory" was not even necessary, since Hoover is allowed to testify that he has a wealth of corroborating evidence against the Rosenbergs that cannot be declassified for use in the trial because of the ongoing investigation. Hoover's false witnessing thus does not even need to be verbalized, merely insinuated, to be effective. The government, the media, and the agencies of law enforcement are all implicated in the creation of social fictions whose artificiality cannot be acknowledged, since to do so would undermine their capacity to maintain ideological unity and its attendant political power.

After the Rosenbergs' final appeal for clemency is denied, Nixon comes to believe that he can personally intervene to save Ethel Rosenberg from execution at the last minute, and he goes to Sing Sing prison with this intention. As he does throughout the novel, Coover intentionally conflates politics and sexuality. Nixon fumblingly attempts to seduce Ethel and is subsequently surprised by her vigorous response, failing to recognize that her reaction to his advances seems disingenuously warm. He becomes so engrossed in their mutual groping that he is forced to retreat hurriedly into the execution chamber when the jailers arrive to lead Ethel off to carry out her death sentence. As Sing Sing and Times Square phantasmagorically merge into the same locality, Nixon finds himself backing onstage, bare bottomed in front of an audience that includes Uncle Sam, Nixon's immediate family, and a compendium of luminaries from American politics and entertainment (which Coover implies are nearly indistinguishable). To compound Nixon's embarrassment, Ethel has lipsticked the phrase "I AM A SCAMP" on his exposed posterior. In addition to commenting on Nixon's current mischief, this phrase also hearkens back to Ethel's participation in a labor dispute earlier in her life. Nixon recalls this episode prior to his ill-fated trip to Ossining, demonstrating his political sympathies in the process: "She *was* pretty goddamn tough, all right. Once, when she was only nineteen years old, she led 150 fellow women workers in a strike that closed down National Shipping. This was during the Depression and the company was fighting for its life, so naturally they hired a new staff and tried to keep operating. But Ethel led the girls in an illegal riot that terrorized the non-union girls and shut the plant down again, in spite of the protective efforts of the whole New York City police force. When a delivery truck tried to crash the picket line, Ethel and the girls hauled the driver from his cab, stripped him bare and lipsticked his butt with I AM A SCAB. My own butt tingled with the thought of it" (304). Nixon's prescient tingling is, of course, borne out later after he tries to break the ideological picket line represented by the Rosenbergs' refusal to confess to the espionage charges of which they have been convicted.

Caught literally and figuratively with his pants down in a moment of fraternization with the ideological enemy, Nixon wraps a piece of bunting (which turns out to be a circa-1789 American flag) around his naked waist. He then resorts to a speech in which he regains the shocked crowd's confidence by appealing to the simple binary logic of their rabid anti-Communism: "'*I tell you, we are on the brink,*' I screamed—I *had* to scream: the uproar in the Square was deafening, and on top of it radios were blaring away, bands playing, generators humming, and police helicopters were rattling overhead, taking pictures and dropping booze parcels. '*Look at Korea!*' I cried. '*Look at China! Eastern Europe! Our own State Department! Even the Supreme Court! We're exposed on all sides by this insidious evil! this sinister conspiracy! this deadly infection! Let me assure you, the Phantom isn't changing! He isn't sleeping! He is, as always, plotting, screaming, working, fighting! Scheming, I should say!*'" (474). Nixon cannot properly "recall that lecture that Uncle Sam had given [him] about the wall-eyed harbinger who thirsted for Christian blood" because he is "too overwrought and afraid [he] would fuck it up," so instead he falls back on standard anti-Communist rhetorical flourishes (which he calls "a touch of the old Dick Nixon"): "*We owe a solemn duty, not only to our own people but to free peoples everywhere on both sides of the Iron Curtain, to roll back the Red Tide which to date has swept everything before it! We cannot allow another Munich!*" (474). In this brief excerpt, Nixon invokes almost all the elements that constitute Hirshberg's American cold war schema, including the various positive associations contained in the American patriotic schema (freedom, democracy, good, self, United States) and the transference of diametrical opponent status from the Nazis to the Soviets (achieved through the reference to the Allies' appeasement of Hitler at Munich).

Coover's presentation makes it clear that Nixon is only parroting the words of Uncle Sam in an effort again literally and figuratively to cover his ass by wrapping it in the flag. His trysting with Ethel is clearly "counter-schematic information" in terms of his reputation as a confirmed anti-Communist, and this speech (like his famous "Checkers" speech that helped him extricate himself from scandal during the 1952 election campaign) is an attempt to salvage his career by redirecting attention away from his own transgressions. His mistake in repeating the formula (saying "screaming" instead of "scheming"), though, points out Nixon's lack of real comprehension of the words that he is shouting at the frenzied crowd. In this regard Coover's technique again resembles that of Aleshkovsky. In *The Hand* Bashov retells a story in which Stalin, in a moment of revolutionary zeal, attempts to appeal to the spirit of Karl Marx: "'I see, I see,' Stalin said quietly. 'Constipation. . . . Lambs. . . . My gut. . . . The shish kebab of world revolution. . . . This is a call to Louis Bonaparte's 18th Humidor" (108).[29] This nonsensical melange of words and misquotes that issues from Stalin's mouth points out, as Booker and Juraga note, the fact that the "new Soviet man . . . far from being superior to his predecessors, was utterly devoid of any moral character because of his lack of connection to any meaningful cultural or moral tradition . . . [as demonstrated by his] almost complete ignoran[ce] of history" (105–6). Coover and Aleshkovsky not only accuse Nixon and Stalin, respectively, of using oversimplified and faulty binary logic, but also of being largely incapable of understanding it themselves.

Nixon calls for the crowd to join him in his vulnerable state to demonstrate their patriotism, again using the rhetoric of ideological warfare to persuade:

> *Now, my friends, I am going to suggest a course of conduct—and I am going to ask you to help! This is a war and we are all in it together! So I would suggest that under the circumstances, everybody here tonight should come before the American people and bare himself as I have done! . . . I want to make my position perfectly clear! We have nothing to hide! And we have a lot to be proud of! We say that no one of the 167 million Americans is a little man! The only question is whether we face up to our world responsibilities, whether we have the faith, the patriotism, the willingness to lead in his [sic] critical period! I say it is time for a new sense of dedication in this country! I ask for your support in helping to develop the national spirit, the faith that we need in order to meet our responsibilities in the world! It is a great goal! And to achieve it, I am asking everyone*

tonight to step forward—right now!—and drop his pants for America!
(482)

The crowd responds enthusiastically to his entreaties, removing their pants and shouting a series of slogans consistent with the constituent parts of the patriotic schema (several of which contain, as Nixon's original plea did, unrecognized double entendres):

> "IT'S A SHOWDOWN!" they cried.
> "PANTS DOWN FOR GOD AND COUNTRY!"
> "PANTS DOWN FOR JESUS CHRIST!"
> "WHOOPEE!"
> "FOR THE COMMON MAN!"
> "DEEDS NOT WORDS!"
> "*PANTS DOWN FOR DICK!*"

Everyone in his audience, from Billy Graham and Joseph Kennedy to Nixon's father and the women of the Mormon Tabernacle Choir, begins removing their clothing, leading Nixon to remark, "I knew that, whatever the cost, I'd won the day, the victory was mine!" (483).

But Nixon becomes hubristic in the wake of his success and overreaches. Uncle Sam tries to regain the spotlight and resume the festivities by forcing Nixon from the stage, dismissing him with a flippant gesture that only incites Nixon to greater rhetorical excess: "'Wait a minute!' I hollered through the freshly unleashed crash of derisive laughter. 'Wait just a goddamn minute!' The laughter subsided for a moment, and there was a moment of grinning silence, waiting to be filled. Even though I was still dangling by the scruff of my neck, I plunged right into it: 'MY pants are down! YOUR pants are down! EVERYBODY'S pants in AMERICA are down! Everybody's—EXCEPT HIS!' This stunned the Square. A deadly hush fell over everybody. That, I thought, is what you call putting a cap on it" (484). Nixon's rash demand that Uncle Sam expose himself—thereby literally unclothing the American "emperor" and revealing what lies beneath the American myths in which he is figuratively dressed—causes Uncle Sam to ask the crowd, now chanting for his pants to come down, "What mad project of national sooey-cide *is* this?" As Uncle Sam's pants hit the floor, Nixon relates, "There was a blinding flash of light, a simultaneous crack of ear-splitting thunder, and then—BLACKOUT!!" (485).

The subsequent chapter, narrated by the more omniscient voice that has alternated with Nixon's throughout the novel, recounts the crowd's hysteria as they attempt to function in the darkness. The early pages of this chapter are filled with terrified and often illogical exclamations such as "*IT'S THE END OF THE WORLD!*" and "*WE SHOULD HAVE NEVER BROKEN THE SOUND BARRIER!*" and "*THE PHANTOM'S KILLT UNCLE SAM!*" (486–87). An encyclopedic compendium of American social anxieties, historical and fictional, is unleashed in the absence of light (that is, the absence of virtue, Uncle Sam, God, and the other positive aspects of the American patriotic schema):

> In the ever deepening nighttime of the people, the shapes of their fear are drawn from ever deepening wells, roiling visions of the imminent imbalance of terror commingling now with shades of half-forgotten nightmares from all their childhoods: V-2s and gas ovens and kamikazes, the hurricane that tore through Overlord, the holocaust at the Cocoanut Grove, gremlins and goose-steppers, malaria, unfaithful wives, starvation at Guadalcanal, U-boat wolfpacks and Jap Snipers and warplanes over Pearl Harbor, vampires and striking workers, hoboes, infantile paralysis, bread lines, bank failures, mortgage foreclosures and dust storms, King Kong and Scarface Al, Wobblies, werewolves, anarchists, Bolsheviks and bootleggers, Filipino guerrillas and Mexican bandidos, the Tweed Ring, earth tremors, the Cross of Gold! (488)

This litany of American terrors goes on for another dozen lines, demonstrating the way in which the fear of the dark (that is, Communism) feeds on and reinforces an almost inexhaustible list of past bogeymen. As the narrator says, "Down they [the crowd] spiral into irrational panic, as upward swirl the spooks of terrors past!" (488).[30] The scene is reminiscent of Yossarian's Dantean trip through Rome near the end of *Catch-22* in that it presents a distinctly hellish vision of reality that has been corruptively influenced by American ideology.

As the darkness continues, the frightened crowd realizes that they "have passed through their conventional terrors and discovered that which they fear most: each other!" (490). The easy moral distinctions made available by the binaries that support the patriotic schema disappear along with Uncle Sam and the people begin to intermingle simply out of their forced proximity: "And inevitably, in all this hysterical jangling around, flesh is finding flesh, mouths mouths, heat heat, and the juices, as Satchel Paige would say, is flowin'. The people are no less beset with confusion and panic, horrendous anguish and pain, like to the throes of travail, but they are also suddenly as hot as firecrackers—or maybe it's not so suddenly, maybe it's just the culmination of that strange randy unease they've been feeling all day. . . . Now . . . the people seek, with distraught hearts and agitated loins—a final connection, a kind of ultimate ingathering, a tribal implosion, that will either release them from this infinite darkness and doleful sorrow or obliterate them once and for all and end their misery" (492). As all manner of sexual mores begin to break down, the crowd seems to be breaking free of its reliance on prescriptive ideas and is actively seeking new sexual experiences, not only with each other but also with "any animal, vegetable, artifact, or other surface irregularity" (492). As was the case with Nixon's attempted seduction of Ethel

Rosenberg, sexual behavior outside the established bounds of propriety becomes associated with political subversion.

When Uncle Sam returns to the scene, though, he interrupts the crowd "in the mind-shattering throes of what might have been some ultimate orgasmic fusion" and restores "their old isolate and terrified selves" by relighting the scene with a "spark from the sacred flame" (493) from Yucca Flat, Nevada.[31] The narrator's description of the returned Uncle Sam not only associates him with Superman, another fictitious character with strong nationalistic associations for an American audience, but also reverts to the artificial language of the patriotic schema: "When [the crowd] open their eyes again, it is to see their Star-Spangled Superhero standing stark and solemn above them on the Death House stage, cradling freedom's holy light in his outstretched hands and gazing down upon them with glittering eyes sunk in deeply shadowed sockets" (493). Freely and willfully conflating Christian religious imagery, comic-book fantasy, political rhetoric, and hyperalliterative (and thus plainly contrived) language, Uncle Sam's restoration of order is as much a verbal act as physical, since it reintroduces what Maltby calls the "discourse of America" (103), this time unmistakably buttressed by the power of the bomb.

Once the square is again lit and under Uncle Sam's indisputable control, he turns the proceedings over to Betty Crocker and the preexecution spectacle proceeds. Julius's electrocution goes off without a hitch, although the merriment of the earlier scenes has abated somewhat, especially among those who have to face the actual repercussions of their patriotic fervor: "[Julius's death] is duly cheered . . . less enthusiastically up front, where the disquieting presence of Death can still be felt like a sticky malodorous fog, more warmly as it spreads out toward the periphery, traveling like a happy rumor, merging finally into a drunken exultant uproar out at the far edges, where everyone is having a terrific time without exactly knowing why" (511). When Ethel's initial electrocution fails to kill her, the crowd's unease momentarily becomes widespread. Uncle Sam rectifies the situation by exhorting the executioner to try again, upon which "virtually the entire VIP section . . . scrambl[es] up over the side of the stage, fighting for position as though their very future depended on it, racing for the switch" (517). It is not clear who actually throws the switch, and the narrator suggests both Nixon and John F. Kennedy as potential "victors" in this race. In doing so he presages the hotly contested 1960 presidential election (in which Kennedy and Nixon would each attempt to seize the anti-Communist high ground) and implicates both parties—and thus the whole scope of establishment politics—in the Rosenbergs' deaths.

All that remains is Nixon's own anointment as the next incarnation of Uncle Sam. This is accomplished through a heavily sexualized scene that likely contributed to the book's lengthy delay in being published. Uncle Sam comes to Nixon in his bedroom and makes his intentions clear in yet another parody of American patriotic iconography:

> "Come here, boy," he said, smiling frostily and jabbing his recruitment finger at me with one hand, unbuttoning his striped pantaloons with the other: "*I want* YOU!"
> "But—!"
> "Speech me no speeches, my friend! I had a bellyfulla baloney—what I got a burnin' yearnin' for now is a little humble toil, heavenward duty, and onmittygated cornholin' whoopee! So jes' drap your drawers and bend over, boy—you been ee-LECK-ted!" (530)

Uncle Sam, having essentially turned Nixon's previous "PANTS DOWN FOR DICK!" rhetoric back on its author, proceeds to sodomize Nixon savagely while telling him that uncritical acceptance of Uncle Sam's personality (that is, American ideology) is necessary if Nixon truly wishes to be president: "You want to make it with me . . . you gotta love me like I really am: Sam Slick the Yankee Peddler, gun-totin' hustler and tooth-'n'-claw tamer of the heathen wilderness, lusty and in everything a screamin' meddler, novus ball-bustin' ordo seculorum, that's me, boy" (531–32). Uncle Sam's graphic commentary *in flagrante delicto* makes one final connection between sexual power and political power in the cold war: "They's a political axiom that wherever a vacuum exists, it will be filled by the nearest or strongest power! Well, you're lookin' at it, mister: an example and fit instrument, big as they come in this world and gittin' bigger by the minute!" (532). After Uncle Sam has finished with him, Nixon reflects that he now understands the true origins of "Hoover's glazed stare, Roosevelt's anguished tics, Ike's silly smile" (533). Gradually overcoming his feelings of having been violated, Nixon finally admits his love for Uncle Sam, thus signaling the end of his questioning of Uncle Sam's reasoning. Hume asserts that the "parallel to George Orwell's Winston Smith realizing that he loves Big Brother is unmistakable" (181), which not only lays bare the grim satirical implications of this final scene but accurately places *The Public Burning* among satires that examine the enormous, even dystopian potential for abuse within intentional distortions of language.

The Public Burning looks backward to a fictionalized version of the 1950s—and even further back via the character of Uncle Sam[32]—for the origins of the societal corruption that Coover believes to be running rampant in Nixon's America. As such the novel serves as a metaphorical examination of the deformed American body politic that Uncle Sam represents. In a similar vein, Don DeLillo diagnosed the cultural malignancies caused by the cold war well in advance of its end. Beginning in 1972, when he deliberately confused the languages of nuclear warfare and football in *End Zone,* DeLillo's fiction has been marked by mediations upon the lasting ramifications of the cold war on both the collective conscience of the United States and the individual psyches of its citizens. This process reaches its peak in 1985's *White Noise,* in which DeLillo offers a portrait of the numbing and dehumanizing effects of the constant fear of death that was inherent in the cold war mindset. As Joseph Dewey compellingly argues in his *In a Dark Time,* DeLillo accomplishes this by exposing the panoply of ineffectual linguistic strategies that American culture offered up as both palliative and justification for unsettling concepts such as the "balance of terror" deterrence theory.[33]

For more than thirty years, historian/psychiatrist Robert Jay Lifton has examined the after effects of the 1945 atomic bombings of Hiroshima and Nagasaki. His *Death in Life* (1969) was the first extensive study of the atomic bombs' psychological ramifications on their Japanese survivors. Directly relevant to consideration of DeLillo's fiction is Lifton's 1995 work (coauthored with Greg Mitchell) *Hiroshima in America: Fifty Years of Denial,* which puts forth the argument that governmental disinformation and/or misinformation coupled with collective societal aversion to face up to the intricate and often unpleasant historical consequences of the bomb's use led to "a collective form of psychic numbing" among the American populace. Lifton and Mitchell contend that the concerted official effort to "justify the use of the bomb on ethical grounds, to hide its grotesque effects on people, and to deny the weapon's revolutionary significance . . . represented an inability to confront the full truth of Hiroshima, an insufficient recognition in our policies and our attitudes that nothing was the same after Hiroshima—that human survival was now at issue" (xiv). This national inability to confront the reality of life in the nuclear age is for Lifton and Mitchell reminiscent of the reaction of patients to a potentially traumatic medical condition: "We construct what Edith Wyschogrod calls a '*cordon sanitaire*' around Hiroshima— a barrier designed to prevent the spread of a threatening disease, the 'illness' that we block off in his case being what we did in Hiroshima. That *cordon sanitaire* was transmitted, as official policy, throughout American society. One was supposed to be numbed to Hiroshima" (338). Extending their medical analogy to post-Hiroshima society, Lifton and Mitchell argue that this numbing is only a superficial and fleeting balm against the complex assortment of anxieties that the bomb unleashed in its aftermath. The net result of this "psychic numbing" is that the cold war became, in essence, a five-decade period of denial, a stage that must be transcended before recovery from trauma can occur.

Jack Gladney, the protagonist of *White Noise,* participates in the process of maintaining the kinds of illusions that perpetuate the problem of psychic numbing. His colleagues at the College-on-the-Hill are all complicit in fostering an academic environment that disproportionately values trivia such as Elvis Presley and supermarket culture. The subjects they study are almost wholly commodified, whether or not such a context is warranted. Even

Gladney's study of Adolf Hitler is significantly removed from its grim and violent historical context and refashioned largely as admiring respect for Hitler's power over death.[34] Gladney's relatively amoral recontextualization of Hitler resembles the general American cultural shift that resulted in the demonization of a new enemy (the Soviet Union) during the cold war to take the place of the old enemy (Nazi Germany) from World War II. The social and political reputation of the Western portion of Germany had largely been rehabilitated by 1985—thanks not only to its repudiation of its Nazi past but also to its general willingness to oppose the Soviets as part of the NATO alliance. Gladney's Hitler Studies program extends this revisionist attitude in an attempt to distill virtue from one of history's greatest tyrants and murderers. In his scholarly work, Gladney abrogates the purely negative cognitive associations that stem from Hitler's now-obsolete wartime classification as a national enemy, although whether he does so consciously or not is debatable.[35]

Nevertheless Gladney is financially and academically secure thanks to his unusual intellectual specialty, even going so far as to claim that "death was strictly a professional matter" (74) at College-on-the-Hill. In this regard, the college is a microcosm of the United States in general, since the lion's share of the national budget during the early 1980s (when the novel was written) was devoted to defense spending, a fact that had been justified to the nation throughout the cold war as necessary for combating "the Evil Empire." Such bellicose rhetoric and the stockpiling of weapons of mass destruction that accompanied it professionalized, politicized, and even familiarized the prospect of death on an enormous scale in the United States. This created an atmosphere in which the continued existence of the "American way of life" was allegedly threatened at all times with extinction and safeguarded by an identical reciprocal threat. Lifton and Mitchell contend that such a constant state of vigilance is likely to desensitize one eventually to the real dangers of destruction, since remaining in a state of alert anxiety for long periods eventually leads to neurosis without some form of sedative coping mechanism (such as a cordon sanitaire). Dewey, like Lifton and Mitchell, argues that such a situation has its roots in unpleasant ground: "The manipulators of language—from Hitler to Stalin to the scientists obtaining data from the rubble of Hiroshima—have made death generic" (206).

The lunchtime discussion among several of the school's faculty members early in the novel demonstrates that nearly everyone at the College-on-the-Hill is engaged in some field of study that concurrently analyzes and contributes to the "white noise," that is, the "static [and] interference that jams the information trying to get through" (Dewey 206). Gladney's colleague Alfonse Stompanato is introduced in a context that suggests at least the potential for informational excess: "He knew four languages, had a photographic memory, did complex mathematics in his head" (DeLillo, *White Noise* 65). Stompanato laments the "incessant bombardment of information" to which

Americans are subjected and claims that the only relief available is "an occasional catastrophe." He goes on to enumerate a list of "good" and "untapped" resources for such catastrophes, noting that options are limited by the fact that "for most people there are only two places in the world. Where they live and their TV set." Murray Siskind, another of Gladney's colleagues, explains that this binary phenomenon is the result of what he calls a collective "brain fade": "They've forgotten how to listen and look as children. They've forgotten how to collect data. In the psychic sense a forest fire on TV is on a lower plane than a ten-second commercial for Automatic Dishwasher All. The commercial has deeper waves, deeper emanations. But we have reversed the relative significance of these things. This is why people's eyes, ears, brains and nervous systems have grown weary. It's a simple case of misuse" (65–66). The fact that the faculty participates almost subliminally in this "misuse" while apparently recognizing the deleterious consequences of "brain fade" speaks both to the pervasiveness of the condition and to the powerful potential for ideological control contained in the simple home/television dichotomy that Stompanato describes.

The brain fade / psychic numbing in the cold war United States is the calculated result of policies that have covert economic and/or political motivations, unrelated or even contrary to the overt moral and/or ethical language in which they are couched. American society of the early 1980s took refuge in the benefits of materialism and anti-Communism that had been "sold" to them as righteous. The fact that this pitch came from a government and a media who profited financially and politically from the propagation of these same values, makes them inherently suspect.[36] DeLillo's satirical depiction of Blacksmith and the College-on-the-Hill (whose name parodically deflates John Winthrop's seventeenth-century identification of America as a "city upon a hill") suggests that he believes this sense of comfort to have been overly credulous and, as a result, superficial and injurious.

The disturbing absurdity of instances in which the realms of the fictional and the real overlap provides DeLillo with much of his satirical power in this regard. Gladney's daughters begin exhibiting the physical symptoms of exposure to a toxic chemical cloud issuing from an industrial accident after merely hearing about it on the radio for example. Although psychosomatic illness and/or hypochondria are neither uncommon nor necessarily the product of disinformation, the ease with which the girls seem to succumb to the broadcast version of reality (which, as Gladney's oldest son Heinrich points out, is riddled with glaring inconsistencies) suggests the degree to which they have been conditioned to be receptive to propaganda. The governmental officials in charge of evacuating Blacksmith, moreover, repeatedly compare the results of their actual evacuation with a simulation of a comparable disaster. One of these officials even complains to Gladney, who has by this point been exposed to the toxic chemical, that the actual event is frustrating them because it does not correspond closely enough with the model to provide illuminating data. Philip E. Simmons notes the ways in which the reality of the cloud is immediately appropriated and altered by the dual linguistic controls of government and the media: "Rather than unequivocally assert the existence of a material reality beyond the realm of the image, the 'airborne toxic event' is quickly absorbed by the image-making apparatus of the media and forced to conform to the bureaucratic imperatives of the official and quasi-official agencies that respond to the catastrophe. On the other side, we see that 'information' itself can be a material cause of 'real' events. What has happened is not that the referent for mass-media images has disappeared but that the binary opposition between the real and imaginary has itself broken down" (60). DeLillo's narrative makes it clear that such a breakdown has happened, yet few if any of the characters recognize it, thereby ensuring—as in Derrida's assessment of the cold war as a self-sustaining fable—that those who control the "imaginary" also control the "real."

For all its utility in perpetuating social, political, and economic objectives, this sort of linguistic control can only serve as a temporary panacea against the specter of violence and death that it is intended to obscure. Despite his nonchalant demeanor and seeming contentedness, Gladney is afflicted by a sort of morbid fascination shared by his own family and seemingly everyone else in Blacksmith. His wife Babette takes a suspect drug called Dylar designed to suppress fear of death (a pharmaceutical supplement to the linguistic numbing process); Heinrich obsessively tracks the progress of the "airborne toxic event" that threatens the city and also corresponds with an imprisoned killer; Gladney's elder daughter Denise constantly chides her parents (especially Babette) for their litany of unhealthy behaviors; and the whole family, but especially the younger daughter Steffie, is "totally absorbed by documentary clips of calamity and death" that they watch on television while eating dinner. They become engrossed in these programs, and Gladney adds that "every disaster made us wish for more, for something bigger, grander, more sweeping" (64). The family's insatiable desire for the spectacle of death and suffering is presented as a conditioned response to the total saturation of semantically empty forms of discourse implied by the novel's title. Nearly all forms of language in the book—from the endless repetitions of brand names that crop up in the text to the pop culture topics that dominate the curriculum at the College-on-the-Hill, and from the radio broadcasts that fail to provide either accurate or substantive information about the "airborne toxic event" to Siskind's attempt to "explain . . . any number of massacres, wars, and executions" through a dubious theory that claims "violence is a form of rebirth" (277)—are either unsuccessful at providing relief from the death-fear that tacitly dominates society or appallingly serve to amplify it.

The fact that the Gladneys desire "something bigger, grander, more sweeping" as a spectacle of death also ties in with the progressively increasing violence of the twentieth century's major conflicts. The history of the century is one that offers ample satisfaction for the kind of exponentially expanding appetite for death that the Gladneys exhibit. The simultaneously cyclical and escalating nature of the world's capacity to destroy itself is evinced by Heinrich's conversation with his father as they watch the progress of the toxic cloud together from their attic window:

> "It doesn't cause nausea, vomiting, shortness of breath, like they said before."
> "What does it cause?"
> "Heart palpitations and a sense of *déjà vu*."
> "*Déjà vu?*"
> "It affects the false part of the human memory or whatever. That's not all. They're not calling it the black billowing cloud anymore."
> "What are they calling it?"
> He looked at me carefully.
> "The airborne toxic event." (112)

The sense of déjà vu that Heinrich mentions associates the danger of the cloud with prior, similar events even as its novelty makes it inherently more engrossing for the Gladneys. The redesignation of the "black billowing cloud" as "the airborne toxic event" also reflects, as Hilgartner, Bell, and O'Connor point out in *Nukespeak,* the tendency of official rhetoric of the nuclear age to sugarcoat or to completely obscure potentially unpleasant aspects of its reality (compare "Sunshine units"). The cloud, therefore, not only represents an intensification of violence in keeping with the times but also reveals the official practice of intentionally masking such intensification. The family's fascination with carefully commodified death must not be allowed to lapse into criticism of that "commodity," and this positive relationship is ensured (or at least fortified) by disingenuous use of language on the part of the powers that control Blacksmith and its environs.

Dewey sees Gladney's physical exposure to the toxic cloud as a positive development since it finally cuts through the "white noise" and removes death from its "fabulous" linguistic context by reconnecting him to "something universal" beyond the "finite, deceptive nature of human systems": "DeLillo offers a tough lesson, a tough avenue to hope. He performs, perhaps unknowingly, the healing most particular to traditional apocalyptic literature. He reminds a people, anchored in time, of a scale far beyond the measure of minutes, days, years (which so profoundly frightens Gladney). He reconnects that people with the elemental, in which endings are simply a phase of living itself" (Dewey 223).

As the novel closes, Gladney and a large crowd including his family silently watch a beautiful sunset, one whose beauty is ironically attributable to light refraction caused by the toxic cloud, from an overpass. Dewey interprets this moment as representing "a measure of human connection with something greater, a recognition of something vaster" because all of the distractions caused by the myriad fictions that provide spurious order for the cold war world have been removed. It is too late for Gladney to change the fact of his exposure to Nyodene, the book's analogue to nuclear fallout, and Dewey is correct in suggesting that there is a sense of "reconnecting with a living cosmos" (222–23) in Gladney's Ecclesiastes-like observation that the "sunsets linger and so do we" (*White Noise* 308).

A pall is cast over this supposed revelation by Gladney's continued withdrawal—"I am taking no calls"—and fear—"I am afraid of the imaging block. . . . Afraid of what it knows about me" (309), both of which suggest that his cordon sanitaire has not yet been dismantled. Moreover there is a foreboding sense at the end of the book that the postcloud respite, symbolically described in the commodified lingo of the novel as "the supermarket shelves hav[ing] been rearranged" (309),[37] will be not only fleeting but also ultimately impotent in terms of affecting real deliverance. Gladney and all the rest "slowly begin to disperse . . . restored to [their] separate and defensible selves" after their communal silence at the overpass, yet the processes and the language of the culture that has dominated them also reassert themselves in the book's final paragraph: "In the altered shelves, the ambient roar, in the plain and heartless fact of their decline, they try to work their way through confusion. But in the end it doesn't matter what they see or think they see. The terminals are equipped with holographic scanners, which decode the binary secret of every item, infallibly. . . . And this is where we wait together, regardless of age, our carts stocked with brightly colored goods. A slowly moving line, satisfying, giving us time to glance at the tabloids in the racks. Everything that we need that is not food or love is here in the tabloid racks. The tales of the supernatural and extraterrestrial. The miracle vitamins, the cures for cancer, the remedies for obesity. The cults of the famous and the dead" (310). The novel ends with the beginnings of yet another of its signature copia of banality and a suggestion that such illusory miracles, cures, and remedies have become a "need" on par with food and love that will overwhelm any other process of coming "through the confusion" engendered by the cloud and its aftereffects. In this manner DeLillo is less apocalyptic in the manner of John the Revelator (or Dewey) and more in the manner of Walter Miller Jr. and *A Canticle for Leibowitz,* in which the repetition of willful self-destruction is seemingly inexorable, even with the knowledge of past apocalypse.

If there is a message of hope at the end of the novel, however, it is (as in the film version of *On the Beach* or in *Fail-Safe*) that the reader still has the chance to act in an attempt to avoid a similar fate. Interpreted this way *White Noise* acts in concert with the rest of DeLillo's body of fiction as a cautionary prescription, a call to reject all aspects of the artificial and obfuscating culture of the cold war thrust upon people by those who stand to gain from the "brain fade." In *This Mad "Instead"* (2000), Arthur M. Saltzman summarizes DeLillo's project of contesting various forms of American cultural logic: "DeLillo is peculiarly conscious among contemporary American writers of predicating his fictions in environments hostile to the individual's capacity to use words that have not been irrevocably sworn to prior manipulations, whose forms include official communiqués and press releases (*Libra*), conventional bigotry (*End Zone*), commercialism (*Americana*), pedantry and jargon (*Ratner's Star*). To combat wholesale manipulation of language into 'lullabies processed by intricate systems' [*End Zone* 54], DeLillo proposes a creed of resistance. . . . In *White Noise* it is seen in the spell that seems to render the post-toxic-event sky incandescent. . . . What is certain is that people linger, exchange, participate—instead of pressing heedlessly, habitually onward, they are moved to interpret and dwell upon the defamiliarized heavens" (46). DeLillo argues that only by adopting this more skeptical and judicious creed— and, perhaps more important, maintaining it in the face of the enormous pressures to backslide into the "lullabies processed by intricate systems" like Coover's Nixon does—will his angst-ridden characters (and by extension his readers) also rid themselves of the accompanying fear of death.

"When life and Socialist Realist art converge":
Questioning the Story of Soviet History

Much in the way that Coover and DeLillo invent fictionalized simulations of American history—that is, seemingly recognizable historical narratives that constantly and conspicuously announce their own fictionalized nature—as vehicles for their cultural satire, several Russian satires of the cold war create counterhistories whose structure and/or narrative call attention to their own fictionality. Like Aksyonov's *Our Golden Ironburg*, both Aleshkovsky's *Kangaroo* and Sokolov's *Astrophobia* (1984; *Palisandriia*) are first-person narratives whose content and structure destabilize official Soviet versions of reality. Mark Lipovetsky's assertion that *Astrophobia* "model[s] an *idyllic simulacrum* of Soviet history" (175) applies equally well to *Our Golden Ironburg* and *Kangaroo*. Lipovetsky's comment underscores both the intentionally idealized tone and the patent artificiality of *Astrophobia*'s narrative. When presented in a parodic context, such characteristics become easy targets for a satirical reductio ad absurdum due to their egregious logical flaws. All three novels widely subvert Soviet culture by creating historical milieus that achieve two interrelated goals: first, they parody genres that express the unremittingly optimistic Soviet view of history resulting from strict adherence to historical determinism; second, they satirize the very processes by which the elaborately veiled social fictions that are required to maintain such a view are created.

In her "Sokolov's *Palisandriya*: the Art of History" (2000), Karen L. Ryan claims such an approach is innate to postmodern Russian satire: "Russian

post-modern texts evince a particularly acute insistence on the need to re-
think history; this tendency is, perhaps, not surprising, considering Soviet
culture's tradition of manipulating and distorting history. Thus Russian postmodernism's questioning of historical myths and the possibility of a final
'knowable' truth dovetails with satire's scepticism about the viability of an
officially sanctioned truth" (216). The reemergence of neo-Stalinist rhetoric
under Brezhnev, a clear stimulus for the parodic *sots-art* movement with
which Ryan and others have associated *Astrophobia,* created an ideological
environment ripe for (if not necessarily accepting of) satirical questioning of
the largely uncritical official rehabilitation of the Soviet past.

   As discussed previously[38] Aleshkovsky's *The Hand* similarly couches satire
intended for its author's present within an altered but still distinctly Stalinist chronotope. Edward J. Brown's assessment of *The Hand* provides a useful
framework for discussing Aleshkovsky's later novel *Kangaroo.* Of the former,
Brown writes, "The novel offers a fascinating fictional hypothesis to explain
certain events in Soviet history that are not yet fully understood, and though
Aleshkovsky's hypothesis may seem a fantastic invention, it makes about as
much sense as any that have yet been offered" (314). Overshadowed within
Brown's otherwise perceptive reading of *The Hand* is the point that Aleshkovsky's "fantastic invention" differs qualitatively from the others "that have yet
been offered" insomuch as it provides readers with constant reminders of its
status as both "fantasy" and "invention." Bashov repeatedly reveals the artifice behind his work as an officer in the KGB to his prisoner/listener, just as
Aleshkovsky openly displays his novelistic techniques to reiterate his book's
status as a satirical work of art and *not* an objective counterhistory. In doing
so he demonstrates one of the essential qualities of historiographic metafiction: "The reader is forced to acknowledge not only the inevitable textuality
of our knowledge of the past, but also both the value and the limitation of
the inescapably discursive form of that knowledge" (Hutcheon 127). Aleshkovsky deflates the claims to veracity made by other versions of history, especially the dominant Soviet ones, by contending that they are at least as fictive
as his own outlandish scenarios.

   This subversive process is even more pronounced in *Kangaroo,* the entire
plot of which revolves around the experiences of a petty criminal named Fan
Fanych[39] within the legal system of the Soviet Union. Fan Fanych's apolitical and largely innocuous career as a criminal intersects on numerous occasions with the highest echelons of power. He becomes a less naive and much
less fortunate Soviet version of Forrest Gump, unintentionally altering the
course of Soviet and even world history at a number of critical junctures.
Aleshkovsky uses Fan Fanych's presence, for example, in the same Berlin
beer hall as Hitler in 1929 (where he unintentionally provokes Hitler into
burning down the Reichstag) and at the Yalta Conference in February of 1945

to create a ridiculous alternative historical narrative whose purpose is ultimately parodic and satirical in regard to accepted Soviet versions of history.

At the start of the novel, Fan Fanych addresses (as he does throughout) his unseen friend Kolya, describing his arrest in the late 1920s by a Cheka lieutenant named Kidalla in connection with the apparent contract killing of an NEP-era businessman. A series of bizarre circumstances led both to Fan Fanych's exoneration (he is guilty of accepting the blood money, but never actually committed the murder) and the end of private enterprise in the Soviet Union.[40] Fan Fanych also incurs a debt to Kidalla, who allows him to go free but also says that he "is saving [Fan Fanych] for a very important case" (17).

Fan Fanych explains to Kolya that he spent years afterward waiting for this "very important case" to arrive. He runs through a litany of occasions during the 1930s and 1940s that he thought could have put an end to his waiting, among which are some of the most infamous episodes of the Stalin era (the murder of Kirov, the terrors of 1937–38, and Hitler's surprise invasion of the Soviet Union) as well as occasions (basic necessities being unavailable, crop failures, failure to meet production quotas during the so-called Stakhanovite year of 1936) for which the Soviet propaganda mechanism would have been compelled to provide expedient explanations. Fan Fanych's disgraceful compendium reveals how the legal system was often used to concoct an ideologically consistent cover for developments that ran contrary to the national ideology, much as Nixon in *The Public Burning* comes to realize that the Rosenbergs' execution (if not their initial conviction) is intended to repair Americans' sense of patriotism in the wake of seeming Communist gains.

When Fan Fanych is summoned to appear before Kidalla, now a prosecutor for the KGB, Fan Fanych explains that "finally—[his] historical necessity arrived": "There's a job for you. In three months our section will celebrate the anniversary of the First Case. *The Very First Case.* Case Number One. By that day we can't have a single very important case left unsolved. Not one. You can't wriggle out of this, so don't fuck around. Any questions?" (20). Fan Fanych immediately asks Kidalla how many important unresolved cases remain and whether he will be charged with all of them in an effort to clear the docket in one stroke. Kidalla's response provides the fictionalized context for the remainder of the novel's plot: "We make them all up anyway, so there's an unlimited quantity of unsolved cases. . . . You have about ten to choose from" (21).[41] Kidalla, moreover, explains that because Fan Fanych is "an artist [who] can make these proceedings a brilliant dramatic performance" he is indispensable to the KGB. He also preempts Fan Fanych's potential objection to the concept of "historical necessity" saying that it is a "state, party, philosophical, and military secret" (21).

Dismayed by the seemingly monolithic forces thus arrayed against him, Fan Fanych begins going through his options. He notes that all the cases carry a fairly standard punishment from the era of the purges: "twenty-five years in stir, plus five of disenfranchisement, five of internal exile, five of exclusion from responsible jobs, and a denunciation at Lenin Stadium" (21).[42] As he recounts the various cases he rejected before getting to his eventual choice, Fan Fanych explains how a computer was used to generate cases for the KGB: "They fed it various data about me, the all-conquering teachings of Marx-Lenin-Stalin, the Soviet era, the Iron Curtain, Socialist Realism, the struggle for peace, cosmopolitanism, the subversive activities of the CIA and the FBI, the number of workdays on collective farms, Tito the hireling of imperialism, and it brought up the very important case that yours truly got involved in" (22). The clichéd overtones—"the struggle for peace," "cosmopolitanism," "the hireling of imperialism"—and absurd disjunctions among this input data helps explain the strange nature of the computer's output. The cases Fan Fanych declines include the typical kinds of charges that were used in the purges and in the show trials of the 1930s (including plots to assassinate Stalin or other politburo members, which are not coincidentally precisely the kinds of fabrications depicted in *The Hand*) but also feature a bizarre melange of "offenses" whose supposed criminality is utterly dependent on the politically motivated legal reasoning of the Soviets: "I took a closer look at a scheme for printing bank notes with portraits of Peter the Great on the hundreds, Bobrov the soccer player on the fifties, and Ilya Ehrenburg on the thirties, but I changed my mind. As for swiping one of the Mongolian prime minister's kidneys when he's under the knife, forget it. Trying to stage *The Brothers Karamazov* in the Central Theater of the Red Army—no way. Wrecking, poisoning rivers and seltzer water in areas where tank troops were stationed, sabotage, praising the theory of relativity, agitation and propaganda, infiltrating literary journals with far-reaching aims like *Novy Mir,* destroying plans and timetables, years of sabotage activity in the U.S.S.R. Meteorological Center, spying for seventy-seven countries, including Antarctica" (23). The implausible and outlandish case he ultimately chooses—"[The] case of the vicious rape and murder of an aged kangaroo in the Moscow Zoo on a night between July 14, 1789 and January 5, 1905" (23)[43]—is perhaps the most unusual of all these. However, it also seems, due to its strange temporal boundaries, to be removed from the Soviet political context (for which Fan Fanych has no use) and accordingly appeals to him the most.

The first thing he reads in the case file is the supposed testimony, apparently completely computer generated, of a "Doctor of Philology" improbably named Perdebabaev-Valois.[44] This document is composed almost entirely of fragments of Soviet clichés, obscene phrases, zoological details, and vaguely legalistic phraseology, none of which coheres enough to be articulate as legal testimony or anything else. Kidalla acknowledges that the statement is hopelessly corrupted and promises to interrogate its inventor. When Fan Fanych asks him why the KGB is using a computer, "when any of your Sholokhovs could turn out this thing without your having to change a word?" (23),[45] Kidalla claims that using the computer is both necessary to keep up with the technology of the enemy and a more equitable means of justice: "We can jump straight from the enemy's sometimes unconscious criminal intent to the right punishment, bypassing the actual crime altogether, with its blood, horrors, cynicism, information leaks, pain, tears of the relatives of those who've suffered, and damage to our military might. We've totally eliminated investigation's indifference to the evolution of a crime, and we've thrown the notorious assumption of innocence on the garbage heap of history along with the productions of that White Guardist whore Akhmatova and that faggot Zoshchenko" (26).[46] Kidalla's description of the supposed improvements in the legal system point out its complete distortion in the service of ideology, as questions of guilt and innocence have been refined entirely out of existence. Aleshkovsky puts the KGB's historical modus operandi of convicting suspects on fabricated charges into an absurdly embellished context with Fan Fanych's case, thereby satirizing the system that would condone, encourage, and develop such a practice.

Once Kidalla explains the kangaroo case's provenance, Fan Fanych is told to assist in the preparation of his fate: "Start getting into your role as kangaroo murderer and rapist. Make up a scenario of the case along the lines of Stanislavsky's Method, and think up some versions and variations. Be happy, scumbag: you've immortalized yourself, you'll go down in *The Secret History of the Cheka* along with me. And it shall be written someday! They *shall* write about our labors! They'll tell how we helped to change the world, not explain it!" (29). Kidalla's exclamation makes it clear that he sees control, not justice, as the Cheka's mission. With the fantastic outlines of Fan Fanych's world established, the remainder of the novel details the process of writing the "script" for the trial at which Fan Fanych will be convicted of the rape and murder of the kangaroo, conducting the trial, and executing Fan Fanych's sentence, all of which continue Aleshkovsky's blending of fiction and history.

Fan Fanych is imprisoned in a "Deluxe" cell furnished with luxuries confiscated from past "enemies of the people," where he is observed by Beria and Kidalla as he composes his script (with the dubious assistance of a zoologist specializing in kangaroos). When Fan Fanych attempts to undermine the scripting process, he is drugged and unwillingly subjected to an experiment involving an attempt to condition him into believing that he is a kangaroo.[47] He momentarily succumbs and teeters on the edge of both madness and submission, but eventually overcomes his captors' efforts, at which point he is returned to his normal cell.

When Fan Fanych is brought forth to be tried for a crime deemed so heinous that the prosecutor claims that *all* parts of Article 58 pertain to it, he steps into a Soviet version of the all-American throng assembled in Times Square for the Rosenbergs' executions in *The Public Burning*: "In the front rows were representatives from all the Soviet republics, in national dress: turbans, kerchiefs, Caucasian sheepskin hats, felt cloaks, side-buttoned Russian blouses, high boots, Central Asian skullcaps, caftans, and a lot of daggers. Behind them were workers straight off the assembly lines, wiping their hands on their overalls. Peasants with sickles. Intellectuals with note pads. Writers. Generals. Soldiers. Violinists. A lot of famous movie stars. A ballerina. Film directors. Surkov. Fadeev. Khrennikov [three renowned 'official' Soviet authors]. Behind them were representatives of the fraternal Communist parties and daughter Chekas" (76).[48] The main piece of evidence against him is an elaborate cinematic recreation of his alleged crime (apparently based on the "screenplay" he produced in his cell), footage recalling both the falsified film testimony used against Conceptiev in *The Hand* and the home movies shown to the crowd as Ethel Rosenberg is led to the electric chair in *The Public Burning*. The prosecutor introduces the film by discussing the "creative" process behind this "radically new cinematic genre" in a manner filled with Soviet-style clichés:

> The author of the screenplay is the accused himself, C.U.N. Tarking-ton. Obviously the investigators, who for a short time had to act as screenwriters, and the screenwriters, who became investigators, made some corrections in the accused's criminal concept. Not everything went smoothly, and not everything conformed to the aesthetic norms of Socialist Realism, the artistic movement of the century. But the collective overcame all the problems and is submitting the fruit of its effort to the people's judgment today. For the time being, its creators will all remain anonymous. They will all receive the Stalin Prize, first class. Long live the greatest friend of the most important art of all, long live the brilliant successor to the work of Marx and Chaplin, Engels and de Sica, Lenin and all-the-Pudovkins—the great Stalin. Death to Hollywood! (83)[49]

The prosecutor's blatant attempt to equate Chaplin (a fellow traveler at *best*), Italian neorealist director Vittorio de Sica (a non-Soviet Communist), and director Vsevolod Pudovkin (one of the giants of early Soviet film, along with Sergei Eisenstein) reverberates with his overall rhetorical strategy of reserving exclusively for the Soviets film's capacity for social change. The apparently intentional eradication of the distinction between investigators and screenwriters (that is, those who attempt to discern reality and those who create fictions) in concocting the evidence against Fan Fanych shows how this rhetoric manifests itself in practice.

Fan Fanych's trial supports Uncle Sam's declaration in *The Public Burning* that "*all* courtroom testimony about the past is ipso facto and teetotaciously a baldface lie" and that it is "like history itself—all more or less bunk" (86). The prosecutor tells the audience that they are "witnessing the trial of the future" and cites the fact that "Soviet jurists have cooperated amicably with engineers, scientific scholars, the accused, and his guard" as the secret to its glorious success. As a result of this "greatest moment in legal history, when life and Socialist Realist art converge" (102–3), Fan Fanych is sentenced to be shot, having literally and figuratively received a show trial that called on the best officially sanctioned artistic, scientific, technological, and juridical skills the country has to offer (that is, "any signifying practices . . . operative in a society" [Hutcheon 137]). Aleshkovsky's satire makes it clear that he finds *all* of these areas of Soviet life to be thoroughly diminished or even completely invalidated by their obedient participation in the wholesale fictionalization of reality.

Fan Fanych is not shot, however, but subjected to a series of bizarre punishments. First he is unwittingly forced to participate in another scientific experiment; this time his captors attempt to convince him that he has been sent into space and is traveling near the speed of light to test whether the human biological clock can be made to conform to Communist ideology. Next he is sent to a prison camp where he is billeted with a collection of unreconstructed Bolsheviks (including one who either is or believes himself to be the nineteenth-century Russian socialist philosopher and novelist Nikolai Chernyshevsky) who were imprisoned during the purges of 1937. They still fervently believe the rhetoric of the revolution—even going so far as to justify their own imprisonment—and their dutiful enthusiasm makes them easy prey for Fan Fanych's fantastically exaggerated lies about the victories of Communism during their incarceration.[50] While in the camps he recalls his chance encounters with Hitler and Goehring in Berlin in 1929 and his unnoticed presence at the Yalta Conference in 1945. Both instances present him with opportunities for telling Kolya (and the reader) an alternative account of actual events, which, given the novel's complete and seemingly intentional lack of historical verisimilitude to this point, must be considered the product of an individual trapped within a society that as a whole can no longer (nor seems to care to) discriminate between fiction and reality.

Booker and Juraga are right in pointing out that "*Kangaroo* critiques the [Stalinist] system from without, through its focus on Fan Fanych, a marginal figure who is very much outside official circles of power" (115), but his narrative is nevertheless clearly tainted by association with this system. Unlike Kitousov in *Our Golden Ironburg*, Fan Fanych has complete ideological control of his story, in large part because he is telling it in retrospect, at a time when most of the major players are no longer around to exert their influence. Like Aleshkovsky himself, Fan Fanych is released from his prison sentence upon Stalin's death in 1953. Unable to find any trace of Kidalla after being freed, he returns to his apartment and begins life anew, apparently taking the time to relate his picaresque adventures to Kolya, his erstwhile partner in crime, during a prodigious drinking bout. No outside force steps in at any point in the novel either to contradict or to corroborate the wild tales he tells, thus making them as *narratively* monologic (literally and in the Bakhtinian sense) as the Soviet perspective that his recollections undermine.[51] Aleshkovsky's novel, though, is dialogic in that it presents its reality as a parodic-satirical amplification of Soviet history. Fan Fanych's story is itself also dialogic in that it presents both the rigid ideological orthodoxy of characters such as Kidalla, Beria, and Chernyshevsky and Fan Fanych's resistance to the system. However, the manner in which his narrative is a closed and self-affirming system mirrors the rhetorical position of the Soviets, a point designed to keep readers' sympathy for Aleshkovsky's roguish hero from being mistaken for blind trust in his story.

The inherent inadequacies of *any* subjective attempt to arrange the details of existence into an authoritative narrative are a central concern of Sokolov's *Astrophobia,* perhaps the quintessential work of Russian historiographic metafiction. Composed in the early 1980s and first published in 1984 (nearly a decade after Sokolov's emigration from the Soviet Union), *Astrophobia* is one of the most comprehensive satires of Soviet society. Like *Our Golden Ironburg* and *Kangaroo,* Sokolov's novel couches its social criticism within extreme formal avant-gardism, demanding not only a high degree of diligence in its readers but also extensive familiarity with minutiae of Russian history and literature. In her article "Sasha Sokolov and His Literary Context," Olga Matich calls it "a postmodern encyclopedia of contemporary Russian life in its various discourses" (315). Booker and Juraga add the qualification that "almost everything in this brilliant text is addressed in one way or another to previous texts and especially to the ways those texts address the events of Soviet history" (145). They go on to write that the privileged (and impossible) position within Soviet history that Sokolov gives to Palisander Dahlberg, his protagonist and narrator, allows "his story to shed light on aspects of Soviet history that might otherwise have remained hidden." The object of this disclosure is not to "recover the real truth of the Soviet past" but to create "an outrageous parody of such efforts that ultimately suggests the impossibility of knowing the truth of history" (147–48).[52] Sokolov's narrative thus undermines both unrelentingly positive pro-Soviet and unrelentingly negative anti-Soviet accounts of history by self-consciously pointing out the fictionalizing impulse behind both such ideologically charged historical perspectives.

The chief difference between Sokolov and his fictional narrator is that Sokolov never allows the line between fiction and history to be blurred. As a novel, *Astrophobia* repeatedly calls attention to its own fictional (and parodic) nature by overt allusions to other texts or by similarly exposed literary devices. Sokolov makes no effort to characterize his novel as a plausible counterhistory of the Soviet Union; in fact, as with Aleshkovsky's *Kangaroo,* the outrageous episodes and unmistakable anachronisms in this novel undermine any such claim a priori. As an autobiography, supposedly completed in

A.D. 2044 and compiled by an unnamed biographer more than seven hundred years later, Palisander's narrative does not make the same kind of admission, claiming instead that its odd construction does not affect its potential to be a precise record of events. Iser's claim that "concealment of fictionality endows an explanation with an appearance of reality" (3) sheds light on the important distinction between Sokolov and Palisander as authors. Sokolov's criticism is directed at those, whether pro-Soviet or anti-Soviet, who mask their fictionalized texts as objectively true accounts of reality.

As a number of critics have pointed out, and Sokolov himself has vigorously asserted, the actual plot details of this novel are largely inconsequential to understanding the novel's themes since they do not cohere in accordance with the rationalist aims of conventional Soviet fiction. D. Barton Johnson provides a succinct summary[53] of Palisander's outlandish life story that illustrates its chaotic nature:

> Palisandr, an orphan, is heir apparent to the leadership of the mysterious secret Order of Watchmen [Keleinaia organizatsiia chasovshchikov], a hereditary group that rules Russia. Palisandr is a universally adored lad of vast and diverse sexual capacities whose welfare is supervised by a Guardian Council consisting of Stalin, Beria, Khrushchev, Brezhnev, and Andropov. The leadership is rumored to be subject to the authority of certain forces abroad, possibly the Masons. In his memoirs, Palisandr recounts his many bizarre, often comic, adventures and misadventures, including childhood sexual escapades with elderly kin and Kremlin wives and widows, a boyish prank that results in Stalin's death, internal exile as a steward of the Government Massage Parlor (located in Novodevichii Convent), an attempt on Brezhnev's life, a pseudo-espionage adventure in western Europe to free Russia from secret Masonic control, and exile abroad from forces that fear his accession to power in Russia. In the west, Palisandr, who proves to be an enthusiastic hermaphrodite, becomes a wandering bisexual courtesan—intimate with the great and near-great, a wealthy writer of scabrous best-sellers, and the owner of the graves of all Russians who have died in exile and emigration. Upon his triumphant return to assume his rightful position, he is accompanied by the coffins of the exiled Russian dead. ("Twilight Cosmos" 639–40)

Elsewhere Johnson sums up both Palisander's self-characterization and Sokolov's external characterization of him even more compactly, noting that although he is "a passive figure who sees himself as History's amanuensis, he is in fact a self-deluded graphomaniac" ("Galoshes" 167). Because of this discrepancy, the *manner* in which the plot is narrated becomes a much more important vehicle for Sokolov to convey his overriding satirical points. Palisander claims to be a faithful recorder of history, rather than openly acknowledging his active participation in shaping both historical events and historical narratives. Likewise, Soviet Communism posited itself as the egalitarian end to which history was inevitably proceeding via conflict between Communism and capitalism—in other words, not a created ideology, but a predestined stage of human development. By the time Sokolov wrote the novel, this benevolent ideological self-image had been discredited by (among other things) Stalinism, the cold war, and the *zastoi* under Brezhnev. Sokolov's literary parody of Palisander's persona and narrative thus also carries within it a satirical critique of the Soviet system that encouraged the various literary and nonliterary styles and genres parodied in the novel.

One of the most common Soviet methods of fictionalizing history involved the aggrandizement of relatively ordinary deeds to heroic status, a practice exemplified by the Stakhanovite movement that began in the 1930s. Such exaggerations often occurred in a military context, whether in terms of actual armed conflict or, as was more common in the cold war, in terms of ideological warfare against a domestic or foreign class enemy. As Clark and others have noted, a common trope in Socialist Realist literature is the often grandiloquent use of epic formulae to aggrandize the deeds of rather ordinary individuals in times of grievous struggle. Soviet rhetoric is filled with examples of this overly epic tone, from ideological "shock workers" or "shock troops" (*udarnie voiska*) to "heroes of socialist labor" (*geroi sotsialisticheskogo truda*), model workers who demonstrated exceptional efficiency. As Alexander Zholkovsky points out, the original Russian title of Sokolov's book begins the parodic critique of this mode of discourse, simply by appending a Homeric suffix to the protagonist's name (381).[54]

The introductory note, supposedly written by Palisander's posthumous biographer, helps frame the ensuing narrative in a hyperbolic context reminiscent of the excessive and toadying praise heaped upon the intellect of Soviet leaders:[55] "Palisander Dahlberg traversed a glorious road, Napoleonic in scope, from simple Kremlin orphan and steward of the Government Massage Parlor to head of state and commander of the powers that were. The seven centuries dividing us from the memoirist's demise have diminished neither the historical significance of his immense stature nor the ideological and artistic merits of his seminal works. Indeed, they stand today as permanent spiritual treasures of the so-called Age of Transition. None of his books is any less precious to us, but this one is infinitely more precious than the rest. Wholly succumbing to the fever of confession, Dahlberg races from first line to last; his pen never stops for mere convention" (*Astrophobia* viii). After the first paragraph, though, it becomes clear that Palisander's narrative relies heavily on elements of "mere convention" taken from a host of different genres and reconstituted, not as the "meticulously reconstructed fragments" (vii) that the biographer attributes to him, but as a self-serving hodgepodge of dubious details.

As Palisander narrates the fictional suicide of Beria, identified not only as the head of the KGB but as Palisander's great uncle, the disharmony between his cocksure narrative tone and the available facts becomes more pronounced: "All at once literally the following happened. Uncle Lavrenty, maligned by minions, hanged himself in despair from the Kremlin's Salvation Tower clock. And though all the chroniclers view the loss in the light of the fatal and unbridgeable gap it left behind, they disagree as to the particulars. Some claim he used the minute hand, others insist on the hour. The guard at hand, however, not only refrains from all claims but omits such details as his own name, first, sur, et caetera. And yet the confidential investigatory report prepared by a specially appointed governmental commission makes it clear that the attempts of one and all dissectors in the laboratory of history to split this particular hair are thoroughly laughable: the time was sixteen minutes to nine" (1). Palisander's haughty dismissal of historians' efforts to study Beria's suicide—a situation made ironic by the real-life circumstances of his death, given that he was executed in December of 1953 for supposedly plotting to overthrow the state after Stalin's death—is problematic on several levels. First, Palisander notes that the extant explanations (that is, the work of "all the chroniclers") differ on the facts but nevertheless agree on their ideological interpretation, which suggests that the latter overrides the former. Second, Palisander fails to realize that the supposedly substantiating detail he cites—itself taken from an internal, and thus potentially distorted, investigation—is no more historically enlightening than the "hairs" he claims are being split by the historians. Finally it certainly does not (and *cannot*, given the missing details) provide the "literal" (*bukval'nyi*) account that his opening sentence implies. As he does throughout the novel, Palisander tries to overcome a lack of definitive information by using a self-assured tone to establish the authority of his dubious version of events.

The fantastic tale Palisander spins in recounting Beria's last hours is so replete with parodies—intentional on Sokolov's part, unintentional on Palisander's—of Soviet hagiography ("The General-General's [Beria's] kindness knew no bounds, and his troops loved him as best they could" [3]) that it actively resists interpretation as anything other than a subjective reconstruction with an ulterior motive. Palisander appears to be aware of his story's credibility problems and frequently interrupts the narrative in an effort to convince readers that these shortcomings in no way affect its authenticity. Immediately after waxing rhapsodic over the alleged uprightness of "Horse Marine officer Yakov Nezabudka,"[56] the same guard singled out for censure only a few lines earlier for having failed to include his own name in his report of Beria's suicide, Palisander directly addresses his reader to defend his narrative against potential charges of misrepresentation: "But, you may ask, have we not slipped into matters mythopoeic, are we not juggling the facts, do we not make an idol unto ourselves of this—how shall I put it—unknown seahorseman? Not in the least. Ensign Nezabudka is, in a sense, more real than the celestial beings we have become. We are cut off from reality; he is manifest, day-to-day, down-to-earth" (2–3).

Palisander's language here is an unwitting parody of the common Soviet practice of glorifying a common soldier, peasant, or worker as the exemplary Soviet man. His words make explicit the substantive separation of the Soviet ruling classes from the populace, in spite of rhetorical efforts to mask them. Propagandistic biographical accounts of Soviet leaders—such as those that called attention to Stalin's alleged populism—attempted to obscure this separation by claiming that the leaders were simply and benevolently first among equals, all of whom embodied the same Communist ideals. Palisander downplays or even attempts to negate the effect of his use of qualifying phrases like "in a sense" (*esli khotite*, or, literally, "if you wish"), claiming that this largely fictive reality is entirely legitimate. Ensign Nezabudka seems to exist, as Palisander consults official documents containing his vital statistics, but the version that Palisander inserts into his story is almost entirely a carefully wrought and, yes, mythopoeic (*mifotvorcheskii*) narrative construct.

From the earliest days of the Soviet Union, Bolshevik heroes of fictionalized *ocherki*[57] such as Dmitrii Furmanov's *Chapaev* (1923), Feodor Gladkov's *Tsement* (1925; *Cement*), or Aleksandr Fadeyev's *Razgrom* (1927; *The Rout*) embodied values that would later be exaggerated even further in the "positive hero" (*polozhitel'nyi geroi*) of Socialist Realism. In his *The Positive Hero in Russian Literature* (1958), Rufus W. Mathewson notes that this genealogy can be traced back even further to Russian socialist writers of the 1860s such as Chernyshevsky, who proposed a model of a "new man" in his novel *Chto delat'?* (1863; *What Is to Be Done?*). The "positive hero" of *sotsrealizm* is a fictionalized cousin to the "hero of socialist labor" in that he "should be a paragon, a builder of a new life, a person capable of leadership, a man without any doubts, that is, a model Communist" (Kasack 389). Palisander presents himself (and selected others) largely along these lines, but his overwhelming control over the narration of his autobiography (repeatedly pointed out to the reader in chatty asides) emphasizes his unreliability and reveals the double-voiced parody at work in the book.

Palisander's attempts at identifying with Nezabudka (and thereby providing further verification for his narrative) expose the false humility behind his words: "[Nezabudka's] year, month, and even day of birth corresponded to the year, month and day of birth of yours truly. 'Coevals!' I thought in amazement, 'but what different fates.' I hope this heartrending coincidence helps you accept the fact that Nezabudka did exist, in flesh and blood, height, age, and sex, that he was—let us not mince our words, bromidic as they may be—human. Though of course a first-class careerist" (3).[58] Despite his earlier protestation, Palisander is very much "juggl[ing] the facts" and "minc[ing] his words" here as throughout his narrative. The "heartrending coincidence" is largely irrelevant, since it does not establish Nezabudka's identity any more firmly, and Palisander's closing jibe of "careerist" (*sluzhbist*, a favorite Soviet slur) is an empty and unsupported claim that retroactively attempts to validate his remark about their "different fates." He "varnishes reality" to his own advantage and his comments about the nature of conventional history shed light on why he feels compelled to tinker with his narrative in such a manner: "Assuming that one discounts a certain apocalyptic ring to its otherwise apoplectic intonations, the first thing one notices is the perhaps not entirely fortuitous fact that it is filled, glutted, with scrupulously dated but unknown and unknowable events. Taken separately, they perplex; taken together, they dismay. In the end, one has no idea what to think. . . . Insofar as one must come to a decision, form some sort of minimally informed ranks, one bites the bullet and formulates a credo" (19).

Palisander claims, furthermore, that "there have always been people and nations that publicly harbor positive or negative feelings toward one another; and not far off there have been people writing about such interrelations. . . . No wonder we begin to yawn and nod and whatever we happen to be holding, despite the esteem in which we hold it, falls from our hands, our academic mortarboard slips down over our eyes, and we doze off yet again" (19).[59] The ubiquity of history has led to perplexity and boredom, and Palisander intends for his history-with-credo to rectify this by making history both comprehensible and interesting again.

By itself, this approach would not present a problem, except that Palisander maintains, as the Soviets did both before and during the cold war, that basing a historical perspective on a particular ideology does not alter its epistemological nature. Also, Palisander's solution for the complaint that consideration of historical facts can "dismay" changes the goal of history from rational analysis to emotional inspiration. When such a tainted history is used to reendorse the ideology that informed it in the first place, the logic becomes circular, and thus invalid and untenable. Much like the deliberate intermingling of reality and fable that Derrida finds central to the nuclear arms race, Palisander's method of composing history eradicates the possibility of distinguishing between *doxa* and *épistémè* and similarly generates a self-sustaining fiction. Sokolov's parodic presentation equates Palisander's logic with Soviet rhetoric in general, claiming that both *invariably* value form over substance, credo over fact, utility over veracity.

The conclusion of the section on Beria's suicide finally exposes the credo at work behind the scenes in Palisander's retelling:

> [Beria's] final thought was of his great-nephew, whom, the peripeteias in their relationship notwithstanding, he loved dearly like a father.
>   "Dare, Palisander!" He shouted in the direction of the Convent of the New Virgin and at the top of his mental lungs. "Dare!" he shouted,

balancing on the threshold of nothingness. And with a child-like clasp
of the hands he crossed over. (8)

Palisander ennobles Beria as a tragic suicide who was driven to kill himself
out of despair at his colleagues' lack of social conscience. All but the most
rigidly conformist Soviet reader can recognize this as an outright fabrication,
but the sheer discontinuity between Beria's execution at the end of a notorious tenure as head of the KGB and this anecdote of an altruistic martyrdom
begins to cast doubt on Palisander's subsequent arrangements. This doubt
is heightened by the nonsensicality of some of Palisander's phrases, such as
the odd adverb *umoglasno,* translated as "at the top of his mental lungs" but
literally meaning something along the more paradoxical lines of "publicly,
within his mind." Finally the maudlin sentimentality of Beria's exhortation to
Palisander would strike Soviet readers as a clear borrowing from Socialist
Realism, in which the example and sacrifice of the "positive hero" provide
both emotional uplift and encouragement to continue working toward the
"radiant future." Palisander's formal adaptation of the impoverished rhetoric
of Socialist Realism, a genre whose status even within official Soviet literature had been devalued by the time Sokolov wrote *Astrophobia,* finalizes his
demise as a reliable narrator and frames the rest of the novel as metahis-
tory/metafiction. The reader has been made blatantly aware of Palisander's
tendency to alter information to correspond to his credo and is much more
likely to notice its manifestations in the remainder of the novel, thus allowing Sokolov to concoct an encyclopedic series of parodic and satirical episodes
that cover an expansive, albeit thoroughly implausible, Soviet history.

The self-apparent although strenuously denied artifice of Palisander's congenial characterizations of Beria, Stalin, Brezhnev, himself, and others reveals
the parodic-satiric intention of Sokolov's novel. The often grotesquely sentimentalized portraits that Palisander paints of such unquestionably distaste-
ful figures as Stalin and Beria are, as Booker and Juraga point out, "quite
consistent with the representations . . . in socialist realist works of the time"
(150). Such supposedly objective representations appear not only in Socialist
Realist fiction, but also in ostensibly nonfictional (auto)biographies, as Palisander's narrative claims to be. Matich's discussion of the subversive function of the anecdote helps explain how fiction and nonfiction intersect in
Soviet-era satire: "Related to the satire in content and form, the anecdote
performs an analogous function in Soviet culture. Voinovich's *Life and Extraordinary Adventures of Private Ivan Chonkin* . . . is patterned on the anecdote, except that what is anecdote in Soviet reality is life in the satirical novel.
The result is a reversal of the life/art relationship, according to which art becomes more real than life because Soviet life is so fantastic" ("Is There" 186).
Voinovich himself echoed this statement concerning the "reversal of the
life/art relationship" in a 1990 interview, stating that "it's not that the book

[*Moscow 2042*, in this case] reflects reality, but that reality is beginning to reflect fiction" (quoted in Ryan-Hayes 215).

While Matich's analysis does not explicitly share Morson's view that parody achieves satire by recontextualizing a nonparodic original in an absurd setting, her interpretation of Voinovich's novel, an exemplar of Soviet-era satire, clearly is conversant with it. Her definition of the "anecdote" being transformed into parody by the simple fact of its describing an absurd or "fantastic" society, is essentially the same as Morson's Bakhtin-derived notion of "double-voiced" parody, since both imply a superficial straightforward reading and a satirical subtext. Thus Palisander's story is not only a mock epic and a mock autobiography but also, specifically, a travesty of Soviet epic and biographical forms that are already themselves perverted by the distorting influence of Soviet ideology. In *Astrophobia* Sokolov simultaneously subverts the aesthetics of Socialist Realism and the false heroic rhetoric behind it by "repeating the original in a significantly inappropriate social or literary setting" (Morson 112).

The works discussed in this chapter exemplify most thoroughly the humanistic subversion of the cold war's cultural logic through satire. Few if any aspects of the fictionalized societies they depict remain untouched by distortions than can be justified—by those who benefit from them, at least—to some perceived necessity within the grand-scale ideological struggle of the cold war. The wholesale revelation of such distortions is intended to remind the reader that the costs of the cold war cannot be measured simply in the dollars and rubles expended on military budgets, but also in terms of any authentic understanding of the world and one's own place in it. Whether propping up a myth of American exceptionalism (as in *The Public Burning*) or recasting Beria's participation in mass murder as heroism (as in *Astrophobia*), such deceits serve only to perpetuate the power structures responsible for the grotesque, dangerous, and dehumanized worlds of these novels. None of these authors offers a definitive view of reality to replace the ones they critique in their works, but all of them accomplish Pynchon's goal of putting "more humanistic concerns" before their readers, both by showing them the perils of *not* addressing these concerns and by exposing unacknowledged fabrications that they believe to be damagingly permeating American and Russian culture during the cold war. Neither of these techniques offers a guarantee of escape from the snares of cold war cultural logic—after all, as Pynchon noted, we "average poor bastards are completely outclassed"—but they are a first step without which meaningful resistance and reform are impossible.

Epilogue

THERE IS STILL TIME

Late in Walter M. Miller Jr.'s apocalyptic cold war novel *A Canticle for Leibowitz* (1959), Abbot Jethrah Zerchi addresses the Brethren of the Order of Leibowitz, a group of Catholic monks devoted to preserving fragments of documentary knowledge from a previous age. Outside the monastery's walls, an international incident threatens to once again unleash nuclear weapons, eighteen hundred years after the "Flame Deluge" that nearly eradicated human life from the planet and precipitated the Order's mission. Miller's novel ambiguously presents the monks as both martyrs in the fight against (self-)destructive ignorance and custodians of information that allows the seemingly inevitable cycle of mass destruction to repeat itself.[1] Dom Zerchi's speech provides a context for a retrospective reading of *A Canticle for Leibowitz* in the context of all the cold war fictions that expressed a combination of fear, anger, perplexity, and strained faith in humanity—which would include most of the works mentioned in this study: "Brothers, let us *not* assume that there is going to be war. Let's remind ourselves that Lucifer [that is, nuclear weapons] has been with us—this time—for nearly two centuries. And was dropped only twice, in sizes smaller than megaton. We all know what *could* happen, if there's war. . . . Back then, in the Saint Leibowitz' [*sic*] time, maybe they didn't know what would happen. Or perhaps they did know, but could not quite believe it until they tried it—like a child who knows what a loaded pistol is supposed to do, but has never pulled a trigger before. They had not yet seen a billion corpses. They had not yet seen the still-born, the monstrous, the de-humanized, the blind. They had not yet seen the madness and the murder and the blotting out of reason. Then they did it, and then they saw it" (255). He is still hopeful that a recurrence of the previous disaster can be averted in this situation, in part because the technological ability to wage all-out nuclear war is this time coupled with firsthand knowledge of the consequences of such behavior: "Now—*now* the princes, the presidents, the praesidiums, now they know—with dead certainty. They can know it by the children they beget and send to asylums for the deformed.

They know it and they've kept the peace. Not Christ's peace, certainly, but peace, until lately—with only two warlike incidents in as many centuries. Now they have the bitter certainty. My sons, they cannot do it again. Only a race of madmen could do it again" (255–56). The novel's ending would indicate that humanity *is* a race of madmen, since they do in fact scorch the planet a second time with nuclear fire despite knowing the inevitable consequences of such an action.

Miller's novel fictionally addresses a question that recurs nonfictionally twenty years later in Carl Sagan's book and television series *Cosmos* (1980). Sagan states that "there are not yet any obvious signs of extraterrestrial intelligence and this makes us wonder whether civilizations like ours always rush implacably, headlong, toward self-destruction" (318). He doubts that even a remnant of human society would survive a nuclear war, writing, "Full-scale nuclear war has never happened. Somehow this is taken to imply that it never will. But we can experience it only once. By then it will be too late to reformulate the statistics" (330). *A Canticle for Leibowitz* makes the claim (in many ways more grim that Sagan's) that humanity might be able to experience the horrors of nuclear war and its aftermath more than once. However, it presents the survival of the species as the ultimate pyrrhic victory, given the inexorable repetition of past mistakes. Miller essentially argues that "reformulat[ing] the statistics" would make no difference if "a billion corpses" are not compelling enough reasons by themselves.

Miller and Sagan both wrote during times—the late 1950s and late 1970s, respectively—at which the ideological tensions of the cold war seemed increasingly likely to touch off a cataclysmic nuclear exchange.[2] That likelihood remained remote even during the most tense moments of the cold war, but as McGeorge Bundy stated in downplaying the severity of the Cuban Missile Crisis, the "objective risk of escalation to the nuclear level may have been as large as 1 in 100 . . . [but] in this apocalyptic matter the risk can be very small indeed and still much too large for comfort" (quoted in Gaddis 269). Thus Sagan's contention that "the development of nuclear weapons and their delivery systems will, sooner or later, lead to global disaster" (328) arises from a similar cultural context as Miller's grim prediction that experience only forestalls self-annihilation instead of preventing it. Both argue that the mere presence of weapons of such unparalleled destructive power is neither the calculated risk nor the bargaining tool that strategists and politicians on both sides made it out to be, but a powder keg of epic proportions waiting only to be lit.

The end of the cold war undoubtedly lessened the threat of all-out nuclear war both by eliminating the direct confrontation between the United States and the Soviet Union (and their corresponding nuclear arsenals) and by accelerating the nuclear arms reduction process. However, the capability for nearly instantaneous large-scale devastation will continue to exist just as long as the bombs and missiles do. Furthermore, as *A Canticle for Leibowitz* eloquently illustrates, the knowledge of how to make such weapons alone presents a threat that cannot be eliminated, only managed in a reasonable fashion. Lifton and Mitchell suggest in *Hiroshima in America* that such management involves "properly stigmatizing the weapons" so that their use becomes inherently and incontrovertibly absurd. They argue that such a perspective would also allow a more genuine appraisal of the influence nuclear weapons have had on the development of society: "We can return to human agency in controlling our lethal technology. And we can 'disenthrall ourselves' from the nuclear deity and from the Hiroshima narrative that has so long shielded and promoted that deity. We can come to recognize the extent to which that Hiroshima narrative has blunted our senses and subverted our moral imagination" (354–55). The satires discussed in the preceding chapters questioned the effects of the "Hiroshima narrative" amid numerous other cultural narratives that (de)formed U.S. and Soviet culture of the cold war era. The overriding aspiration of this collective effort was to subvert the jingoistic philosophies that promised either a capitalist or a Communist utopia that they could not (and perhaps never intended to) deliver.

Because the historical reality of the cold war was predicated on fictional constructs presented as truth—that is, Derrida's "fables" or Iser's "non-literary fictions"—it is only through scrutiny and, if necessary, renunciation of such dishonest cultural fictions that humanity can again achieve some measure of serenity and assurance that living with the knowledge of the bomb is not simply a matter of waiting for the end. Lifton and Mitchell's prescription for "renewal" reveals the significance of a candid attitude toward the past, an element that they, like Russian and American subversive satirists, argue has been missing. They offer this prognosis: "It can enable us to emerge from nuclear entrapment and rediscover our imaginative capacities on behalf of human good. We can overcome our moral inversion and cease to justify weapons or actions of mass killing. We can condemn and then step back from acts of desecration and recognize what Camus called 'a philosophy of limits.' In that way we can also take steps to cease betraying ourselves, cease harming and deceiving our own people. We can also free our society from its apocalyptic concealment, and in the process enlarge our vision. We can break out of our long-standing numbing in the vitalizing endeavor of learning, or relearning, to feel. And we can divest ourselves of a debilitating sense of futurelessness and once more feel bonded to past and future generations" (356). Lifton and Mitchell contend that the end of the cold war should not simply occasion a celebration of survival akin to the sigh of relief that follows a successful turn at Russian roulette, especially since continued participation in *either* situation dramatically increases one's odds of eventually losing. Rather, it should lead to solemn and honest reflection on the reasoning that unleashed the nuclear genie with which the world must henceforth contend.

This process of reflection is abetted not only by a review of past expressions of dissent, but also by study of artistic engagements with the cold war that are afforded the perspectival benefits of hindsight. In the decade since the end of the cold war, novelists such as DeLillo, Heller, Lydia Millet, Pynchon, Phillip Roth, Gerald Vizenor, Vonnegut, Aksyonov, Mark Kharitonov, Vladimir Makanin, Viktor Pelevin, Vladimir Sorokin, and Svetlana Vasilenko have collectively produced a substantial body of work that continues to reexamine the assumptions of recent history with a skeptical eye in order to avoid repeating the missteps of the past. Makanin's *Laz* (1990; *Escape Hatch*) and *Dolog nash put'* (1991; *The Long Road Ahead*), Kharitonov's *Linii sud'by* (1992; *Lines of Fate*), Pelevin's *Omon Ra* (1992) and *Zhizn' nasekomykh* (1994; *The Life of Insects*), Heller's *Closing Time* (1994), Sorokin's *Norma* (1994; *The Norm*), Pelevin's *Chapaev i pustota* (1996; *Chapaev and Void*),[3] DeLillo's *Underworld* (1997), Pynchon's *Mason & Dixon* (1997),[4] Vonnegut's *Timequake* (1997), Aksyonov's *Novyi sladostnyi stil'* (1997; *The New Sweet Style*), Vasilenko's *Durochka* (1998; *Little Fool*), Roth's *I Married a Communist* (1998), Voinovich's *Monumental'naia propaganda* (2002; *Monumental Propaganda*), Vizenor's *Hiroshima Bugi* (2003), Millet's *Oh Pure and Radiant Heart* (2005), and Pynchon's *Against the Day* (2006) are just some of the post–cold war works that fit this description. I can readily foresee a study that continues the comparative analysis of this project by examining the variety of techniques that American and Russian writers have used as part of a wider cultural convalescence after the cold war. For the time being, however, such a project remains a scheme for the future; in other words, it is the kind of prospect that the authors of the cautionary tales and darkly satirical diatribes dealt with in these pages hoped to ensure for their descendants. Humanity has been granted a reprieve— perhaps temporary, perhaps not—from self-extinction. In light of this, we cold war survivors have a communal responsibility to recognize that, as the banner at the end of *On the Beach* proclaims, there *is* still time to learn from the errors of the past in order to create a future world that ends with *neither* a bang nor a whimper of our own devising.

APPENDIX

Time Line of Events and Publications

1896   Radioactivity is discovered.

1905   Revolution takes place in Russia, resulting in moderate political and social reforms.

1906   Adams publishes *The Education of Henry Adams*.

1914–18   World War I.

1917–21   Revolution and civil war occur in Russia.

1917   The Soviet Union is established.

1919–20   American and British vessels blockade ice-free Soviet ports.

1919   Cabell publishes *Jurgen*.

1921–29   New Economic Policy (NEP).

1922   Treaty of Rapallo is concluded between Germany and the Soviet Union. Lewis publishes *Babbitt*.

1924   Lenin dies. Stalin consolidates power gradually over the next five years. Zamyatin publishes *My* (*We*).

1925   Bulgakov publishes *Diavoliada* (*Diaboliad*) and writes *Sobach'e serdtse* (*The Heart of a Dog*), which remains unpublished until 1968.

1927   Olesha publishes *Zavist'* (*Envy*).

1928   Il'f and Petrov publish *Dvenadsat' stul'ev* (*The Twelve Chairs*). Mayakovsky first produces *Klop* (*The Bedbug*).

1929   Mayakovsky first produces *Bania* (*The Bathhouse*).

1930   Stalin begins policies of collectivization and "dekulakification."

1932   Writers' Union replaces RAPP as the official Soviet literary organization. Huxley publishes *Brave New World*.

1934   Kirov is murdered.

1935   Stakhanovite labor movement begins in the Soviet Union. Lewis publishes *It Can't Happen Here*.

1936–38   The "great terror," or *yezhovshchina*.

1936   The show trials of Zinoviev and Kamenev are conducted in response to Kirov murder.

1938   Hahn and Strassmann discover atomic fission.

1939–45   World War II.

1939   Ribbentrop and Molotov sign the German-Soviet nonaggression agreement.

1940   Britain sets up Maud Committee to investigate feasibility of atomic bomb.

1941   Germany invades the Soviet Union. The Soviet Union joins the Allies.

1942   Fermi achieves self-sustaining atomic chain reaction. The Manhattan Project begins.

1943   The Soviet atomic bomb project under Kurchatov begins.

1944   Allies invade occupied France. Soviets begin full-scale counteroffensive against Germany.

1945   The Yalta Conference convenes with Roosevelt, Stalin, and Churchill taking part. Roosevelt dies, and Truman becomes president. Nazi concentration camps are liberated. The Trinity test at Alamogordo, New Mexico, marks the first successful atomic bomb explosion. The United States explodes atomic bombs over Hiroshima and Nagasaki.

1946   The first fully electronic digital computer (ENIAC) is developed. Churchill gives his "Iron Curtain" speech. Akhmatova and Zoshchenko are singled out for censure in speech by Zhdanov. U.S. Operation Crossroads nuclear tests are conducted on Bikini atoll. Atomic Energy Act automatically classifies nuclear information. Hersey publishes *Hiroshima*.

1947   The Truman Doctrine is formulated. The Marshall Plan is enacted to help rebuild Europe. HUAC begins large-scale investigation of suspected Communists in government and the arts.

1948   Israel declares independence. Soviets begin blockade of West Berlin. British and American planes airlift supplies to the city. Hiss accused of spying.

1949   The blockade of West Berlin ends after 321 days. NATO is established. The Soviet Union tests its first atomic bomb. People's Republic of China is established. Orwell publishes *Nineteen Eighty-Four*.

1950–53 Korean War.

1950   U.S. Federal Civil Defense Administration is established. Senator McCarthy claims to have a list of "known Communists" working in the State Department. National Security Council Resolution 68 recommends nuclear arsenal buildup and aggressive military containment policy toward Communism. Klaus Fuchs is convicted of espionage. Hiss is convicted of perjury.

1952   The United States detonates hydrogen bomb at Eniwetok atoll. Eisenhower is elected president. Vonnegut publishes *Player Piano*.

ca.   The Thaw (*Ottepel'*), a period of relaxed governmental control in the
1953–64 Soviet Union.

1953   Stalin dies, and Khrushchev succeeds him as general secretary. The Rosenbergs are executed as Soviet spies.

1954   The Communist Party is outlawed in the United States. The SEATO military alliance is formed. The U.S. Senate censures McCarthy. Simonov openly questions Socialist Realism at Writers' Congress. Golding publishes *Lord of the Flies*.

1955   The Warsaw Pact military alliance is formed. The Geneva Summit includes Khrushchev, Eisenhower, and British prime minister Eden. The liberal journal *Iunost'* (*Youth*) is established.

1956   Khrushchev gives "secret speech" denouncing Stalin at the Twenty-fifth Party Congress. Soviets forcibly put down Hungarian insurrection. Khrushchev makes "We will bury you" comment.

1957   Soviet Union launches Sputnik, the first artificial satellite. Both the Soviet Union and the United States successfully test ICBMs. Pasternak publishes *Doktor Zhivago* in the West, for which he receives the Nobel Prize in 1958. Shute publishes *On the Beach*.

1958   Khrushchev becomes Soviet premier. The Soviet Union, the United States, and Britain suspend atmospheric nuclear testing.

1959   Communists' revolt is successful in Cuba. Vice President Nixon visits the Soviet Union, and Khrushchev visits the United States. Miller publishes *A Canticle for Leibowitz*. Kramer's film of *On the Beach* released. Sinyavsky (as Abram Tertz) publishes *Chto takoe sotsialisticheskii realizm? (What Is Socialist Realism?)* and *Sud idyot (The Trial Begins)* in the West.

1960   An American U-2 spy plane is shot down over the Soviet Union. Kennedy is elected president. Kahn publishes *On Thermonuclear War*.

1961   Soviet cosmonaut Gagarin orbits the earth. U.S.-sponsored Bay of Pigs invasion fails in Cuba. The Berlin Wall is erected. The Soviet Union resumes atmospheric nuclear testing. Aksyonov publishes *Zvezdnyi bilet (A Ticket to the Stars)*. Heller publishes *Catch-22*. Vonnegut publishes *Mother Night*. *The Twilight Zone* episode "The Shelter" airs on televison.

1962   American astronaut Glenn orbits the earth. The United States resumes atmospheric nuclear testing. The Cuban Missile Crisis takes place. Burdick and Wheeler publish *Fail-Safe*. Sinyavsky/Tertz publishes *Liubimov (The Makepeace Experiment)*.

1963   "Hot line" between the Kremlin and White House is established. Kennedy visits Berlin. The Limited Test-Ban Treaty is signed. Kennedy is assassinated, and Johnson becomes president. Pynchon publishes *V.* Vonnegut publishes *Cat's Cradle*. Kubrick's *Dr. Strangelove* is released.

1964–73 Vietnam War.

1964   The Gulf of Tonkin Resolution allows increased U.S. military presence in Southeast Asia. Khrushchev is ousted and replaced by Brezhnev and Kosygin. China successfully tests its first atomic bomb. Johnson is elected president.

1965   Daniel and Sinyavsky are arrested for publishing abroad.

1966   U.S. Senate hearings on the Vietnam War begin. Daniel and Sinyavsky are tried and imprisoned. Barth publishes *Giles Goat-Boy*. Pynchon publishes *The Crying of Lot 49*. Watkins produces *The War Game* for BBC television. Iskander publishes *Sozvezdie kozlotura (The Goatibex Constellation)*.

1967   Stalin's daughter Svetlana Alliluyeva defects to West. Israel and Egypt fight the Six-Day War. China successfully tests its first hydrogen bomb. Barth publishes "The Literature of Exhaustion." Barthelme publishes *Snow White*. Lifton publishes *Death in Life*.

1968   American military involvement in Vietnam peaks. Dr. Martin Luther King Jr. and Robert Kennedy are assassinated. The Nuclear Arms Nonproliferation Treaty is signed. Soviets invade Czechoslovakia to put down the "Prague Spring." Nixon is elected president. Barthelme publishes *Unspeakable Practices, Unnatural Acts*.

1969   Armstrong walks on the moon. Strategic Arms Limitation Talks (SALT) begin. Vonnegut publishes *Slaughterhouse-Five*.

1970   Paris Peace Talks begin between the United States and Vietnam. The United
        States deploys first MIRVed missiles (Minuteman III). The United States
        invades Cambodia. Solzhenitsyn is awarded Nobel Prize for Literature.

1971   China joins the UN. Percy publishes *Love in the Ruins*. Tanner publishes
        City of Words. Carl and Ellendea Proffer found Ardis Publishers in Ann
        Arbor, Michigan.

ca.

1972–79 Détente.

1972   Nixon visits China. Nixon and Brezhnev sign Anti-Ballistic Missile (ABM)
        Treaty and SALT I agreement. Brodsky emigrates. DeLillo publishes *End
        Zone*. Reed publishes *Mumbo Jumbo*.

1973   Last American combat troops leave Vietnam. Sinyavsky emigrates. Pynchon
        publishes *Gravity's Rainbow*. Iskander publishes *Sandro iz Chegema* (*Sandro
        of Chegem*).

1974   India successfully tests atomic bomb. Nixon resigns from office after Water-
        gate scandal and is replaced by Ford. Solzhenitsyn is expelled from the
        Soviet Union. Limonov emigrates.

1975   Saigon falls, and the United States evacuates embassy. U.S. astronauts and
        Soviet cosmonauts cooperate in *Apollo-Soiuz* linkage. Helsinki Accords are
        signed. Soviets deploy first MIRVed missiles. Sakharov wins Nobel Peace
        Prize. Sokolov emigrates.

1976   The United States celebrates its bicentennial. The United States and Soviet
        Union sign agreement limiting underground testing. Carter is elected presi-
        dent. Zinoviev publishes *Ziiaiushchie vysoty* (*The Yawning Heights*).

1977   New Soviet constitution is ratified, making Brezhnev president. Robert
        Coover publishes *The Public Burning*. Voinovich publishes *Zhizn' i neoby-
        chainye prikliucheniia soldata Ivana Chonkina* (*The Life and Extraordinary
        Adventures of Private Ivan Chonkin*). Zinoviev emigrates.

1978   Dovlatov emigrates and publishes *Nevidimaia kniga* (*The Invisible Book*).
        Zinoviev publishes *Svetloe budushchee* (*The Radiant Future*).

1979   Camp David Accords are signed. A major nuclear incident occurs at Three
        Mile Island, Pennsylvania. The SALT II agreement is signed by Carter and
        Brezhnev. The Soviet invasion of Afghanistan prompts Carter to call for
        U.S. military buildup, thus effectively ending détente. Aksyonov, Iskander,
        Aleshkovsky, and others are involved in the production of the unofficial lit-
        erary almanac *Metropol'*. Aleshkovsky emigrates. Voinovich publishes *Pre-
        tendent na prestol* (*Pretender to the Throne*) and *Putiom vzaimnoi perepiski*
        (*In Plain Russian*).

1980   Sakharov is sentenced to internal exile. The United States boycotts the Mos-
        cow Summer Olympics. Reagan is elected president. Hoban publishes *Ridd-
        ley Walker*. Aksyonov and Voinovich emigrate. Aksyonov publishes *Ozhog*
        (*The Burn*) and *Zolotaia nasha zhelezka* (*Our Golden Ironburg*). Aleshkovsky
        publishes *Ruka* (*The Hand*). Aitmatov publishes *I dol'she veka dlitsia den'*
        (*The Day Lasts More Than a Hundred Years*). Zinoviev publishes *Gomo Sovi-
        etikus* (*Homo Sovieticus*).

1981   Martial law is imposed in Poland in response to Solidarity movement actions. Aksyonov publishes *Ostrov Krym (The Island of Crimea)*. Aleshkovsky publishes *Kenguru (Kangaroo)*. Dovlatov publishes *Kompromiss (The Compromise)*.

1982   Strategic Arms Reduction Talks (START) open in Geneva. Brezhnev dies and is replaced by Andropov. Iskander publishes *Kroliki i udavy (Rabbits and Boa Constrictors)*.

1983   Reagan proposes Strategic Defense Initiative (SDI). The MX missile program begins in the United States. Korean Air Lines Flight 007 is shot down by the Soviets. Dovlatov publishes *Nashi (Ours)*.

1984   Alliluyeva returns to the Soviet Union. Andropov dies and is replaced by Chernenko. Derrida publishes his essay "No Apocalypse, Not Now" in *Diacritics* issue devoted to "nuclear criticism." Pynchon publishes "Is It O.K. to Be a Luddite?" and *Slow Learner*. Sokolov publishes *Palisandriia (Astrophobia)*.

1985   Chernenko dies and is replaced by Gorbachev. A summit meeting is held between Reagan and Gorbachev in Geneva. DeLillo publishes *White Noise*. Aksyonov publishes *Skazhi izium (Say Cheese!)*.

1986   Gorbachev announces glasnost and perestroika policies. A major nuclear disaster occurs at Chernobyl. A summit meeting is held between Reagan and Gorbachev in Reykjavik. Sakharov is released from internal exile. Voinovich publishes *Moskva 2042 (Moscow 2042)* and *Antisovetskii sovetskii soiuz (The Anti-Soviet Soviet Union)*.

1987   A summit meeting is held between Reagan and Gorbachev in Washington, D.C. Percy publishes *The Thanatos Syndrome*.

1988   A summit meeting is held between Reagan and Gorbachev in Moscow. A U.S. naval vessel shoots down Iran Air Flight 655. George H. W. Bush is elected president.

1989   Soviet troops withdraw from Afghanistan. Prodemocracy demonstrations are suppressed with force in China. Numerous Eastern European nations renounce ties with the Soviet Union. The Berlin Wall is torn down.

1990   Germany unifies. Previously revoked Soviet citizenship of Aksyonov, Voinovich, Solzhenitsyn, and others is reinstated. Pynchon publishes *Vineland*.

1991   The Persian Gulf War is fought between a U.S.-led international coalition and Iraq. The START Treaty is signed by Bush and Gorbachev. An attempted coup against Gorbachev is mounted by hard-line Communists. Several Soviet republics declare independence. The Commonwealth of Independent States (CIS) is formed. Gorbachev resigns. The Soviet Union ends.

NOTES

Introduction

1. This time frame is not intended to suggest that nuclear anxieties existed only during the years in which both the United States and the Soviet Union possessed the capacity to explode a nuclear weapon. Clearly the fear of Nazi Germany developing the bomb helped spur the Manhattan Project and concern over "rogue states" possessing the bomb still guides American foreign policy. The span indicated here simply represents the boundaries of the most intense and relatively sustained period of *public* nuclear anxiety.

2. Yelstin's own long career as a devoted Communist was largely ignored, for example, a process that would be largely repeated with former KGB officer Vladimir Putin a decade later.

3. Especially noteworthy writers in this category include Chingiz Aitmatov, Anna Akhmatova, Isaak Babel, Olga Berggolts, Yuli Daniel, Yevgeny Yevtushenko, Evgenia Ginzburg, Vassily Grossman, Ilya Il'f, Fazil Iskander, Osip Mandelshtam, Bulat Okudzhava, Yuri Olesha, Boris Pasternak, Boris Pilnyak, and Mikhail Zoshchenko. The degree to which these writers identified themselves as non-Russians varies widely, though. Akhmatova's Ukrainian background (her given name was Anna Gorenko) is hardly evident in her writing, for example, whereas Aitmatov's Kirghiz identity and Babel's Jewishness are intrinsic to their respective works.

4. For the sake of brevity, I will hereafter refer to this organization simply as the Writers' Union.

1. The Role of Literature during the Cold War

1. For more on this initial response, see Moylan, *Scraps of the Untainted Sky,* and Seed, *American Science Fiction and the Cold War.*

2. It should also be noted that the merits of the Thaw itself were far from universally lauded. Nearly every instance of publication of controversial works such as *Not by Bread Alone* and *One Day in the Life of Ivan Denisovich* led to a virulent and publicly expressed backlash (often organized from above by conservative party cadres) against the liberal atmosphere that allowed such a book to appear in print. The accumulation of such sentiments ultimately helped bring about Khrushchev's removal from power.

3. Recently declassified documents that shed considerable light on the political and military machinations behind the crisis are available at George Washington University's

National Security Archive (available online at http://www.gwu.edu/~nsarchiv/nsa/cuba_mis_cri/).

4. See Boyer, *Fallout*, 120–28; Henriksen, *Dr. Strangelove's America*, 281–86.

5. Boyer is not alone among prominent critics and historians in making such a contention. Spencer Weart, in *Nuclear Fear*, is similarly insistent about the disappearance of the bomb from the American conscience: "The 1958–1965 spate of films, novels and magazine articles about accidental war brought down the curtain on the long series of important nuclear fiction and nonfiction published since 1945. Debate over accidental war was the final burst of serious argument before attention turned elsewhere" (279).

6. Even Aksyonov's early works initiated a harsh conservative backlash following the end of the Thaw, by which time he had begun to write in a much more experimental and openly critical manner. Voinovich's early career as an author featured the odd (given the general arc of his career) distinction of having penned a song about the Soviet space program that became widely popular after Nikita Khrushchev sang it atop the Lenin Mausoleum in 1960. Neither could be said to have ever been part of the mainstream of Soviet literature, but both were accepted at least by the more liberal branches of Soviet criticism in their formative years as authors.

7. For compendia and further discussion of these themes in American science fiction, see Brians, *Nuclear Holocausts*; Bartter, *Way to Ground Zero*; and Booker, *Monsters*, 65–104.

8. Yuz Aleshkovsky's *Kenguru* (1981; *Kangaroo*), for example, contains a number of explicit references to the atomic bomb development program under Kurchatov.

9. Among the works she discusses are Daniil Granin's novels *Iskateli* (1954; *Those Who Seek*) and *Idu na grozu* (1964; *Into the Storm*); Andrei Voznesensky's poem "Monolog bitnika" (1962; "A Beatnik's Monologue"); Aitmatov's *I dol'she veka dlitsia den'* (1980; *The Day Lasts More Than a Hundred Years*); Alexander Chakovsky's *Pobeda* (1980–81; *Victory*); and Solzhenitsyn's *V kruge pervom* (1968; *The First Circle*) and *Arkhipelag GULAG* (1973–75; *The Gulag Archipelago*).

10. Boyer's *By the Bomb's Early Light* and Stone's *Literary Aftershocks* both present excellent documentary evidence of the anxious and conflicted years after the bombings. The former focuses on a wider social context while the latter contains a chapter expressly treating fictional and nonfictional literary works from 1945 to 1963.

11. The United States exploded the world's first hydrogen bomb at Elugelab atoll in the South Pacific late in 1952. The Soviet Union followed suit just after the end of the Korean War in September 1953. According to the *Bulletin of the Atomic Scientists*, over the course of the Korean War years (1950–53), the number of operational warheads in the United States grew from 369 to 1,436, while the Soviet arsenal expanded from 5 to 120. These numbers would grow to 20,434 and 1,605, respectively, by the end of the decade (Norris and Kristiansen, "Nuclear Notebook," 64–66).

12. Szilard even tried his hand at writing antinuclear satirical fiction, publishing a collection of five stories (composed between 1948 to 1960) titled *The Voice of the Dolphins and Other Stories* in 1961. He also is indirectly (or perhaps directly; see Grant, *Companion*, 89–95) connected to another prominent cold war satire, having formulated a refutation to the "Maxwell's Demon" theory that plays a prominent metaphorical role in Pynchon's *Crying of Lot 49*.

13. Spencer Weart discusses Sakharov's role in the limited Soviet antinuclear campaign of the late 1950s in *Nuclear Fear*: "Doubts about government bomb tests were stirring even in the Soviet Union. Although Soviet officials discouraged all talk of technological danger, some biologists privately discussed genetic risks. Backed up by the statements of foreigners such as [Albert] Schweitzer and [Linus] Pauling, they won quiet support from leading nuclear physicists and especially from Andrei Sakharov, who wrote Khrushchev to warn against the tests. These private concerns became public when the Soviet government backed up its peace propaganda with a 1958 announcement that it would cease all tests. Now the Supreme Soviet openly stated that testing meant 'the poisoning of human organisms.' At once Sakharov and other scientists began to publish, in the Soviet press, Pauling-style warnings about the thousands or millions of babies who would be born defective if other nations continued to test bombs" (204–5).

14. U.S. opposition to Soviet-backed regimes in Latin America, Asia, and Africa, for example, had little or nothing to do with any potential threat of nuclear weapons bases being installed there, as they nearly were in Cuba during the early 1960s. Carol R. Saivetz and Sylvia Woodby skillfully discuss the nonnuclear nature of the peripheral cold war among client states of the two superpowers in their *Soviet–Third World Relations*.

15. Seed's *American Science Fiction and the Cold War* and Henriksen's *Dr. Strangelove's America* are two excellent works that adopt this broader perspective of the cold war in an American context.

16. Richard Chapple's *Soviet Satire of the Twenties* provides a more detailed examination of the complexities underlying the production of satire during this period.

17. Ironically, Valentin Kataev's 1926 satirical novel *Rastratchiki* (*The Embezzlers*) won official praise for its author despite its negative caricature of life under the NEP. Kataev's satire is admittedly less biting than Bulgakov's or Zoshchenko's, and it places the blame for problems with NEP on antirevolutionary elements instead of on its planners. The disparity in reaction nonetheless demonstrates that subjects were not necessarily taboo to Soviet satirists as long as their treatment served the normative ideological function.

18. The continued publication and popularity of Il'f and Petrov's works during the mid-1930s, despite an outcry over their generally unflattering portrait of the NEP period, indicates that some ideologically aberrant satire still managed to slip through the cracks.

19. Unlike in the Soviet Union, occasions of direct governmental intervention in literary matters in the United States are generally more local (as in school boards banning particular books from libraries) than national phenomena, although Herbert Mitgang's *Dangerous Dossiers* suggests that federal surveillance and occasional harassment of authors for ideological reasons was hardly uncommon.

20. She does, of course, discuss the related concept of parody at length in *Poetics of Postmodernism,* and many of her claims about the purposes of postmodern fiction clearly contain an understanding of their satirical implications.

21. This is the case with most genres with a lengthy lifespan. If interpreted within the tradition of the historical novel, the differences among Sir Walter Scott's *Ivanhoe*, Tolstoy's *War and Peace*, and Charles Frazier's *Cold Mountain* stem in large part from

the differences in their respective cultural and temporal contexts, even though all three conform to the genre's conventions (see Holman and Harmon, *Handbook to Literature*, 229–30).

2. The Intersection of Literature and Politics during the Cold War

1. Some Slavists dispute this view, claiming that the positive effects of the Thaw were powerful enough to cause a greater tolerance for ideological divergences in official literature even during the 1970s. See Hosking's *Beyond Socialist Realism* and Peterson's *Subversive Imaginations*.

2. Voinovich cites specific individuals ("KGB agent Tsvigun," "professional [writer Vadim] Kozhevinkov," and "Marshal Brezhnev") as examples of this corrupted system in the Russian original. The published English translation mistakenly renders *milit-sioneri* (Soviet policemen) as "millionaires" (*millioneri*), an error I have corrected here.

3. In this vein Gary Saul Morson (writing as Alicia Chudo) only half-jokingly defines Aesopian language as follows in his satirical piece "The Devil's Dictionary of Received Ideas": "A Russian method of using apparently innocent words and gestures to express subversive meanings. Often practiced and always suspected. Thus the Russian cautionary habit of checking to make sure nothing one writes could possibly be taken as alluding to a Soviet leader; under Brezhnev, eyebrows disappeared from literature" (Chudo, *And Quiet Flows the Vodka*, 180).

4. See Clowes, *Russian Experimental Fiction*; Ryan-Hayes, *Contemporary Russian Satire*; Booker, *Dystopian Impulse*, 115–40; Morson, *Boundaries of Genre*, 102–3; and Porter, *Russia's Alternative Prose*, 20–26.

5. In the cultural environment of the early twenty-first century, such a skeptical/cynical view of political utterance may seem almost commonplace, given the scrutiny—in popular if not governmental forums—of the premises upon which the 2003 invasion of Iraq was based. The relative ease with which the American populace accepted the official version of the Gulf of Tonkin incident as a *cassus belli* in 1964 serves as a powerful reminder that such a view has not always been as prevalent.

6. As I illustrate in later chapters, the strategies for this approach vary widely, from Zinoviev's narrator musing on how to define the genre of the book he is writing in *Homo Sovieticus* to Coover's incorporation of actual quotes from Eisenhower's speeches and transcripts from the Rosenberg espionage trial into *The Public Burning*.

7. The Russian Civil War is an "international" conflict from the standpoint of this schema in the sense that the secessionist Confederacy represents a quintessentially "un-American" worldview.

8. Thomas Moore's remarkably concise summary runs as follows: "[Laszlo] Jamf of Darmstadt came to Harvard on an academic grant, sometime in the late 1920s, where, on the model of the Watson-Raymer experiments in which an 'Infant Albert' had been conditioned to feel reflex terror of all furry things, he conditioned Infant Tyrone to respond to a certain mysterious smell by getting an erection. . . . Broderick Slothrop [Tyrone's father] agreed to let the I. G. Farben cartel of Germany pay for Tyrone's future education at Harvard and signed a contract committing the Slothrop Paper Company to manufacture the Notgeld banknotes of the calamitous German inflation of the 1920s. Linkages for these various deals ran through Massachusetts businessman Lyle Bland, who had 'arrangements' with German financier Hugo Stinnes.

. . . During the inflation, Laszlo Jamf sat on the board of directors of the Swiss Grössli Chemical Corporation, a firm soon to be incorporated into the Farben cartel. The Farben cartel in turn had linkages with German General Electric and, therefore, with American GE 'under Swope, whose ideas on matters of "control" ran close to those of Walther Rathenau, of German GE,' and later German foreign minister" (72).

9. Although he mentions Soviet attitudes about the United States in passing, he does not outline any specific Soviet cognitive schemata.

10. I will briefly address some of these instances in this section in the process of exporting Maltby's template to Soviet society. More detailed explication of each can be found in subsequent chapters.

11. See Riasanovsky, *History of Russia,* 593; Remington, *Truth of Authority,* 118–20.

12. Turonok, Dovlatov's editor in the story, uses the word *polnotsennyi,* literally "fully valued," to describe the ideal child he seeks. He enumerates the specific characteristics of such a child as follows: "No damaged goods, nothing gloomy. No cesarean [*sic*] sections. No unwed mothers. A complete set of parents. A healthy boy meeting all the social requirements" (*Compromise,* 27).

13. One need look no further than the general American public's somewhat shocked reaction to the revelation in early 2002 of the propaganda campaigns run by the Pentagon's Office of Strategic Influence to see how durable this association remains.

14. *Ziiaiushchie vysoty* is a distortion of *siiaiushchie vysoty sotsializma,* "the gleaming heights of socialism."

15. Consistent with Soviet patterns of giving villages new "Soviet names," the name of the town has been changed from the very apt Griaznoye, "dirty" or "muddy," to Krasnoye, which means both "red" and, in a folksy colloquialism, "beautiful." Golubev's name also carries a mixture of connotations, from "dove" (*golub'*) to "light blue" (*goluboi,* which is also a slang term for homosexuals, roughly corresponding to "gay"), as well as a pun on the word *golova* (head), which is, as in English, often used figuratively to denote the "head" of a department, for example.

16. The Ghost Shirt Movement's opposition to machines is reminiscent of the Mephi in Zamyatin's *We.* The Mephi, who live outside the technocratic and rigidly organized society of the "One State," also unsuccessfully attempt to foment a revolt against the mechanization of human life, though unlike Vonnegut, Zamyatin ends his novel with a minute glimmer of hope that his revolutionaries are not utterly defeated.

17. See chapter 4 for further discussion of this concept.

18. The puns are even more obvious in the original because of the close similarity among the verbs *byt'* (to be), *pit'* (to drink), and *bit'* (to beat).

19. Vonnegut echoes the sentimental yet sensible philosophy espoused by jazzman McClintic Sphere in Pynchon's *V.,* which is (not coincidentally, in my view) articulated in the context of cold war geopolitics: "There's no magic words. Not even I love you is magic enough. Can you see Eisenhower telling Malenkov or Khrushchev that? Ho-ho. . . . Keep cool, but care. . . . If my mother was alive I would have her make a sampler with that on it" (*Cat's Cradle,* 366).

20. Boyer treats civil defense during the late 1940s and early 1950s in detail in *By the Bomb's Early Light,* including quotes from popular magazine articles and books with titles such as *How to Survive an Atomic Bomb* or "You Can Live Despite A-Bomb" (see 319–33). Henriksen in turn extensively discusses the shelter-building phase of civil defense during the early 1960s in *Dr. Strangelove's America,* 202–12, 231–34.

21. It was released instead as a feature film and, despite limited numbers of available prints and considerable negative press attention, received the Academy Award for Best Documentary in 1966.

22. Although civil defense documents from the late 1960s were generally more forthright in discussing these topics, they still included statements that were questionable at best, especially after Carl Sagan and Richard Turco's formulation of the "nuclear winter" theory. A 1968 pamphlet published by the Office of Civil Defense titled *In Time of Emergency*, for example, contains the following predictions as part of its advice to citizens: "After a nuclear attack, food and water would be available to most people, and it would be usable" (9); "even in communities that received heavy accumulations of fallout particles, people soon might be able to leave shelter for a few minutes or a few hours at a time in order to perform emergency tasks" (13); "milk contamination from fallout is not expected to be a serious problem after an attack" (16).

23. This normalcy apparently includes singing "Waltzing Matilda" for hours on end. Neither the filmmakers nor Shute had particularly well-developed notions about Australian culture beyond certain highly superficial aspects. Both the novel and the film nevertheless managed to tell compelling, if often sentimentalized, stories about the demise of humanity.

24. Critics such as Weart who have derided the sentimentality of the novel and the film have largely overlooked the decidedly unsentimental episodes within it: Julian's impassioned speeches about the meaninglessness of the war, the stinging satirical absurdity of a scene in which two stuffy gentlemen discuss the foolishness of their club's wine committee for not stocking better reserves of port before they became unavailable, the government's tight-fisted control over information even as the radiation approaches, and so on.

25. Two other episodes with nuclear themes were also aired, "Time Enough at Last" in 1959 and "No Time Like the Past" in 1963.

26. This applies at least to Randy Bragg, the novel's protagonist, and his associates, all of whom in some way transcend (if not radically, by today's standards) the race, gender, and class norms of the time in an idealized depiction of American values. Not without its blind spots, the book is nevertheless more complex than some of its detractors claim; it is neither a jingoistic affirmation of blind patriotism (despite its conclusion that a war that sets American society back a thousand years could be won in any meaningful way) nor ignorant of the deus ex machina tropes it uses in depicting its heroes' survival. While undoubtedly patriotic, especially when compared with an unabashedly humanistic work like Mordecai Roshwald's *Level 7* (which also came out in 1959), Frank's novel also defines patriotism considerably more expansively than Eisenhower did, to say nothing of McCarthy or Nixon.

27. See chapter 4.

28. Mordecai Roshwald's dystopian novel *Level 7* had already dramatically illustrated the potential problems with the kind of underground system that Strangelove suggests. In that novel each side in an atomic conflict has built an elaborate hierarchy of underground shelters intended to allow portions of its population—mostly the military, economic, and political elite—to survive an all-out nuclear war. The gradual failure of each level of protection and the slow descent of the narrator into insanity deftly underscore the futility of any civil defense scheme that presumes not only the capacity to survive a nuclear war but the desire to do so.

3. "The Bind of the Digital" and Other Oversimplified Logic

1. Compare the excerpts from Tanner, Iser, Maltby, Hirshberg, and Rojecki in the previous chapter.

2. Hence the incorrect identification of political dissenters with the enemy in both the Soviet Union and the United States. U.S. history during the cold war is rife with instances in which political dissenters have been inaccurately (and intentionally) branded as Communists in order to mobilize the strong negative reaction that this term carries, thanks to the cold war schema. Spencer Weart notes, for example, that Oppenheimer's opposition to U.S. nuclear policy in the 1950s—which resulted in the removal of his security clearance—had an "impact on public opinion as great as if he had been condemned for treason" (180). Many of those who questioned Oppenheimer's motives, including former Manhattan Project colleagues such as Edward Teller, accused him of directly or indirectly aiding the Soviets. In the Soviet Union, political dissidents, including scores of writers who violated the regulations of the publication system, were similarly vilified as enemies of the state and/or collaborators with the forces of capitalist imperialism (regardless of the nature or the validity of their transgressions) for most of that country's existence.

3. The fact that he or she has also rejected "bad" becomes irrelevant since, as the historical practice and recurrent satirical trope (see *Babbitt, Nineteen Eighty-Four, The Public Burning*, and others) of having individuals recite loyalty oaths or other patriotic propaganda demonstrates, claiming to be on the side of right is a performative act that demands constant reinforcement to steel oneself against infiltration.

4. For further discussion of the mundane milieu of Pynchon's suburbia in the novel, see Molly Hite, *Ideas of Order in the Novels of Thomas Pynchon* (Columbus: Ohio State UP, 1983); and Maurice Couturier, "The Death of the Real in *The Crying of Lot 49*," *Pynchon Notes* 20–21 (Spring/Fall 1987): 5–29.

5. See chapter 5 for further discussion of *White Noise* in this context.

6. Barth undoubtedly satirizes aspects of the statesmanship and rhetoric that led to the "Quiet Riot" (the academic analogue for the cold war) in *Giles Goat-Boy*, but his satire strikes me (as well as critics such as Maltby and Tanner) as less of a subversion of a *particular* historical and political rhetoric than a leery examination of the cultural values that guide the post–World War II age in general.

7. Billy/George's heavily framed autobiography itself is written from a retrospective viewpoint that alludes to epic literature from its opening lines: "George is my name; my deeds have been heard of in Tower Hall, and my childhood has been chronicled in the *Journal of Experimental Psychology*. I am he that was called in those days Billy Bocksfuss—cruel misnomer" (*Giles Goat-Boy*, 41).

8. Barth accentuates the parallels with Oppenheimer's life via indirect reference to Oppenheimer's loss of security clearance in apparent retribution for questioning U.S. nuclear policy: "All [Spielman] asked was that the flunking Computer not be programmed to EAT [that is, kill] its enemies automatically. So they call him a Student-Unionist, and they *strip* him of his privileges" (*Giles Goat-Boy*, 69).

9. Robinson provides an extensive discussion of Barth's use of "The Hero-Myth as Story," drawing direct connections with the scholarship on heroic archetypes produced by Lord Raglan and Joseph Campbell. Compare John Barth's *Giles Goat-Boy*, 179–258.

212 *Notes to Pages 67–74*

10. The latter two of these strategies are especially common in the mid-1950s, when the House Un-American Activities Committee (HUAC) was at its peak. The linguistic aspect remains fairly consistent throughout the period leading up to *Giles Goat-Boy's* publication.

11. A number of Barth's critics (Robert Scholes, Charles B. Harris, Jac Thorpe, James Gresham) have accentuated the dialectical drive of the novel, claiming that it is composed of various diametrical pairs (such as the hyper-American Peter Greene and the Socialist Leonid Alexandrov, or the atavistic Croaker and the superrational Eblis Eierkopf) that are more or less synthesized by the novel's end. Indeed, George's entire enlightenment is predicated on such a dialectical progress. As Stan Fogel and Gordon Slethaug note in *Understanding John Barth,* though, this sort of reading both undervalues the self-discrediting epilogues and fails to recognize that many of the dialectical resolutions are incomplete: "The balances of those resolutions are not equally achieved in all instances: Max and Eierkopf cannot really be integrated, nor can East and West" (95). Their interpretation not only supports their argument that the novel is primarily a "satire . . . of the literary conventions that serve to shore up the presentation of heroic deeds" (95) but also helps bolster the assertion that Barth's satire is subversive rather than normative, since he argues that synthetic solutions like George's are incomplete at best and thoroughly unreliable at worst.

12. The multiple postscripts that threaten to cancel each other out demonstrate Barth's awareness that confirmation of the existence of paradox is itself paradoxical, since all it proves is that nothing can be conclusively proved due to paradox's inherent resistance to logic.

13. As his later essays "The Literature of Exhaustion" and "The Literature of Replenishment" demonstrate, Barth shares Iser's wonder at the persistence of human interest in literary fictions despite their recognized "inauthenticity."

14. The late 1920s and early 1930s witnessed a number of actions that served to divide the population of the Soviet Union more rigidly into clearly discernible pro and con factions. The Party Resolution of 1932 on literature codified Socialist Realism as *the* ideologically acceptable literary mode and officially abolished the unmistakably *un*binary concept of the "fellow traveler." Similarly the campaign against the *kulaki* (relatively wealthy peasant farmers) was used to weed out opponents of collectivization among the peasants in general, regardless of their economic status.

15. Zinoviev's novels include considerable satire of various classes of dissidents and Voinovich's *Moscow 2042* includes a character widely interpreted, despite Voinovich's continuous denials, as a satire of Solzhenitsyn's nationalistic brand of dissidence. Aksyonov's *Say Cheese!* fictionalizes the events surrounding the publication of the *Metropol'* literary almanac and uses them to satirize the unwillingness of some writers who claim the dissident title to engage in genuine protest when given the chance.

16. In her *Border Crossings* (1983), Carol Avins broadly and reflexively defines this nineteenth-century notion of the West (which she states denotes only the countries of Western Europe before 1917) as "the accumulated ideas about it—assumptions and images included in every intellectual's cultural baggage." After the revolution, she notes, the word "West" (*zapad*) became synonymous with capitalism, although "its other meanings . . . are not submerged by this one: it continues to have dimensions beyond the political and economic" (4).

17. Mayakovsky's poem "150 Million" (1920) satirizes Woodrow Wilson as a dull-witted and antiquated capitalist, while Marietta Shaginian's novel *Mess-Mend, ili ianki v Petrograde* (1924; *Mess-Mend, or a Yankee in Petrograd*), written under the pseudonym Dzhim Dollar (Jim Dollar), is an anticapitalist parody of Western adventure novels. Alayne P. Reilly's *America in Contemporary Soviet Literature* (1971) provides insightful commentary on several other works of "Propagandist Caricature" (1) from the 1920s and 1930s, such as Pilnyak's *O-kei, amerikanskii roman* (1933; *Okay: An American Novel*) and Il'f and Petrov's *Odnoetazhnaia Amerika* (1937; *One-Storied America*).

18. See Clark, *Soviet Novel*, 255–63; Marsh, *Soviet Fiction since Stalin*, 197–206; and Kasack, *Dictionary of Russian Literature*, 73, 181–82, 193–94.

19. Booker makes a similar claim; see *Dystopian Impulse*, 130–37. I discuss Voinovich's engagement with dystopia in *Moscow 2042* at length in the next chapter.

20. Olga Matich and M. Keith Booker have both discussed *The Island of Crimea* as a dystopian text that parodies not only official Soviet versions of Communist reality but also "the more strongly utopian orientation of many of Aksyonov's earlier works" (Matich, "Vasilii Aksenov and the Literature of Convergence"; quotation from Booker, *Dystopian Impulse*, 130). The general dystopian tenor of Soviet dissident writing is treated more substantially in the next chapter.

21. Voinovich's *Chonkin* novels also strongly resemble two previous satirical (or at the very least parodic) portraits of common soldiers, the Czech writer Jaroslav Hašek's masterpiece *Osudy dobrého vojáka Švejka za sv tové války* (*The Good Soldier Schweik*) and Alexander Tvardovsky's verse novel *Terkin na tom svete* (1954–63; *Tyorkin in the Other World*). While Voinovich's work contains clear thematic similarities to Hašek's, the comparison with the latter is perhaps more relevant, since Tvardovsky directly mentored Voinovich during the late 1950s and early 1960s in his position as editor of *Novyi Mir*, one of the leading Soviet literary journals. *Tyorkin in the Other World* is largely self-parody, as Tvardovsky uses his own Stalin Prize–winning wartime poetry cycle *Vasilii Terkin* (1941–45) as the original text. Much as his writing influenced Voinovich's early style, Tvardovsky's transformation from an exemplary Socialist Realist author to one of the leading liberal figures of the Thaw provided a potential model for Voinovich's personal development as well.

22. The types she identifies are "the production novel plus five other types: the historical novel, the novel about a worthy intellectual or inventor, the novel of war or revolution, the villain or spy novel, and the novel about the West." She goes on to note that the "differences between these types are not as great as they might seem, since all involve, minimally, a 'road to consciousness' pattern and usually a 'task' as well" (Clark, *Soviet Novel*, 255).

23. Occasional exceptions to this rule do exist, ranging from Khrushchev's approval of the publication of *One Day in the Life of Ivan Denisovich* to works by official writers such as Aitmatov or Iskander that contain comparatively mild criticisms of Soviet policy toward non-Russians. On the whole, though, dissent in the official publication system of the post-Stalin Soviet Union required approval of the state organs, making it a pyrrhic victory at best (and, consequently, making it dubious in the eyes of many émigrés).

24. Gordon Clough's "Translator's Preface" to the 1978 American edition of the novel offers a good explanation of this largely untranslatable pun: "[Ibansk] is a double pun, deriving partly from the commonest Russian forename Ivan, and part from the coarse

verb *'yebat"*—to fuck. So Ibansk means, broadly speaking, a fucktown or fuckland for the Ivans" (Zinoviev, *Yawning Heights,* 7).

25. The characters Truth-Teller (Pravdets), Singer (Pevets), and the Boss (Khoziain) function, for example, both as representatives of common character types found in Soviet society and as representations—sometimes parodic, sometimes not, depending on Zinoviev's somewhat capricious sympathies—of Solzhenitsyn, Alexander Galich, and Stalin, respectively.

26. Zinoviev may be alluding to Yuri Olesha's *Envy* in this passage. As Janet Tucker notes, two characters in *Envy* also find a piece of literature that has been discarded, a symbol with political overtones: "Kavalerov and Ivan stumble on a page . . . from Gogol's *Taras Bul'ba*. Writers, Kavalerov and Ivan, notice what everyone else ignores— the truth behind surface reality. And they find the page cast away, and in a vacant lot, not [in] the garbage. A vacant lot is a space ignored by urban development. Marxism (along with the city and industry) has passed it by—so the vacant lot is to urban space as writers are to Marxist society" (*Revolution Betrayed,* 87). By the time, fifty years later, when Zinoviev is writing, the vacant lot of *Envy* has become the garbage heap of *The Yawning Heights,* as writers who refused to play by the state's rules were not only ignored but also often cast out, literally or figuratively (compare Dovlatov's ref- erence to Kozlov, the editor who threw out manuscripts unread to cut down his work- load, in *The Invisible Book*).

27. Thus Ibansk is a utopia in only the negative sense of More's original Greek pun. It is *ou topos* but by no means *eu topos*.

28. The first English-language edition consists of 829 pages and nearly as many chapters.

29. Literally, "a little page of heroic history" (*stranichka geroicheskoi istorii*). *Stra- nichka* is a diminutive form of *stranitsa* (page) and thus heightens the irony of this passage, since genuinely "heroic" history is presumably deserving of more than a pass- ing mention.

30. The accent with which the Boss speaks, an exaggerated form of the Georgian lilt with which Stalin (that is, "the Boss") spoke Russian, is almost impossible to ren- der into English, but the translation quoted here does manage to convey Zinoviev's derisive intention.

31. The word (*sdokh,* derived from the infinitve *sdokhnut'*) that Zinoviev uses to refer to the Boss's death is usually reserved for animals, especially cattle, although it is colloquially (and somewhat pejoratively) used to refer to humans as well. It would certainly be inappropriate in reference to a "heroic" figure such as the Boss in the kind of writing Zinoviev is parodying in this section.

32. For more detailed discussion of this novel, see chapter 4.

33. Although it does not appear in the original, the English translators add the word "victors" into the second line, an emendation that generally corresponds with the rhetoric Iskander is parodying.

34. The interrogative used in the original Russian (*kakoi*) is more akin to "what sort of" rather than "when," but the context of "when" in this sentence (that is, "in what situation" rather than "at what time") generally retains this meaning in translation.

35. This scene echoes—unintentionally, in all likelihood—the scene in *Dr. Strange- love* in which Group Captain Mandrake attempts to bring General Ripper the "good news" that he has discovered a radio broadcasting civilian programming, which would

suggest that a Russian attack is not underway as he had been told. Ripper reacts not with relief but by berating Mandrake for "questioning his orders" and then by locking him into his office. Mandrake's discovery that Ripper's order to attack Russia is not a relatively benign misunderstanding but the result of Ripper's insanity comes too late to prevent the film's ultimate apocalypse.

36. Iskander's sentence contains two Russian words that are translated into English as "truth," *istina* and *pravda*. These words' semantic weight is similar, although not identical, in Russian; *istina* is often rendered into English as "verity" and connotes an eternal truth, whereas *pravda* stems from the same grammatical root (*prav*) as the word *pravednost'* (righteousness) and connotes "correctness." The latter, however, was famously the name of the official Communist Party newspaper founded in 1912 and thus bears additional satirical connotations in this context (that is, that "boring, but comforting" *Pravda* can be used to artificially obscure or supersede "alarming" *istina*).

37. Evidence indicates that Stalin first arranged for Kirov's assassination and then blamed the assassination on followers of Grigory Zinoviev and Lev Kamenev, two of Stalin's former rivals in the power struggles that followed Lenin's death in 1924. As was the case with Zinoviev and Kirov, Sharpie is subjected to a show trial as an enemy of the state, after which he is sentenced to exile, which ultimately leads to his death (Zinoviev and Kamenev were shot). Furthermore, as Stalin did for Kirov, Ponderer is posthumously given heroic status by the very person responsible for his death, an act of political alchemy that transmuted dissidence into political orthodoxy. Robert Conquest's *Stalin and the Kirov Murder* (1989) gives a full, if not always unbiased, account of this complicated episode in Soviet history.

38. The original Russian reads something akin to "out-patriotize and out-rage the patriot."

39. The mummified Great Python is actually described as having "vigilant" (*bdiashchii*) eyes rather than simply "open" (*otkrytyi*) ones, a much more typical propagandistic phrasing.

40. Although it is not explicitly mentioned in the text, one of the problematic aspects of Bashov's biography (in terms of his potential acceptance within Soviet society) that is tidied up via his new naming is the apparent Jewishness of his father's patronymic. Vasily Vasilievich is a thoroughly Russian name, just as Trotsky was a more suitably Russian-sounding surname for a member of the party elite than Bronshtein.

41. This translation from the original retains the paronomasic intent of the Russian name Poniat'ev, which is derived from the word *poniatie* (concept) and the verb *poniat'* (to understand). Given the close association of both Gurov and his father (consistently called Conceptiev/Poniat'ev) with "the Idea" (*Ideia*), Bashov's name for Soviet Communism, this linguistic linkage is appropriate. Gurov and his father both claim to live their lives according to the Idea/Concept of the revolution, even as they profit financially from their status as party elites, a fact that runs totally contrary to the egalitarian rhetoric of Communism.

42. Significantly Gurov kills her on November 7, 1939, the anniversary of the Bolshevik Revolution. He marries Electra before the end of the year and then kills (or at least is complicit in the murder of) the doctor who falsified Brutnikova's death certificate. His actions thus parallel Stalin's in that Gurov murders a loyal Communist out of egocentric motives and then eliminates his accomplice, just as many of Stalin's executioners from the 1930s eventually found the tables turned on them.

43. This is never stated explicitly in the novel, although it can be inferred from the fact that Bashov at one point cites records that indicate that Brutnikov assumes his wife's name at marriage, a reversal of the norm in Russian society (10). The origins of the name Gurov are further complicated by the fact that Electra's last name presumably should also be Brutnikova, which hints that Collectiva's last name (like her first name) is adopted rather than familial. Aleshkovsky does not clarify this situation in the novel, leaving the origins of at least one and possibly two of Conceptiev/Brutnikov/Gurov's last names in ontological limbo.

44. Bashov mockingly refers to him using the anachronistic and decidedly un-Communist phrase "solidly enthroned" (164).

45. Aleshkovsky revisits the notion of a fictive filmed record being used as part of a legal proceedings in *Kangaroo* (see chapter 5).

46. When Bashov's biography is idealized, his date of birth is altered to coincide with the exact beginning of the Soviet Union. Both come into existence on November 7, 1917, according to Aleshkovsky's fictionalized accounts of history.

47. The particular issue he votes on thus is ultimately irrelevant, since the opposing vote is intended to be purely symbolic rather than representative of actual dissent.

48. The reference to the "Supreme Con of all times and all peoples" parodically links Satan directly to Stalin, since this title (with "Ruler" in place of "Con") was one of the latter's favorite honorifics.

49. The English translation makes the Russian etymology of Gusev's name (it is derived from *gus,* the word for "goose") clearer to non-Russian readers by spelling it Goosev. I have chosen to retain the standard transliteration of the original Russian here because some of the common English connotations with geese (silliness, stubbornness) that are likely to be conveyed by this spelling are, in my view, not intended.

50. This date is potentially significant, since it marks the feast day of St. Basil the Confessor, an eighth-century martyr, in the Russian Orthodox tradition. Bashov's first name (Vasily) is the Russian version of Basil, and the story of Gusev's actions on this day seem to cause him by the end of the novel to seek a righteous martyrdom akin to St. Basil's.

51. David M. Bethea discusses both serious and satirical uses of the train/locomotive as a Socialist, and later Communist, metaphor in Russian culture in *The Shape of Apocalypse in Modern Russian Fiction.* From the time of Herzen and Belinsky (that is, the mid-1800s) onward, the metaphorical horse-versus-train debate became one that divided Russian intellectuals roughly along Slavophile and Westernizer lines. Tolstoy's extremely negative train symbolism in *Anna Karenina* (1873–77) and Dostoyevsky's similarly unfavorable associations in *The Idiot* (1868) were among the most prominent early criticisms of the locomotive as a symbol of progress.

52. Outraged Reason's rhetoric in the original Russian text is considerably more inflammatory and profuse, including claims to be prepared for "a bacillus of chaos prepared for the West, a bacillus of Peoples' Liberation movements" (my translation of "My gotovim dlia Zapada batsillu khaosa, batsillu Narodno-Osvoboditel'nykh dvizhenii").

53. The novel's 1983 setting would place the start of this war in 1968, making it roughly contemporary to the height of American involvement in Vietnam. The South-versus-North distinction Percy makes between the warring sides furthers this allegorical association.

54. Such a situation recurred in the Reagan administration's unflinching support of the anti-Communist Contra rebels in Nicaragua during the early and mid-1980s. Despite considerable evidence that the Contras were as capable of committing atrocities as the Communist Sandinista faction, American support was so steadfast as to include potential violations of the Constitution and disregard for prohibitions on international weapons trade. As H. W. Brands points out, American support for Angolan rebel leader Jonas Savimbi, the mujahideen in Afghanistan, and the Cambodian resistance coalition (which included the Khmer Rouge) during this period was equally spurious in terms of "the distance between the noble ends America pursued and the ignoble means it employed to pursue them" (*Devil We Knew,* 171).

4. Cold War Critiques of Utopia

1. Critics such as Alexandra Aldridge, M. Keith Booker, Edith Clowes, John Glad, Gary Saul Morson, and David Sisk.

2. This formula can be expressed in two basic ways: (1) the utopia is a "good" society—the best, in fact—while all others are flawed, or (2), the present is "bad" whereas the future according to the utopian model is "good."

3. The essays collected in Rafaella Baccolini and Tom Moylan's *Dark Horizons* come to a similar conclusion, though they exclusively concern themselves with dystopias in the broadly defined genre of science fiction. Some, though not all, of the works I discuss here fit within that category.

4. This, of course, is the form of the three best-known twentieth-century dystopias, Zamyatin's *We,* Huxley's *Brave New World,* and Orwell's *Nineteen Eighty-Four.*

5. Novels such as Vonnegut's *Cat's Cradle,* Aksyonov's *The Burn,* and DeLillo's *White Noise.*

6. See the previous chapter for more detailed discussion of these cultural binaries in Russian history.

7. While not (in my opinion) absolutely watertight, Bethea's argument in this regard has much to recommend it. This is not, alas, the time or the place for a more thorough dissection of his interpretive logic.

8. Aleshkovsky often (though not always) advocates for pre-Communist social values such as Russian Orthodox Christianity, for example, while Voinovich and Aksyonov are more ambivalent about or downright opposed to such retrograde cultural motion. Voinovich even directly satirizes one form of "apocalypticist" nationalism in the character of Sim Simych Karnavalov in *Moscow 2042* (see below).

9. The seventeenth-century flourishing of utopian writings that followed More's *Utopia* (1516), including such works as Johann Andreae's *Christianopolis* (1619), Tommaso Campanella's *City of the Sun* (1623), Francis Bacon's *New Atlantis* (1627), and John Harrington's *Oceana* (1656), can be (and have been) attributed in part to the "discovery" and exploration of the American continent.

10. These are, not surprisingly, also among the most prominent forces within C. Wright Mills's "power elite," a concept articulated in 1956 at the height of the "first" cold war. Russell Hoban satirizes the power elite in his postapocalyptic novel *Riddley Walker* through the character of Lissener, a blind genetic mutant. Lissener is initially a sympathetic character because he is grievously mistreated by Goodparley, the political head of Hoban's postnuclear Britain. However, Lissener quickly merits derision for his steadfast insistence that his people were the "Power Leat" before the

nuclear war in the book's distant past, missing the point that this makes them culpable in the development of the very weapons that have made the world as it is. His
efforts to rediscover the secret of gunpowder and overthrow Goodparley, reinforce the
potential for destruction within the desire to be among a power elite defined primarily
by its control of knowledge and weaponry.

11. Howard P. Segal's *Technological Utopianism* is a magisterial overview of more
than twenty Americans dating back to the nineteenth century who have been instrumental in promulgating notions of utopian futures predicated on technological innovation.

12. The fact that German troops were occupying Paris and establishing Jewish ghet-
tos in Poland and Czechoslovakia (although the latter may not have been known to
the author) at the time of this article's publication makes Langer's references to the
potential abilities of "industrious, powerful nations" and "aggressive, clever races"—
phrases that resonate with the Nazis' propagandistic image of Aryans—a highly unfortunate irony.

13. Boyer identifies the United Nations, whose charter predated the use of the
atomic bomb by two months, as a continuation of a "dream of world government—
from Tennyson's great parliament of mankind to Wendell Wilkie's visionary 1943 best-
seller *One World*" (*By the Bomb's Early Light*, 34). He cites a somewhat fleeting but
significant groundswell of support for global government schemes as one of the most
noticeable immediate results of the development and use of the bomb. For a full discussion of this theme, see *Bomb's Early Light*, 33–45.

14. The United States is not exempt from the kinds of dystopian charges that are
easily leveled at the Soviet Union because of Stalinism. Without overstating the point,
it bears mention that the cold war period saw events such as the rise (and, admittedly,
also the fall) of McCarthy and HUAC, the Gulf of Tonkin Resolution, a rancorous
(and incomplete) process of granting civil rights to all citizens, and a marked increase
in covert (and often illegal) government activity, such as counter intelligence programs
(COINTELPRO). None of these, nationalistic rhetoric aside, corresponds particularly
well to the basic principles of the Constitution. The United States was formed with
the semiutopian intent of "establish[ing] a more perfect Union," but at least *some* of its
official actions during the cold war had a directly opposite (that is, dystopian) effect.

15. For thorough bibliographies of dystopian works from this period, see the works
mentioned at the beginning of this chapter: Brians, *Nuclear Holocausts,* and Moylan,
Scraps of the Untainted Sky.

16. At the Trinity test, Oppenheimer famously quoted from the *Bhagavad Gita* ("Now
I am become death, the destroyer of worlds"). The comment that Vonnegut para-
phrases in the novel (see below) was not actually made by Oppenheimer until 1948.

17. Oppenheimer adamantly opposed the development of hydrogen bomb in the
early 1950s, leading to a vicious attack on his national loyalty that ultimately resulted
in the revocation of his security clearance in 1953. Richard Rhodes provides a succinct
yet detailed account of Oppenheimer's hearing in his *Dark Sun,* 530–59. The text of
the hearings was also published by the United States Atomic Energy Commission
as *In the Matter of J. Robert Oppenheimer.* It should be noted that Oppenheimer's
views regarding the atomic bomb after 1945 were by no means unequivocally negative.
Oppenheimer's comments to W. L. Laurence in 1965 demonstrate more pride than
regret: "I never regretted, and do not regret now, having done my part of the job. . . . I

also think that it was a damn good thing that the bomb was developed, that it was recognized as something important and new, and that it would have an effect on the course of history" (quoted in Lifton and Mitchell, *Hiroshima in America,* 226). Lifton and Mitchell conclude that Oppenheimer's mixed messages were a result of "struggling with his own survivor emotions . . . [that] had not only to do with creating a murderous weapon but, just as importantly, with having embraced that weapon as a beneficent force" (225).

18. A number of private companies reaped a substantial profit from producing components, machinery, or raw materials for the Manhattan Project, even if they were not privy to the details of what their products were being used to create.

19. This laboratory is located in Ilium, Vonnegut's frequent fictional double for Troy, New York. As such, it becomes a cousin (in terms of both the fictionalized geography of Vonnegut's United States and the technologically dystopian tenor of both novels) to the Ilium Works that Paul Proteus manages in *Player Piano.*

20. Manhattan Project physicist I. R. Rabi wrote that the bomb represented "a new understanding of man, which man had acquired over nature" (quoted in Rhodes, *Dark Sun,* 201), one of many comments by principals involved in the development of the atomic bomb who describe that knowledge as somehow *beyond* nature.

21. Brother is described as "hid[ing] manuscripts of protest letters in his home" while at the same time testifying against dissident authors. When his colleagues claim that Brother is "an informer" and "a provocateur," Chatterer insists instead that he "works on no-one's behalf" in order to "bring everyone down to his own level" (528–29).

22. Zinoviev offers an early clue regarding his attitude toward the narrator's job when he notes that the institute where the narrator works (which was responsible for the Slogan's installation) "occupies the upper floors of the Yellow House" (11). The phrase "yellow house," *zheltyi dom,* is a euphemism for a madhouse in Russian and also serves as the title for Zinoviev's first postemigration novel, *The Madhouse* (1980).

23. Perhaps coincidentally a road rally occurs in both *On the Beach* and *The Island of Crimea* on the eve of apocalypse, although the element of wish fulfillment that the race contains in *On the Beach* is notably absent from Aksyonov's novel.

24. In an interview published in 1986, poet Natalya Gorbanevskaya uses the same zoological metaphor of rabbits and boa constrictors (without referencing Iskander explicitly) to describe Aksyonov's depiction of the West in *The Island of Crimea*: "[He] saw . . . how the West, like a rabbit, is gazing at the Soviet boa constrictor which has hypnotized it. In *The Island of Crimea* Aksyonov built a model of the West in one separate country. The question is whether or not the West is able to survive." She also describes Luchnikov's dream of a unified Russia in terms of the "visible decay" of Western life: "The envy, the neurosis, the longing for wholeness, for a beautifully monolithic world—even if we have to enslave or be enslaved, let's become beautiful and whole, the way the communist world is beautiful and whole" (quoted in Możejko, Briker and Dalgård, *Vasiliy Pavlovich Aksënov,* 30).

25. Marlen's name—a combination of Marx and Lenin—is another example of superficial adherence to ideology dominating identity. A number of Soviet satires use characters with similar names (which were not uncommon during the Soviet era, especially among children born in the 1920s and 1930s)—see the discussion of Aleshkovsky's novel *The Hand* in the previous chapter—to comment on the totality with which Soviet rhetoric suffused everyday life.

26. In her article "Vasilii Aksenov and the Literature of Convergence," Matich argues that the entire novel is Aksyonov's repudiation of the philosophy of convergence (which is clearly expressed in Luchnikov's article) that he himself had espoused earlier in his career. She summarizes this position as follows: "Like many western and Soviet liberals in the 1960s, young Aksenov believed in the peaceful coexistence of socialism and capitalism and the eventual convergence of the two political systems. Developed in the 1950s by western social scientists, the convergence thesis was a response to postindustrial society as shaped by modern science and technology. According to the theory, in the space age capitalism and socialism would become indistinguishable in spite of ideological differences. . . . In the Soviet Union, the reformist intelligentsia adopted it in the hope that Stalinist Russia could be transformed into a democratic, technologically advanced society" ("Vasilii Aksenov," 642). She argues that Aksyonov uses *The Island of Crimea* to "demythologiz[e] his literary persona of the 1960s and the many layers of ambiguity associated with his generation. He is saying farewell to Russia and preparing himself for dissident politics and, eventually, emigration" (643–44).

27. While Voinovich has repeatedly denied that Karnavalov is intended to be a parody of Solzhenitsyn—a denial he repeats in his *Portret na fone mifa* (2002; *Portrait in a Myth's Setting*), despite spending most of the remainder of that work criticizing Solzhenitsyn for self-aggrandizement—there are simply too many biographical and philosophical correspondences between the two to invalidate this interpretation altogether.

28. The parody of Solzhenitsyn, whose cycle of historical novels about the Russian Revolution titled *The Red Wheel* (*Krasnoe koleso*) is divided into several "knots" (*uzly*), is unmistakable here.

29. This name is typical of Soviet bureaucratic shorthand and stands for Moscow Republic. In the original the name is *Moskorep*, short for *Moskovskaia respublika*.

30. Voinovich's play with the time frame in the novel makes "text" refer in this manner not only to Kartsev's account of the trip, but to the trip itself, since the book he has not yet written based on his experiences (presumably also the one the reader has in hand) appears in the future Moscow and influences both his decision making and the unfolding plot.

31. This unusual portmanteau title's origins are explained to Kartsev by one of the Moscowrep officials in the kind of extravagant terms that were used to laud Stalin: "The Genialissimo is simultaneously the general secretary of our party, holds the military rank of generalissimo, and, moreover, stands apart from everyone in the scope of his genius. In view of all his ranks and attributes, people used to call him 'our general secretary, genius, and generalissimo.' Well, as everyone knows, among his other virtues, our leader is also distinguished by his exceptional modesty. And he asked us many times to call him by a name that was simpler, shorter, and more modest. And so, in the end, it was that simple and natural name that caught on—Genialissimo" (125).

32. In this regard Bukashev is like Bashov in Aleshkovsky's novel *The Hand* (see next chapter), although his reasons are more intellectually than personally motivated. Whereas Bashov recognizes the irrationality of the Soviet system largely as a result of his quest for vengeance, Bukashev seems to have understood it from the start (although he does not begin to rebel against it immediately).

33. In the published English translation, *druzhok* is rendered as "little fool." It actually means something more along the lines of "pal" (*druzhok* is a diminutive of the word *drug* [friend]), whereas *durachok* (the diminutive form of *durak* [fool]) carries the meaning given in the translation.

34. The English translation adds the final line, which explains the combined acronyms more clearly.

35. In the Russian original, this organization is named BEZO (short for *"organy gosbezopasnosti,"'* or "organs of state security"), a name that contains a satirical connotation with the word/particle *bez*, which means "without" or "the absence of" (for example, *bez-* modifies *opasnost'* [danger] into *bezopasnost'* ["security" or "absence of danger"]). Since the NKVD and the KGB were important tools in achieving the *physical* absence of people and things considered dangerous to the Soviet state, the emphasis placed on this particle in the name BEZO accentuates this negative association. The parallel between Siromakhin's and Bukashev's ranks in BEZO and the KGB, respectively, also supports this connection. Siromakhin's first name—Dzerzhin, a clear reference to the Cheka's first leader, Felix Dzerzhinsky—also alludes to his secret police bloodlines. There is further irony in BEZO's very existence, given that the absorption of the KGB into the Communist Party has apparently left a vacuum that requires at least nominal filling.

36. Whereas the English translation renders Kartsev answer to Siromakhin's "OK?" ("O'kei?" in the original), also as "OK," the Russian text reads "Shiur," an approximation of the English "sure." Voinovich makes sure his Russian readers understand this answer—whose unfamiliarity points out Kartsev's doubts as to whether Siromakhin is actually an American agent or a Russian one—by providing a footnoted explanation of how "sure" would be used in this context.

37. The word Voinovich coins in Russian is "kabesot," which is short for "kabinet estestvennykh otpravlenii" (*Moskva*, 114), a term that sounds as bureaucratically euphemistic in Russian as "Bureau of Natural Functions" does in English.

38. Voinovich is not alone in using this combination for satirical effect, either in Russian literature or cold war fiction in general. In Aleshkovsky's *Hand*, Bashov tells of how his father, a wealthy peasant who resisted collectivization in the 1920s and was killed as a result, foretold the corruption that Bashov's current prisoner would engage in as a member of the Soviet elite: "Even the fact that sausage would be made practically from shit at your meat-packing plants, Citizen Gurov—that too Poppa foretold" (17). Early in *Catch-22*, Heller describes a heavily bandaged patient in Yossarian's hospital ward who is connected to two jars in a manner that similarly effaces the distinction between food and waste: "Sewn into the bandages over the insides of both elbows were zippered lips through which he was fed clear fluid from a clear jar. A silent zinc pipe rose from the cement on his groin and was coupled to a slim rubber hose that carried waste from his kidneys and dripped it efficiently into a clear, stoppered jar on the floor. When the jar on the floor was full, the jar feeding his elbow was empty, and the two were simply switched quickly so that the stuff could drip back into him" (10).

39. Karnavalov's edict is a direct reversal of Peter the Great's order to shave the beards of the clergy and gentry in the early eighteenth century.

40. The English translation does not convey the clear association with Soviet terminology, but the Russian words for "emergency board" (*Chrezvychainaia kollegiia*) can be readily transformed via portmanteau into "Cheka."

41. Siromakhin's comments (like the policies of Karnavalov's new regime themselves) contain an echo of Marx's *Eighteenth Brumaire of Louis Bonaparte* (1852). Marx's argument in that work is that most revolutionaries fail to accomplish true revolution because they simply imitate previous revolutionaries (as Louis Bonaparte, a.k.a. Napoleon III, imitated Napoleon Bonaparte, who himself imitated the Roman emperors) and, like their models, eventually became tyrants who uphold or even strengthen the bourgeois status quo. For Marx this was one of the salient differences that would arise from a genuinely proletarian revolution.

42. Detailed analyses of each of these works in terms of their dystopianism/anti-utopianism is already extant, so I will not reproduce that work here. See, for example, Babenko, "Fazil Iskander," 131–34; Clowes, *Russian Experimental Fiction*, 136–39 and 165–71; McGuire, *Red Star*, 73–75; Booker, *Dystopian Impulse*, 120–27; Nepomnyashchy, *Abram Tertz*, 130–47; and Howell, *Apocalyptic Realism*, 83–100.

5. Totalized Distortions and Fabrications

1. The Herero recur in *Gravity's Rainbow* as the Schwarzkommando, whose story of unintended consequences is "a lurid tale . . . of Hitler's scheme for setting up a Nazi empire in black Africa, which fell through after Old Blood 'n' Guts handed Rommel's ass back to him in the desert. . . . Well, the black cadres had no more future in Africa, stayed on in Germany as governments-in-exile without even official recognition, drifted somehow into the ordnance branch of the German Army, and pretty soon learned how to be rocket technicians. Now they were just running loose" (Pynchon, *Gravity's Rainbow*, 287–88).

2. Despite his distinctly military outlook on life and his stalwart opposition to Communism, Eisenhower at least gave some thought to the potential dangers of certain forces in American society. In his farewell address on January 17, 1961, he gave the following warning: "In the councils of government, we must guard against the acquisition of unwarranted influence, whether sought or unsought, by the military-industrial complex. The potential for the disastrous rise of misplaced power exists and will persist." Of course Eisenhower did not necessarily follow his own advice in this regard while in office, as Coover was quick to satirize in *The Public Burning* (see below).

3. Compare "nuclear normality" (Lifton and Markusen, *Genocidal Mentality*) and "nuclear mindset" (Hilgartner, Bell, and O'Connor, *Nukespeak*) (both discussed in chapter 4) as well as Pynchon's comment above about an "unblinking acceptance of a holocaust running to seven- and eight-figure body counts."

4. As mentioned in passing in the introduction to this volume, Betonie's comment in Silko's *Ceremony* about how "witchery works to scare people, to make them fear growth" (116) echoes this sentiment.

5. See chapter 2.

6. The same holds true for the Soviet Union through the 1970s, where the nuclear elite (both strategists and developers) was separated from society intellectually and physically, just as the Manhattan Project scientists had been. The strict control over information that was commonplace in everyday Soviet policy was even more evident in nuclear matters, necessitated both by the inherent sensitivity of atomic weapons research and the desire to mask Soviet nuclear inferiority until the arms race could be equalized. Khrushchev and Brezhnev were keenly aware of the futility of a nuclear

war for both sides but also needed to maintain a position of political and military strength to effectively continue the cold war as a standoff. Gaddis, *We Now Know;* Brands, *Devil We Knew;* Rhodes, *Dark Sun;* and Holloway, *Stalin and the Bomb* all discuss the Soviet nuclear program and policies surrounding it.

7. In the latter stages of the cold war, nuclear accidents in both countries precipitated this process of disclosure. Although opposition to nuclear energy was not absent in the United States before the 1979 accident at Three Mile Island or in the Soviet Union before the 1986 accident at Chernobyl, its effect on public consciousness (and thus the effectiveness of its demands for more candid information) of the two societies was markedly greater afterward.

8. See chapter 2.

9. Despite continual failures and massive expenditures on elaborate programs such as Reagan's Strategic Defense Initiative (SDI, nicknamed "Star Wars"), such antimissile defense systems are still an integral part of the United States Missile Defense Agency's plans as of 2010.

10. Mike Moore writes that MIRVs increased the potential for nuclear war by shortening the response time available to an attacked nation in order to retain a strong enough nuclear counterforce: "In this new post-*Strangelove* world, an enemy who struck first would have a clear advantage, said nuclear strategists. Because one MIRVed ICBM could theoretically knock out several enemy missiles in their silos, the side that struck first could retain many of its missiles for a possible second strike. . . . In a MIRVed use-'em-or-lose-'em world, the U.S. and Russian commanders might have just minutes to make a launch–no launch decision, even if the information they had was muddled and ambiguous" ("Midnight Never Came," 21).

11. As Boyer and others have pointed out, though, few of Kubrick's characters are simple parodies of particular historical figures, functioning instead more like Barth's parodic composites in *Giles Goat-Boy.* Turgidson voices the sentiments of noted nuclear hawk Curtis LeMay—perhaps making General Ripper a stand-in for Thomas Power, LeMay's even more bellicose successor as SAC commander—and Strangelove amalgamates aspects of Edward Teller, Wernher von Braun, and Henry Kissinger (Boyer, *Fallout,* 98–99).

12. See chapter 2.

13. Katerina Clark claims that this genre is "the most common type of Stalinist novel by far" and "more or less originated with [Fyodor Gladkov's] *Cement*" (*Soviet Novel,* 256). This genre is concerned with "how the plan was fulfilled or the project was constructed" and features a predictable master plot that Clark summarizes in *The Soviet Novel,* 255–60.

14. In a 1984 piece titled "Who's Braver—the Cosmonaut or the Dissident?" Aksyonov describes details of Akademgorodok that he clearly adapted in creating Pikhty in *Our Golden Ironburg:* "According to the authorities, these were meant to be 'fortresses' of scientific productivity set far away from the dissipation of the big cities. The authorities never foresaw that these towns would turn into 'nests of sedition.' . . . One of the most remarkable of [these towns] in this respect was a Siberian town where amidst the vast void of the taiga nonconformist art was encouraged. There were exhibitions of avant-garde art, performances of forbidden jazz and presentations by controversial young poets and balladeers. . . . There was a famous café, the Integral [presumably not named for the rocket in Zamyatin's *We*], where for a short time an

independent discussion club was set up. The discussers, jokingly fencing with foils, argued some pretty serious questions, such as the competence—if any—of a one-party system" (143).

15. See Kustanovich, *Artist and the Tyrant,* 102–6; Kuznetsov, "Vassily Aksyonov's Parody of *V,*" 181–85.

16. In the original this reads *dabl'-f'yu,* a roughly phonetic Russian rendering of the English letter "W," which has no equivalent in Russian. Because of the shared atomic research aspect, it is perhaps tempting to interpret the Ironburg institute as being analogous to the Soviet bomb program established under the leadership of Yuli Khariton at Sarov in the 1940s, but I resist such a reading for two reasons. First, the temporal setting of Aksyonov's novel is much too late for such a comparison to make sense, especially given the importance of the specific historical time frame to bomb research (that is, moving a program to develop the atomic bomb the 1970s makes little sense). Second, details about the program at Sarov were unavailable to all but the upper echelons of Soviet officials, whereas propagandistic reports about the achievements of "cities of science" like Akademgorodok were common during the time Aksyonov wrote the novel. This is not to say that the potential value of systematic scientific endeavors like those established at Akademgorodok was not spurred at least in part by the success of the Soviet Los Alamos set up at Sarov, but Aksyonov is not likely to have had that specific project in mind in creating this novel.

17. His name, like almost all the others in the novel, contains semantically absurd elements. Veliky-Salazkin literally means "Great-Toboggan," and as Kolesnikoff points out, his hyphenated name "is . . . ironic for it suggests an aristocratic background, when in reality he comes from a poor family" (197). This irony is heightened by the fact that the *last* thing a hero of Soviet science should affect is an aristocratic air, especially if his proletarian credentials are legitimate, as Veliky-Salazkin's are. Other unusual names, such as Kitousov (suggestive of *kitovyi us,* "whalebone"), Morkovnikov (carrot-man), Mohrsitzer (a Germanic name connoting "carrot-sitter"), and Slon (elephant), all parody the rigid rationality of Socialist Realism by resisting positive or even sensible metaphorical associations.

18. Memozov causes Ironburg to disappear in a dream world that temporarily displaces the "real" one that Kitousov narrates as the setting of the novel. The scientists merely start over after finding a new piece of metal (a new *zhelezka*) and in the process reassert the primacy of Kitousov's point of view.

19. All of the quotations from Kessler are my translations of his original German text.

20. Kolesnikoff singles out "the overstated praise of individual achievements or achievements of the whole country" among a number of particularly ripe sources of parody-ready materials for Aksyonov ("*Our Golden Hardware* as a Parody," 198–200).

21. This period lasted roughly from the late 1920s through the mid-1950s, although a substantial number of novels praising the accomplishments of Soviet science (especially the space program) and industry still appeared in the 1960s and even the 1970s.

22. The scientists' almost mechanical desire to rebuild Ironburg after Memozov causes it to disappear is possibly meant as a satirical commentary on the recurrence of Stalinist traits in Brezhnev's Soviet Union.

23. See chapter 3.

24. In *The Public Burning* Coover avoids any overt commentary on the matter of the Rosenbergs' guilt, which subsequent evidence appears to have demonstrated fairly unquestionably in Julius's case, although less completely in Ethel's (see the 1997 revised edition of Ronald Radosh and Joyce Milton's *Rosenberg File*). As Weisenburger states, "*The Public Burning* submits no brief for either side . . . because it is more concerned with anterior matters: specifically, whether or not the Rosenbergs were given a fair trial, and more generally, whether a fair trial was even possible, given the intense anxieties and sense of impending crisis skewing American politics during the McCarthy Era" (*Fables of Subversion*, 192). The fact that evidence released to the public from the American and Soviet archives after the end of the cold war clearly implicates the Rosenbergs does not alter the fact that there were substantial irregularities in both the investigations and trials that led to the executions in 1953. The post facto justification of the verdict (and the unusually severe sentence) does not render Coover's criticisms invalid since the evidence that was presented in the actual case against the Rosenbergs has been questioned even by some legal historians who have long asserted the Rosenbergs' guilt.

25. All emphases and other unusual typographies in the passages quoted from *The Public Burning* are Coover's, not mine.

26. In the book's prologue the narrator notes that the global "score" changes from "1,625,000,000 people for Uncle Sam, only 180,000,000 for the Phantom" at the end of World War II to a situation in which "the Phantom has a score of 800,000,000 to Uncle Sam's 600,000,000 and the rest—about 600,000,000 so-called neutrals—are adrift" (13–14) by the end of the 1940s. The somewhat pejorative use of the qualifier "so-called" in describing nonparticipants in the binary conflict demonstrates the cynicism with which an either/or system views *any* dissent, much less antagonism.

27. Nixon's anti-Communism contributed greatly to his election to the senate and his selection as Eisenhower's running mate, but Coover's presentation of Nixon at this stage seems to imply that his actual political acumen was still rather undeveloped in 1953. Since superficial anti-Communism was rarely challenged at this time, Nixon has not had to elaborate his thoughts in the manner that Uncle Sam demands.

28. Such a ring, including such figures as Klaus Fuchs, Herbert Gold, David Greenglass, Julius Rosenberg, and others *did* exist, of course, as Rhodes exhaustively catalogues in *Dark Sun*. Nevertheless Nixon's 1949 claim seems to have been predicated more on impressing Joseph McCarthy, on whose House Committee on Un-American Activities Nixon had recently been appointed to serve. The figures, including J. Robert Oppenheimer and his brother Frank, that Nixon interrogated as part of his inquiries into an atomic spy ring were all exonerated, whereas the actual atomic spies were apprehended in wholly separate investigations, many of which were undertaken by the British MI5 service in addition to Hoover's FBI. See Rhodes, *Dark Sun*, especially 411–15, 420–22.

29. Stalin's references and mistakes in the original are somewhat different, although the translation retains the sense of thorough misunderstanding and wild combination: "Tak, tak—tikho skazal Stalin . . . —Zapor . . . Barashki . . . Moia utroba . . . Shashlyk mirovoi revoliutsii . . . Bronenosets ≪Potemkin≫ . . . Èto uzhe prizyv k vosemnadtsatomu pomidoru Lui Bonaparta" (Aleshkovsky, *Ruka*, 131). Literally translated, this quote reads as follows: "'Well, well,' Stalin said quietly. "Constipation . . . Lambs . . .

My belly . . . The shish kebab of world revolution . . . The Battleship 'Potemkin' . . . This is certainly a call to the Eighteenth of Tomato of Louis Bonaparte." If Stalin's cannot even correctly recall the title of Marx's *The Eighteenth Brumaire of Louis Bonaparte,* one is obviously inclined to doubt his comprehension of its ideas.

30. Although the lengthy list seems incoherent in some regards, there is a consistency in that almost all of its constituent parts are marginalized from the idealized American vision of the 1950s as embodied by Eisenhower. Whether in terms of race (where the narrator's mention of "spooks of terrors past" carries a doubly cynical meaning), class, gender, sexuality, ethnicity, religion, political affiliation, or philosophy, disparate factors from "CREEPING SOCIALISTS[S]" and "SANTY ANNY" to "COMANCHES" and "REDCOATS" are cast as blood enemies of America who are attacking under cover of the dark (488–89).

31. That is, the light of an atomic blast from the Nevada Test Site. Uncle Sam's rout of the Phantom in Times Square thus represents the use of the bomb as a deterrent threat, an association that is ultimately made clear by the narrator's statement that the "darkness lifts off the square like a great mushroom cloud rising high into the lightening sky and sucking the fears and phantasms of the people's nighttime up with it" (494).

32. While the origins of Uncle Sam are still somewhat unclear, a 1961 congressional proclamation officially weighed in on the side of a long-standing story that attributed the moniker to a Troy, New York, meatpacker named Sam Wilson, who supplied provisions for U.S. troops during the War of 1812. By the late nineteenth century, especially during the Spanish-American War, Uncle Sam had frequently become a tool of satire employed by political cartoonists such as Thomas Nast to criticize U.S. foreign policy. The iconic, unambiguously patriotic Uncle Sam that Coover's description evokes dates back to James Montgomery Flagg's military recruitment posters that were used during both world wars.

33. DeLillo picks up this theme again in 1997's *Underworld,* in which he takes the reader through virtually the entire history of the nuclear arms race in order to trace the development of U.S. cold war angst in its entirety. More important, though, *Underworld* also makes clear the ways in which this condition outlives the end of the cold war in much the same manner as the physical detritus of the conflict does. *White Noise* thus serves as the diagnosis of cold war trauma, and *Underworld* as the prognosis for the future if that trauma is left "untreated."

34. To further demonstrate the emotional remove of the faculty of the College-on-the-Hill, Gladney's Jewish colleague Murray Siskind even calls this power of Hitler's "a wonderful thing" (that is, a thing to be marveled at) without a hint of irony (except, of course, for the reader).

35. Gladney does seem genuinely repulsed by Hitler's anti-Semitism, for example, despite the fact that it obviously facilitates the exertion of the power over death that he finds so fascinating and even estimable.

36. Rojecki's *Silencing the Opposition* again provides a sound analysis of how the objectivity of news coverage of nuclear issues by television networks such as CBS and NBC (both of whose corporate owners—Westinghouse and General Electric, respectively—derive substantial revenues from government defense contracts) shows evidence of having been undermined by financial considerations.

37. DeLillo (*Underworld*) suggests this practice is as irrelevant to solution of the larger problem as rearranging the deck chairs of the *Titanic,* the cliché to which his construction here seems to allude.

38. See chapter 3.

39. He assumes a dizzying array of aliases and pseudonyms within the novel, so many that one of his aliases is Etcetera (in the original Russian, his unusual-sounding alias is "Ted," a close homophone of *i.t.d.*, the common abbreviation for *i tak dalee,* which translates into English as "and so on"). This first name and patronymic combination seems to be his preferred moniker.

40. A severed hand that Fan Fanych uses in deceiving the woman who wants her husband killed turns out to belong to a party member and sets a strange series of events into motion. After the hand has served its purpose of misleading the would-be victim's wife, Fan Fanych feeds it to a tiger at the zoo. However, a zookeeper finds a finger of it in the tiger's cage and takes it straight to Yezhov, the head of the Cheka. Yezhov recognizes the finger and claims that its owner was killed by members of "the right-wing and Leninist bourgeoisie." Stalin, in turn, tells Yezhov to "brush up on industrialization and collectivization" (13–14) and declares NEP to be over.

41. A point left out of the English translation is that Kidalla also flatly notes that the fact that the cases are made up is an "unrevealed matter" (16).

42. In the original, Aleshkovsky has Fan Fanych use phrases from the Russian idiom of the camps (with which he was familiar as a former prisoner) to describe the penalty that these cases carry. Consequently the English translation contains additional context and more familiar references that help make his meaning clear. The original reads as follows: "chetvertak [a slang term for a quarter-ruble but denoting a twenty-five-year, that is, quarter-century, prison term], piat' po rogam [literally, "five over the horns," a common camp slang term for disenfranchisement], piat' po rukam [literally, "five on the arms," a pun on the noun *poruka,* meaning "parole" or "bail"], piat' po nogam [literally, "five on foot" or "five on your legs," presumably referring to the fact that a former prisoner would likely have to work in heavy labor upon his or her release] i gnevnyi miting na zavode ≪Kalibr≫ ["and an angry rally at the 'Caliber' factory"]" (17).

43. The dates that form the temporal boundaries of this case are, respectively, Bastille Day and Bloody Sunday, two of the more important benchmarks in the pre-Soviet history of European revolutionary movements.

44. The Perdebabaev portion of this name contains echoes of both the verb *perdet'* (to fart) and *baba* (a colloquial term used to refer to women, comparable to the English "chick"). The French name Valois is derived from the verb *valoir* (to be worth), which makes his complete last name suggestive of "worth a woman's fart," a potentially apt designation given the nonsensical testimony that is attributed to him.

45. The original Russian text refers to Kornei Chukovsky rather than Mikhail Sholokhov, who is a more familiar representative of official Soviet literature for American readers because of his novel *And Quiet Flows the Don* (1934; *Tikhii Don*). Chukovsky provides a more apt association, however, since he is best known for his fairy tales for children.

46. Kidalla's closing comments echo those of party functionary Andrei Zhdanov, who denounced Akhmatova as "half-nun and half-harlot" and Zoshchenko as "a vile hooligan" at the 1946 party congress.

47. The connection with the conditioning experiments conducted on the young Tyrone Slothrop in *Gravity's Rainbow* appears to be largely coincidental here, but the theme of behaviorist psychological conditioning recurs in a variety of ways in cold war literature (see Orwell's *Nineteen Eighty-Four*, Vonnegut's *Sirens of Titan*, Burgess's *Clockwork Orange*, Kesey's *One Flew Over the Cuckoo's Nest*, and Zinoviev's *Madhouse*) as an analogue of ideological conformity. At least in the Russian instances, this theme has clear historical connections: the Soviets commonly used psychotropic drugs and other forms of psychological "persuasion" to condition (or often simply to punish) political dissidents.

48. The translation of *kolkhoznitsy* as "peasants" loses the distinctly Soviet overtones of that word (especially given the sickles they are carrying), which is more accurately rendered as "collective farm workers."

49. The preposterous pseudonym under which Fan Fanych is tried suggests a somewhat different obscenity in Russian than the English rendering of "C. U. N. Tarkington." In addition to providing clear association with one unmistakable center of capitalist culture (New York), the initials of the name Kh. U. Iork spell out the word *khui*, which is roughly equivalent to the English "prick" or "cock."

50. If so this creates yet another chronological inconsistency—presumably intentional on Aleshkovsky's part—since Chernyshevsky died more than sixty years earlier in 1889.

51. He even becomes annoyed with Kolya at one point early in the narrative when the latter apparently makes an unrecorded protestation against some aspect of Fan Fanych's narration: "Shut your mouth, Kolya. Quit telling me to cool it or you can find some other international crook to spout his memoirs" (19). The original Russian here relies heavily on idiomatic expressions, but the general sense is retained accurately in the translation.

52. One of Booker and Juraga's central assertions in their analysis of *Astrophobia* is that "Palisander's carnivalesque revisions of history . . . function not so much as a parody of official versions of Soviet history as of the recent retellings of that history by dissident writers such as Solzhenitsyn" (*Bakhtin*, 150). They also single out Eduard Limonov as a target of Sokolov's parody in the novel, noting that "Palisander's outrageous sexual adventures often read almost as an attempt to out-Limonov Limonov" (153). While I acknowledge that this element clearly seems present in the work, I also feel that Booker and Juraga oversell their point somewhat by interpreting this parody of dissident counterhistory as the *primary* intention of *Astrophobia*. Sokolov's parody uses models from both pro- and anti-Soviet texts, thus suggesting that the satire contained within this parody is reserved more for the fictionalizing technique that these two perspectives share, rather than their individual messages.

53. I quote it here at considerable length since paraphrasing it or producing another similar summary would simply repeat work that has already been done well.

54. Before the novel was translated into English as *Astrophobia*, English-speaking critics often referred to it using the working title *The Epic of Palisandr* because of the distinctively epic *-iia* ending.

55. Gregory L. Freeze singles out Andropov's praise of Brezhnev's speeches ("[He] brilliantly reveals the paths and prospects of communist construction in the USSR and inspires new heroic feats of labour in the name of strengthening our multinational state, the unity and solidarity of the Soviet people") and the justifications for Brezhnev's

receipt of the Lenin Prize for his memoirs ("For their popularity and their educational influence on the mass of readers, the books of Leonid Ilich are unrivalled") as some of the most heinous examples of this sort of absurd flattery ("From Stalinism to Stagnation," 372). Of Brezhnev's memoirs, Katerina Clark writes, "They remind one of the Stalinist variety of autohagiography, where 'all the threads' of the administration pass through the hands of one man, who is constantly achieving what by normal reckoning is impossible" (*Soviet Novel*, 238). As part of Sokolov's critique in this regard, *Astrophobia* contains a scene in which Palisander loses a literary prize competition to both Stalin and Brezhnev, whose poem, quoted in the text, is wholly without merit (34).

56. His unusual last name refers to the flower the forget-me-not.

57. The word *ocherk* (often translated into English as "sketch") is defined by Marc Slonim in *Soviet Russian Literature* as "a genre between a journalist's report and an essay" whose purpose was "accurate and faithful reproduction of people and conditions of labor with an emphasis on industrial, agricultural, military, and other achievements of the country's economic and social life" (166). Many of the realistic and naturalistic novels of the 1920s with revolutionary themes are essentially fictionalized examples of this genre.

58. Palisander even uses the diminutive form of Nezabudka's first name (*Iasha*) here to affect a greater degree of familiarity. Palisander seems to intend the diminutive as a sign of his amity toward his "coeval" (*rovesnik*). The context of the passage in which the diminutive appears, however, causes it to function much as the use of a diminutive form by a landowner toward one of his peasants in a nineteenth-century novel would, that is, to accentuate the social inequality between the two.

59. The hat Palisander refers to in the original (the "murmolka") is not technically equivalent to a graduate's "mortarboard," as the English translation reads. The murmolka is a traditional style of Russian hat dating back to the seventeenth century. This potentially makes Palisander's reference to it even more uncomplimentary, since a murmolka would not only be perceived as inappropriately plebeian headgear for an academic but also somewhat antiquated.

Epilogue

1. Seed discusses the trope of preserved knowledge leading to a renewed cycle of destruction in his *American Science Fiction and the Cold War*. He primarily treats this theme in Hoban's *Riddley Walker* and *A Canticle for Leibowitz*, although he also mentions Leigh Brackett's 1955 novel *The Long Tomorrow* (157–67).

2. The "Doomsday Clock" in the *Bulletin of the Atomic Scientists* was set at two minutes before midnight when *A Canticle for Leibowitz* was released and moved from seven to three minutes before midnight in the years that bracketed the publication of *Cosmos*. These two instances represent the two most dire assessments of the nuclear threat since the clock's inception in 1947.

3. This is the literal translation of the Russian title. The book has been translated into English under the titles *The Clay Machine-Gun* (United Kingdom) and *Buddha's Little Finger* (United States).

4. David Cowart notes in his article "Pynchon and the Sixties" (1999) that *Mason & Dixon* is filled with anachronistic references that bring the symbolic analogue of Pynchon's mock eighteenth-century novel into clear focus: "Those small reflections in history's distant mirror highlight a much larger congruence between the 1760s and

the 1960s, for Pynchon ultimately reads the eighteenth century much as he reads the twentieth. As in one era the struggle to resist the totalizing tide of reason manifested itself as a taste for Gothic, a nostalgia for magic, and an embattled spirituality, so, in the 1960s, enormous numbers of American citizens resisted the logical-yet-monstrous coercion of cold war rationality as embodied in the military-industrial complex, the Vietnam war, the policy of Mutual Assured Destruction, and so forth" (5). As such *Mason & Dixon* provides a retrospective consideration of Anglo-American history that spans more than two centuries.

BIBLIOGRAPHY

Primary Texts

Adams, Henry. *The Education of Henry Adams*. 1919. Boston: Houghton Mifflin, 1961.

Aitmatov, Chingiz. *The Day Lasts More Than a Hundred Years*. Translated by F. J. French. Bloomington: Indiana University Press, 1983.

Aksyonov, Vassily. *The Burn*. Translated by Michael Glenny. New York: Random House, 1984.

———. *The Island of Crimea*. Translated by Michael Henry Heim. New York: Random House, 1983.

———. *The New Sweet Style*. Translated by Christopher Morris. New York: Random House, 1999.

———. *Ostrov Krym*. Ann Arbor, Mich.: Ardis, 1981.

———. *Our Golden Ironburg: A Novel with Formulas*. Translated by Ronald E. Peterson. Ann Arbor, Mich.: Ardis, 1989.

———. *Say Cheese!* Translated by Antonina W. Bouis. New York: Random House, 1989.

———. *The Steel Bird and Other Stories*. Ann Arbor, Mich.: Ardis, 1979.

———. "Who's Braver—the Cosmonaut or the Dissident?" In *Andrei Sakharov and Peace*, edited by Edward D. Lozansky, 141–44. New York: Avon, 1985.

———. *Zolotaia nasha zhelezka: Roman s formulami*. Ann Arbor, Mich.: Ardis, 1980.

Aksyonov, Vassily, Viktor Yerofeyev, Fazil Iskander, Andrei Bitov, and Yevgeny Popov, eds. *Metropol: A Literary Almanac*. New York: Norton, 1982.

Aleshkovsky, Yuz. *The Hand, or, The Confession of an Executioner*. Translated by Susan Brownsberger. New York: Farrar, Straus and Giroux, 1990.

———. *Kangaroo*. Translated by Tamara Glenny. New York: Farrar, Straus and Giroux, 1986.

———. *Kenguru*. Ann Arbor, Mich.: Ardis, 1981.

———. *Ruka: (povestvovanie palacha)*. New York: Russica, 1980.

Barth, John. *Giles Goat-Boy*. New York: Doubleday, 1966.

———. "The Literature of Exhaustion." *Atlantic Monthly*, August 1967, 29–34.

Barthelme, Donald. *The King*. Harper and Row, 1990.

———. *Snow White*. 1967. New York: Atheneum, 1972.

———. *Unspeakable Practices, Unnatural Acts*. New York: Farrar, Straus, 1968.

Bulgakov, Mikhail. *The Diaboliad and Other Stories*. Translated by Carl R. Proffer. Bloomington: Indiana University Press, 1972.

————. *The Heart of a Dog.* Translated by Michael Glenny. New York: Harcourt, Brace and Wolff, 1968.

Bulychev, Kirill. *Half a Life.* Translated by Helen Saltz Jacobson. New York: Macmillan, 1977.

Burdick, Eugene, and Harvey Wheeler. *Fail-Safe.* New York: McGraw-Hill, 1962.

Cabell, James Branch. *Jurgen: A Comedy of Justice.* New York: McBride, 1919.

Chakovsky, Alexander. *Pobeda: Politicheskii roman.* Moscow: Izvestiia, 1985.

Condon, Richard. *The Manchurian Candidate.* New York: McGraw-Hill, 1959.

Coover, Robert. *The Origin of the Brunists.* New York: Putnam, 1966.

————. *The Public Burning.* New York: Viking, 1977.

DeLillo, Don. 1971. *End Zone.* New York: Penguin, 1986.

————. *Underworld.* New York: Scribner, 1997.

————. *White Noise.* 1985. New York: Penguin, 1999.

Dovlatov, Sergei. *The Compromise.* Translated by Anne Frydman. Chicago: Academy Chicago, 1990.

————. *The Invisible Book (Epilogue).* Translated by Katherine O'Connor and Diana L. Burgin. Ann Arbor, Mich.: Ardis, 1979.

————. *Kompromiss.* New York: Serebrianyi Vek, 1981.

————. *Nevidimaia kniga.* Ann Arbor, Mich.: Ardis, 1978.

————. *Ours.* Translated by Anne Frydman. New York: Weidenfeld and Nicolson, 1989.

Eliot, T. S. *Collected Poems, 1909–1962.* New York: Harcourt, Brace, 1991.

Frank, Pat. *Alas, Babylon.* 1959. New York: HarperCollins, 2005.

Gogol, Nikolai. *Tchitchikoff's Journeys; or Dead Souls.* Translated by Isabel Hapgood. New York: Thomas Y. Crowell, 1886.

Granin, Daniil. *Into the Storm.* Translated by Robert Daglish. Moscow: Progress, 1965.

————. *Those Who Seek.* Translated by Robert Daglish. Moscow: Foreign Languages Publishing House, 1955.

Hašek, Jaroslav. *The Good Soldier Schweik.* Translated by Paul Selver. Garden City, N.Y.: Doubleday, Doran, 1930.

Heller, Joseph. *Catch-22.* New York: Simon and Schuster, 1961.

————. *Closing Time.* New York: Simon and Schuster, 1994.

Hoban, Russell. *Riddley Walker.* New York: Summit, 1980.

Huxley, Aldous. *Brave New World.* 1932. New York: Harper and Brothers, 1946.

Il'f, Ilya, and Evgeny Petrov. *The Twelve Chairs.* Translated by John H. C. Richardson. 1966. Evanston, Ill.: Northwestern University Press, 1997.

Iskander, Fazil. *The Goatibex Constellation.* Translated by Helen Burlingame. Ann Arbor, Mich.: Ardis, 1975.

————. "Kroliki i udavy." In *Stoianka cheloveka: Povesti I rasskazy,* 439–580. Moscow: Kvadrat, 1995.

————. *Rabbits and Boa Constrictors.* Translated by Ronald E. Peterson. Ann Arbor, Mich.: Ardis, 1989.

Kataev, Valentin. *The Embezzlers.* Translated by Charles Rougle. Ann Arbor, Mich.: Ardis, 1975.

Kharitonov, Mark. *Lines of Fate.* Translated by Helena Goscilo. New York: New Press, 1996.

Kochetov, Vsevolod. *Sekretar' obkoma.* Moscow: Molodaia gvardiia, 1962.

Kozhevnikov, Vadim. *Znakom'tes,' Baluev.* 1960. Moscow: Vysshaia Shkola, 1988.

Kramer, Stanley, dir. *On the Beach.* Perf. Gregory Peck, Ava Gardner, Fred Astaire, Anthony Perkins. United Artists. 1959.

Kubrick, Stanley, dir. *Dr. Strangelove, or How I Learned to Stop Worrying and Love the Bomb.* Perf. Peter Sellers, George C. Scott, Sterling Hayden, Slim Pickens. Columbia Pictures Corporation, 1964.

le Carré, John. *The Secret Pilgrim.* New York: Knopf, 1990.

Lewis, Sinclair. *Babbitt.* 1922. New York: New American Library, 1961.

———. *It Can't Happen Here.* Garden City, N.Y.: Doubleday, Doran, 1935.

Makanin, Vladimir. *Escape Hatch and The Long Road Ahead.* Translated by Mary Ann Szporluk. Dana Point, Calif.: Ardis, 1996.

Mayakovsky, Vladimir. *The Complete Plays of Vladimir Mayakovsky.* Translated by Guy Daniels. New York: Washington Square Press, 1968.

Miller, Walter M., Jr. *A Canticle for Leibowitz.* 1959. New York: Bantam Books, 1961.

Millet, Lydia. *Oh Pure and Radiant Heart.* 2005. Orlando, Fla.: Harcourt, 2006.

O'Brien, Tim. *The Nuclear Age.* New York: Knopf, 1985.

Olesha, Yuri. *Envy.* Translated by T. S. Berczynski. Ann Arbor, Mich.: Ardis, 1975.

Orwell, George. *Nineteen Eighty-Four.* New York: Harcourt, Brace, 1949.

Pelevin, Viktor. *Buddha's Little Finger.* Translated by Andrew Bromfield. New York: Viking, 2000.

———. *The Life of Insects.* Translated by Andrew Bromfield. New York: Farrar, Straus and Giroux, 1998.

———. *Omon Ra.* Translated by Andrew Bromfield. New York: Farrar, Straus and Giroux, 1996.

Percy, Walker. *Love in the Ruins: The Adventures of a Bad Catholic at a Time Near the End of the World.* New York: Farrar, Straus and Giroux, 1971.

Pynchon, Thomas. *Against the Day.* New York: Penguin, 2006.

———. *The Crying of Lot 49.* Philadelphia: Lippincott, 1966.

———. *Gravity's Rainbow.* 1973. New York: Penguin, 1987.

———. "Is It O.K. to Be a Luddite?" *New York Times Book Review,* October 28, 1984, 1, 40–41.

———. *Mason & Dixon.* New York: Henry Holt, 1997.

———. *Slow Learner.* Boston: Little, Brown, 1984.

———. *V.* 1963. New York: Modern Library, 1966.

———. *Vineland.* Boston: Little, Brown, 1990.

Reed, Ishmael. *The Free-lance Pallbearers.* 1966. London: Allison and Busby, 1990.

———. *Mumbo Jumbo.* 1972. New York: Atheneum, 1988.

Roshwald, Mordecai. *Level 7.* London: Allison and Busby, 1959.

Roth, Philip. *I Married a Communist.* Boston: Houghton Mifflin, 1998.

"Shelter, The." *The Twilight Zone.* Directed by Lamont Johnson, September 29, 1961.

Shute, Nevil. *On the Beach.* New York: William Morrow, 1957.

Silko, Leslie Marmon. *Ceremony.* 1977. New York: Penguin, 2006.

Sokolov, Sasha. *Astrophobia.* Translated by Michael Henry Heim. New York: Grove Weidenfeld, 1989.

———. *Palisandriia.* Ann Arbor, Mich.: Ardis, 1984.

Solzhenitsyn, Alexander. *The First Circle.* Translated by Thomas P. Whitney. New York: Harper and Row, 1968.

————. *The Gulag Archipelago, 1918–1956: An Experiment in Literary Investigation.* Translated by Thomas P. Whitney and H. T. Willetts. London: Collins-Harvill, 1974–78.

————. *One Day in the Life of Ivan Denisovich.* Translated by Ralph Parker. New York: Dutton, 1963.

Sorokin, Vladimir. *Norma.* Moscow: Tri Kita / Obscura viti, 1994.

Stephenson, Neal. *Snow Crash.* New York: Bantam, 1992.

Strugatsky, Arkady, and Boris Strugatsky. *Prisoners of Power.* Translated by Helen Saltz Jacobson. New York: Macmillan, 1977.

————. *Roadside Picnic / Tale of the Troika.* Translated by Antonia W. Bouis. New York: Macmillan, 1977.

————. *The Ugly Swans.* Translated by Alice Stone Nakhimovsky and Alexander Nakhimovsky. New York: Macmillan, 1979.

Szilard, Leo. *The Voice of the Dolphins and Other Stories.* New York: Simon and Schuster, 1961.

Tertz, Abram [Andrei Sinyavsky]. *The Makepeace Experiment.* Translated by Manya Harari. Evanston, Ill.: Northwestern University Press, 1989.

————. *"The Trial Begins" and "On Socialist Realism."* Translated by Max Hayward and George Dennis. Berkeley and Los Angeles: University of California Press, 1960.

Vasilenko, Svetlana. *Shamara and Other Stories.* Translated by Elena V. Prokhorova. Evanston, Ill.: Northwestern University Press, 1999.

Vizenor, Gerald. *Hiroshima Bugi.* Lincoln: University of Nebraska Press, 2003.

Voinovich, Vladimir. *Antisovietskii sovietskii soiuz.* Ann Arbor, Mich.: Ardis, 1985.

————. *The Anti-Soviet Soviet Union.* Translated by Richard Lourie. San Diego: Harcourt Brace Jovanovich, 1986.

————. *In Plain Russian: Stories.* Translated by Richard Lourie. New York: Farrar, Straus and Giroux, 1979.

————. *The Life and Extraordinary Adventures of Private Ivan Chonkin.* Translated by Richard Lourie. New York: Farrar, Straus and Giroux, 1977.

————. *Monumental Propaganda.* Translated by Andrew Bromfield. New York: Knopf, 2004.

————. *Moscow 2042.* Translated by Richard Lourie. San Diego, Calif.: Harcourt Brace Jovanovich, 1987.

————. *Moskva 2042.* Moscow: Vsia Moskva, 1990.

————. *Portret na fone mifa.* Moscow: Eksmo, 2002.

————. *Pretendent na prestol: Novye priklucheniia soldata Ivana Chonkina.* Paris: YMCA Press, 1981.

————. *Pretender to the Throne: The Further Adventures of Private Ivan Chonkin.* Translated by Richard Lourie. New York: Farrar, Straus and Giroux, 1981.

————. *Zhizn' i neobychainye prikliucheniia soldata Ivana Chonkina.* Paris: YMCA Press, 1976.

Vonnegut, Kurt, Jr. *Cat's Cradle.* 1963. New York: Dial, 2006.

————. *Player Piano.* 1952. New York: Delacorte, 1973.

————. *Slaughterhouse-Five, or the Children's Crusade: A Duty-Dance with Death.* New York: Delta, 1969.

————. *Timequake.* New York: Putnam, 1997.

Voznesensky, Andrei. "Beatnik's Monologue." In *The New Russian Poets: 1953–1968*, translated by George Reavey, 202–3. New York: October House, 1968.

Watkins, Peter, dir. *The War Game*. British Broadcasting Corporation, 1965.

Zamyatin, Evgeny. *We*. Translated by Bernard Guilbert Guerney. London: Jonathan Cape, 1970.

Zinoviev, Alexander. *Gomo Sovietikus*. Lausanne: L'Age d'Homme, 1982.

———. *Homo Sovieticus*. Translated by Charles Janson. Boston: Atlantic Monthly Press, 1985.

———. *The Madhouse*. Translated by Michael Kirkwood. London: Victor Gollancz, 1986.

———. *The Radiant Future*. Translated by Gordon Clough. New York: Random House, 1980.

———. *Svetloe budushchee*. Lausanne: L'Age d'Homme, 1978.

———. *The Yawning Heights*. Translated by Gordon Clough. New York: Random House, 1979.

———. *Ziiaiushchie vysoty*. Lausanne: L'Age d'Homme, 1976.

Secondary Texts

Aldridge, Alexandra. *The Scientific World View in Dystopia*. Ann Arbor, Mich.: UMI Research Press, 1984.

Avins, Carol. *Border Crossings: The West and Russian Identity in Soviet Literature, 1917–1934*. Berkeley and Los Angeles: University of California Press, 1983.

Babenko, Vickie. "Fazil Iskander: An Examination of His Satire." *Russian Language Journal* 30, no. 106 (1976): 131–42.

Baccolini, Rafaella and Tom Moylan, eds. *Dark Horizons: Science Fiction and the Dystopian Imagination*. London: Routledge, 2003.

Bartter, Martha A. *The Way to Ground Zero: The Atomic Bomb in American Science Fiction*. New York: Greenwood Press, 1988.

Bethea, David. *The Shape of Apocalypse in Modern Russian Fiction*. Princeton, N.J.: Princeton University Press, 1989.

Booker, M. Keith. *The Dystopian Impulse in Modern Literature: Fiction as Social Criticism*. Westport, Conn.: Greenwood Press, 1994.

———. *Monsters, Mushroom Clouds, and the Cold War: American Science Fiction and the Roots of Postmodernism, 1946–1964*. Westport, Conn.: Greenwood Press, 2001.

Booker, M. Keith, and Dubravka Juraga. *Bakhtin, Stalin, and Modern Russian Fiction: Carnival, Dialogism, and History*. Westport, Conn.: Greenwood Press, 1995.

Boyer, Paul. *By the Bomb's Early Light: American Thought and Culture at the Dawn of the Atomic Age*. Rev. ed. Chapel Hill: University of North Carolina Press, 1994.

———. *Fallout: A Historian Reflects on America's Half-Century Encounter with Nuclear Weapons*. Columbus: Ohio State University Press, 1998.

Brands, H. W. *The Devil We Knew: Americans and the Cold War*. New York: Oxford University Press, 1993.

Brians, Paul. *Nuclear Holocausts: Atomic War in Fiction, 1895–1984*. Kent, Ohio: Kent State University Press, 1987.

Brown, Edward J. "Zinoviev, Aleshkovsky, Rabelais, Sorrentino, Possibly Pynchon, Maybe James Joyce, and Certainly *Tristram Shandy*: A Comparative Study of a Satirical Mode." *Stanford Slavic Studies* 1, no. 1 (1987): 307–25.

Bundy, McGeorge. *Danger and Survival: Choices about the Bomb in the First Fifty Years.* New York: Vintage, 1990.

Campbell, Joseph. *The Hero with a Thousand Faces.* Princeton, N.J.: Princeton University Press, 1949.

Chapple, Richard L. *Soviet Satire of the Twenties.* Gainesville: University Press of Florida, 1980.

Chudo, Alicia [Gary Saul Morson]. *And Quiet Flows the Vodka, or, When Pushkin Comes to Shove: The Curmudgeon's Guide to Russian Literature and Culture, with the Devil's Dictionary of Received Ideas.* Evanston, Ill.: Northwestern University Press, 2000.

Ciuba, Gary M. *Walker Percy: Books of Revelations.* Athens: University of Georgia Press, 1991.

Clark, John R. "Vapid Voices and Sleazy Styles." In *Theorizing Satire: Essays in Literary Criticism,* edited by Brian A. Connery and Kirk Combe, 19–42. New York: St. Martin's Press, 1995.

Clark, Katerina. *The Soviet Novel: History as Ritual.* Chicago: University of Chicago Press, 1981.

Clowes, Edith W. *Russian Experimental Fiction: Resisting Ideology after Utopia.* Princeton, N.J.: Princeton University Press, 1993.

Connery, Brian A., and Kirk Combe. "Theorizing Satire: A Retrospective and Introduction." In *Theorizing Satire: Essays in Literary Criticism,* edited by Brian A. Connery and Kirk Combe, 1–15. New York: St. Martin's Press, 1995.

———, eds. *Theorizing Satire: Essays in Literary Criticism.* New York: St. Martin's Press, 1995.

Conquest, Robert. *Stalin and the Kirov Murder.* Oxford: Oxford University Press, 1989.

Cowart, David. "Pynchon and the Sixties." *Critique: Studies in Contemporary Fiction* 41, no. 1 (1999): 3–12.

Cunningham, Hugo C., ed. *Article 58, Criminal Code of the RSFSR (1934).* http://www.cyberussr.com/rus/uk58-e.html (accessed May 28, 2009).

———. *Sekciya 58, Ugolovnyj Kodeks RSFSR (1934).* http://www.cyberussr.com/rus/uk58-r.html (accessed May 28, 2009).

Dalgård, Per. *The Function of the Grotesque in Vasilij Aksenov.* Translated by Robert Porter. Aarhus, Denmark: Arkona, 1982.

Derrida, Jacques. "No Apocalypse, Not Now (Full Speed Ahead, Seven Missiles, Seven Missives)." *Diacritics* 14, no. 2 (1984): 20–31.

Dewey, Joseph. *In a Dark Time: The Apocalyptic Temper in the American Novel of the Nuclear Age.* West Lafayette, Ind.: Purdue University Press, 1990.

Engelhardt, Tom. *The End of Victory Culture: Cold War America and the Disillusioning of a Generation.* New York: Basic Books, 1995.

Epstein, Mikhail. "Postmodernism, Communism and Sots-Art." In *Endquote: Sots-Art Literature and Soviet Grand Style,* edited by Marina Balina, Nancy Condee, and Evgeny Dobrenko, 3–31. Evanston, Ill.: Northwestern University Press, 2000.

Ezrahi, Sidra DeKoven. *By Words Alone: The Holocaust in Literature.* Chicago: University of Chicago Press, 1980.

Fogel, Stan, and Gordon Slethaug. *Understanding John Barth.* Columbia: University of South Carolina Press, 1990.

Freeze, Gregory L. "From Stalinism to Stagnation, 1953–1985." In *Russia: A History*, edited by Gregory L. Freeze, 347–82. New York: Oxford University Press, 1997.

Gaddis, John Lewis. *We Now Know: Rethinking Cold War History*. Oxford: Clarendon Press, 1997.

Gakov, Vladimir, and Paul Brians. "Nuclear War Themes in Soviet Science Fiction: An Annotated Bibliography." *Science Fiction Studies* 16 (March 1989): 67–84.

Garrard, John, and Carol Garrard. *Inside the Soviet Writers' Union*. New York: Free Press, 1990.

Gery, John. *Nuclear Annihilation and Contemporary American Poetry: Ways of Nothingness*. Gainesville: University Press of Florida, 1996.

Glad, John, ed. *Literature in Exile*. Durham, N.C.: Duke University Press, 1990.

Goldman, Marshall. *The Soviet Economy: Myth and Reality*. Englewood Cliffs, N.J.: Prentice-Hall, 1968.

Grant, J. Kerry. *A Companion to "The Crying of Lot 49."* Athens: University of Georgia Press, 1994.

Gray, Chris Hables. *Postmodern War: The New Politics of Conflict*. New York: Guilford Press, 1997.

Guilhamet, Leon. *Satire and the Transformation of Genre*. Philadelphia: University of Pennsylvania Press, 1987.

Harris, Charles B. *Passionate Virtuosity: The Fiction of John Barth*. Urbana: University of Illinois Press, 1983.

Henriksen, Margot A. *Dr. Strangelove's America: Society and Culture in the Atomic Age*. Berkeley and Los Angeles: University of California Press, 1997.

Hersey, John. *Hiroshima*. New York: Knopf, 1946.

Highet, Gilbert. *The Anatomy of Satire*. Princeton, N.J.: Princeton University Press, 1962.

Hilgartner, Stephen, Richard C. Bell, and Rory O'Connor. *Nukespeak: Nuclear Language, Visions, and Mindset*. San Francisco: Sierra Club Books, 1982.

Hirshberg, Matthew S. *Perpetuating Patriotic Perceptions: The Cognitive Function of the Cold War*. Westport, Conn.: Praeger, 1993.

Holloway, David. *Stalin and the Bomb: The Soviet Union and Atomic Energy, 1939–1956*. New Haven, Conn.: Yale University Press, 1994.

Holman, C. Hugh, and William Harmon. *A Handbook to Literature*. 6th ed. New York: Macmillan, 1992.

Hosking, Geoffrey. *Beyond Socialist Realism: Soviet Fiction since Ivan Denisovich*. London: Granada, 1980.

Howell, Yvonne. *Apocalyptic Realism: The Science Fiction of Arkady and Boris Strugatsky*. New York: Peter Lang, 1994.

Hume, Kathryn. *American Dream, American Nightmare: Fiction Since 1960*. Urbana: University of Illinois Press, 2000.

Hutcheon, Linda. *A Poetics of Postmodernism: History, Theory, Fiction*. New York: Routledge, 1988.

Iser, Wolfgang. "The Significance of Fictionalizing." *Anthropoetics: The Electronic Journal of Generative Anthropology* 3 (Fall 1997 / Winter 1998): 1–7. Also available online at http://www.anthropoetics.ucla.edu/apo302/iser_fiction.htm (accessed May 28, 2009).

Johnson, D. Barton. "The Galoshes Manifesto: A Motif in the Novels of Sasha Sokolov." *Oxford Slavonic Papers* 22 (1989): 155–79

———. "Sasha Sokolov's Twilight Cosmos: Themes and Motifs." *Slavic Review* 45, no. 4 (1986): 639–49.

Jones, Peter G. *War and the Novelist: Appraising the American War Novel.* Columbia: University of Missouri Press, 1976.

Kahn, Herman. *On Thermonuclear War.* Princeton, N.J.: Princeton University Press, 1961.

Karl, Frederick R. *American Fiction, 1940–1980: A Comprehensive History and Critical Evaluation.* New York: Harper and Row, 1983.

Kasack, Wolfgang. *Dictionary of Russian Literature since 1917.* New York: Columbia University Press, 1988.

Kennan, George F. "The G.O.P. Won the Cold War? Ridiculous." *New York Times,* October 28, 1992, A21.

Kessler, Stephan. *Erzähltechniken und Informationsvergabe in Vasilij Aksenov's "Oûog, Zolotaja nasha ûelezka" und "Poiski ûanra."* Munich: Verlag Otto Sagner, 1998.

Kharpertian, Theodore. *A Hand to Turn the Time: The Menippean Satires of Thomas Pynchon.* Cranbury, N.J.: Associated University Presses, 1990.

Kirkwood, Michael. "Ideology in the Works of A. A. Zinoviev." In *Alexander Zinoviev as Writer and Thinker: An Assessment,* edited by Philip Hanson and Michael Kirkwood, 44–60. London: Macmillan, 1988.

Kolesnikoff, Nina. "*Our Golden Hardware* as a Parody." In *Vasiliy Pavlovich Aksënov: A Writer in Quest of Himself,* edited by Edward Możejko, Boris Briker, and Per Dalgård, 193–204. Columbus, Ohio: Slavica, 1986.

Kustanovich, Konstantin. *The Artist and the Tyrant: Vassily Aksenov's Works in the Brezhnev Era.* Columbus, Ohio: Slavica, 1992.

Kuznetsov, Sergey. "Vassily Aksyonov's Parody of V." *Pynchon Notes* 32–33 (Spring/Fall 1993): 181–85.

Laird, Sally. *Voices of Russian Literature: Interviews with Ten Contemporary Writers.* Oxford: Oxford University Press, 1999.

Langer, Lawrence L. *The Age of Atrocity: Death in Modern Literature.* Boston: Beacon, 1978.

———. "On Reading and Writing Holocaust Literature." Introduction to *Art from the Ashes: A Holocaust Anthology,* edited by Lawrence L. Langer, 3–10. New York: Oxford University Press, 1995.

Lenin, V. I. *The Collected Works of Lenin.* Vol. 17. Moscow, 1925.

Lifton, Robert Jay, and Eric Markusen. *The Genocidal Mentality: Nazi Holocaust and Nuclear Threat.* New York: Basic Books, 1990.

Lifton, Robert Jay, and Greg Mitchell. *Hiroshima in America: Fifty Years of Denial.* New York: Putnam, 1995.

Lipovetsky, Mark. *Russian Postmodernist Fiction: Dialogue with Chaos.* Armonk, N.Y.: M. E. Sharpe, 1999.

Lotman, Yuri, and Boris Uspensky. "Binary Models in the Dynamics of Russian Culture (to the End of the Eighteenth Century)." In *The Semiotics of Russian Cultural History,* edited by Alexander D. Nakhimovsky and Alice Stone Nakhimovsky, 30–66. Ithaca, N.Y.: Cornell University Press, 1985.

Maltby, Paul. *Dissident Postmodernists: Barthelme, Coover, Pynchon.* Philadelphia: University of Pennsylvania Press, 1991.

Marsh, Rosalind J. *Soviet Fiction since Stalin: Science, Politics and Literature.* London: Croom Helm, 1986.

Mathewson, Rufus W. *The Positive Hero in Russian Literature.* New York: Columbia University Press, 1958.

Matich, Olga. "Is There a Russian Literature beyond Politics?" In *The Third Wave: Russian Literature in Emigration,* edited by Olga Matich and Michael Heim, 180–87. Ann Arbor, Mich.: Ardis, 1984.

———. "Sasha Sokolov and His Literary Context." *Canadian-American Slavic Studies* 21, no. 3–4 (1987): 301–19.

———. "Vasilii Aksenov and the Literature of Convergence: *Ostrov Krym* as Self-Criticism." *Slavic Review* 47, no. 4 (1988): 642–51.

Matich, Olga, and Michael Heim, eds. *The Third Wave: Russian Literature in Emigration.* Ann Arbor, Mich.: Ardis, 1984.

McConnell, Frank D. *Four Postwar American Novelists: Bellow, Mailer, Barth, and Pynchon.* Chicago: University of Chicago Press, 1977.

McGuire, Patrick L. *Red Stars: Political Aspects of Soviet Science Fiction.* Ann Arbor, Mich.: UMI Research Press, 1985.

McHoul, Alec, and David Wills. *Writing Pynchon: Strategies in Fictional Analysis.* Urbana: University of Illinois Press, 1990.

Miller, Stephen Paul. *The Seventies Now: Culture as Surveillance.* Durham, N.C.: Duke University Press, 1999.

Mitgang, Herbert. *Dangerous Dossiers: Exposing the Secret War Against America's Greatest Authors.* New York: D. I. Fine, 1988.

Moore, Mike. "Midnight Never Came." *Bulletin of the Atomic Scientists* 51, no. 6 (1995): 16–27.

Moore, Thomas. *The Style of Connectedness: "Gravity's Rainbow" and Thomas Pynchon.* Columbia: University of Missouri Press, 1987.

Morson, Gary Saul. *The Boundaries of Genre: Dostoevsky's Diary of a Writer and the Traditions of Literary Utopia.* Evanston, Ill.: Northwestern University Press, 1981.

Moskovich, Wolf. "Alexander Zinoviev's Language." In *Alexander Zinoviev as Writer and Thinker: An Assessment,* edited by Philip Hanson and Michael Kirkwood, 89–104. London: Macmillan, 1988.

Moylan, Tom. *Scraps of the Untainted Sky: Science Fiction, Utopia, Dystopia.* Boulder, Colo.: Westview Press, 2000.

Możejko, Edward, Boris Briker, and Per Dalgård, eds. *Vasiliy Pavlovich Aksënov: A Writer in Quest of Himself.* Columbus, Ohio: Slavica, 1986.

Nepomnyashchy, Catharine Theimer. *Abram Tertz and the Poetics of Crime.* New Haven, Conn.: Yale University Press, 1995.

Norris, Robert S., and Hans M. Kristensen, "Nuclear Notebook: Global Nuclear Stockpiles, 1945–2006." *Bulletin of the Atomic Scientists* 62, no. 4 (July/August 2006): 64–66.

Office of Civil Defense. *In Time of Emergency: A Citizen's Handbook on Nuclear Attack and Natural Disasters.* Washington, D.C.: USGPO, 1968.

Oppenheimer, J. Robert. "Physics in the Contemporary World." *Bulletin of the Atomic Scientists* 4, no. 3 (1948): 65–68.

Peterson, Nadya L. *Subversive Imaginations: Fantastic Prose and the End of Soviet Literature, 1970s–1990s*. Boulder, Colo.: Westview Press, 1997.

Piller, Charles. *The Fail-Safe Society: Community Defiance and the End of American Technological Optimism*. New York: Basic Books, 1991.

Porter, Robert. *Russia's Alternative Prose*. Oxford: Berg, 1994.

Proffer, Ellendea. "The Prague Winter: Two Novels by Aksyonov." In *The Third Wave: Russian Literature in Emigration*, edited by Olga Matich and Michael Heim, 131–36. Ann Arbor, Mich.: Ardis, 1984.

Radosh, Ronald, and Joyce Milton. *The Rosenberg File*. 2nd rev. ed. New Haven, Conn.: Yale University Press, 1997.

Reilly, Alayne P. *America in Contemporary Soviet Literature*. New York: New York University Press, 1971.

Remington, Thomas F. *The Truth of Authority: Ideology and Communication in the Soviet Union*. Pittsburgh, Pa.: University of Pittsburgh Press, 1988.

Rhodes, Richard. *Dark Sun: The Making of the Hydrogen Bomb*. New York: Simon and Schuster, 1995.

Riasanovsky, Nicholas V. *A History of Russia*. 5th ed. New York: Oxford, 1993.

Robinson, Douglas. *John Barth's "Giles Goat-Boy": A Study*. Jyväskylä, Finland: University of Jyväskylä, 1980.

Rojecki, Andrew. *Silencing the Opposition: Antinuclear Movements and the Media in the Cold War*. Urbana: University of Illinois Press, 1999.

Rorty, Richard. *Achieving Our Country: Leftist Thought in Twentieth-Century America*. Cambridge, Mass.: Harvard University Press, 1998.

Roszak, Theodore. *The Making of a Counter Culture: Reflections on the Technocratic Society and Its Youthful Opposition*. Garden City, N.Y.: Doubleday, 1969.

Ryan, Karen L. "Sokolov's *Palisandriya*: The Art of History." In *Twentieth-Century Russian Literature: Selected Papers from the Fifth World Congress of Central and East European Studies*, edited by Karen L. Ryan and Barry P. Scherr, 215–27. London: Macmillan, 2000.

Ryan-Hayes, Karen L. *Contemporary Russian Satire: A Genre Study*. Cambridge: Cambridge University Press, 1995.

Sagan, Carl. *Cosmos*. New York: Random House, 1980.

Saivetz, Carol R., and Sylvia Woodby. *Soviet–Third World Relations*. Boulder, Colo.: Westview Press, 1985.

Saltzman, Arthur M. *This Mad "Instead": Governing Metaphors in Contemporary American Fiction*. Columbia: University of South Carolina Press, 2000.

Schulz, Max F. *Black Humor Fiction of the Sixties: A Pluralistic Definition of Man and His World*. Athens: Ohio University Press, 1973.

Seed, David. *American Science Fiction and the Cold War: Literature and Film*. Chicago: Fitzroy Dearborn, 1999.

———. *The Fictional Labyrinths of Thomas Pynchon*. Iowa City: University of Iowa Press, 1988.

Segal, Howard P. *Technological Utopianism in American Culture*. Chicago: University of Chicago Press, 1985.

Simmons, Philip E. *Deep Surfaces: Mass Culture and History in Postmodern American Fiction*. Athens: University of Georgia Press, 1997.

Sinyavsky, Andrei. *Soviet Civilization: A Cultural History.* Translated by Joanne Turn-
bull with the assistance of Nikolai Formozov. New York: Arcade, 1990.

Sisk, David W. *Transformations of Language in Modern Dystopias.* Westport, Conn.:
Greenwood Press, 1997.

Slonim, Marc. *Soviet Russian Literature: Writers and Problems.* New York: Oxford
University Press, 1964.

Solomon, J. Fisher. *Discourse and Reference in the Nuclear Age.* Norman: University
of Oklahoma Press, 1988.

Stone, Albert E. *Literary Aftershocks: American Writers, Readers, and the Bomb.* New
York: Twayne, 1994.

Tanner, Tony. *City of Words: A Study of American Fiction in the Mid–Twentieth Century.* London: Jonathan Cape, 1971.

Tucker, Janet G. *Revolution Betrayed: Jurij Oleša's Envy.* Columbus, Ohio: Slavica,
1996.

United States Atomic Energy Commission. *In the Matter of J. Robert Oppenheimer.*
Cambridge, Mass.: MIT Press, 1954.

Weart, Spencer R. "The Heyday of Myth and Cliché." In *Assessing the Nuclear Age,*
edited by Len Ackland and Steven McGuire, 81–90. Chicago: Educational Foundation for Nuclear Science, 1986.

———. *Nuclear Fear: A History of Images.* Cambridge, Mass.: Harvard University Press,
1988.

Weisenburger, Steven. *Fables of Subversion: Satire and the American Novel, 1930–1980.*
Athens: University of Georgia Press, 1995.

White, E. B. *The Wild Flag: Editorials from "The New Yorker" on Federal World Government and Other Matters.* Boston: Houghton, 1946.

White, Hayden. *Figural Realism: Studies in the Mimesis Effect.* Baltimore: Johns Hopkins University Press, 1999.

Whitfield, Stephen J. *The Culture of the Cold War.* 2nd ed. Baltimore: Johns Hopkins
University Press, 1996.

Zholkovsky, Alexander. "The Stylistic Roots of *Palisandriia.*" *Canadian American Slavic
Studies* 21, no. 3–4 (1987): 369–400.

INDEX

ABOUT THE AUTHOR

DEREK C. MAUS is an associate
professor of English at the State University of New York at Potsdam. He
has published many articles and essays on satire and American and Russian culture. He is also the coeditor
of *Finding a Way Home: A Critical
Assessment of Walter Mosley's Fiction.*

GAYLORD